History of Crime and Criminal Justice Series

Social Control in Europe
Volume 1, 1500–1800

EDITED BY

HERMAN ROODENBURG

AND

PIETER SPIERENBURG

The Ohio State University Press
Columbus

Library of Congress Cataloging-in-Publication Data

Social control in Europe.
    p. cm. — (History of crime and criminal justice series)
  Includes bibliographical references and index.
  ISBN 0-8142-0971-8 (set : alk. paper) — ISBN 0-8142-9048-5 (CD-
ROM) 1. Social control—Europe—History. I. Roodenburg, Herman. II.
Series.
  HN373.S563 2004
  303.3'3'094—dc22

                              2004005763

Volume 1 ISBN: 0-8142-0968-8
Volumes 1 and 2 are available as a two-volume set: 0-8142-0971-8

Cover design by Dan O'Dair.
Type set in Adobe Garamond.
Printed by Thomson-Shore, Inc.

9 8 7 6 5 4 3 2 1

Contents

Acknowledgments

This volume results from a project for which Herman Diederiks took the initiative shortly before his death. In the course of that project, the contributions were discussed in three successive meetings: in Menaggio, Italy (1997), Amsterdam (1998), and Berlin (1999). The project was funded by the Volkswagenstiftung in Germany and the N.W. Posthumus Institute (with funds obtained from the Netherlands Organization for Scientific Research, NWO). The editors greatly appreciate the support given by these institutions. We are also grateful to Bernd Roeck for organizing the meeting in Menaggio and to Heinz Schilling for organizing the one in Berlin.

Social Control and History:
An Introduction

Pieter Spierenburg

What is social control? If anything, it is a classic concept, which many scholars use as a matter of course. Few, however, care about providing an explicit statement of what they understand it to be. This book, like its companion volume on the modern period, scrutinizes this classic notion. The two volumes examine formal and informal types of control over the last five hundred years of European history, thus providing an integral perspective on the efforts at control by various agencies and the responses to them. Yet, each contributor deals with more than just institutions or impersonal mechanisms. Both volumes focus on real people, some more powerful, some less, in Europe's past and present.

Although, over the last few decades, much work has been done on a variety of separate institutions that sought to change or influence people's behavior, these institutions have never been examined in their totality. For example, the history of crime and justice and that of church discipline have coexisted as largely unconnected subdisciplines. We know much about the state machinery of control (courts, police, prisons), but less about its relationship to popular sanctions. We can see how consistories and fraternities corrected the behavior and molded the beliefs of their members, but we are less informed about how these efforts related to official law enforcement. Finally, separate studies exist of such subjects as charity, labor, and communal life, but there is no overall analysis of how these settings operated as informal structures of control by way of scrutinizing the habits of the poor, for example, or through popular sanctions in villages and neighborhoods. This collection brings all these elements together in a comparative manner.

Social Control: The Concept's Origins

Although a classic concept, none of the classical European sociologists included social control in their scholarly vocabulary. It is absent from the work of Durkheim and Weber. The concept's origins are unequivocally American; it appears

1

to have become popular in Europe only after the Second World War. Popularity was instant in the United States from May 1901 when a thirty-four-year-old professor named Ross first introduced the idea in a book. The date of its appearance makes social control a decidedly twentieth-century notion, which needs fresh scrutiny at the start of the twenty-first century. Such an exercise could begin with the person of its intellectual father. Although historians—but less so sociologists— routinely cite Ross as the author who introduced the idea of social control, very rarely do they take account of the intellectual and political context in which he did so.

Edward Alsworth Ross (1866–1951) was a farmer's son from Virden, Illinois.[1] An orphan at age nine, he was raised in the home of a local justice of the peace. His foster parents cared enough for him to send him to college in Iowa. As a graduate student, Ross spent two years in Germany, studying philosophy in Berlin, but there is no record of his meeting any of that country's young generation of social scientists. Back in America he turned to economics, which he taught at several universities and from the mid-1890s at Stanford. There he gradually redirected his attention to sociology. The switch of disciplines was one reason for a conflict with the university's cofounder and governor, Jane Stanford, widow of Leland Stanford, who finally fired him in 1900. Ross developed the concept of social control more or less simultaneously with becoming a sociologist. From 1896 onward he published a series of articles as a preview (so the idea actually dates from just before the twentieth century). By the time he collected the articles in a book, the concept of social control had already gained notoriety. Ross applied for a chair at the University of Wisconsin, which at the time housed the largest sociology department in the United States, but the state legislature withdrew the post's funding. He finally became a professor at Wisconsin in 1906.

Social Control reads as an erudite essay on human society, with an emphasis on the problem of social order. The book discusses a wide range of societies, from ancient Greece and various non-Western nations to the United States in the author's own days. The bibliography includes such classic figures as Herbert Spencer, Emile Durkheim, and Ferdinand Tönnies. Intriguingly, Ross concludes that social control will be all the more necessary as we move from "community" to "society," adding in a footnote that he developed this thought before becoming acquainted with Tönnies' book but that the ideas are similar.[2] Essentially, however, Ross is concerned with classifying and labeling institutions and practices, much like Max Weber a few years after him. The crucial passage, summarizing the overall thesis, is tucked away in a discussion two-thirds of the way through the text. Ross first admits that society is a kind of fiction: There is nothing to it but people affecting one another in various ways. "The thesis of this book is that from the interactions of individuals and generations there emerges a kind of collective mind evincing itself in living ideals, conventions, dogmas, institutions, and religious sentiments which are more or less happily adapted to the task of safeguarding the collective welfare from the ravages of egoism."[3] This is a remarkably modern statement, to the extent that it acknowledges that society is an abstract, not an actor who can "do" things, and that processes of change are "blind," not set in motion consciously by powerful individuals or groups. It is also an outdated statement, to the extent that it minimizes the role of conflict in social relations and unabashedly expresses personal contentment.

Order, then, is equated with peaceful social relations and a degree of collective harmony. It is the opposite of an aggressive assertion of self-interest. It is equally the opposite of a ruling class's exploitation of subordinate groups, which Ross calls class control, not social control. Ross admits that order has not always prevailed historically, but he seems to consider episodes of disorder as the exceptions. The book's first page addresses the problem of order with a metaphor: The flow of traffic at a crowded city junction is orderly when persons and vehicles move in different directions but do not collide with each other. Similarly, all members of society have different interests, but they share conventions for avoiding collisions most of the time. Why is this so since, after all, it would be more logical to assume a state of disorder? Surely, people are not born with a set of commandments etched upon their souls or with inherited cooperative instincts. At that point, social control enters the picture. Ross first identifies its sociopsychological foundations, each operating in different situations: sympathy, sociability, sense of justice, and resentment (which another person may show if we injure him). The means of social control are rather variegated, the primary ones being public opinion and the law, in that order. In other words, people act more or less peacefully because they value others' judgments and because the state coerces them toward it. Although the latter comes second, Ross nevertheless concludes that the law "however minor its part at a given moment in the actual coercion of citizens, is still the cornerstone of the edifice of order."[4] The entire selection of the various means of social control is unsystematic; it further includes religious beliefs and sanctions (among which are notions of brotherhood), education, custom, and a host of minor sources, one of which is a sense of honor.[5] Throughout the book, finally, Ross mixes analysis with considerations of policy and recipes for ameliorating institutions. When discussing criminal justice, for example, he advocates a "scientific penology" that graduates punishments according to both the harmfulness of the offense to society and its attractiveness to the criminal.[6]

Although *Social Control* must be judged first of all on its own merits, any evaluation of the book should take the author's later work and his political beliefs into account. Ross's personal ideology was far from consistent over time. During the 1890s he advocated "state socialism" and supported Populist causes. After 1900 he turned to a more moderate advocacy of federal intervention and mediation in labor conflicts. At the same time, he called for restrictions on immigration, particularly of Asians. Despite this, he traveled to China for six months in 1910, to acquaint himself with Chinese culture. When the First World War broke out, he championed international arbitration by disinterested third parties as a solution, but when Wilson called for war in April 1917, Ross and other intellectuals with pacifist leanings rallied behind their president. Ross visited Russia in the crucial years 1917–1918, but in the 1920s he became a great admirer of Taylor and Ford. His Russian contacts were good enough to persuade the Soviets to release his fellow sociologist Pitirim Sorokin, whom he got a job in the United States. During the depression Ross again advocated federal intervention, supporting the "other" Roosevelt's New Deal. As late as 1935, a committee investigating communism on campuses summoned Ross to its meeting. Generally, then, he appears as a man of contrasts. He supported women's rights, but he was convinced of the racial superiority of Anglo-Saxons. He advocated a strong government, but he cosponsored a speech on the Madison campus by the anarchist Emma Goldman, which almost got him fired again.

A bullet fired at his predecessor made Theodore Roosevelt president in the same year that *Social Control* appeared. He became Ross's most influential political friend. They shared the conviction that large corporations, the latter-day "sinners," should be kept in check for the public benefit. Roosevelt initiated antitrust measures, and his "square deal policy" sought compromises between employers and workers without favoring either party. Advocating government as compromise, Ross considered the square deal as a form of social control forced upon workers and employers. His *Sin and Society* (1907), a mixture of sociological observations and political statements, diagnosed a basic condition of the world he lived in: The interdependence that characterized modern society meant that all members of the social body were at each other's mercy to a greater extent than ever before.[7] This situation created the opportunity for new forms of wrongdoing, the quintessential "sinners" being the large corporations. Unlike traditional small businessmen, the managers of corporations had no moral scruples and hardly felt restrained by public sentiment. So they had to be kept in check by state intervention, seen as a form of beneficial social control.[8] The preface to *Sin and Society* was a personal letter signed by Roosevelt. The president called *Social Control* an impressive work, adding he had read everything published by Ross since.

The presidential attack on corporate capitalism was short-lived. William Howard Taft, Roosevelt's successor, wooed the business community by instituting a committee on monopolies that proclaimed the inevitability of corporations in 1912. Ross expressed his intense disappointment with this "dirty deal." The outcome was predetermined, he noted, since there were no social scientists on the committee. Taft had ignored "scholars and social workers who have given twenty years or more of their lives to the disinterested and impartial study of the problem of industrial peace."[9] This statement provides the final key to Ross's scholarly and political concerns. No doubt, he had wished to be on that committee himself. He viewed the sociological mission as providing practical insights into social problems and giving policy makers expert advice. A major goal was to promote the majority's welfare and security without endangering social tranquility. In this project, social control was a crucial factor, but note that it included state control.

Ross's Legacy

It would take a lifetime to work through the vast number of books and articles on social control published in the twentieth century, and especially after the Second World War, when sociology had become a well-established discipline. This section, then, is certainly not a discussion of social control theory or of the way the concept has been handled within various schools of social science. It merely samples a few collective volumes, sociological and historical, in order to show the wide range of applications to which the concept has been put.[10] This is evident from even a cursory look. Take one of the earliest textbooks on the subject by Roucek and "associates," first published in 1947. Meant as reading for introductory courses in sociology and social psychology, it takes a broad view of agencies of social control. The book opens with the principal "institutions" involved (state, law, and government; religion; marriage, home, and family; education) and continues with elements of social control in areas such as the economy, art, literature, and the mass media. The preface to the second edition of 1956 proudly announces a new chapter on television, "this ever-more-important means of public communication and control." Had it been the 1990s, the new chapter, no doubt, would have dealt with the Internet. The introduction defines social control as "those processes, planned or unplanned, by which individuals are taught, persuaded, or compelled to conform to the usages and life-values of groups."[11] Essentially, it comes down to "attempts to influence others," or everything that is not self-control. Thus, despite the broad view taken, the insight that the formation of self-control also is a social process is lacking.

A volume entitled *Social Control and Social Change* exemplifies the move away from a static perspective in the social sciences, which became manifest by the late 1960s. Sociologists, social psychologists, and even biologists contributed to this collection. A chapter on the biological basis of social behavior, for example, offers sections on "the physiological and genetic bases of social control." In the chapter on changing concepts of masculinity and femininity, the emphasis is on culture rather than biology. Its central concept is the sex role, as one type of "social role," which men and women acquire through learning. The word "gender" was not yet fashionable! Chapters on play and games (involving "ludic controls"), the American radical Right, and the growth of populations indicate that, for this team of authors, social control is virtually everything. The concept gets no formal definition, but chapter 1 delineates the field on the basis of a few practical problems: "that of producing constructive social change without the use of destructive methods, . . . that of inducing individuals to take up desirable kinds of social behavior within the framework of what is presumably a well-organized society, . . . that of the undesirable effects of social control" (in particular its "misuse" for exploiting others or enforcing rules that run counter to human biology).[12] In line with the broad approach, the preface states "many people understand control to mean only restriction of action rather than the positive interstimulation that is the chief subject of this book."[13]

Historians turned to social control a little later. In *Social Control in Nineteenth-Century Britain* (1977), A. P. Donajgrodzki, the editor, claims that this is "the first collection of historical essays making use of the concept."[14] To date, it is probably the best-known historical work with "social control" in its title. In this collection, the emphasis clearly lies on nonstate control. The contributions deal with, among other things, charity organizations, educational policy, metropolitan fairs, and the Salvation Army. To justify this emphasis, the editor cites a passage from Ross's work, without paying any further attention to it. According to Donajgrodzki, his contributors share the belief "that social order is maintained not only, or even mainly, by legal systems, police forces and prisons, but is expressed through a wide range of social institutions, from religion to family life, and including, for example, leisure and recreation, education, charity and philanthropy, social work and poor relief."[15] In this case, too, we miss a formal definition; Donajgrodzki is content with the observation that the institutions his book deals with "contributed to social order."[16]

We find the emphasis exactly reversed in the collection *Social Control and the State* (1983), edited by Stanley Cohen and Andrew Scull. Although not apparently from its title, this volume contains historical perspectives, some of them going back to the eighteenth century. They focus on either crime and prisons or insanity and its treatment, the latter equally with reference to the state and the social order. The introduction, entitled "social control in history and sociology," firmly links our concept with state agencies (the very first words are "the interrelationships between the modern state and its apparatus of social control"). Another revealing sentence accuses authors who use the word "reform" of cherishing a naive, value-laden view of a continuous movement "from barbarism to enlightenment, from ignorance to expertly guided intervention."[17] For Cohen and Scull, it seems, social control is mainly a negative category, which refers to checking deviant people and labeling deviance; it is the opposite of "benevolent intentions." This perspective necessarily leads to a disproportionate emphasis on control from above.[18] In contrast to Donajgrodzki, Cohen and Scull, even though they appear to dislike it, do believe that social order is maintained primarily by legal systems, police forces, asylums, and prisons.

In a study published two years later, Stanley Cohen put his emphasis on the control of crime and delinquency, in particular the interventionist strategies of state-sponsored professionals. He comments on (then) recent developments in a cynical tone. The cynicism extends to the notion of social control itself, which he calls a Mickey Mouse concept, but not after he has provided us with a formal definition, again in the very first sentence. Social control refers to "the organized ways in which society responds to behaviour and people it regards as deviant, problematic, worrying, threatening, troublesome or undesirable in some way or another."[19] The problem with this definition, of course, is that it represents society as an actor. Who actually does the responding? Aren't the deviants and undesirables part of the very society that supposedly deals with them? Don't they interact with others? Or are we to assume that "society" in reality means the state and its agents and institutions? Then, what about social control in stateless societies? Clearly, the various pathways and trajectories taken by the concept of social control have led us to another dead end here.

Are we to conclude, then, that Ross's legacy is totally confusing and worthless? In 1901, social control already referred to many things, and it has become more of a container concept ever since. Moreover, whereas some authors consider it primarily a by-product of all kinds of institutions and social interaction, others connect it squarely with the mighty apparatus of the state. Nevertheless, social control has been a successful concept, providing scholars with a convenient term whose connotations they understand. Let me underline again that Ross himself clearly meant it to cover both the formal institutions of the state and all kinds of nongovernmental arenas, some of them at the "bottom" of society. Thus, Ross allowed for top-down as well as bottom-up perspectives on social control. In this, we can still follow him today, but we need an updated and sharper focus. We cannot simply adopt all of Ross's premises a hundred years later. As historians considering the period beginning 1500, we must reject the prima facie equation of order with peaceful social relations and the idea that social control functions most smoothly in democratic societies. In fact, early modern communities tolerated a relative amount of interpersonal violence, if they thought it justified, and twentieth-century totalitarian regimes, known for their organized violence, still had to reckon with public opinion and accept a measure of compromise. Finally, Ross's notion that social control is often based on a degree of consensus and ideals of harmony can be adopted and used to analyze communities and voluntary associations in the more distant past.

Social Control As Conflict Settlement

The misleading notion of society as an actor is absent from the work of criminologists such as Donald Black (1984) and Alan Horwitz (1990). They do identify the controllers—as persons and groups who act upon other persons and groups.

They acknowledge, moreover, that social control involves both formal control emanating from the state and a host of informal reactions and interventions at nongovernmental levels of society, including, for example, the power of gossip. Notably, Horwitz emphasizes that social control does not require the existence of consensus regarding the definitions of appropriate behavior.[20] A recent book by Mark Cooney builds upon this work. Although it deals primarily with violence, it is relevant for our task of updating the concept of social control.

Cooney, too, acknowledges that the state, where it exists, forms merely a part of society and that top-down and bottom-up perspectives are equally important. His aim is to outline a formal theory of conflict. In particular, he addresses the question "when do conflicts erupt into violence and when do they end peacefully, through mediation, reconciliation or by still other means?" Admittedly, social control involves more than just regulating, repressing, or preventing the strife between two parties. The policing of men's and women's morals, for example, even in the absence of discord, falls outside Cooney's framework. Yet, for a large part, social control has to do with regulating conflicts in one way or another. So-called third parties are the central feature in Cooney's theory. These may encourage the contestants to fight or to facilitate physical aggression, but alternatively they may mitigate the contestants' violence, stop it, or even prevent it from happening. As third parties Cooney considers "all those who have knowledge of a conflict, actual or potential."[21] They include not only the principals' friends or enemies, bystanders, and possible mediators but also the police who can arrest one or both contestants (or decide not to intervene) and the judge who may punish them. Thus, "private" persons are included in the same category along with state agents. Whether social control proceeds top-down or bottom-up, the controllers are viewed consistently as a third party in a conflict.

Whether third parties are official law enforcers or self-appointed mediators, the status difference with the contestants is of crucial importance. According to Cooney, the judgment of third parties is most readily accepted if their social status is moderately superior to that of the principals. Thus, a too hegemonic state agency finds itself no less at a disadvantage than a mediator from the contestants' peer group. Besides status, other factors affect the degree of effectiveness of informal as well as state-based third-party settlement. An analysis of the strengths and weaknesses of both comes down to a series of "yes-buts." One advantage of state control, for example, lies in its broader jurisdiction. Informal control often operates in a local setting only, so outside it people must resolve conflicts in a different way. On the contrary, some stateless societies boast well-developed systems of informal settlement. However, they have no way of handling the minority of "intractably violent people"—those who constitute a persistent threat to their neighbors and won't listen to any palaver. Obviously, state agents are better equipped to deal with such persons. The state may use coercion in settling disputes between ordinary people not especially bent on fighting or even force two parties to comply with its ruling if they both find it totally unacceptable. However, whereas state coercion is backed by greater force, it can alienate people and breed resentment or even protest and resistance. Informal settlement, by contrast, has greater acceptance potential, but it depends on cooperation and consensus. The moral authority of one's community, to be sure, often ensures compliance. "Disputants may well find it harder to disobey the consensus of informal tribunals than the mandates of judges and police officers."[22]

Up to now, this is a formal analysis, with few historical-processual dimensions. The only element implying change is the proposition that reliance on the state to settle conflict may cause systems of informal settlement to wither away. Paradoxically, this statement alerts us to the historical situations in which it does not apply. Historians easily imagine the growth of state supervision supplanting or suppressing ecclesiastical discipline, community sanctions, and other forms of informal or semiformal control. However—as not only this collection but even more so its companion volume on the modern period shows—if informal means of conflict settlement decline before an advancing state, new informal controls often take their place. For example, the nineteenth century not only witnessed the establishment of the police but also industrialization, which brought industrial paternalism with it in some cases and, in others, a set of informal controls at the workplace. Simultaneously, community sanctions and ecclesiastical discipline remained alive in many regions of Europe. On the other hand, some modern inner-city neighborhoods witness both an ephemeral presence of state institutions and a decline of the moral authority of community elders. Thus, it is not always a question of either–or.

Having completed his survey, Cooney concludes that we lack a clear-cut answer to the question whether state or informal settlement is more effective. Therefore, "from the point of view of reducing violence, the optimal social system would combine the moderate status superiority of informal settlement with the extensive jurisdiction of the state."[23] This is policy advice not unlike that offered by Edward Ross, with its implementation left undiscussed. A more adequate knowledge of the historical development of social control and conflict settlement in various sectors of society could help implement such proposals. One obvious amendment to Cooney's scheme is the observation that in early modern communal settings with little state intervention, the community refrained from acting as a third party in certain situations. In particular, members would view some cases of violence as a form of redress by one principal upon another. Conversely, community leaders might act and pass judgment over single individuals thought to show improper behavior, sexually or otherwise, as they did in England already from the end of the fourteenth century.[24] These amendments notwithstanding, Cooney's analysis has been helpful in furthering our discussion. Notably, his concept of third parties has made us alert to the fact that social control, when also based upon community consensus, always concerns interaction between a number of people, each of whom may have his own particular interest at stake.

To conclude, social control involves a variegated set of practices and beliefs. Sometimes it has the character of conflict settlement, at other times it can be viewed more adequately as the enforcement of norms or the regulation of behavior. Always it concerns people or groups acting upon other people or groups. There are at least two parties involved, but often a third party plays a crucial role. Settlement or regulation can be obtained through care and relief, through arbitration, or through containment and punishment of behavior judged unacceptable. The set of norms and values involved in all these processes is subject to change over time. Social control, then, essentially constitutes a sensitizing concept: It draws attention to the relationships between various mechanisms inducing people to act in a way that is desirable according to a certain standard or ideal. In all societies social control constitutes a major key to understanding violence, conflict, and problems related to the formation and acceptance of social norms. As the present collection shows, this crucial function of social control is operative regardless of the period one examines or a country's political system. It works in the early modern period as well as in recent times and in both democratic and authoritarian societies.

The Historiographical Background

The present book—and its complementary volume on the modern period—could not have been completed without the existence of several traditions of research, even though the concept of social control played only a minor role in each of them. For this volume, three were especially important: the historical study of crime and criminal justice, the history of church discipline, and the study of popular culture in the past. Two other branches of research, the social history of industrialization and the analysis of totalitarianism, also formed a significant background, but to the modern volume in particular.

The history of crime and criminal justice was first developed as a field of research in the mid-1970s. Historians discovered the value of court records as a major source to uncover the social world of the people who transgressed the law as well as to understand the development of judicial practices and official responses to deviant behavior. This resulted in an interdisciplinary effort in which historians were joined by sociologists, lawyers, and a few anthropologists. Their investigations covered a broad period from the later Middle Ages until World War I. Less work has been done for the twentieth century though. Beginning in France, England, and the Netherlands, the study of court records later spread to countries and regions like Scandinavia, Germany, and Italy. Understandably, this research covered the crime as well as the control side of deviance. To the extent that it dealt with the latter, major themes include: the criminal law in its social context;[25] the origins and development of the police;[26] the impact of state justice on local communities;[27] punishment as a cultural and political factor;[28] the life of marginal groups and attitudes toward them;[29] and banditry.[30] The result was an increased understanding of the methods used, over time, to deal with criminal and illegal behavior as well as new insights into the sociocultural environment of lawbreakers.

It followed from the nature of its subject that the history of crime and criminal justice concentrated on the institutions of formal control: courts, police, and other state agencies. This was especially so until the beginning of the 1990s. Since then, however, a shift of focus has become visible. For one thing, crime historians began to take lower courts, like the French *prévotés* or German village courts, into consideration.[31] Notably in rural areas during the ancien régime, but also in urban environments, such courts dealt for a large part with petty conflicts among neighbors. Accusations of slander, for example, mostly brought forward by women, often were numerous. The studies emanating from this type of research focused on the character of communal relations, with gender, honor, and neighborliness as central issues. A second recent trend concerns the history of violence, both quantitative and qualitative. Especially studies of the sociocultural context of violence have alerted us to its Janus-faced nature, as a producer of both disorder and order, in past communities.[32] These recent trends in the historiography of crime and justice make it easier to link up with the second and third traditions identified here.

The history of church discipline began as a largely independent field of study. A number of investigations concerned the disciplinary efforts by consistories or presbyteries in Protestant parts of Germany, the Dutch Republic, and among Huguenot communities in France. Originally, this research was performed from the perspective of socioreligious history, focusing on the Reformation and the process of confessionalization.[33] More recently, historians studying consistorial discipline have viewed it from a sociocultural angle in which the focus was, among other things, on social relations among church members, their notions of honor, and the "civilizing" efforts of the church elite.[34] Another important question concerned the differentiation, both analytically and in the minds of contemporaries, between crime and sin.[35] Especially in the latter case, the opportunity offered itself for linking up with the history of criminal justice. In England, moreover, a strong link between crime history and the history of ecclesiastical discipline already existed because of the peculiar institution of the Church courts. These dealt with matters related to marriage and the family, their jurisdiction coming close to formal control.[36]

Although post-Tridentine Catholicism lacked a church discipline in the strict sense, it offered various functional equivalents, such as Jesuit missions and episcopal visitations. Historians have also debated about the extent to which the sacrament of confession functioned as an instrument of social control.[37] Finally, in the countries of southern Europe, the Inquisition remained active throughout the early modern period. Studies of this institution, in several regions of southern Europe, have contributed to our knowledge of popular culture and the elite offensive against such popular practices as love magic or unorthodox devotion.[38] Again, the state backing that the Inquisition enjoyed made the activities of its tribunals akin to formal social control. The contrast between ecclesiastical discipline in Protestant and Catholic parts of Europe naturally is an important theme in this book Although church discipline was on the wane already by the eighteenth century, it revived in some regions, the northern provinces of the Netherlands for example, in the following century. Apart from this, the ideological and institutional hold of church leaders, as well as common priests and pastors, over their flock remained an important source of informal social control well into the twentieth century.

In the wake of ecclesiastical discipline, poor relief agencies have functioned as agents of social control. During the early modern period, charity was often, but not always, a church matter. Poor relief functioned as a control mechanism to the extent that the people applying for assistance had to adjust their behavior to the norms and rules of those distributing relief. In the nineteenth and twentieth centuries, charity was transformed into welfare, distributed by the state as a rule. However, social control remained an important feature of the relations between welfare agencies and their recipients.

The third research tradition, dealing with popular culture and elite attitudes, has obvious connections with the previous two, if only because judicial and consistorial records reveal a lot about the life of common people. Overviews of the history of popular culture date from the late 1970s.[39] Although the sixteenth and seventeenth centuries constitute the heyday of Europe's traditional popular culture, much work has been done also on the workers' culture of the nineteenth and early-twentieth centuries. Local communities—rural villages and, increasingly, urban neighborhoods—were a central focus of this research. The popular culture embedded in these settings involved a shared world view and much feasting and merrymaking, but also the supervision of behavior. Charivari is only the most obvious mechanism of informal social control operating within local communities.[40] In fact, control was an aspect of virtually all communal relationships. We may think of gossip, informal supervision, dispute settlement by community elders, and the negotiation of honor. Urban neighborhoods, moreover, sometimes knew formalized associations, which among other things regulated the common life of the inhabitants. Complementarily to communal agencies, guilds and fraternities exercised similar functions.[41]

Here we have the clearest example of a bottom-up perspective on social control. Unorganized communities as well as neighborhood associations, guilds, and fraternities, although exercising control functions, worked according to consensual concepts such as brotherhood, friendship, and harmony, rather than hierarchy and authority, which were the key concepts of formal control. All these communal institutions were also social phenomena in their own right, with a firm basis in everyday life and as such having specific meanings for the groups and individuals involved. Ideas about social harmony were important even at the level of the lower official institutions, such as English local courts, which applied charivari-like sanctions until the middle of the seventeenth century.[42] That kind of symbiosis of popular culture and official justice, however, rapidly declined afterward. Most historians agree on the eighteenth-century withdrawal of the elites from popular culture, which meant that local communities lost a number of functions to overarching organizations. Community life remained vigorous nevertheless. A couple of studies focusing on the modern period have shown that neighborhood ties continued to be strong and coherent until at least the early-twentieth century.[43] In this case, too, neighborly life involved both shared pleasures and mutual scrutiny.

The existence of official associations and the symbiosis of popular sanctions and the business of the lower courts warn us that a focus on social control at the community level cannot simply be equated with a bottom-up perspective. Similarly, not everything connected with the law and criminal justice should be viewed as top-down social control. Whereas the state was more than just an instrument of repression or acculturation, the structure of local communities comprised power differences and social inequality. In this connection, the notion of legal pluralism may be relevant. Scholars using that term emphasize the wide spectrum in the settling of disputes, from processes of negotiation to processes of adjudication. They view both the courts and a broad range of semiformal and informal institutions as suppliers of services, to which people may or may not choose to turn when they are in conflict.

The two types of research left to discuss are more specific, regarding subject and period, than the first three. The social history of industrialization has dealt with, among other issues, industrial paternalism and the control of workers—important themes in this book's companion volume. In the modern period, industrial employers often embarked upon "civilization offensives," while the leadership of labor movements had their own disciplinary agenda. Although regulating the behavior of members was not the principal or original function of economic institutions, they have exercised social control from an early date. This was true of the guilds and journeymen's associations of the ancien régime no less than the industrial establishments of a more recent period. The historiography of totalitarian regimes, finally, comprises numerous studies, but the focus on social control is relatively novel.[44] That focus has the additional advantage of remedying a neglect of the first tradition discussed. As explained above, the historiography of crime and justice has hardly extended to the twentieth century. The chapters in this book's companion volume make a start with that enterprise.

Different as they are, the last two research traditions complement each other nicely to the extent that they concern nonstate and state institutions, respectively. Thus, they reproduce the contrast between informal and formal social control, a distinction prominent in our discussion up to now. For the nineteenth and twentieth centuries, such a dichotomy appears sufficient, that is, as long as we realize that absolute dichotomies, without overlaps or cross ties, never exist in history. For the early modern period, however, we may have to distinguish an intermediate category of semiformal social control. The tripartite division following from this loosely parallels the first three research traditions identified above. Church discipline and the supervision of behavior through charity must be regarded as semiformal control, in particular in situations in which the former was exercised by an official or favored church and the latter was politically influenced.[45] Consequently, for the early modern period, a large part of the top-down perspective is represented by the semiformal control of ecclesiastical discipline. This justifies its prominent place in the present volume, at the expense of the familiar story of secular criminal justice. The lesser role of the latter subject here is also justified because several theoretical works and synthetic overviews concerning early modern law enforcement and punishment have already been published.[46]

Phases in the History of Social Control

At this stage, it is possible to provide a rough outline of the chronology of social control in Europe. Five phases can be distinguished. Between about 1200 and about 1500, a system of criminal justice developed in Europe's core areas under the aegis of princes and urban patriciates. Originally, the higher courts were merely complementary to community-based institutions for resolving conflicts. For example, the higher courts punished thieves whom the community could not handle or they dealt with outsiders not rooted in a city. Among the community-based institutions, local lower courts have to be included. Marjorie McIntosh demonstrates their importance for social control in England from 1370 onward. They dealt with such matters as scolding, secretly overhearing the conversations of one's neighbors, disorderly alehouses, taking wood from hedges for use as fuel, playing illegal games, and sheltering vagabonds. McIntosh stresses the relative continuity in England from the later-fourteenth century until the end of the sixteenth century and the fact that many early modern institutions of social control originated in the Middle Ages.[47] In a similar vein, several contributors to this volume deal with the Middle Ages as a prelude to early modern developments. For practical reasons of manageability, however, this volume has the year 1500 as its starting point.

For continental Europe at least, the sixteenth and seventeenth centuries can be considered as a separate phase, because the three main forms of control—state justice, church discipline, and community supervision—all operated together. The late-sixteenth and the seventeenth centuries constituted the high point for church discipline. Thus, semiformal and informal means of control loomed large in the lives of villagers and townspeople. The state's penal system, however, was attuned to social control at a general level, that of maintaining public peace and order. Courts primarily dealt with serious violence and property offenses, next to challenges to the state's authority. The eighteenth century actually saw much continuity with the preceding phase. The fact that church discipline—certainly in matters of daily life—declined, justifies the identification of the years 1700–1800 as a separate phase in the history of social control. In addition, the eighteenth century witnessed an increasing social gulf between the elites and the popular classes.

Since the end of the ancien régime, according to the conventional view, the impact of penal law on the lives of the population became greater.[48] The fourth phase, roughly from 1800 to 1950, covers the period when an industrial economy emerged as well as the European system of nation-states. In the wake of these developments, a new system of formal social control became firmly established. However, informal types of control did not suddenly vanish. As this book's follow-up volume shows, the activities of economic and moral entrepreneurs, among others, ensured a degree of informal supervision of behavior. Village and neighborhood controls declined in some places but remained vigorous in others. Even Reformed church discipline was revived or had stayed alive in certain parts of Europe.[49] It should be added that, with the shift from the small world of the guilds to the larger one of industrial paternalism, social control at the workplace lost much of its bottom-up, consensus-based character. Finally, both formal and informal types of control continued to be permeated by patriarchal views of social order.[50]

During the fifth and last phase, from about 1950 until today, formal control clearly predominated. Under the impact of the emergence of the welfare state, the principal overall development of this period, informal controls receded rapidly. State agencies, however, soon proved unable to exercise effective supervision in all social arenas. For one thing, they now face problems of control because of globalization. In particular, international criminal groups are organized more efficiently than the institutions of cross-state police cooperation set up to confront them. In this matter, informal controls are marginal, and it seems unlikely that in the future their role can become significant to any degree. This may be different in the case of the second arena in which problems of supervision have become apparent in recent decades: inner cities with a heterogeneous population. The disappearance of informal controls has been noted and deplored since the 1980s, by administrators at the national level and leaders of local communities. In every major European city, they are faced with an increasingly complex, multicultural variety of groups who share the urban space, giving rise to specific problems. Administrators have responded with a renewed interest in control, also, and especially by means other than the official state apparatus backed by criminal law. The development of future policies in this area might be served by a better understanding of longitudinal processes of shifting forms of social control, as discussed in this book and its companion volume.

Theoretical Frameworks and Orientations

The richness of the subject under scrutiny means there is no single master theory capable of accommodating every finding. Indeed, the contributors refer to various theorists as they see fit. It would be wrong, however, to view the present collection as entirely eclectic. A few broad orientations and theoretical perspectives recur throughout the book, shared more or less by most contributors. One of these centers on the concept of *Sozialdisziplinierung* (social disciplining), developed by German historians. According to them, early modern society was characterized by an ever increasing and expanding set of disciplines in every social arena.[51] This process operated partly from above, at the level of church and state, but it could be guided and modified from the bottom up. *Sozialdisziplinierung* comes close to social control itself (with the "social" actually redundant in both cases), but the former concept implies a continual increase in controls. It is not always clear, though, who was disciplining whom.

The effort of naming the groups involved in disciplining is made easier with the help of the concept of civilization offensives. This concept has the additional advantage of not being restricted to the early modern period; in fact, these campaigns were especially characteristic of the phase 1800–1950. "Civilization offensive" refers to the more or less conscious efforts by powerful groups to change the norms and conduct of others in the direction of the former's standards of civilized behavior. The term leaves open the extent to which they are successful, if at all. Political elites, church people, philanthropists, and moral entrepreneurs are among the groups who have launched civilization offensives in the past. The concerted campaign, in the late-nineteenth and early-twentieth centuries, to improve the housing conditions of the poor constitutes an example. Through it, the campaigners hoped, the moral standards of the targeted group, regarding cleanliness and sexuality, would be uplifted as well. Civilization offensives are top-down phenomena almost by definition. Standards of conduct, however, may also become more "civilized" without such offensives, through pressure from below or from one's peers. That is the case, for example, when elite groups raise their own standards because they feel that imitation of their conduct by others makes them less distinctive or when a religious community wishes to demonstrate its purity in the eyes of the rest of the population.

A third general theme refers to the importance of conflict. As has been stressed before, notably in early modern villages and neighborhoods, social order was not simply the equivalent of peace and quiet. Social control was sometimes achieved by individuals behaving violently toward other individuals. When this happened, and in case of conflict generally, notions of honor were intricately involved. As several contributors argue, honor itself served as a vehicle to maintain order within local communities, relegating to everyone his or her proper place. Yet, the people's honor games—or the "honor trade" (*Ehrenhandel*) as German historians call it—could be disruptive at times, setting up community members against each other. It may also be asked to what extent the institutions of formal control could build upon honor-based informal control. In some cases, local people's notions of honor were in line with the conceptions of legal order cherished by the representatives of the state. At other times, the community's definition of honor ran counter to official views of public order. This is perhaps most evident in the German guilds' opposition to governmental measures and ordinances that they felt threatened their *Ehrlichkeit* ("honorable status"). Thus, local conceptions of honor and order were Janus-faced.

A final general theme is that of the negotiation concerning imposed rules. It is firmly acknowledged in this book that the regulation of behavior is always a two-way process. Previous scholars have often viewed disciplinary efforts (reforms of popular festivals by religious leaders, for example, or policemen's activities as domestic missionaries) as a top-down phenomenon: The "superiors" had specific ideas about a godly life, the obedient worker, or the law-abiding citizen, with which they impregnated the "inferiors." Viewed from this angle, the principal research question concerns the degree of rule enforcement's success: How far did the inferiors live by the rules the superiors held up to them? However, as this collection demonstrates, people seldom act as passive recipients of social control. Sometimes they resist; more often, they negotiate and bend the rules of the game. Such a top-bottom interaction is equally characteristic for preindustrial local communities as for twentieth-century authoritarian states. To conclude, considerable negotiation has always existed between the people and the state as well as between ordinary churchgoers and ecclesiastical institutions, workers and employers, and so on. Consequently, informal social control has been equally, or perhaps more, forceful than formal social control in all societies over the past five centuries, independent of whether they were monarchical, democratic, authoritarian, or totalitarian.

The negotiation concerning imposed rules might be illuminated with the help of the concept of power resources. Certain social situations provided the objects of control more room for maneuvering and negotiating with their controllers than other situations. Conversely, the power resources of the agents of control were not the same in every context. The agents could be bound by institutional agreements, such as those existing in biconfessional cities and regions, or by their own ideological beliefs, for example if their adherence to an ideal of social harmony and consensus limited the means at their disposal or the severity they were prepared to exhibit.

Themes in the Contributions

The contributions that follow elaborate on and extend the major themes discussed up to now. This volume consists of two parts. The first focuses on the interplay of ecclesiastical institutions and the emerging states, with special attention for church discipline. As Heinz Schilling emphasizes in his introduction, this is a still expanding field, in which even the history of art can be integrated. Little attention is paid in this part to the already familiar story of prosecution by secular courts and their repertoire of punishments, from the scaffold to banishment. Instead, the focus is on the relationships between institutions and the people. Thus, James Sharpe underlines the symbiosis of the state's penal system on the one hand and informal social control within the household and the workplace on the other in early modern England. He extends his analysis to the ideological level by examining a popular play teaching a moral lesson to apprentices in particular. Manon van der Heijden's contribution on Dutch cities deals with the efforts of both urban magistrates and the Reformed consistory at regulating marital behavior (including premarital and extramarital affairs) and the expectations that urban dwellers cherished in their contacts with both these institutions. Indeed, marriage and the family constituted a target for the disciplinary efforts of state and church throughout early modern Europe. This equally emerges from Susanna Burghartz's contribution on the regulation of marriage and sexuality in southern Germany and Switzerland. In the moral politics of Protestant as well as Catholic reformers, she argues with reference to Mary Douglas, a pervasive discourse of (ritual) purity constituting a central element.

Even though the first part deals mostly with the level of official institutions, the importance of notions of harmony and consensus frequently shines through. This is obvious in the peculiar situation of Ireland, with a Protestant state church ineffectively claiming ecclesiastical jurisdiction over the entire population and a Catholic church de facto representing the majority. Ute Lotz-Heumann shows that the Catholic church's priests and bishops—relying on informal regulation within families, villages, and urban neighborhoods as well as the support of Catholic landowners—were considerably more capable of enforcing conformity than the helpless Church of Ireland.

The first part closes with two essays exploring the ways in which early modern art has functioned as a vehicle for social control. Because one focuses on Spain and the other deals primarily with Italy and southern Germany, these contributions also serve to redress the geographic balance toward Catholic southern Europe. Michael Scholz-Hänsel examines art works created in the service of church and state as well as the extent to which painters were able to negotiate within the Inquisition system—in the latter case continuing our general theme of the negotiation of norms. Bernd Roeck focuses on architecture. In particular, he shows that the designs of grand palaces and official buildings formed part of a conscious effort to buttress the "magnificence" and superiority of territorial rulers and urban patriciates alike. By impressing subjects and citizens, architecture indirectly served to uphold the existing social order. Surprisingly perhaps, here is an extreme example of social control from above, yet without any involvement of the courts or the police and perhaps of an informal rather than a formal sort.

Although the interaction between various social and institutional levels is a guiding principle throughout the book, the second part looks more explicitly at discipline from a bottom-up perspective. First, Herman Roodenburg's introductory essay provides a comprehensive view of social control at the communal level, which he considers a valuable new direction of research. Martin Dinges further extends the perspective from below by examining the discriminating ways in which ordinary people had recourse to the institutions of justice in early modern Europe. He concludes that local inhabitants often considered these institutions supplementary to extrajudicial ways of solving conflicts, through reconciliation or arbitration. Indeed, for the study of social control from below, local communities, urban as well as rural, are of crucial importance. Even the parishes of a metropolis like London, as Martin Ingram makes clear, were to a large extent self-governing communities, whose aldermen shared with the inhabitants a vision of social control through shaming. Well into the seventeenth century, popular sanctions— in particular charivari—operated in a symbiotic relationship with "official" shame punishments imposed by local magistrates. This applies to England and probably to other European countries as well. On the other hand, local communities were not always homogeneous. In England as well as Germany, as Robert von Friedeburg shows, minorities of "godly" villagers acknowledged only their own religious norms as a guideline to life—a situation that impinged upon the effectiveness of communal social controls.

Voluntary associations constituted another setting for informal social control from below. This emerges from the contributions by Maarten Prak on the guilds of early modern Europe and Katherine Lynch about religious associations, the family, and poor relief. Associational social control could even be a feature of urban neighborhoods, to the extent that they had a semiofficial existence. Carl Hoffmann touches upon this aspect in his contribution, which compares neighborhoods in early modern Germany with those of the Netherlands and Paris. We must conclude that the system of discipline and control in the context of neighborhoods was Janus-faced. On the one hand, it consisted of the inhabitants themselves exercising a degree of mutual control, and on the other, it involved neighborhood corporations functioning as instruments of control by a superior agency. In the Netherlands, these corporations often constituted a "subauthority" employed by urban governments to ensure order and discipline in the city and to enforce the magistrates' conceptions of peace and security.

Whenever mutual discipline and self-discipline were operating, within neighborhoods as well as rural settings, personal honor was the axis around which they revolved. This is a central issue in several contributions. We now know that a sensitivity to one's reputation characterized early modern northern Europe as much as it did southern Europe, once considered the heartland of honor. Nevertheless, although anthropologists and historians have written much about honor in the Mediterranean world, they have hardly considered its role within local communities and its relationship to discipline. Tomás Mantecón remedies that defect, analyzing the interrelationships between patriarchy, community, and informal control in early modern Spain. In an earlier article, he had already explained that the Spanish language differentiated between *honor,* related to social position and the reputation of one's family, and *honra,* one's personal prestige that one constantly needed to guard.[52] Closely related to personal honor is the subject of violence. According to the traditional male honor code, widely acknowledged throughout Europe in the early modern period, encroachments upon one's honor could only be repaired through physical aggression against the offender. To the extent that the community approved of this aggression, it effectively functioned as informal control. Thus, as Gerd Schwerhoff argues, violence can be a tool of social control as well as its target; whereas originally it was both, by the end of the early modern period it had become an object of social control only.

Together, the two parts take us back to the conclusion reached by Edward Ross just over a century ago: Social control operates at various levels and through a number of institutions within society.

Notes

I am grateful to Clive Emsley and Astrid Ikelaar for their comments on the draft version. Some ideas developed by Herman Roodenburg, while he was working with me on various introductory texts, also resound in this introduction.

1. Unless otherwise mentioned, the biographical data on Ross are taken from McMahon, *Social Control and Public Intellect.*

2. Ross, *Social Control,* 432. This 1939 edition, the only one available to me, is an unaltered reprint of the 1901 original.

3. Ibid., 293.

4. Ibid., 125.

5. On honor: Ibid., 239–40.

6. Ibid., 110.

7. Ross, *Sin and Society,* 4.

8. We find this idea already in Ross, *Social Control,* 87–88: In "the century we are just entering on" the state should be strengthened in order to counter powerful private interests.

9. Ross, quoted in McMahon, *Social Control and Public Intellect,* 97.

10. The sample refers to works devoted exclusively to social control. Of course, major sociological theorists such as Talcott Parsons amply discussed the subject in their general works.

11. Roucek et al., *Social Control*, 3 (this 1970 edition is a reprint of the 1956 edition).

12. Scott and Scott, eds., *Social Control and Social Change*, 1.

13. Ibid., x.

14. Donajgrodzki, ed., *Social Control in Nineteenth-Century Britain*, 9.

15. Ibid.

16. Ibid., 16.

17. Cohen and Scull, eds., *Social Control and the State*, 2.

18. Yet, Mayer's contribution to the volume (17–38) criticizes such a top-down view, without mentioning the editors.

19. Cohen, *Visions of Social Control*, 1.

20. Horwitz, *The Logic of Social Control*, 9. Black wrote the foreword to Horwitz's book.

21. Cooney, *Warriors and Peacemakers*, 6.

22. Ibid., 63.

23. Ibid., 66.

24. On England: McIntosh, *Controlling Misbehavior*.

25. Hay et al., *Albion's Fatal Tree;* Faber, Strafrechtspleging en criminaliteit; Beattie, *Crime and the Courts;* Diederiks, *In een land van justitie;* Huussen, *Veroordeeld in Friesland.*

26. Bayley, "The Police and Political Development in Europe"; Storch, "The Plague of the Blue Locusts"; Storch, "The Policeman As Domestic Missionary"; Emsley, *Policing and Its Context;* Emsley, *Gendarmes and the State.*

27. Castan, *Honnêteté et relations sociales;* Castan, *Justice et répression;* Kent, *The English Village Constable;* Schulte, *Das Dorf im Verhör;* Roeck, *Als wollt die Welt schier brechen.*

28. Spierenburg, *The Spectacle of Suffering;* Zysberg, *Les galériens;* Gatrell, *The Hanging Tree;* Evans, *Rituals of Retribution.*

29. Hufton, *The Poor of Eighteenth-Century France;* Küther, *Menschen auf der Strasse;* Beier, *Masterless Men;* Spierenburg, *The Prison Experience;* Geremek, *Het Kaïnsteken.*

30. Cobb, *The Police and the People;* Danker, *Räuberbanden im alten Reich;* Blok, *De Bokkerijders;* Egmond, *Underworlds.*

31. See, among others, Frank, *Dörfliche Gesellschaft;* Gowing, *Domestic Dangers.*

32. One example is Spierenburg, ed., *Men and Violence.* See also Schwerhoff in this volume.

33. Van Deursen, *Bavianen en slijkgeuzen;* Estèbe and Vogler, "La genèse d'une société protestante; Monter, "The Consistory of Geneva"; Schmidt, *Konfessionalisierung.*

34. Münch, "Kirchenzucht und Nachbarschaft"; Mentzer, "Disciplina Nervus Ecclesiae"; Mentzer, *Blood and Belief;* Roodenburg, *Onder censuur;* and several contributions to Friess and Kiessling, eds., *Konfessionalisierung und Region.*

35. Compare Schilling, "History of Crime" and Schilling, ed., *Kirchenzucht und Sozialdisziplinierung.*

36. See especially Houlbrooke, *Church Courts;* and Ingram, *Church Courts.*

37. Briggs, "The Sins of the People"; de Boer, *Sinews of Discipline.*

38. Bennassar et al., *L'Inquisition;* Haliczer, ed., *Inquisition and Society;* Monter, *Frontiers of Heresy.* For an overview of all Inquisitorial activities in three countries, see Bethencourt, *L'Inquisition.*

39. Burke, *Popular Culture;* Muchembled, *Culture populaire;* Yeo and Yeo, eds., *Popular Culture.*

40. Le Goff and Schmitt, eds., *Le charivari;* Rooijakkers and Romme, eds., *Charivari.*

41. See, among others, Garrioch, *Neighbourhood and Community;* Brennan, *Public Drinking;* Roodenburg, "Freundschaft." Ongoing research by Aries van Meeteren into 17th-century Leiden will increase our understanding of the mechanisms of control at the neighborhood level.

42. Ingram, "Juridical Folklore" and, more elaborately, in this volume.

43. In particular: Burdy, *Le soleil noir.*

44. Aspects of social control are discussed in Gellately, *The Gestapo;* Gellately, *Backing Hitler;* and Johnson, *Nazi Terror.* The article by Jan T. Gross "Social Control under Totalitarianism" is rather superficial and focuses only on Poland at the beginning of Soviet hegemony.

45. Ecclesiastical discipline and criminal justice had a particularly symbiotic relationship in early modern Scandinavia, a region not represented in this volume. A recent collection (Österberg and Sogner, eds., *People Meet the Law*) offers an excellent overview.

46. See, among others, Spierenburg, *The Spectacle of Suffering;* and Sharpe, *Judicial Punishment.* For a concise overview of early modern punishment: Spierenburg, "The Body and the State."

47. McIntosh, *Controlling Misbehavior.* See also the discussion in *Journal of British Studies* 37, 3 (1998): 231–305 with contributions by Paul Seaver, Barbara Hanawalt, R. H. Helmholz, Shannon McSheffrey, Peter Lake, and a reply by the author. Most contributors find McIntosh's crossing of the medieval early modern divide valuable.

48. A recent assessment of the growth of state control in the German world is Härter, "Soziale Disziplinierung."

49. For the Netherlands: Sleebe, *In termen van fatsoen;* for Davos: Schmidt and Brodbeck, "Davos zwischen Sünde und Verbrechen."

50. See Miller, *Transformations of Patriarchy.*

51. For a recent overview: Behrens, "Sozialdisziplinierung."

52. Mantecón, "Honour and social discipline" in Schilling, ed., *Institutionen.*

Part One

INSTITUTIONAL PERSPECTIVES:
STATE, CHURCH, AND THE PEOPLE

CHAPTER I

Discipline:
The State and the Churches in Early Modern Europe

Heinz Schilling

Translated by Jeremy Gaines

We can summarize the results of the decades of debate on Gerhard Oestreich's concept[1] of a "fundamental process" of social disciplining in early modern times primarily controlled by the state—and it is a debate that has most recently taken place on an international level—by citing the formula expressed by Fernand Braudel back in 1959 in opposition to Otto Brunner, namely that today "to cross the multiple thresholds of history, all doors are good."[2] Indeed, as to researching social control and disciplining in Old European—or, if that smacks too much of Otto Brunner, in Medieval and early modern times—any door is good today for historians as long as it offers an unobstructed path to a better understanding of the exceptionally complex and varied occurrences that they endeavor to grasp with these or similar concepts.

Initially, in the sometimes fierce debate with Gerhard Oestreich, any focus on state or otherwise institutionally steered disciplining "from above" was immediately suspected of being ideological—at least in German research circles. Today, a consensus is once again possible on integrative methods that try to interweave micro- and macrohistorical approaches in social and cultural history.[3] Even the once so fiercely contested question on the "correct" terminology and concepts can now be viewed more flexibly and liberally, as is shown not least by the concept behind the essays in this volume.[4] On this basis we can now discern once more which of Oestreich's observations, irrespective of how they were conditioned by the time when they were written, were trailblazing and can be taken up in the current perspective, whereby today's vantage point is far more wide ranging in terms of subject matter and theoretical edifice.

Formal social control and the institutions of early modern discipline are thus the object addressed in the essays in the first part of this volume on social control in early modern Europe.[5] Methodologically speaking, here the usual choice of perspective is "from above." At the same time, the context addressed is highly complex and diverse—proof that in recent years in this institutional segment of research into social disciplining the focus of study and observation has been expanded greatly. Originally, attention concentrated almost exclusively on the state as well as its institutions and agents, in other words the political elite, the judiciary, police, and so forth. In particular, scholars scrutinized absolutist and authoritarian forms, while social control by the Estates and Republican modes were only rarely considered. By contrast, the spectrum presented below is broader and more differentiated, both geographically and in terms of constitutional typologies, as well as with regard to subject matter and themes. The articles are primarily concerned with nonabsolutist societies such as Ireland, the Netherlands, and Switzerland. Alongside the state institutions and control mechanisms in the narrow sense, the articles also look at the Church and ecclesiastical discipline, legislation on marriage and families, art and architecture, and that is also only a selection from an even larger diversity of topics that are currently at the center of interest in this sector of research on disciplining.

Social Control and Church Discipline

As early as the nineteenth century, historians started to concern themselves with the Church and ecclesiastical discipline as institutions of social control—and in this volume it is in particular Ute Lotz-Heumann who focuses on these through the example of the history of Ireland,[6] an area to date hardly treated in this context at all. In other words, scholars tackled the subject long before the emergence of a social and criminal history that addressed law enforcement, deviance, and punishment in the secular, civil domain. However, this early interest in Church discipline tended to center on the *causes celèbres* of a history of the sinfulness of those who had turned their backs on a purely Christian life, viewed as a *histoire scandaleuse*.[7] Church discipline started to attract the attention of a professional social history and history of mentality as of the 1960s, encouraged by the Annales School in France, not to mention the church and social historians in the English-speaking world who were interested in investigation of the history of mentality through statistics.[8]

Initially, the interest homed in almost exclusively on the explicit Church discipline of the Calvinist or reformed Presbyterians of France, Switzerland (specifically Geneva), the Netherlands, the British Isles, and colonial North America. This did not change until the research into confessionalization arose at the end of the 1970s in German faculties of the humanities. This approach assumed that the confessionalization to be observed in Europe since the mid-sixteenth century (i.e., the formation of intrinsically closed systems of worldviews on the basis of the Lutheran, Tridentine, or Reformed, including Anglican, confessions) pursued similar or identical goals, for all known and manifest differences in the phenomena themselves. Above all, they developed comparable institutions and forms of action, and the consequences they had for history in general were functionally similar. All these confessional churches aspired to lay down norms for and control the respective faith, thought, emotions, and above all the actions and behavior of their members, and to impose sanctions in the case of corresponding deviations. In this way, researchers started to study not only Presbyterian Church discipline as practiced by the Calvinists but also the entire spectrum of clerical and religious norms, controls, and discipline.

This also amounted to the first instance of the social discipline by the state being overcome—given the proof that, generally speaking, in the European countries nonstate agencies, as well as state institutions and agents, played a role in the introduction of social norms and controls in early modern times. Henceforth, alongside the state or semistate organized imposition of norms through laws and punishments (and it was on this that not only Oestreich's paradigm of social discipline but also criminal history concentrated), Church and community ecclesiastical discipline had to be considered. It has been postulated that this form of Church discipline, for all the overlaps and mixed forms with state and political social controls that actually occurred, was in principle independent in that unlike secular criminal jurisdiction (that envisaged punishment as the sanction) it concentrated "discipline of sin" on the perpetrators' understanding of their misdemeanor and their doing penance.[9] This is an ideal typical difference that is discussed by Manon van der Heijden in this volume and given closer definition by comparing it with historical reality.

Today, a large number of studies exist on the factually very different disciplining activities of the various confessional churches and of the nonconfessionalized or non-Christian religious communities such as the Baptists or the Jews.[10] The view from above likewise preferred by most of the studies on Church discipline that have a nonstatist thrust was supplemented by microhistorical studies that examine (in particular using Swiss examples) the communal basis and the contribution by parishes and individuals to "disciplining sin" in early modern times.[11]

Marriage and the Family

In recent years, the scope of studies on norms imposed by and control processes exerted by marriage and the family has been expanded and differentiated in a similar way, with a plurality of methods now being applied. These have been complemented by studies on the related subject of the education system (in part they overlap perfectly with studies on the family and the household), which strangely enough for many years played only a marginal role in research into old European disciplining processes. Initially, procedures for asserting norms and for social formation within marriages and the family were usually addressed in connection with Church discipline or other Church activities, and education thus came into focus, at least to the extent that it took place within the family and the household.[12] The complementary secular matrimonial jurisdiction and other activities by the state or authorities were at best considered only in passing.

Today, marriage and the family are researched from a much broader perspective in terms of subject matter, methodology, and the source materials consulted. Here, too, the vantage points of "from below" and "from above" and the focusing on "communities" and "institutions" are complementary. Both approaches are represented in this volume—by the essay by Katherine Lynch in the second part and the essay by Manon van der Heijden and Susanna Burghartz in this part. By contrast, education has not been integrated into it in the same way. This has to do with the fact that the history of education and upbringing is still overly construed as a specialist subject and thus customarily written not by general historians but by pedagogues interested in history who work in departments of education studies—this is at any rate the case in Germany. What benefit research into both social controls and discipline, not to mention general social and cultural history, can draw from integrative research into education and upbringing conducted by professional historians can be seen from a number of the publications by Stefan Ehrenpreis.[13]

Marriage, the family, and education comprise perhaps that part of early modern discipline influenced by the most institutions and actors. Traditionally, above all, extended families and neighborhoods were active in this regard. Moreover, the small circle of friends, close relatives, and the godfather and godmother of the couple also always played a certain role. Since the end of the Middle Ages, increasingly the Church, the early modern state, or the municipal magistrates became the authorities imposing the norms, exercising social control and empowered to punish, without the older social circles and institutions ever completely losing their influence.

Several monographs and essays have been published on this subject, including by two authors in this volume.[14] In her chapter published here, Manon van der Heijden convincingly demonstrates with reference to Dutch examples how church and state interests formed a coalition regarding the introduction of norms and regulation of marriage and the family, ensnaring such in a kind of pincer movement as of the Reformation. I increasingly feel it doubtful whether one should in this context speak of "private misdemeanors" (as I myself have done)[15] and thus suggest that "consistories and criminal courts both meddled in private affairs."[16] As has been shown not least by Susanna Burghartz in her analysis of the discourse on purity and as my own observations on the purity of Intercommunion as the foundations of early Church discipline in Emden should have taught me[17], sexual purity and the corresponding order of marriage were anything but a private matter—and this definitely went beyond the closer circle of the Christian communities. Indeed, these factors were considered to impact directly on the common weal and (as the famous Utrecht homosexual scandal in the early-eighteenth century proved) applied even in the Netherlands, where the respective domains of the state and the Church were separated to a greater extent than elsewhere in Europe at that time.

However, such an eschatological linkage of "private" and individual morality to communal salvation and the common good in the early-eighteenth century was only possible in extreme or exceptional situations. For we will no doubt encounter in identical or similar form elsewhere in Europe the periods of the "moral campaign" as developed by Susanna Burghartz using Swiss examples with its heyday and turnaround in the confessionalization as of the mid-sixteenth century, the more rigid nature of the same during the seventeenth century, in particular in Pietist circles, and the paradigm change from "morality to welfare" as of the early-eighteenth century. This applies at any rate to the Calvinist-Reformed regions, of which we could say: "Emden is everywhere."[18]

Art As a Form of Social Control

Studies in art history, such as the essays by Michael Scholz-Hänsel on painters and painting and by Bernd Roeck on the theory and practice of architecture, are at present probably the most fascinating innovation in terms of methodology and subject matter to occur in research into early modern disciplining and social control. Through these studies, the base of source matter consulted has been broadened considerably. Indeed, the researchers have put their finger on a new medium of psychological control, namely vision: "Works of art, texts without letters, can only be looked at" is how Bernd Roeck puts it and he proposes that this type of "soft" influence be construed as "conditioning"—a convincing terminological supplement to discipline and social control.

Michael Scholz-Hänsel cautiously (in fact experimentally) introduces the perspective of discipline into the study of early modern painting, primarily as he wishes to access a new "instrument of interpretation" for art history. At the same time, he expands the field covered by discipline research, which likewise pays attention to the resistance to such disciplining, in this case the actual free scope open to the painter who depended on those who commissioned him and was subject to state and Church control in the Catholic confessionalized domain of the Spanish and other Mediterranean cultural region. Scholz-Hänsel's ideas, as put forward here and in earlier essays, form important stepping stones for an interdisciplinary melding of general history and art history, one that is by no means as well developed as it should be. Given the close linkage between early modern confessionalization and social formation (specifically discipline), renewed evidence of which is provided in this volume, it will come as no surprise that, like other art historians who take an interdisciplinary approach, Scholz-Hänsel concentrates in particular on the confessional age, which is more or less identical with the Baroque age in art history.[19]

Periods and Regions

In temporal and chronological terms, the essays collected here center on the sixteenth and seventeenth centuries, outlining the prospects for the eighteenth century and, in the case of architectural history, discussing the entire premodern age. From the perspective of conditioning through seeing, Bernd Roeck convincingly demonstrates the relative constancy of the latter compared with the "flood of the media and before increasing communication and transportation links" set in. Within the early modern age, the different periods identified by Susanna Burghartz in her study of marriage and matrimonial discipline in Reform Switzerland probably apply more or less to the other regions in Europe. The Reformation in the narrower sense was followed from about 1550 through 1650 by confessionalization as the first phase of more intense formal control and disciplining "from above." In the course of the first half of the seventeenth century, a change gradually took place, away from the orthodox in favor of more open, but by no means weaker or even "more liberal," forms and justifications. At the beginning of the eighteenth century, a paradigm shift started toward enlightened, more strongly secular models and mechanisms of controls and disciplines.

Needless to say, we can assume temporal and substantive variations on this Swiss periodicization regarding the other European countries and confessional zones, and these variants were influenced by other agents and currents in intellectual history—for example the Jesuits with their spiritual exercises and the Marian congregations of a Catholic persuasion, or Jansenism instead of Pietism in certain Protestant communities. Nevertheless, within each respective phase, functional equivalents between discipline and social control can indeed be discerned—as was recently demonstrated in a volume of essays comparing French and German society—between the specific educational concepts of the French Jansenist schools, with their focus on individualization, and similar tendencies in Protestant Brandenburg-Prussia.[20]

In geographical terms, the examples are primarily chosen from central and northern European regions—albeit with important exceptions, such as the Mediterranean countries discussed in the essay by Tomás Mantecón in the second part of this book and those by Michael Scholz-Hänsel and Bernd Roeck in the first part. Yet it should be sufficiently clear on this basis that the institutions, mechanisms, and trends in the history of social control and discipline differed both within Europe and regionally. They need to be investigated both as an expression of the "Latin European" type of civilization and as firm reflections of national and territorial societies and nations.

Important opportunities for historical comparisons of society arise at both levels and have not to date been sufficiently explored. I refer here to the comparison with non-European and non-Christian civilizations but primarily to comparisons within Europe, namely between developments in Roman/Latin Europe, which were exposed by confessionalization to profound changes and differentiation in the sixteenth century, and Greek/Russian/Orthodox Europe, which did not undergo comparable dynamic changes and had given rise in the Middle Ages to quite different institutions and concepts for society. Inevitably, in Orthodox eastern Europe the history of discipline and social control moved in quite a different direction and with quite different results than did the disciplining in Latin Europe presented in this volume. However, we need to make comparisons within a civilization, that is, between different national and regional models of discipline and social control within Latin Europe itself. The objective is to identify the different conditions, types, and consequences of the respective form of disciplining, also with a view to the different consequences for the respective society up until the present day.

A wide spectrum of factors was responsible for this early modern disciplining within Europe. These factors include the political order and the particular form of early modern state formation, such as the consensus-bound Estates in England, the Netherlands, and Switzerland, as well as Poland and the other east central European states, prior to the intervention by the Habsburg dynasty or authoritarian or absolutist states, particularly France and the larger German territorial states. The list must also include the respective strength or weakness of communal or republican traditions and structures; the role of neighborhood associations, of extended families, of marital and marriage circles; the form of legislation, above all laws of inheritance and the legal position of women (important specifically, but not exclusively, regarding the control of sexuality, marriage, and the family); the degree of urbanization, urban networks, and density of communications, relations between cities and rural areas; the economy and economic conditions; the degree to which political and cultural formation had permeated society, for example in the case of policies on language; and finally (although it is difficult to define this in scholarly terms) the differences in mentality or temperament between populations in the various regions of Europe, between north and south, the mountains and the plains, and so forth.

Religious and Church institutions and disciplining measures, above all in more emphatically sharper confessionalizing form as of the mid-sixteenth century, played a particularly important if not predominant role in early modern Europe, as is shown by many of the essays in this volume. This concurs with the underlying basic structures of the premodern Latin type of civilization from the point of view of a sociology of religion—typified by the duality of church and state, of religion and politics, as well as the dialectical dovetailing of religious and secular change.[21] Irrespective of the aforementioned pan-European character, "social control" and "social disciplining" in early modern times were confessionally influenced. This also implied geographical division and differentiation therein: roughly speaking, between a north and northwest European, primarily Protestant model and a south and east central European, primarily Catholic model of social control and discipline. Central Europe, with the Netherlands, Switzerland, and Germany, formed a hybrid zone, in which both models existed side by side. Specifically in Germany, the European subdivision is reflected at the microlevel: with a Protestant north and a Catholic south, with the dividing line more or less in the middle in the shape of the Main river.

The differences between these models and the actual consequences they had, on the one hand, on the success of discipline from above and, on the other hand, for the acceptance from below at the grassroots level need to be investigated more closely and duly weighted. For example, we can look at the conditions and longer-term impact of the Reformed Church discipline compared with discipline by the Lutheran paterfamilias or chaplaincy or the Catholic confessional, or we can examine the differences between discipline in the Protestant societies, which was primarily effected through the word, and disciplining among the Catholics, which Bernd Roeck calls conditioning conveyed through seeing.

All this and much more besides must be charted on the early modern map of European discipline and social control. Until such an atlas of confessionalization and discipline has been prepared, we can still resort to literature to shed light on such landscapes of feelings, thought, and action: In her short story "Our Friend Judith," Doris Lessing (hardly renowned for overweighting religion or confession) finds the causes of the failed love of Judith, an Englishwoman, and Luigi, an Italian, in the fact that the northerner, with her Puritanical Protestant upbringing, "has no sense of sin: but she has guilt," while the Italian, with his Mediterranean Catholic roots, has "no sense of guilt, but a sense of sin."[22]

Perspectives for Further Research

The essays in this volume focus on only a selection of the institutions and mechanisms of early modern social control and discipline. The overall spectrum is far greater, and today additional research work is still required in order to cover the totality of the disciplining measures influencing individuals and the various social groups from approximately 1500 through 1800 and to detail the overall reach of such influence and the pressure to change customs regarding thought and behavior. I wish for reasons of space to mention but a few examples.

In connection with the control of marriage and sexual behavior it would, for instance, be necessary to pay attention to midwifery. Older studies have already dealt with the formal and institutional side of midwifery, specifically its regulation by the Church and the state. More recent studies rooted in cultural history have now expanded the focus here to include the history of corporeality and the role of gender-specific or communal factors.[23] The same is true of the general systems of health and hygiene as well as welfare for the poor, the old, and the sick—in the light of recent studies in cultural history, they evidently had a far greater impact on early modern discipline than the formal regulation by Church and state as described in past investigations.

Another area that has hardly been examined is the connection between discipline and environmental protection policies by early modern magistrates and authorities. In the late Middle Ages, and above all in the mining regions of central Europe, but also in the industrial centers of the highly urbanized zones of southern and western Europe, local authorities issued decrees against noise, malodors, pollution of the air and water, and other environmental damage, such as the thoughtless felling of complete forests, and these inevitably entailed discipline and social control of individuals or business groups in favor of the overarching interests of the community as a whole. A very striking and almost burlesque example was the prohibition on urinating in rivers upstream from breweries on days when the brewery was drawing water—already to be encountered in municipal decrees in Medieval times.

Little research has as yet been done into the disciplining functions of, primarily (though not exclusively), religious rites, ceremonies, symbols. Most recently, scholars have pointed to the normative and intellectually and physically disciplining nature of joint pilgrimages to a particular destination or processions for a specific reason, particularly pilgrimages proper, the number of which surged in the course of Catholic confessionalization, leading to their more pronounced formation. Freitag writes that "the uncontrolled procession of individuals or small groups gave way to a disciplining holy practice allowing control to be exercised."[24]

Last but not least, the early modern formation processes to which language was subjected in almost all European societies also had a normative and disciplining role—once Latin had started to recede as the preferred medium of communication by the educated and once each centralized state as well as the confessional churches became interested in repressing dialects and regional idiosyncrasies, certainly as part of official communications. Wolfgang Reinhard has shown just what cognitive insights can be gained from historical linguistics with a focus on the socio-historical context in his study of colonialization and the process of the world's Europeanization.[25] For Germany, Martin Luther's normative linguistic achievements are something like a "*lieu de mémoire.*" However, to date there has been insufficient research into the exact mechanisms and phases during which, above all in northern Germany, the Low German dialect gave way to a normative High German, first of all from the pulpits, then among communications by local authorities and the educated, and finally among the broader population. The same applies to the impact of other "high" languages competing with High German, such as Dutch, which penetrated northwestern Germany in the seventeenth century, or Latin, which held its ground in the Catholic regions, especially in southern Germany, for quite some time to come. It is clear that in each case a major struggle revolving around linguistic standardization and an intellectual monopoly on interpretations was involved, something that must have had far-reaching consequences not only for people's thought and faith but also on their actions and behavior. It is also evident that specifically the institutional and formal normativization and control of language was only one side of the coin and that a decisive role was also played by the "stubbornness" of the speakers themselves. Language was and is both a medium of discipline and trammeling as well as a means of resistance and self-assertion.

Thus, specifically the example of language reminds us that the entire spectrum of early modern discipline and control can only be grasped using an integrative methodology or through the dual perspective of "from below" and "from above," of formal and informal, of macro- and microhistorical, of institutional disciplining from outside and internalized self-discipline. The essay by James Sharpe shows this emphatically using English source material, and he advocates "the need for a broad perspective." Manon van der Heijden takes up a similar demand by Martin Ingram and highlights both Church and secular marital discipline. In general, scholars love to focus either on a close-up view of their object or on a panoramic perspective of the same. As this volume shows, with its division into two parts, this is usually for analysis or presentation. In historical reality, both sides take place at once.

Something else can also be seen from language, something which applies well beyond language alone: Individualizing and collective trends complemented each other in early modern discipline. Just as the individual finds his personal language within the collective language and thus adapts collective norms set externally, early modern discipline in Europe did not lead in the final instance to the decline of the individual in the collective, but to the individual's being strengthened and receiving a sharper profile. This did not, conversely, lead to society's bounds being exploded. Seen in this way, Immanuel Kant's categorical imperative has a direct role to play in our topic: "Act as if the maxims of your will could at all times also be valid as the principle for general legislation." For this new secular anchoring of the individual within society, or (to put it in modern terms) within civil society, assumes as it were that the individual has internalized discipline and is accustomed to being responsible for his own actions.

The history of social control and discipline in early modern times is thus suited to provide a key contribution to a current field of research on which social scientists have especially concentrated most recently, namely the origins and nature of modern individualism and the relation between individualism and the civil society that arose parallel to it and complemented it factually.[26] It is well known that this did not occur to the same extent in all European societies at once. The collaboration between historical research into social control and early modern discipline, on the one hand, and deliberations on individualization and the civil society model in the social sciences, on the other hand, could help shed new light on the reasons and conditions that led in nineteenth-century Europe to certain societies instituting an authoritarian and later Fascist or Communist "order," while others remained committed to civil society.

Notes

1. Most recently, plausible arguments were brought that raised doubts as to whether Oestreich's elaborations on social disciplining even constituted a concept in the strict scholarly sense; see Freitag, "Mißverständnis."

2. "toutes les portes paraissent bonnes pour franchir le seuil multiple de l'histoire": Braudel, "Sur une conception," 318.

3. On this point, see the discussion between Heinz Schilling and Heinrich-Richard Schmidt in *Historische Zeitschrift* 264 (1997), 675–91; and *Historische Zeitschrift* 265 (1997), 639–82.

4. For a suggestion on a flexible and far-reaching open terminology, see my introduction to Schilling, ed., *Institutionen*.

5. For simplicity's sake, in the following I mainly use the term "disciplining" in line with the justification in Schilling, ed., *Institutionen*.

6. Cf. also Lotz-Heumann, *Konfessionalisierung in Irland* and her contribution to Schilling, ed., *Institutionen*.

7. By way of example I would simply cite the corresponding chapters on the Frisian communities in Cuperus, *Kerkelijk leven* (esp. vol. 2, 54–126).

8. This and the following are elaborated on in detail and proven in the introduction and bibliography of Schilling, ed., *Kirchenzucht und Sozialdisziplinierung.*

9. Schilling, "Geschichte der Sünde"; Schilling, "History of Crime."

10. I refer the reader here solely to the essays in Schilling, ed., *Kirchenzucht und Sozialdisziplinierung.* A prime example that, regardless of the problems of finding source material, it is possible to generate key insights into Catholic discipline through the confessional is offered in Myers, *Poor, Sinning Folk.*

11. Worthy of mention, because they take the methodology and subject matter further, are primarily the studies by Heinrich-Richard Schmidt, above all Schmidt, *Dorf und Religion.* See also Schmidt, "Die Ächtung des Fluchens"; Schmidt, "Das Bernische Sittengericht"; Schmidt and Brodbeck, "Davos zwischen Sünde und Verbrechen; and Schmidt, "Über die Tätigkeit von Berner Kurgerichten."

12. See my contribution in Mentzer, ed., *Sin and the Calvinists.* Specifically on education, see Schilling, "Sündenzucht"; and Schilling, *Civic Calvinism,* 43 et seq. (table 2–2).

13. See Ehrenpreis, "Französische Uniformität"; and Ehrenpreis, ed., *Konfessionelle und säkulare Trends.*

14. I refer the reader here only to the monographs by van der Heijden, *Huwelijk in Holland* and Burghartz, *Zeiten der Reinheit.*

15. Among others in Schilling, "Sündenzucht," 277, 290.

16. Cf. van der Heijden in this volume.

17. Burghartz, *Zeiten der Reinheit;* Schilling, "Reformierte Kirchenzucht als Sozialdisziplinierung," 272 et seq. The purity of intercommunion as the underlying idea behind church discipline was recently taken up again in Schilling, "Urban Architecture," 22 et seq.

18. Schmidt, "Emden est partout."

19. Scholz-Hänsel, "The Social Meaning"; Scholz-Hänsel, "Neapolitanische Malerei," vol. 93 of the Archive for the History of the Reformation offers as a focal point for that year "Confessionalization and Art." See also Göttler, *Die Kunst des Fegefeuers;* and Leineweber, *Bologna nach dem Tridentinum.*

20. "Mager, Jansenistische Erziehung," in Schilling and Gross, eds., *Minderheiten und Erziehung,* 313–55. Winter, "Die Hugenotten."

21. The developments mentioned in this paragraph and the previous one are discussed more elaborately in Schilling, *Die neue Zeit,* esp. 457 et seq.

22. Lessing, *The Temptation,* 18.

23. For older studies, see, among others: Schilling, *Religion, Political Culture,* 353–412 (orig. ed. 1980). Another macrohistorical study, if with a different thrust is Donnison, *Midwives.* For studies in cultural history, see, for example, Labouvie, *Andere Umstände;* Schlumbohm et al., eds., *Rituale der Geburt.* A fundamental work with a wide range: Laqueur, *Making Sex.*

24. Freitag, *Volks- und Elitenfrömmigkeit,* 100 et seq.

25. Reinhard, "Sprachbeherrschung und Weltherrschaft" (first ed. 1987).

26. See, for example, van Dülmen, ed., *Entdeckung des Ich;* Münkler and Bluhm, eds., *Gemeinwohl und Gemeinsinn;* Keane, *Civil Society;* Hildermeier et al., eds., *Zivilgesellschaft.*

CHAPTER 2

Social Control in Early Modern England: The Need for a Broad Perspective

James A. Sharpe

I n 1985, toward the beginning of a book entitled *Visions of Social Control: Crime, Punishment and Classification,* the British sociologist of deviance Stanley Cohen made the following comments:

> The term "social control" has lately become something of a Mickey Mouse concept. In sociology textbooks, it appears as a neutral term to cover all social processes to induce conformity ranging from infant socialization through to public execution. In radical theory and rhetoric, it has become a negative term to cover not just the obviously coercive apparatus of the state, but also the putative hidden element in all state-sponsored social policy, whether called health, education or welfare. Historians and political scientists restrict the concept to the repression of political opposition, while sociologists, psychologists and anthropologists invariably talk in broader and non-political terms. In everyday language, that concept has no resonant or clear meaning at all.

It is therefore not surprising that Cohen should comment "all this creates some terrible muddles."[1] Yet the various contributions gathered here in this volume are dedicated to discussing historical aspects of this "Mickey Mouse concept" and, it is to be hoped, creating some sort of cosmos from the chaos of the "terrible confusion." If I may state my own position, the term "social control" is one which I have not used much in works I have written, largely because of an awareness of its imprecision: I have generally found the term "social discipline" a more useful one, although I accept that this term too entails a fair degree of confusion, while I am aware that the term enjoys little currency among historians of early modern England. I have, more particularly, been anxious not to employ the term "social control" when discussing law enforcement and the punishment of crime, despite the tendency for historians to use the concept when discussing such matters, simply because of my awareness of the breadth of its connotations. Indeed, historians' usage of this term has frequently reflected a distressing tendency for practitioners of history to borrow and apply concepts from another social science without sufficient precision and without proper awareness of the resonances of those concepts.[2] What I would like to do in this essay is to explore some of the complexities of what social control in some of its broader ramifications might involve in the historical context I know best, early modern England.

The term seems to have entered sociological discourse largely through the writings of Edward Alsworth Ross, one of the founding fathers of American sociology (see introduction to this volume). His book *Social Control: A Survey of the Foundations of Order*, published in 1901, gave a broad definition to the concept and delineated both the formal and the informal ways in which society constrains the individual, bringing together the influence of both external norms and internalized processes. His objective in writing the book, it has been claimed, was "to synthesise the old and the new, to infuse an impersonal industrial society with the idealized virtues of the face-to-face community in which he grew up."[3] Raised in the moralistic and agrarian Midwest, Ross's sociology seems to have been the outcome of a personal transition that he made from *Gemeinschaft* to *Gesellschaft* as United States society became more urban, more sophisticated, and more overtly racially and culturally complex.

Thus the concept of social control, in its original form, places Ross's work firmly in the context of the major concern of the classic sociology: namely, attempting to understand and explain the workings of that allegedly new and complex industrial and urban society of the nineteenth century that had apparently replaced the pre-existing traditional forms of social organization. Indeed, the concept of social control for Ross seems to have performed roughly the same function as did the *conscience collective* for Durkheim as an explanation of social cohesion. The concept whose usage had become so loose by the time Cohen wrote as to render it, in his opinion, almost useless, was in fact central to the United States' sociological tradition.[4] Thus, social control was a concept of major importance to the Chicago School of the 1920s, not least for Robert E. Park, one of the major figures in that school. In the weighty *Introduction to the Science of Sociology*, which Park published with E. W. Burgess in 1924, it was commented that "all social problems turn out finally to be problems of social control" and that social control should be "the central fact and the central problem of sociology."[5] Currently, even in the United States, social control has lost this primacy in the pantheon of sociological concepts. But for many years it provided, in both North America and elsewhere, a means of getting a grip on the multifaceted ways in which societies attempt, consciously or otherwise, to achieve some form of coherence, taking in such primary institutions of social control as the family, the neighborhood, and the community, and such secondary ones as the police, the courts, the press, and political machines. I would argue that, in our efforts to consider social control in its historical context, we should attempt to bear in mind this broad usage. To return to a point made earlier, we must deplore the way, as one scholar has put it, that "historians have borrowed the sociological concept of social control as applied to the control of deviant behaviour: thus the strong emphasis, in historical writing, on coercion."[6]

The State and Religion

But to begin our discussion of social control in early modern England let us, nevertheless, turn to an act of coercion. In 1680 a man called John Marketman was publicly executed at West Ham in Essex after being convicted for murdering his wife. This is, perhaps, social control at its rawest: an assertion of the power of the monarch's law, with the convicted felon dying before what was described as "some thousands of sorrowful spectators." Yet embedded in the rituals of execution was a view of what we might call social control that went far before the simple act of public execution. Stanley Cohen, as we have noted, when pondering the problematically open-ended nature of the concept of social control, commented that one problem is the way in which sociology textbooks tend to include under social control "all processes to induce conformity from infant socialization to public execution."[7] John Marketman, who had certainly never read a sociology textbook, would have shared this view. According to a pamphlet describing his death, he made a speech from the gallows in which he declared that

> he had been very disobedient to his too indulgent parents, and that he had spent his youthful days in profanation of the Sabbath and licentious evils of debaucheries beyond expression, and that he had been over penurious in his narrow observance of his wive's ways, desirous that all should pray to the Eternal God for his everlasting welfare, and with many pious expressions ended this mortal life.[8]

This was, in fact, the standard gallows speech of the type that is recounted in pamphlet after pamphlet describing the public execution.[9] And, on almost every occasion, those on the brink of being executed told how the crimes that had led to their terrible but deserved fate had been prefaced by disobedience to parents as a child and by youthful debauchery, while like Marketman they usually followed the clergymen who offered them spiritual advice in their last hours and recast their experience in the context of the ongoing battle between good and evil, ending their personal narrative with an epilogue on repentance and redemption. The public execution, therefore, serves as a useful introduction to some of the broader dimensions of social control in our period.

Public executions do, of course, focus our attention on one of the main agencies of social control: the state. This entity remains difficult to define for early modern England, but it remains clear that with the public execution of convicted felons, the public whipping of petty thieves, and the public setting on the pillory of speakers of seditious words, we—like the contemporaries attending these spectacles—are witnesses to displays of state power in which the social control ambitions of central authority and its local representatives seem all too overt. Yet the influence of the state was working in ways more subtle than these open manifestations of the power of the authorities. Perhaps the most accessible evidence on this point lies in the way in which local communities, or sections of those communities, found it useful to invoke higher authority when faced with troublesome neighbors.

Consider, for example, a scrap of evidence from the obscure Worcestershire village of Feckenham. In 1612 a number of the inhabitants of that village sent a set of "articles" to the county justices about the misdoings of John Leight, a laborer of that parish, whom they wished the justices to bind over to keep the peace. Leight was fairly typical of the disorderly nuisance offender of the period. He was an alehouse haunter, a drunkard, a blasphemous swearer, and would spend money in the alehouse rather than go home to his wife and children, who were in receipt of poor relief. He was a slanderous person, a man of lewd life and conversation, and a man who would sooner lurk in the alehouse than go to church on the Sabbath. He gossiped about his neighbors in the alehouse and eroded family and household discipline by encouraging the sons and servants of his more respectable neighbors to join him in his drinking. That his neighbors were anxious to invoke the county bench to act against this local nuisance is a neat, and very typical, illustration of how "community" notions of social control as offered by the agents of the state was something that was sought from below as much as it was imposed from above.[10] And on the level of more serious crime, many of those who died on the scaffold suffered this fate not because of the action of some "police" agency, but rather because of the action of the person offended against, who had decided to invoke the state law.

But as John Marketman's dying speech from the scaffold makes clear, social control involved not only the input of the state but also that of religion. The Reformation and the Catholic Counter-Reformation are two very old friends for historians of the early modern period, and in earlier generations considerable time was devoted to attempting to discern connections between the new religious ideas and the social structure of the period, the most celebrated outcome of these musings being the rather different sets of connections between Protestantism and capitalism made by Max Weber and Marxist thinkers. Among English historians at least, there has been something of a retreat from this type of paradigm, but nevertheless there is considerable value in addressing the social control, or perhaps more accurately the social discipline, aspects of Protestantism.

I would contend that current thinking here runs along two tracks, and that these two tracks serve handily to lead us to two areas of major importance. The first of these is the social. The old connections between Protestantism, or more specifically that English brand of Protestantism known as Puritanism, and a rising middle class are no longer tenable. There has been, however, a more subtle analysis of the differential appeal of Puritanism to various social groups that is centered on considerations of power rather than wealth (and, of course, it was the wealthy who tended to wield power, frequently in the very overt and direct form of local office holding). A religion that stressed the need to preserve God-given social hierarchies and that also laid considerable emphasis on humankind's innate sinfulness would make a lot of sense to the justices of the peace who ruled England's shires, the merchant elites who governed England's towns, and—in at least some cases—the parish constables and churchwardens who were responsible for law enforcement in local communities.[11] In the post-Reformation official mind set that equated the good Christian (as defined in England by the Church Settlement of 1559) with the good subject, religion would obviously have a crucial role in the control of crime and delinquency: witness that innovation of the Tudor period, the active presence of the clergy on the gallows when felons were executed.[12]

Yet religion is essentially about personal belief, and in effect the Reformation's most important battlefield was the mind of the individual believer. Thus one of the objectives of the Reformation was to create a new human being and to promote in the individual Christian a rational and internalized view of Christianity that would inform his or her everyday belief.[13] Puritanism as a social force is very familiar in English historical writing. But if we are to understand the full impact of the Reformation as an agency of social control, we have to recognize its psychological dimension: the control of human beings best came from within, rather than from an external coercive agency. I would contend that realization of this point should be of central importance to any broad study of social control in early modern Europe or in any other social context.

But individuals, for the most part, are raised in families. In almost all societies, one suspects, the family is the primary institution of socialization, the milieu where culture is transmitted from generation to generation, and society thus made possible. Despite considerable work on the history of the family in our period, however, there is still some uncertainty as to how exactly the processes of socialization (certainly of very young children) operated, while such sources as we have bearing on this issue are very heavily skewed toward the rich: how a Suffolk weaver and his wife or their equivalents among the Yorkshire yeomanry might have gone about socializing their children are, as yet, uncertain matters. There is a large amount of contemporary normative literature on family life (notably the "conduct books" that were so frequently published in the Elizabethan period and the seventeenth century), but this is usually very conventional and nonspecific, while such memories as we have of the experience of childhood were written many years after the experience took place, of necessity missing the early months or even years of childhood, and were—to return to a point I have just made—very much the product of the middling and superior strata of society.[14] Conversely, what is obvious from the books of instruction on how to raise families (many of which were, in fact, written by clergymen) was that the widespread belief in the family as an agent of socialization was becoming more focused and was constantly reiterated.[15] The image of the godly household supplemented and reinforced existing notions of the family as the primary unit of political organization. But in this period, the "family" did not just include kin. The presence of apprentices in many households, and the common custom of sending adolescents out to work as live-in servants, meant that the family as a unit of control and socialization affected others than the immediate blood or affinal kin of the head of the household. The phenomenon of apprenticeship was of central importance in the early modern period: an examination of it would, therefore, seem to offer some deeper insights into the workings of social control in that era.

The World of Work

In England, as in many other European states, apprenticeship was a phenomenon of considerable importance, imbricated into the economic practices and assumptions of the period, and involving a high proportion of young people, especially males. Apprenticeship was thought to offer considerable advantages. It provided a secure future for a child, with a guarantee of employment at the end of training and the benefits of belonging as an adult to a trade or craft organization. The apprentice was legally bound to his master, who during the term of the apprenticeship enjoyed what were essentially parental rights over him. The apprentice lived with his master's family, was provided with food, shelter, and clothing, and thus the child learned not only technical craft skills but also the way of life of the craft or profession that was being entered. Apprenticeship was thus in many ways a method of raising and educating children and had both implicit and explicit social control functions, the most efficient of these being the master's right of "moderate" physical correction over the apprentice.[16]

Apprentices were, in fact, extremely varied in their social composition, although it is possible to divide them into three broad groups. The first of these, the "typical" apprentices, were those boys (and less frequently, girls) who were apprenticed to learn the skilled crafts and trades typical of an early modern economy and who were eventually to become members of what historians of England are now becoming accustomed to think of as the "middling sort." Second, however, there were those boys who were bound apprentice to masters who represented the upper stratum of urban society, the richer merchants and trades-men. In many cases this type of apprenticeship was seen as offering a means of upward social mobility, and it was here that apprenticeship as a means of social-ization into a set of cultural expectations different from that which the appren-tice might formerly have experienced was at its most important. Third, and most problematically, there was, as an aspect of the poor relief system, the enforced binding out of poor children to sometimes unwilling masters.

Ideally, however, the relationship between the apprentice and his master was one into which the apprentice, or at least his parents, and the master entered willingly. And the formal contracts that set out the details of apprenticeships nor-mally included clauses demonstrating that part of the relationship was the assump-tion of control over the apprentice by the master and the imposition of the constraints that the period felt appropriate for youth. Thus, when the Wiltshire husband-man William Selman apprenticed his son Richard to a broadweaver in 1705, the contract set out the following directions for the apprentice: "Taverns and ale-houses he shall not haunt, dice, cards or any other unlawful games he shall not use, fornication with any woman he shall not commit, matrimony with any woman he shall not contract. He shall not absent himself by night or day without his master's leave but be a true and faithful servant."[17] Control was obviously seen as a major concern in this and the countless other contracts of apprenticeship in the early modern period.

The apprenticeship of poor children also had considerable social control over-tones. Let us consider an order made by the Somerset assizes in March 1638. As part of a general clampdown on the disorderly, apparently sparked by "the great increase of bastards that are chargeable to parishes," the court ordered that

> for prevencion of charge that cometh upon parishes by children which live idley and be fitting to be bound forth apprentices, this court doth require all justices of peace that they take speciall care for the byndinge forth [of] apprentices: and yf the parents of poore children shall refuse to have their chil-dren bound forth apprentices in such cases where the officers of the parish shall desire it and the justices of the peace due approve thereof, then the justices of the peace shall send the parents of such children to the house of correccion whoe doe soe refuse or oppose the binding forth of their children . . . such par-ents there to remayne untill they shall willingly submitt themselves to the order and direccon of the justices in that behalfe.

Despite parental objections, the justices were empowered to bind the children of the idle poor as apprentices, while those who refused to take apprentices, or who treated them so badly that they ran away, were to be bound over to the next assizes "there to be dealt withall as this court shall think fitt." In fact, the court envisaged making those refusing to take apprentices pay the costs of their prosecution and also pay "such money as this court shall thinke fitt" to the poor relief funds of their respective parishes, "to the end that others by their punishment may take example not to be soe obstinate and troublesome hereafter."[18]

At the best of times, the relationship between the apprentice and his master was an inherently problematic one, but the practice of enforced apprenticeships meant that many heads of household, perhaps with already strained resources, now had the responsibility of feeding and raising another, and probably recalcitrant, child laid upon them. Details of breakdown in the relationship between master and servant, however, demonstrate that both parish apprentices and those apprenticed by more traditional means were likely to represent problems for the social control aspects of apprenticeship.

Early modern apprentices, like any group of (especially male) young people, attracted the attention of the social commentators and moralists of their time. There was a body of normative literature, although as ever the historian is left uncertain of its impact.[19] Certainly there were contemporary complaints enough about apprentices' unruliness and their tendency to neglect their duties, consort with prostitutes, haunt taverns, and riot. Entries in the court records of the period both add substance to these generalized complaints and also provide examples of ill treatment of apprentices.

Apprentices were sometimes brought to court for stealing from their masters. One such was John Game, who was convicted and branded in 1639 for stealing £5/6/6 (a considerable sum) from his master, Henry Stone, of Minterne Magna in Dorset. Game was apparently a parish apprentice, and the court ordered that he should be discharged from Stone's service (one suspects that Stone was all too glad to see the back of him) but was to be bound to another master as speedily as possible.[20] Another thieving apprentice tried by the South-Western assizes was Joseph Griffen, charged in 1648 with stealing money from his master, Richard Hunt. Griffen was deemed to be below the age of criminal responsibility and was therefore not convicted. Hunt was anxious to get rid of him, yet refused to return to Griffen's father the £5 and three pecks of wheat that had been paid at the time when Joseph Griffen's indentures had been signed.[21]

It is therefore possible to find considerable evidence of apprenticeship malfunctioning. Yet, generally, it seems to have been a widely accepted phenomenon that usually worked reasonably well. And it had, we must reiterate, marked social control functions. In a period when youth was seen as an especially problematic stage in the human life cycle,[22] apprenticeship took young people, especially young males, into a context where they were subjected to the discipline, potentially backed by physical punishment, of a master's control. There they were socialized for adult life by learning a trade, thus preparing them for the world of work and also teaching them those disciplines that would allow them, in turn, to set up as heads of household. Most of what we know about apprenticeship, of course, comes from official and legal records, and we are in need of a study of the phenomenon from the apprentices' point of view. What is obvious is that in London at least, and perhaps in other major English cities, by the seventeenth century there existed an apprentice culture, in which youths in service showed shared values and a shared awareness.[23] And an aspect of this culture was shared leisure activities.

A Popular Play

The institution of apprenticeship is, therefore, clearly one that would be important in any discussion of social control in the early modern period, involving as it does the themes of household discipline, workplace discipline, and the control of young people, especially young males. But, to push my examination of the broader themes that a discussion of social control might involve, let us take apprenticeship as a somewhat unlikely springboard to another dimension of social control, the role of popular entertainment, and in particular the drama, in the enforcement of social norms.

It is possible to see a number of items of cultural production, familiar enough by the eighteenth century, in which the theme of the bad apprentice figured prominently. Perhaps the most striking, in that it depended on visual images, was William Hogarth's *Industry and Idleness* print series. This traced the fortunes of two apprentices, Tom Idle and John Goodchild, who begin service together in the same London workshop. John was the good apprentice, who eventually rose to fame through the time-honored combination of hard work and marrying the boss's daughter. Tom Idle, conversely, displayed the paradigmatic characteristics of the bad apprentice: he neglected his work, fell into bad company, gambled, drank, and consorted with prostitutes, turned to crime to provide the financial support for these activities, and was eventually hanged at Tyburn. The model Tom Idle represented was, in fact, a familiar one, corresponding as it did with the "Last Dying Speeches" made by convicted criminals as they stood on the gallows.[24] These characteristically insisted that it was youthful wrongdoing and the resulting small delinquencies that led inexorably to more serious offenses, and the gallows. Moreover, from the early eighteenth century it was possible to read compendia of criminal biographies in which the theme of the unruly apprentices, and the way in which youthful vices, if unchecked, could lead to serious crime and an untimely death at the end of a rope loomed large.[25] The theme of the idle and delinquent apprentice was absolutely central to cultural concepts of the origins of criminal behavior in the seventeenth and eighteenth centuries, and, as I have suggested, by the mid-eighteenth there was a range of visual and print sources that reinforced this centrality.

From 1731 this range was extended by an unexpectedly popular play, George Lillo's *The London Merchant*. Lillo was one of those recurring figures in the history of the arts, a man who enjoyed massive popularity in his own day, but who is now largely forgotten and whose works are never performed. He was born in London, probably in 1693, of Dutch and English parents, and followed his father by being a goldsmith-jeweler by trade and a Dissenter by religion. He died in 1739, by that time a reasonably prosperous businessman, and was buried at St. Leonard's, Shoreditch. Apart from these details, little is known of his life, except that he spent all of it in London and that he supplemented his business activities by becoming a successful and well-regarded playwright. He wrote eight (or possibly nine) dramatic works, including a ballad-opera, *Sylvia: Or the Country Burial,* a patriotic masque, *Britannia and Batavia,* and *Marina,* a reworking of Shakespeare's *Pericles* written to cash in on a vogue for the Bard's works. He was best known, however, for his domestic tragedies, *The London Merchant* and *Fatal Curiosity,* and for plays written in the heroic tradition, the most noteworthy of these being *The Christian Hero* of 1735. His domestic tragedies in particular were thought of as the prototypes for an important dramatic genre and were regarded on the continent as the model for *tragédie domestique et bourgeoise.* Henry Fielding, who produced Lillo's *Fatal Curiosity,* declared that the play gave its author "title to be the best tragick poet of his age."[26]

It was, however, *The London Merchant: Or, the History of George Barnwell,* first performed at Drury Lane Theatre on Tuesday, June 22, 1731, which made Lillo's reputation. Adapted from a story line provided by a seventeenth-century ballad, the plot told of the downfall of George Barnwell, apprentice to a London merchant called Thorowgood, who developed an attachment for a prostitute named Millwood, robbed his master, and then murdered and robbed his uncle for her, and eventually ended up with her on the gallows. From the first night the play was a great success. Lillo's previous work, his ballad-opera *Sylvia,* had not been well received, and apparently many of those who attended the first night of *The London Merchant* had come to mock. But, as a contemporary newspaper review was to put it, shortly into the production "most profound silence argued the deepest attention, and the sincerest pleasure imaginable—This increased gradually, as the plot advanced, and new circumstances of guilt and distress aggravated the concern of the spectators . . . and I believe there was hardly a spectator there that did not witness his approbation by tears."

The first night success was symptomatic of the play's later popularity. The play was frequently performed at Drury Lane over the next few months, became the subject of a royal command performance, was staged at fairs around London, and until the mid-1770s was one of the five most popular non-Shakespearean tragedies produced in the capital. Details for provincial performances are less easy to come by, but it was clearly a drama that enjoyed widespread popularity, and it is noteworthy that the great actress Sarah Siddons acted in a production in Liverpool in 1776. The play was revived in London in the late-eighteenth century, and there is every indication that it remained popular in both the capital and the provinces well into the nineteenth. There were recurrent rumors, apparently unsubstantiated, that it owed part of its success to financial support from, as a contemporary put it, "eminent merchants and citizens who approved of its moral tendency," but it rapidly acquired a lasting reputation for having been very widely attended by apprentices, many of whom were encouraged to see the play by their masters, who hoped that the important moral messages it attempted to convey would be internalized. It was regularly produced at the time of the Christmas and Easter holidays, being "judged a proper entertainment for apprentices, &c, as being a more instructive, moral and cautionary drama, than many pieces that had usually been given on those days." It was also given the seal of approval of the capital's mercantile elite by being regularly performed in London on Lord Mayor's day in the November of each year, replacing a less edifying work entitled *The London Cuckolds*.[27]

Certainly Lillo wrote the play with a didactic intent. The published version of the work was prefaced by a dedicatory letter from Lillo to Sir John Eyles, member of Parliament for and alderman of the City of London, and subgovernor of the South-Sea Company. In the letter, Lillo wrote of "the end of tragedy, the exciting of the passions, in order to the correcting of such of them as are criminal, either in their nature, or through their excess." Meeting the criticism that *The London Merchant* had debased tragedy by dealing with relatively lowly people and had met with considerable popularity, Lillo commented:

> What I wou'd infer is this, I think, evident truth; that tragedy is so far from losing its dignity, by being accommodated to the circumstances of the generality of mankind, that it is more truly August in proportion to the extent of its influence, and the numbers that are properly affected by it. As it is more truly great to be the instrument of good to many, who stand in need of our assistance, than to a very small part of that number. . . . Plays, founded on moral tales in private life, may be of admirable use, by carrying conviction to the mind, with such irresistible force, as to engage all the faculties and powers of the soul in the cause of virtue, by stifling vice in its first principles.

Lillo, a Christian writing from a clear moral perspective, was convinced of "the usefulness of tragedy in general" in helping to curb vice. In other words, he saw his play, of course among many other things, as a vehicle for social control.

We do not, of course, have any insights into what the generations of apprentices who went to see *The London Merchant* made of the experience, but they were certainly presented with a strong and explicit lesson on the wages of sin. George Barnwell, a youth of eighteen with a promising future before him, was described thus by his friend and fellow apprentice, Trueman: "Never had a youth a higher sense of virtue—Justly he thought, and as he thought he practised; never was a life more regular than his; as understanding uncommon at his years; an open, generous manliness of temper; his manners easy, unaffected and engaging."[28] As well as being admired by Trueman, Barnwell was liked and trusted by his master, while unknown to him, Maria, Thorowgood's daughter whom Barnwell secretly loved, harbored an undisclosed passion for him.

His downfall was occasioned by Millwood, a woman who, noticing his receiving and paying considerable sums of money in the city, decided to pretend to be in love with this clearly inexperienced young man and persuade him to rob his master and bring money to her. Barnwell does so, his actions providing him with opportunities to wrestle with his conscience on stage.[29] Eventually, Millwood persuades him to murder and rob his wealthy uncle. Barnwell does so, and after another passage in which the turmoil of his conscience is displayed, goes to Millwood and tells her that he has done the deed. By this stage, understandably, he is in a rather disturbed state, and in the best traditions of the period, declares that although no human witnessed the murder, "what can we hide from heaven's all-seeing eye?" Taking a more robust attitude, Millwood replies, "No more of this stuff—what advantage did you make of his death . . . what gold, what jewels, or what else of value have you brought me?" Barnwell's response, that he was too conscience-stricken after the murder to take anything, sends Millwood into a passion. Realizing that "in his madness he will discover all, and involve me in his ruin," she sends for a servant and tells him "fetch me an officer and seize this villain, he has confessed himself a murderer, shou'd I let him escape, I justly might be thought as bad as he."[30]

But Millwood's attempts at self-preservation are doomed. Her servant, Lucy, concerned about being implicated in the murder of Barnwell's uncle, had already revealed all to Thorowgood, who gets a constable and goes with him and a number of assistants to arrest Millwood. She and Barnwell meet after their arrests, and Barnwell has his first opportunity to start moralizing about his downfall:

> Be warn'd ye youths, who see my sad despair,
> Avoid lewd women, false as they are fair;
> By reason guided, honest joys pursue;
> To fair, to honour and to virtue true,
> Just to her self, will ne'er be false to you.
> By my example learn to shun my fate,
> (How wretched is the man who's wise too late).[31]

A scene or two later, Millwood is given her own chance to moralize, and returning to a theme she has touched on earlier in the play, declares that women are men's "universal prey" and that every fallen woman could attribute her position to the male sex. "Another and another spoiler came," she declares, and "all my gain was poverty and reproach . . . I found it necessary to be rich; and to that end, I summon'd all my arts. You call 'em wicked, be it so, they were such as my conversation with your sex has furnished me withal."[32]

The play quickly returns, however, to more mainstream morality. Barnwell is reported to have behaved well in court, weeping and expressing sorrow, and accepting the inevitability of the sentence of death placed upon him (Millwood, of course, shows none of these qualities). Thorowgood sends a clergyman to help prepare Barnwell for death, and this minister, as is so often the case in the execution pamphlets of the period, does his job well. Barnwell is visited in prison by Thorowgood and tells him of how receptive he had been to the minister's spiritual guidance: "The word of truth, which he recommended for my constant companion in this my sad retirement, has at length remov'd the doubts I labour'd under. From thence I've learn'd the infinite extent of his mercy; that my offences, tho' great, are not unpardonable; and that 'tis not my interest only, but my duty to believe and to rejoice in that hope—so shall heaven receive the glory, and future penitents the profit of my example."[33] As well as Thorowgood, Barnwell is visited in prison by Trueman and Maria, which provides more opportunities for the development of moralizing themes, and for animadversions on Barnwell's sad condition.

The play ends with the execution of Barnwell and Millwood, who go to their deaths together. As they walk to the gallows, as Millwood's maid, Lucy, puts it, "how humble and composed young Barnwell seems! But Millwood looks wild, ruffled with passion, confounded and amazed."[34] On the gallows Barnwell, by now fully prepared spiritually for death, tries to bring Millwood to a similar state of mind, advising her "add not to your vast account despair: a sin more injurious to heaven, than all you've yet committed."[35] He prays for her, expresses the hope that "she may find mercy where she least expects it, and this be all her hell" and dies hoping that by his and Millwood's example "may all be taught to fly the first approach of vice."[36] The final words go to Barnwell's friend, the good apprentice Trueman:

> With bleeding hearts, and weeping eyes we show
> A human gen'rous sense of others' woe;
> Unless we mark what drew their ruin on,
> And by avoiding that—prevent our own.

As I have suggested, the tone of these concluding scenes is essentially that of the execution pamphlets. Barnwell had been led to an acceptance of his fate by a clergyman, the fact that he is able to warn Millwood of the danger of despair on the point of death demonstrates that he has internalized the basic theological thrust that lay behind the input of clergymen on these occasions, he dies hoping that his example would serve as a warning for others, and this last point is reinforced, in verse, by another character at the very end of the play. Taken at its face value, *The London Merchant* is a powerful warning against youthful mis-deeds, and more particularly, against delinquency by apprentices. This warning was made all the more powerful by the fact that the play's tone and plot would have been very familiar to anybody in the period who read the pamphlets describing the "last dying speeches" of criminals, which were so vital in creating one of the standard images of public execution and the conventional wisdom about what lay behind that phenomenon, in eighteenth-century England.

Yet there was more to *The London Merchant* than that. In the very first scene, where Thorowgood and Trueman are shown conducting business together, Thorowgood presents a brief eulogy of the merchant class, declaring how "honest merchants, as such, may sometimes contribute to the safety of the country, as they do to its happiness," warning Trueman that "if hereafter you should be tempted to any action that has the appearance of vice or meanness in it, upon reflecting on the dignity of our profession, you may with honest scorn reject whatever is unworthy of it."[37] At a later point in the play, Thorowgood returns to this theme. He is again addressing Trueman, and advises him that "the method of merchandize" should not be regarded "merely as a means of getting wealth," but should also be studied as a science, because it is "founded in reason, and the nature of things," and "promotes humanity, as it has opened and yet keeps up intercourse between nations, far remote from one another in situation, customs and religion; promoting arts, industry, peace and plenty; by mutual benefits diffusing love from Pole to Pole." Trueman, in response, develops the theme, commenting that "I have observ'd those countries, where trade is promoted and encouraged, do not make discoveries to destroy, but to improve mankind." Thorowgood agrees, opining that "on every climate, and on every country, heaven has bestowed some good peculiar to it self—It is the industrious merchant's business to collect the various blessings of each soil and climate, and with the product of the whole, to enrich his native country." Turning to Trueman's accounts (ironically, he will turn to Barnwell's next), Thorowgood informs the younger man that "Method in business is the surest guide. He, who neglects it, frequently stumbles, and always wanders, perplex'd, uncertain, and in danger."[38]

On its most obvious level, then, *The London Merchant* is, like the speeches given or allegedly given by condemned felons on the gallows, like the images created a few years after the play's first performance in Hogarth's *Industry and Idleness* series, and like the numerous accounts of the lives of notorious criminals that were so much in vogue by 1731, a warning to apprentices of the dangers and folly of disobedience, delinquency, and the allures of lewd women. As such it clearly had a strong social control message, and one which was in line with a number of others widely available in the culture of the period.

But it also offered something else. Although set in Armada year, 1588, the play clearly related to many of the values that were current at the time of its first performance. By that date, England was coming to the end of the first phase of what has been described as a commercial revolution, the period when England, for the first time in its history, assumed the role of state of the first order of economic importance. In *The London Merchant* we find not simply a reassertion of one of its period's more prominent social control themes, a warning to potentially idle apprentices. Here also is an assertion of the dominant values of what was, in many ways, a newly emergent social order in which the values of mercantile capitalism were, if not actually becoming dominant, at least becoming sufficiently strong to make it essential that they, and the social groups they represented, were accommodated within both the ideological and concrete power structures of the period. Thorowgood's encomium on the importance of trade reminded apprentices in the audience of the importance of the activity that they, and their masters, were involved in. It also reminded them that if "method in business" was neglected, they might stumble, and wander "perplex'd, uncertain, and in danger." We return to George Barnwell standing on the gallows with that great impediment to method in business, Millwood the prostitute.

Conclusion

Thus Lillo's *The London Merchant* reminds us of the importance of the household as an arena of social control, both in its role in socialization and also, crucial to apprenticeship, as a workplace. The historian of England is faced by the phenomenon of the Industrial Revolution, one of whose themes was the disciplining of a labor force of semi-independent artisans and cottage-based workers, used to working according to their own rhythms, into a docile and time-conscious body of factory workers.[39] The supposedly massive changes that the coming of the factories brought have tended, apart from some work on apprenticeship, to obscure labor discipline before the industrial revolution as a subject for historical investigation. But, surely, here is an aspect of the past experience where social control must have been of prime importance, whether that control manifested itself through a system of labor discipline based on fines and penalties, or through those habits of deference that are thought to have been so strong in rural contexts. And lying behind this, of course, is the need for a continued testing of what the very notion of "work" meant, socially and culturally, in the preindustrial period.

As such considerations remind us, any society, early modern England as much as any other, requires the recognition that social life involves a knowledge of, and willingness to observe, sets of rules, norms, and conventions. Arguably, achieving this type of internalization is one of the major objectives of social control, broadly defined. This leads us back to a set of problems hinted at when touching on the social control aspects of religion: the need to take account of how social control was an element in, and something that affected, the human psyche. Social control was one element in the social construction of the self, and thus, more broadly, of what society held to be a decent (that is, well socialized and fully acculturated) human being.

Finding much by way of evidence on how the more intimate, personal, or familial processes of social control operated remains problematic, although it is possible that close reading of the personal memoirs of the period, as well as a broader and more imaginative trawl through various categories of court record, might prove helpful. Until such investigations have been completed, we must depend largely upon printed sources. It should be stressed that there was a large body of moralistic and normative literature in existence in early modern England, much of it, of course, based firmly on Christian teaching. One such example of this genre was Richard Allestree's *The Whole Duty of Man*. Allestree (1619–1681), was a divine and a scholar who survived the disadvantages inherent in taking a royalist position in the Civil Wars and was to enjoy a successful career in the Restoration period, which encompassed being Regius Professor of Divinity at Oxford. His *The Whole Duty of Man* was an entirely conventional tract: its views on apprenticeship and domestic service, for example, demonstrated the essentially patriarchal notions of the period, stressing the responsibilities of masters in providing apprentices with instruction in their trade and also moral and religious instruction, and the virtues of diligence and obedience among apprentices. The work was divided into eighteen chapters, each designed to be read on a Sunday, with the intent that the whole book should thus be read on a rolling basis three times a year. Its objective was to create a balanced, godly, and socialized Christian, sincere in his faith, temperate in his personal habits, and honest in his dealings with his neighbors. The first Sunday's reading, indeed, set out the "three great branches of man's duty: to God, our selves, our neighbours," while the point noted on the work's title page, that the book was "necessary to all families," returns us to that most important of the primary institutions of social control.[40]

We must, of course, be skeptical of the actual impact of this or any other normative text, yet the work's printing history is remarkable. The British Library catalogue lists over fifty editions between the book's first appearance in 1659 and 1842, it was translated into a number of languages other than English, and it encouraged a number of spin-offs, notably *The New Whole Duty of Man,* which had reached its twenty-ninth edition by 1792 and continued to be published well into the nineteenth century. Such works must have had at least some importance in acculturating individuals into the ways of the Christian commonwealth. And of course, it is interesting that this work should analyze basic social relationships in terms of "duties" and that it should nod at Rossian notions of social control in reminding its readers that the Scriptures contained commands, promises of punishments, and promises of rewards.

Commands, punishments, rewards: three of the vital elements of social control as it was defined by Edward Ross in 1901. The problematic, I would contend, lies in the need to embrace the notion of "social control" in a broader sense than that offered by discussions of law enforcement and punishment and to understand social control as an entity that pervades many, if not most, areas of human activity. We must, therefore, accept the necessity of taking a broad view of how social control might be studied. I would contend that we must study a large number of institutions: the family, the community, the workplace, schools and universities, the Church, law enforcement, and, as I hope I have demonstrated, even such popular works of entertainment as George Lillo's *The London Merchant*. These institutions did not operate independently, and the historian must try to ascertain how their operations as agencies of social control meshed. We also need to clarify our ideas on what social control was for; and here, I would reiterate, we need to look at not only the social, but how social control helped create socialized individuals, or how, to put it slightly differently, it helped both the social construction of the individual and the ways in which individuals reproduced the societies in which they lived.

Notes

1. Cohen, *Visions of Social Control*, 2.
2. e.g., Spufford, "Puritanism and Social Control," 41–57.
3. Weinburg, "Ross, Edward A.," 560.
4. Pitt, "Social Control: I The Concept."
5. Park and Burgess, *Introduction*, 785.
6. Mayer, "Notes towards a Working Definition of Social Control," 22.
7. Cohen, *Visions of Social Control*, 2.
8. Anonymous, *True Narrative of the Execution of John Marketman*, 4.
9. Sharpe, "'Last Dying Speeches.'"
10. Willis Bund, ed., *Calendar of the Quarter Sessions Records*, 726A.
11. Wrightson and Levine, *Poverty and Piety*.
12. Sharpe, "'Last Dying Speeches.'"
13. Watkins, *The Puritan Experience*.
14. Pollock, *Forgotten Children*.
15. e.g., Gouge, *Domesticall Duties*.
16. Lane, *Apprenticeship in England*, 2–3.
17. Quoted in Laslett, *World We Have Lost*, 3.
18. Quotations in Cockburn, ed., *Western Circuit Assize Orders*, 144–45.
19. e.g., Richardson, *The Apprentice's Vade Mecum*.
20. Cockburn, ed., *Western Circuit Assize Orders*, 166.
21. Cockburn, ed., *Western Circuit Assize Orders*, 290.
22. Griffiths, *Youth and Authority*.

23. Smith, "London Apprentices."

24. Sharpe, "'Last Dying Speeches.'"

25. e.g., Smith, *History of the Lives;* Johnson, *A General History of the Lives.*

26. Quoted in Steffensen, ed., *Dramatic Works of George Lillo,* xvii.

27. Steffensen, ed., *Dramatic Works of George Lillo,* 120–28; McBurney, ed., *The London Merchant,* ix-xiii.

28. Lillo, *The London Merchant,* Act III, sc. III, 11, 14–20.

29. e.g., Lillo, *The London Merchant,* Act II, sc. I, 11, 1–11; Act II, sc. III, 11, 1–12.

30. Ibid., Act IV, sc. X, 11, 19–44, passim; Act IV, sc. XI, 11, 1–2.

31. Ibid., Act IV, sc. XIII, 11, 9–15.

32. Ibid., Act IV, sc. XVIII, 11, 53, 10–16.

33. Ibid., Act V, sc. II, 11, 10–15.

34. Ibid., Act V, sc. XI, 11, 6–8.

35. Ibid., Act V, sc. XI, 11, 31–32.

36. Ibid., Act V, sc. XI, 11, 56–57.

37. Ibid., Act I, sc. I, 11, 12–16.

38. Ibid., Act III, sc. I, 1, 1–26, passim.

39. Thompson, "Time, Work—Discipline and Industrial Capitalism."

40. Allestree, *Whole Duty of Man.*

CHAPTER 3

Punishment versus Reconciliation: Marriage Control in Sixteenth- and Seventeenth-Century Holland

Manon van der Heijden

Introduction

Recently, Martin Ingram argued that, in order to understand various forms of early modern social discipline, historians should compare a range of secular and ecclesiastical jurisdictions over a long period of time.[1] Focusing on Holland during the early modern period, this article attempts to accomplish exactly what Ingram advocated. Before elaborating on the issues he raised, it might be wise to start with defining the term "social control" and explaining the questions asked and the sources used.

This article follows the broad definition of Herman Roodenburg and Pieter Spierenburg in which "social control" is described as all those practices by which people define deviant behavior and respond to it by taking action.[2] According to their description, "social control" covers formal social control exercised by the state, semiformal control exercised by various institutions such as churches, guilds, and charities, and informal control practiced by family members, neighbors, and friends.

In Holland a broad range of options either to impose social control or to be submitted to social control were in existence. This article deals with two of the most formal modes of social control in early modern Holland: church discipline and secular criminal justice. From 1572 (after the revolt against Spain) onward, both ecclesiastical and secular authorities meddled in domestic matters. Bailiffs brought adulterers, bigamists, and fornicators to court, where judges decided upon the suspect's sentence. For their part, clergymen and elders kept an eye on the members of their church. During their visits to people's homes, they obtained all kinds of information about these members. Whenever they heard of disorderly conduct in their district, clergymen informed the consistory, so that it could take appropriate action.

The main focus of this article is on the ways in which secular and ecclesiastical authorities controlled marriage and behavior related to marriage. I will argue that, despite the fundamental differences that existed between ecclesiastical discipline and criminal justice, comparisons between court cases and church cases yield useful information on early modern social control. First, I will take a brief look at the influence of Reformed thought on marriage regulation and the division of tasks between the secular and ecclesiastical authorities. Second, I am focusing on the enforcement of secular legislation and ecclesiastical regulation in daily practice. Which forms of behavior were actually corrected by the government and the Reformed church, how did both institutions handle their cases, and to what extent did the control they exercised differ? Finally, I will pay attention to the legitimacy of the intervention of church and government. To what extent did people summoned before the consistory or punished by the court accept the interference of these institutions? In which cases did people themselves take the initiative to call upon these institutions to act?

In order to satisfactorily cover both secular and ecclesiastical marriage control, two different sources in the archives of two Dutch cities, Rotterdam and Delft, were examined. First, I investigated three different types of court records: sentence, correction, and confession books. Second, I examined the consistory notes of the Reformed Church. Both sources reveal interesting insights into marriage regulation during the sixteenth and seventeenth centuries.[3]

The sentence books consist of all sentences for serious offenses, while the correction books contain less serious cases. Although the confession books were meant only for the examination of suspect persons, in most cases sentences were also recorded. Where no sentence can be found in the examination books, they were recorded in the sentence books. Furthermore, the confession books contain examinations of all persons who played a role in the case. The examinations of spouses, children, neighbors, and other persons involved were recorded extensively.

The consistory notes contain the records of all Reformed consistory meetings, including disciplinary cases. In particular, the consistory handled matrimonial issues. Regularly, spouses or fiancées asked the consistory to mediate in matrimonial affairs. Besides that, clergymen often questioned relatives, neighbors, and other persons involved, in order to boost their discipline. Therefore, the consistory notes include complaints of fiancées, statements of relatives, and points of view of neighbors.

Marriage Regulation and Reformed Thought

Since the twelfth century, theologians emphasized the spiritual and sacramental character of marriage, and marital issues obtained a good deal of attention from the Catholic Church.[4] However, the Reformers proclaimed marriage to be a political and public matter. In 1566 the Governor-General of the Netherlands, Margaret of Parma, granted freedom of religion, which allowed Protestant clergymen to take over Catholic churches. Although nearly half of the Dutch population remained Catholic after 1572, the Reformed Church became the dominant religion, certainly in the province of Holland.

The most important change concerned the nature of marriage. Since the Reformed Church did not view it as a sacrament, but rather as a political affair, the secular authorities had to take responsibility for it. At least, they ought to draw up regulations. But even though Protestants proclaimed marriage to be secular, it continued to be a divine institution. Consequently, matrimonial matters nevertheless remained a concern for clergymen.

Reformed thought had its consequences: no longer was reproduction the only goal of marriage, as it had been under Catholic rule. Reformers like Luther did not judge reproduction as being of lesser importance, but they viewed it as the work of God himself. Marital love became the most important object of marriage. Love and companionship were to be the bond that kept men and women together.

A second important change concerned parental consent. Because the Reformed Church viewed parental authority as an extension of divine authority, children of minor age (under twenty-five for sons and under twenty for daughters) were supposed to have full consent of their parents when entering into marriage. This also meant that only marriage vows given with the full consent of the parents were valid. Contrary to canon law, the Dutch Reformed rulers claimed marriages without full consent of the parents or proclamation of the banns to be invalid.[5]

Third, Reformers changed the rules concerning the dissolution of marriages. Under Catholic rule, unless one of the spouses died, a marriage was virtually indissoluble. Since the Roman Catholic Church monopolized the jurisdiction and legislation in marital affairs, it had the power to outlaw divorce entirely. The Church only allowed the so-called *divortium quoad thorum*. However, this separation of board and bed did not end the conjugal union; it permitted spouses to split up their household. In other words, it suspended the obligation of living together. After the Reformation the *divortium quoad thorum* remained in existence, but Reformers also allowed divorce. Of course, divorce had strong limitations. Only in case of malicious abandonment or proven adultery could one obtain a divorce.

Although several crucial changes took place after the Reformation, most rules concerning marriage remained the same. Unless Catholic regulations were inconsistent with the Holy Bible of Roman law, Reformers adopted the existing canonical rules. Marriage vows could be broken only by mutual consent or for significant reasons put forward by one of the parties. The Reformers continued to allow this, but illegal breaches did have further consequences. One could be forced to marry when untrue or invalid reasons for breaking the vows were given. Forbidden degrees of kinship, which were instituted by the Catholic Church, remained in existence.

Secular Punishment and Ecclesiastical Discipline

Although many regulations concerning marriage stayed the same, the enforcement of marriage legislation changed fundamentally. Since the Reformers viewed matrimonial matters as a public issue, the secular authorities took control. From a judicial point of view, this meant a switch from civil law to public law.

The secular authorities drew up marriage regulations and executed criminal law. Bailiffs brought charges against those who transgressed the legal rules concerning marriage. Adultery, bigamy, and incest were regarded as serious crimes. Breaking a marriage vow and fornication were usually minor offenses, but still punishable by law. After their arrest, suspects were always subjected to interrogations, in order to make them confess. If it concerned a serious offense, bailiffs used instruments of torture to force the suspect's confession. Surely, the criminal courts did not treat offenders of marital laws any differently from burglars or knife fighters.[6]

Officially, the Church no longer decided in matrimonial affairs, but in practice it still felt the obligation to watch over the married life of its members. Since the Reformed Church lacked the authority to initiate legislation, it was limited in its activities concerning family life. First, it could only deal with people who were members of the Reformed Church. Furthermore, when it found members engaging in deviant behavior, it could only apply ecclesiastical sanctions. This usually meant that offending members were excluded from Holy Communion, until they showed an improvement in their domestic life.

The aims of consistorial discipline differed from those of secular justice. Both Els Kloek and Herman Roodenburg conclude that the consistories of Leiden and Amsterdam focused primarily on reconciliation.[7] Indeed, secular punishment and ecclesiastical discipline constituted two fundamentally different ways of correction. When referring to this distinction, Sir Geoffrey Elton and Heinz Schilling have argued that historians should make a strict factual and methodological separation between the "history of crime" and the "history of sin."[8] Schilling in particular insists that, since the Reformers primarily wished to purify their own group of believers, church discipline focused on the sinner and his reconciliation with the community. The most important aim of the criminal court, however, was merely to punish the crime.

Elton and Schilling are right in arguing that historians should acknowledge the religious essence of church discipline in order to understand its nature. However, their statement that the "history of sin" and the "history of crime" are separate fields should be qualified. As noted at the beginning, Ingram claims that valuable insights into the functioning of early modern social control can be obtained by comparing its different agencies.[9] Although I am restricting myself to the Dutch case, I support Ingram's claim. While keeping in mind that it concerns two essentially different ways of regulating marital conduct, we still can fruitfully compare criminal court cases with cases of church discipline.

In the first place, both institutions exercised social control within an official institutional context, according to regulations that were for the most part codified. Second, it would be wrong to assume that clergymen, elders, and magistrates themselves always made such clear distinctions between "crime" and "sin." Consistories sometimes reaccepted offenders as soon as the case was settled in court. Furthermore, clergymen actively tried to influence both secular regulation and law enforcement where it concerned marital matters. Even though their discipline was primarily aimed at reconciliation, consistories were equally convinced that offenders should be sentenced. Although magistrates might have centered their correction around punishment, they took other considerations, as we shall see, into account as well. Finally, magistrates and clergymen often exchanged letters, debating both the criminal conduct they had to deal with and the proper reaction to it. Apparently, contemporary judges and clergymen themselves found that the cases they dealt with were comparable.[10]

This article does not intend to deny the crucial differences between church discipline and criminal justice. To the contrary, it constantly refers to the diverging objectives, interests, and methods of consistories and criminal courts. I only object to the assumption that the practices of consistories and criminal courts were unrelated altogether. In the next paragraphs I attempt to demonstrate that by comparing ecclesiastical and secular cases, historians can increase their insight into the functioning of and the interconnections between two different types of social control.

Marriage Regulation in Practice

During the period 1550–1700 more than 2800 cases, involving all sorts of conduct related to marriage, can be found in the judicial and ecclesiastical records.[11] Since all sexual acts outside legal marriage were forbidden, other related cases have also been recorded. (See Tables 1 through 6 illustrating criminal court cases and church discipline cases concerning marriage, Rotterdam and Delft, 1550–1700.) In order to illustrate the results as clearly as possible, a distinction has been made between premarital and matrimonial cases. Of the total, 1466 cases were related to premarital matters, and 1372 cases concerned matrimonial offenses.[12] Thus, matrimonial crimes resulted in prosecution almost as often as premarital offenses. However, we shall see that consistories and secular courts handled different cases. While the magistrates dealt with fornication and adultery more often, the churchmen concentrated on broken marriage vows and domestic quarrels. Obviously, the secular court only prosecuted those who had indulged in activities prohibited by criminal law. Consistories, however, interfered with all sorts of conduct they considered inadmissible. Therefore, clergymen and magistrates not only handled cases in a different manner; they also dealt with different types of cases.

However, the difference between criminal justice and ecclesiastical discipline is not merely a function of the fundamental distinction between "crime" and "sin." Various factors played a role in controlling deviant behavior. First, prosecutors and judges did not always handle cases according to the prescripts of the criminal law. Second, economic considerations influenced their judgment as well. Furthermore, where the public image of church members was at stake, consistories were selective in controlling sinful behavior. For example, clergymen were rarely inclined to expose the sinful act of adultery. Finally, accusers and complainants tended to submit certain complaints to the consistory rather than the criminal court, and vice versa. As the next paragraphs will show, only a comparison between church discipline and criminal justices uncovers these mechanisms for controlling marital conduct.

Premarital Matters

By far the largest number of premarital matters concerned sexual intercourse, concubinage, and the contract of marriage. Especially illicit lovemaking, with or without cohabitation, resulted in prosecution and discipline. Magistrates and clergymen dealt with more than 940 illicit love affairs. Since it constituted a criminal act, criminal courts chiefly controlled these matters. Magistrates usually called the crime "carnal conversation."[13]

All sexual acts outside marriage were forbidden, with or without previous marriage vows. Consequently, engaged couples who had made love before their wedding night were guilty of the crime of carnal conversation. However, magistrates did take extenuating circumstances into account. Having made marriage vows influenced their final sentence. Furthermore, the frequency of the carnal conversation was taken into account as well. Whereas some couples had established a long-term relationship, others knew each other for a shorter period, sometimes a single occasion only. As expected, the magistrates considered the first two situations more serious. Besides the questions of frequency and marriage vows, numerous other extenuating or aggravating circumstances were taken into account. Because of this, it is not always easy to assess the grounds on which the magistrates based their verdict.

Carnal Conversation

Premarital sexual acts were forbidden, but having exchanged marriage vows usually extenuated the crime of carnal conversation. Therefore, the majority of the accused claimed to be engaged or stated that they planned to marry. Women

Table 1   Total criminal court cases concerning marriage, 1550–1700

	Men	Women	Total
Premarital cases	215	444	659 (52%)
Marital cases	317	291	608 (48%)
Total	532 (42%)	735 (58%)	1267

Source: Tables 1–6 from Judicial archives of Delft and Rotterdam, sentence books, correction books, examination books, confession books (1550 –1700)

Table 2   Total church discipline cases concerning marriage, 1573–1700

	Men	Women	Total
Premarital cases	325	282	807 (51%)
Marital cases	435	419	764 (49%)
Total	670 (43 %)	901 (57%)	1571

Source: Consistory note s and discipline books of the Reformed Church of Delft (1573–1700) and Rotterdam (1639–1700)

especially used this argument, since their virtue was at stake. In his work about the consistory of Amsterdam, Herman Roodenburg finds that, when referring to sexual intercourse, women were anxious to preserve their virtue. Indeed, young women who lost their virginity without having received a promise of marriage not only risked conviction but they risked losing their honor as well. Behaving unchastely or committing fornication seriously limited a girl's marriage opportunities. These moral judgments were common throughout Europe.[14]

Women who claimed to be engaged usually stated that they had only consented to giving up their virginity after having received a proposal of marriage. In the event that they could substantiate this claim by showing written evidence, by bringing forward witnesses, or persuading with convincing statements, they got away with a reprimand. Not surprisingly, sometimes illegitimate children were born of illicit relationships. However, being pregnant or having an illegitimate child had no influence on the sentence; at least, not until the second half of the seventeenth century.[15] When the bailiff was able to capture both lovers, the magistrates ordered the couple to marry as soon as possible. For example, in 1696 a woman was arrested and accused of carnal conversation with the captain of a barge. It took the bailiff a month to find him, but because he confirmed having made a marriage vow, the court stopped legal proceedings, on the condition that the couple would marry soon.[16]

Although defendants who could prove their statements escaped with a reprimand, this was seldom the case. Most trials were much more complex, especially where married lovers were involved. Someone who entered into a relationship with a married person was formally committing adultery. But what if an unmarried lover had been unaware of the married state of the loved one?

Table 3   Premarital court cases, 1550–1700

	Men	Women	Total
Carnal conversation	115	342	457
Concubinage	52	78	130
Marriage contract	37	24	61
Assault/rape	11	0	11
Total	215	444	659

Table 4   Marital court cases, 1550–1700

	Men	Women	Total
Adultery	188	236	424
Desertion	34	22	56
Maltreatment	50	2	52
Bigamy	30	9	39
Incest	10	17	27
Marital dispute	5	5	10
Total	317	291	608

Table 5   Premarital church discipline cases, 1573–1700

	Men	Women	Total
Carnal conversation	66	253	319
Marriage vows	196	152	348
Concubinage	9	25	34
Other cases	54	52	106
Total	325	482	807

Note: 24.7% of cases concerning marriage vows were related to the consent of parents or guardians.

Examinations show that the magistrates' primary aim was to find out whether defendants had had knowledge of the married state of their partner. Obviously, an offender could easily claim that this was the case. If it was true, the suspect had been unaware of committing a crime and, therefore, was not guilty of adultery. Indeed, the confessions of some defendants and the statements from neighbors or relatives leave no doubt that people sometimes acted in good faith, assuming that a sincere promise of marriage had been given. Geertruyd Jacobs, for instance, sincerely believed that her lover would soon marry her. She had not only received a marriage promise but their engagement was registered as well. Thus, Geertruyd had not been naive, nor had she acted rashly, and she was, therefore, not convicted, whereas her lover was sentenced to a banishment of six years.[17]

A similar attitude is apparent in other cases in which the magistrates were convinced of the sincerity of the statements. The criminal court considered even clandestine marriage vows as an extenuating circumstance. Clearly, in this respect it did not execute the criminal law to the letter. The Estates of Holland had instituted marriage legislation immediately after the Revolt. From 1580 onward, every couple wishing to marry had to report their intended marriage to the magistrate or clergyman of their place of residence. The names of the bride and groom had to be announced three times to make sure there were no objections to the wedding. After these proclamations a couple could marry before the magistrates or a clergyman. The most important aim of these prescriptions was to bring marriage into the public sphere.[18]

Prior to 1580 ambiguity had prevailed concerning the nature of marriage. The Catholic Church held that the mutual consent of a man and a woman constituted a binding marriage contract. Moreover, intercourse meant definitive endorsement of the contract. The Catholic Church had already made proclamation of the banns obligatory in 1535, but at that occasion it did not declare that failing to do so made the marriage invalid. From 1580 onward only legal marriage vows were valid. Nevertheless, the magistrates did not proceed according to these rules in criminal jurisdiction. Both defendants and magistrates did not make a clear distinction between public marriage vows and secret marriage vows. The criminal court considered both types valid. Moreover, magistrates accepted carnal conversation as long as couples married soon after their release from jail.

Due to the continuing acceptance of secret marriage vows, magistrates faced difficulties concerning the items of evidence. Those who had reported their marriage to the magistrate or a clergyman could easily prove their innocence. But it was often difficult to find out whether couples had truly exchanged marriage vows. For that reason, magistrates could only base their judgments on the declaration of the defendants and the statements of relatives and neighbors. Defendants unable to provide evidence of their engagement were convicted for committing carnal conversation or concubinage. The majority of the accused failed to prove their innocence, so they were convicted, usually to the penalties of banishment.

Usually, persons arrested for carnal conversation either were involved in a long-term relationships or they had had intimate relations with many different persons. Both types of offenders were generally punished severely. Most of the accused were sentenced to a banishment of six, ten, or twelve years. Light sentences were given where less serious carnal conversation was concerned. Judges considered sharing a bed together in an inn for one night, or having made love only one time, less serious. When the judges were convinced that it concerned a one-time event only, they sentenced the accused to fourteen days on bread and water, or the accused had only to beg for forgiveness in open court. Persons who had had long-term intimate relations without having the intention to marry their loved one were punished severely. Sentences of twenty-five years of banishment were usually given when the accused, especially if it was a man, had seduced sexually inexperienced minors. The shoemaker Cornelis Jans was even sentenced to a banishment of a hundred years because he had had intercourse with several young girls, seducing them with cake and apples.[19]

Judges definitely considered having sexual relationships from an early age an aggravating circumstance. Conversely, those who had had sex with inexperienced youngsters of good reputation were punished severely. Rape and incest cases show the ambiguity of the magistrates' attitude very clearly. Marital state and sexual experience influenced the judges' attitude toward rape and assault victims.[20] Furthermore, honor and good reputation played an important role in those cases. Unless rape and incest victims proved their sexual innocence and inexperience, judges put equal blame on the victim. In other words, they were guilty of carnal conversation, adultery (when married) or incest by having sexual intercourse. Since some lawyers considered incest a capital crime, judges were even less inclined to give incest victims the benefit of the doubt. A sad example of this attitude is the case of Dirkje Jans, who had been raped and threatened by her stepfather, during her mother's absence. Even worse, as a result of her stepfather's maltreatment, she had become lame. When she declared that she had had sexual intercourse with another man, the magistrates sentenced her.[21] As contemporaries were of the opinion that mature women were sexually insatiable, married women, too, were accessories to any sexual relationship. Therefore, married women who had been raped were usually sentenced for committing the crime of adultery.[22]

Marriage Vows

While the secular court mainly dealt with cases of carnal conversation and concubinage, the Church more often handled marriage contract disputes. This is not surprising, since the two agencies possessed different competencies and functions. The secular authorities enforced the criminal law, but consistories, apart from correcting people, also dealt with all sorts of requests concerning marriage. Almost all premarital offenses handled by the consistories were in some way related to the contract of marriage; in particular double marriage vows, breach of promise, and annulment of a marriage vow were matters in which the consistories played an important role.

Prospective spouses could complain to the consistory and ask for actions in the event that the other party had made marriage vows to more than one person or had tried to break the marriage vow. Men, especially, were accused of having made double marriage vows. Since the banns were announced publicly, earlier lovers could easily discover the implied breach of promise before the wedding took place. Most of the time, a woman objected to a marriage after she had seen the names of her fiancé and another woman announced at the city hall. Neeltje Ymant, accompanied by her mother, appeared before the consistory when she discovered that her fiancé, Pieter, had announced a marriage with Catalijntje.[23] The woman was often accompanied by one of her relatives and sometimes by friends or neighbors who could testify to the promise of marriage she claimed to have received.

The consistories almost always reacted by summoning the accused man to appear and questioning him about the marriage vows he had made. In cases where the young man denied having done anything of the sort and evidence could not be brought forward, both parties were referred to the secular court.

All sorts of reasons were mentioned when marriage contract disputes were brought before the consistory. The elders and clergymen always demanded explanations for a petitioner's behavior, and if possible all parties were heard. Most men accused of double marriage vows or of breach of promise gave the first woman's dishonorable and immoral behavior as a reason. Again, loss of virtue and honor played an important role. Several times, women stated they were less interested in marrying the man to whom they were engaged than in saving their honor.[24] Sometimes, young men gave their age as an excuse. They argued that, since they had entered upon an engagement while a minor and without their parents' consent, it could not be valid, or they claimed they had entered upon it out of ignorance. Women, however, could argue that they wanted to end an engagement because of the disabilities of their prospective spouse.

As discussed earlier, secular courts accepted secret marriage vows as long as couples promised to marry as soon as possible. Consistories, however, dealt with the matter by the book. Clergymen considered only public marriage vows valid. They refused to acknowledge secret vows, both in cases in which youngsters had made double marriage vows and in which they had broken a single promise. Thus, as far as the Reformed church was concerned, women who had intercourse after having received a verbal promise were de facto not engaged. Still, clergymen, like the magistrates, took the sincerity of the offenders into account as well. Where no double vows were involved, a consistory tried to convince youngsters to marry the person they had slept with. Furthermore, it always demanded a statement in writing, in which the alleged fiancé stated that he had not left a girl behind because of her immoral behavior. In that way, at least the girl's reputation and honor were preserved. Finally, a young man who had broken his promise, left his fiancée, or made a double marriage vow, was always excluded for several times from Holy Communion.

Another type of marriage contract dispute concerned parental consent. In cases where parents refused to consent to the marriage, youngsters often tried to obtain the support of the consistory. Conversely, parents who disagreed with their child's choice of partner could simply point out that the Church required parental consent. Although the clergymen indeed placed value on parental consent, the consistory always demanded a valid reason for withholding it. When children had reached majority and parents or guardians failed to come up with a good reason, the consistory decided to allow the marriage. However, when it concerned minors, clergymen followed the rules of parental consent very strictly. With or without valid reasons, children could never ignore their parents' rejection of a partner. Remarkably, clergymen often expressed their regrets about the parents' obstinate refusal. Despite this, they advised youngsters to wait until they had reached majority. In all cases, the consistory attempted to reconcile the parties. But when youngsters disobeyed the rules, they were excluded from Holy Communion.

Morals and Financial Interests

Courts of law and consistories regularly punished or disciplined those who committed carnal conversation and concubinage or who had broken their marriage promise. In the course of the seventeenth century an increasing number of these offenders appeared before them. Both demographic and moral changes lay behind this development.

Several English and German studies have shown that most European countries witnessed an increase in the number of illegitimate children during the second half of the seventeenth century. Data on the Dutch illegitimacy rate are scarce for this period.[25] The Dutch Reformed Church, however, showed a growing interest in the matter. Influenced by English Reformers, the Dutch Reformed Church embarked upon a program of "Further Reformation." With this program, the Church tried to promote the ideal way of living—the Reformed way. The Church's aim was to ban all immoral behavior. Premarital relationships were among the main targets of this campaign.[26] Both the Reformed church and the secular courts intensified their disciplinary actions in the field of sexual intercourse. However, secular courts and consistories seemed to have different interests.

Illegitimacy became the overriding concern in the legal prosecution of premarital intercourse. The magistrates ostensibly paid greater attention to women whose children were born out of wedlock. Besides this, they distinguished more clearly between mere sexual intercourse and having an illegitimate child. In cases of illegitimate birth, women were punished more severely. At least, more severe sentences were imposed on women whose lover remained unknown. This suggests a relationship between the court's judgment and the identification of the father.

Both Martin Ingram and Keith Wrightson have pointed out that a growing concern among the authorities for the problems of poverty resulted in an increase in prosecutions concerning premarital relations.[27] The financial burden of illegitimate children came down primarily on the local authorities, who were responsible for poor relief. Similar motives seem to have influenced the attitude of the Dutch courts. For this reason, midwives who assisted an unmarried mother were obliged to ask for the name of the father. Local authorities did not have to take up the financial care for the child, as they could force the father to do so.

Court cases reveal a neat relationship between the sentence and the possibility of child support. The judges expected single mothers to disclose the name of their lover, and, if they did the court requested financial guarantees from the father. Whether he was married to someone else seemed to matter less. The father's name and his financial support were the most important issues during the investigation. It was not unusual that the authorities provided assistance in such matters and, as one example shows, not only in cases in which honor and virtue were beyond doubt. Anna became pregnant when she was having an affair with Jan Michel, a married man. However, when she delivered the baby, the magistrates not only imposed a fine upon him but he also had to make monthly payments to support the child.[28]

Obviously, financial interests played an important role in court. The consistories, however, never took any financial considerations into account. They based their judgments solely on moral grounds. Cases concerning pregnant maids clearly reveal the divergent interests of the secular court and the consistory. Both institutions considered sexual relationships between masters and maids reprehensible, especially when maids got pregnant. However, when a master supported the child, magistrates considered the matter settled and done, provided of course, that the couple would discontinue their relationship. The consistories, however, continued to intervene as long as the maid and her master shared a household. The clergymen were of the opinion that members of the Reformed church should avoid any suspicion about their moral conduct.

The clergymen disciplined every unmarried couple guilty of sexual intercourse, whether they were engaged or not. In order to avoid having to do so too often, consistories insisted that couples should marry within a month after their third proclamation of the banns. Besides that, in cases where clergymen discovered the couple's premarital activities months after the actual wedding, they disciplined the newlyweds after all. Such cases of belated prosecution never occurred in criminal court. As shown before, judges merely ordered illicit lovers to enter upon marriage as soon as possible. If a couple obeyed that order, the magistrates felt no need to deal with the case any longer. The secular authorities considered premarital intercourse problematic only to the extent that it involved financial interests. As we shall see, the magistrates exhibited a similar attitude toward marital matters.

Marital Matters

By far the greatest number of marital matters concerned adultery and marital conflict. Magistrates and clergymen handled more than 560 cases of adultery and approximately 600 cases related to marital disputes. Besides these offenses, both institutions regularly dealt with issues regarding abandonment, bigamy, and incest as well. Again, secular courts and consistories handled different matters. Evidently, because it concerned a punishable act, the criminal court dealt with adultery in particular. The secular courts' primary aim was to enforce the law. As long as quarrelling spouses refrained from causing disturbance and noise or maltreating each other, they did not commit any criminal act. They did, however, offend Reformed moral rules with regard to marital life. The Reformed ideal of marriage required a peaceful home for both parents and children. This ideal became even more important during the seventeenth century. For that reason, consistories regularly summoned quarrelling and fighting couples to their meetings.

Adultery, Abandonment, and Bigamy

The 1580 ordinance of the Estates of Holland comprised strict rules for penalizing the crime of adultery. If both partners were married, it prescribed a banishment of fifty years, while fines of one hundred or two hundred guilders ought to be imposed if only one of the lovers had a spouse.[29] Despite these clear instructions, magistrates sentenced adulterers to various penalties. They regularly received a banishment of six, ten, or twelve years. Even more striking, perhaps, is that the crime of adultery could be bought off.[30]

Although legally forbidden, buying off one's adultery was a widespread custom in the whole of Holland. The offenders and the public prosecutor both profited from such settlements: bailiffs earned an extra income and adulterers escaped conviction. When adultery was settled out of court, bailiffs only mentioned the crime and the amount of money paid in their account books, without recording the offender's name or the circumstances of the act.[31]

Since most bailiffs' accounts have not been preserved, it is hard to tell exactly how many offenders bought off their adultery, but court records and consistory notes indicate that this was often the case. However, the system had severe limitations. First, since large sums of money were involved, only wealthy offenders were able to buy off their adultery. Second, the deceived spouses had to give their approval to the settlement. Trijntje Jans, for example, had cheated on her husband, but she was rich enough to escape conviction. Unfortunately for her, her husband refused to give his approval, and therefore she was sentenced to a banishment of ten years.[32]

Remarkably, women in particular were convicted for committing adultery. One might conclude that the authorities observed different moral standards for men and women. Women were also more vulnerable because their adulterous behavior could lead to pregnancy. When we take a closer look at the women's statements, however, another picture emerges. Over 25 percent of the female adulterers complained about the long lasting absence of their husbands. The fact that Rotterdam and Delft were trade centers and a large number of the population earned a living by working on ships sailing abroad must have made an imprint on marital life. Indeed, according to the statements, many husbands sailed to the East or West Indies, leaving their wives behind in uncertainty. The husband of Dingenom Dirx had left his wife eleven years ago, and she had heard nothing of him since.[33] Other women presumed their husbands to be long dead.[34] Yet, magistrates always convicted women and men accused of adultery, if they failed to prove that their spouse had died. Most adulterers received a fine or a banishment of fifty years.

Whereas women were accused of adultery more often, men were prosecuted especially for abandonment and bigamy. Again, financial considerations played a crucial role. According to the magistrates' records, abandonment resulted in poverty and unchaste behavior. When Willem deserted his family, his wife was forced to beg or to resort to prostitution in order to support herself and their child.[35] After being deserted by the breadwinner, most families were left behind in poverty and as a result they had to turn to the parish. The financial burden of deserted families lay with the secular and ecclesiastical agencies responsible for poor relief. For that reason, the magistrates prosecuted men more often than women. When bailiffs were able to discover a deserter, they ordered him to return to his family. In addition, some breadwinners were publicly whipped on the scaffold because their families had to rely on poor relief as a result of their desertion. In the event of a deserter committing adultery, however, the magistrates did not treat him any differently from other adulterers.

Lawrence Stone has argued that English magistrates did not pursue bigamy cases intensively. In Holland, however, the strict rules regarding a public wedding limited one's possibilities to commit the crime of bigamy. As a result, clergymen and magistrates generally exposed impostors before their second or third wedding took place. This can be taken as support for Martin Ingram's statement that "there is no real evidence to support Stone's assertion that the practice was both easy and common."[36] In cases of bigamy, notably when a man managed to marry for the third time, magistrates imposed special sentences that symbolized the gravity of the act. Male bigamists were always sentenced to a banishment of fifty years and beaten with distaffs (symbolizing the women they had cheated on) while they were escorted outside town.[37]

Marital Disputes and Maltreatment

Although consistories, too, dealt with adultery and abandonment of a wife at times, this constituted only a minor part of their business. They did, however, frequently handle marital conflict. As many couples were accustomed to physical violence, fights and maltreatment often ensued from marital quarrels. Moreover, domestic violence occurred in combination with the use of alcohol most of the time. Finally, while men were summoned more often for marital disputes, wives were usually disciplined for running away from their husbands. Twice as many women as men were summoned because they wished to separate. These differences are easily explained. According to the consistory's notes, husbands behaved so violently that wives left the house out of sheer necessity.[38]

The question is how consistories handled these matters. Despite the sometimes obvious maltreatment of wives, the clergymen were never inclined to involve the criminal court. They were primarily bent on restoring peace in the family, not on denouncing abusive or quarrelsome spouses to the criminal court. Above all, Reformed discipline was aimed at restoring the sinner's relationship with God and the Reformed church. In order to accomplish that, consistories always tried to reconcile the married partners. Meanwhile, couples who were publicly quarrelling or living separately were excluded from Holy Communion, until they showed an improvement in their behavior.

Men especially were sometimes excluded for years. As long as husbands or wives refused to make an effort to make their marriage work, the Church enforced its discipline. Since the consistories were never inclined to involve the bailiff, couples often felt they could speak about their dissatisfactions freely. Strikingly, most husbands complained about their wives' domineering behavior. They often claimed that their wives' assertive conduct had forced them to take violent action. Married women were often accused of being drunk, neglecting their household, refusing sexual intercourse, and being gadabouts. Furthermore, husbands repeatedly complained about their spouses' unfriendly, obstinate, stubborn, and disagreeable character. Indeed, foreign visitors expressed their surprise when they noted that in the Dutch Republic, wife beating was severely frowned upon.[39] But did this mean that Dutch wives were more free and independent than other married women in seventeenth-century Europe?

Without discussing this extensively, let me just state that the Reformed rules potentially improved women's power position within marriage. As mentioned above, the Reformers permitted divorce in the event of adultery and willful abandonment. Several Dutch studies have shown that women especially requested the magistrates to allow them to divorce.[40] However, the extended opportunities to escape abusive husbands did not in fact result in an increase in divorce. But perhaps they made separation of bed and board and informal separations by mutual consent more acceptable. They might also have made married women's position within the household stronger.

Although officially allowing divorce and separation of bed and board, the Reformed church never permitted their own members to live apart from their marriage partner. Battered women were never advised to divorce, nor did the clergymen help church members in getting a separation order from the magistrates.[41] Instead, they attempted to reconcile the couple and summoned the abusive husband and various relatives in an effort to ameliorate the domestic circumstances. When a husband refused to improve his behavior, the consistory excluded him from Holy Communion. But as soon as a wife left her abusive husband or filed for divorce, she was disciplined as well.

Although, in cases of maltreatment by their husbands, women had access to the legal process, only some of them used that right.[42] It appears that other interests could be of greater importance. First, a convicted husband was unable to support his family, since banishment or imprisonment evidently entailed the loss of one's livelihood. Second, being convicted brought not only shame and dishonor on the accused but on his wife and children as well. Women started legal action against their husbands only where their abusive behavior endangered their lives and that of their children. Frequently, neighbors acted as plaintiffs when husbands molested their wives. Causing noise and disturbance in the neighborhood were reasons for the community to intervene. Perhaps even more important, severe maltreatment could bring shame and dishonor on the whole neighborhood.

Punishment versus Reconciliation

Although both the secular and ecclesiastical authorities considered adultery and abandonment of one's partner criminal acts, the consistories tended not to denounce adulterers to the criminal court. On the contrary, consistories always attempted to keep the immoral and criminal behavior of church members as private as possible. Apparently, the consistory's primary concern was to keep the serious sins and the criminal conduct of church members from public view.

When church members were arrested nevertheless, the clergymen often instructed both the adulterers and their spouses to make arrangements with the bailiff. The consistory of Delft, for instance, advised Heijndrickje Wijnants in 1664 to plead on her husband's behalf in criminal court. She, however, did not at all desire her husband's release, since his mistress was pregnant with his child. Despite his patently obvious adultery, the clergymen kept on telling her that she ought to reconcile with her husband and make their marriage work.[43]

In this case, too, consistories were primarily focused on reconciliation and aimed less at correction. Of course clergymen corrected people by excluding them from Holy Communion, but adulterous members were never excommunicated. Indeed, consistories were never inclined to make church members' adultery or abandonment public. Thus, when the adulterous husband Teen Pauwels accused the clergymen of informing the bailiff about his crime, they reacted with great indignation.[44] Consistories enforced their discipline mildly, as long as couples were prepared to reconcile, showed remorse, and their offense remained private. Members who persisted in their misconduct or crimes were excluded until they improved their behavior. As mentioned above, sinners were sometimes excluded for years. However, when people showed their repentance and regret, they were always readmitted to the church.

Adultery and abandonment cases clearly show the divergent objectives of secular courts and consistories. Whereas the magistrates' final aim was to punish criminals, the clergymen used their discipline only as a means to reconcile members both with each other and the Church. Consequently, deceived marriage partners did not hesitate to inform the clergymen about their spouses' immoral behavior. Evidently, they were well aware that the consistory rarely notified the bailiff. As the clergymen always advised spouses to make up, some members must have been slightly disappointed about the consistory's attitude toward their problems. Trijntje Jacobs, for instance, asked the clergymen to discipline her husband's mistress. However, they rejected her request, arguing that it would only cause renewed dissension between Trijntje and her husband.[45] Clearly, the consistory considered restoring the family peace more important than punishing the criminal.

The discipline by consistories differed from that of the criminal courts in yet another way, since the former more often summoned women leaving their husbands than men leaving their wives. As financial interests took primacy in the criminal courts, the courts prosecuted men more often than women for this offense. The magistrates convicted men more often because, as breadwinners, they had to care for their wives and children. Again, the clergymen rarely mentioned financial motives for disciplining church members. They only referred to the offenders' immoral and sinful behavior, emphasizing that husbands should be dependable and trustworthy. Financial interests surfaced in consistory notes only where it concerned bankruptcy or divorce. At all times, the clergymen aimed at reconciliation between married partners and to a much lesser extent at punishing breadwinners whose abandonment led to poverty.

The Legitimacy of Secular and Ecclesiastical Discipline

Consistories and criminal courts both meddled in private affairs, but to what extent did people accept the interference of these institutions? Roodenburg has rightly argued that historians should distinguish "conflict" from "criminality," because many private settlements of conflicts concerned acts that were not punishable by law.[46] As shown above, criminal courts and consistories not only handled different cases, but each institution also treated similar matters differently. As a result, people did not hesitate to inform the clergymen about the illicit conduct of their spouses, while at the same time they hoped to hide it from the magistrates.

Besides consistories and secular courts, various other arenas for social control and the settlement of conflict were in existence.[47] In order to cover all modes of administration of justice, Roodenburg suggests using the term "legal pluralism," which he defines as a set of rules, linked to a procedure of administration of justice.[48] Indeed, consistory notes sometimes reveal interesting information about other ways to settle conflicts. The clergymen regularly noted that "neighborhood masters" mediated where minor conflicts were involved. Several Dutch historians have emphasized the significant role of the neighborhood masters in settling conflicts among neighbors.[49] This seems to have been the case in Rotterdam and

Delft also. Fifteen-year old Annetje, for instance, asked the neighborhood masters for help, since she had been accused of committing the crime of carnal conversation.[50]

Neighborhood masters might have been respectable citizens or men of influence, but they did not have the competence to execute civil or criminal law. Their judgment concerned an informal procedure only, and it was not in any way linked to the official secular court. As far as legal proceedings were concerned, a neighborhood master could act only as an honorable witness. Nevertheless, they often played a crucial role in settling conflicts among neighbors. Most likely, people complained about their nearby residents to the neighborhood master first.[51] If the latter did not succeed in settling the differences, consistories and secular courts became involved.

Historians have debated the extent of acceptance of the discipline exercised by secular and ecclesiastical authorities.[52] Did people support the authorities in their handling of cases, or were they merely the subjects of discipline from above? Both Leuker and Roodenburg have argued that neighbors themselves often informed the magistrates about the immoral and shameless conduct of nearby residents.[53] Indeed, both secular and ecclesiastical records reveal the involvement of parents, guardians, relatives, friends, and neighbors where premarital and matrimonial matters were concerned. All of them were involved as plaintiffs, witnesses, defenders, or supporters when a person was accused. They also played an important role in the process of reconciliation. In almost all cases, the community showed a great concern for behavior in premarital and matrimonial matters, or in any case, they meddled in such affairs.

Whether it concerned secular or ecclesiastical discipline, the majority of the accused were arrested or summoned because relatives or neighbors had spied on them. Adulterers, bigamists, and youngsters who unlawfully shared a bed were often caught red-handed by the bailiff. Tattlers, gossips, and envious next-door neighbors sometimes notified the authorities, but more often local residents seriously objected to the immoral conduct in their neighborhood. Making noise and causing commotion constituted one of the reasons for the community to intervene, but neighbors were also anxious about the reputation of their community.

Martin Dinges concludes that whenever individual community members crossed the borderline of decent or honorable behavior, the neighborhood as a whole could feel threatened.[54] The records of Dutch criminal courts and consistories clearly confirm his findings. Daniel from Rotterdam was denounced by people from his street because the maltreatment of his wife brought "shame and disgrace" on his fellow neighbors.[55] For the same reason, Leendert was not allowed to return to his former neighborhood. In Rotterdam, people regularly requested the magistrates to expel dishonorable community members from their neighborhood. The accusations could refer to prenuptial fornication, bridal pregnancy, adultery, and severe maltreatment of wives and husbands.[56]

Table 6　Marital church discipline cases, 1573–1700

	Men	Women	Total
Marital dispute	206	217	423
Adultery	66	71	137
Desertion	23	40	63
Bigamy	17	16	33
Incest	13	22	35
Other cases	20	53	73
Total	345	419	764

Marriage control concerned the honor and reputation not only of the victim and the perpetrator but also of neighbors and family members. Although the latter did not stand trial or risk conviction, their good reputation was endangered as well. Therefore, neighbors played an important role in controlling premarital sex and supervising matrimonial conduct. As soon as their honor and reputations were concerned, the inhabitants of neighborhoods directly supported the authorities' regulative actions. Relatives and spouses sometimes supported regulation as well, but again, protection of one's reputation influenced one's decision to take family members to court. Financial interests were also of decisive importance, as banishment or imprisonment of the breadwinner evidently led to the loss of income. Therefore, family members rarely informed the criminal court about their relatives' improper behavior. They rather asked the consistory to assist them in their marital problems and to discipline their sinful and criminal relatives.

Conclusion

My comparison of criminal justice and church discipline has highlighted the differences and resemblances between two types of social control in the early modern period. The evidence shows that the differences between criminal justice and church discipline are not satisfactorily explained by the parallel contrast of "sin" versus "crime." It seems that, with respect to marital conduct, both institutions had various aims and objectives.

First, economic factors influenced the prosecution and sentencing in marital matters. When criminal behavior resulted in poverty causing family members to request urban poor relief, judges tended to punish more severely. Therefore, mothers of illegitimate children and abandoning husbands were punished more frequently and more severely. Second, consistories did not only aim at controlling sin and morality but also at preserving the reputation of their parishes. In dealing with sinful matrimonial behavior, clergymen were rarely inclined to take on adultery cases. Although it concerned a serious criminal act, they rather kept it from public view. Finally, the business of consistories and criminal courts was selectively influenced by the complainant's preference. Accusers preferred to take certain complaints to the consistory rather than the criminal court, and vice versa.

The evidence shows that the urban population was more than just a subject of secular punishment and ecclesiastical discipline. The comparison of criminal justice and church discipline clearly reveals that people played an active role in both prosecution and the reconciliation process. They also understood how to make use of the institutions as a means of resolving their private and public problems.

Besides consistories and secular courts, various modes of social control were in existence. Only by comparing all these types of discipline can historians determine how these institutions operated and how they involved various people.

Notes

1. Ingram, "History of Sin or History of Crime?" 95.

2. See the contributions by Herman Roodenburg and Pieter Spierenburg to this volume.

3. Gemeente Archief Rotterdam (GAR), Oude Rechterlijke Archieven, sententieboeken, inv. nos. 244–52, confessieboeken, inv. nos. 139–43, correctieboeken, inv. nos. 266–68; Kerkenraadsacta van de Nederlands Hervormde Gemeente van Rotterdam, kerkenraadsnotulen, inv. nos. 1–8; Gemeente Archief Delft (GAD), Oude Rechterlijke Archieven, sententieboeken, inv. nos. 46–50, confessieboeken, inv. nos. 58–61; Archief Kerkenraad van de Nederlands Hervormde Kerk te Delft, kerkenraadsnotulen, inv. nos. 1–7, tuchtboeken, 276–77.

4. See for Catholic regulations concerning marriage: Eupen, "Kerk en gezin in Nederland," 7–28; Apeldoorn, *Geschiedenis;* Heijden, *Huwelijk in Holland.* In the whole of Europe: Brundage, *Law, Sex and Christian Society;* Esmein, *Le mariage;* Storme, *Die trouwen wil.*

5. Brink, *De taak van de kerk,* 126–41; Grotius, *Inleidinge,* 16; Ankum, "Le mariage," 204–49.

6. Heijden, "Criminaliteit en sexe," 1–36; Ulbricht, *Von Huren und Rabenmüttern.*

7. Kloek, *Wie hij zij,* 78–121; Roodenburg, *Onder censuur,* 381–82.

8. Eliott, "Introduction"; Schilling, "'History of Crime,'" 289–310.

9. Ingram, "History of Sin or History of Crime?" 87–103.

10. Van der Heijden, *Huwelijk in Holland,* 56–76.

11. Ibid., 29.

12. For figures see tables 1 to 6 on premarital and matrimonial church discipline and criminal court cases in Rotterdam and Delft during the period 1550–1700.

13. In Dutch: *vleselijke conversatie.*

14. Storme, *Die trouwen wil,* 232–34, 367–73; Watt, *The Making of the Modern Marriage,* 90–91.

15. This seemed to be the case in Germany as well: Harrington, *Reordering Marriage*, 239.

16. GAR, confession book 142, 24 February 1696.

17. GAR, sentence book 251, 1697, fol. 175, confession book 142, 24 December 1696.

18. Blécourt and Fischer, *Klein plakkaatboek*, 126–34.

19. RAD, sentence book 47, 1605, fol. 137.

20. Heijden, "Women as Victims," 97–118.

21. GAR, confession book 141, 1688.

22. Heijden, "Women as Victims," 102–3

23. GAR, church council notes 1, 1639.

24. According to Keunen almost all charges against women concerning insults were related to chastity: Keunen, "Ongaarne beticht en bevlekt," 415–31. See also Leuker, "Schelmen, hoeren," 314–39.

25. Shorter, "Illegitimacy," 235–72; Mitteraurer, *Ledige Mütter*, 28–43; Damsma, "De dubbele revolutie," 165–92.

26. About the Dutch Further Reformation: Lieburg, *De Nadere Reformatie*; Groenendijk, *De nadere reformatie*. About English Puritanism: Irwin, *Womanhood*, 70–104; Hill, *Society and Puritanism*; Foster, *The Long Argument*.

27. Ingram, *Church Courts*, 262–63; Wrightson, *English Society*, 86.

28. GAR, sentence book 248, 1649, fol. 81.

29. Heijden, *Huwelijk in Holland*, 48–49.

30. Ibid., 82.

31. Ibid., 83–84.

32. GAR, sentence books, 248, 1646, fol. 24–25.

33. GAR, sentence books 250, 1679, fol. 146; Heijden, "Secular and Ecclesiastical Marriage Control," 51.

34. GAR, sentence books 250, 1679, fol. 166–67.

35. GAR, sentence book 246, 1623, fol. 139.

36. Ingram, *Church Courts*, 149; Stone, *The Family*, 40.

37. Heijden, *Huwelijk in Holland*, 160–63.

38. Ibid., 218–37.

39. Schama, *The Embarrassment of Riches*, 420; Haks, *Huwelijk en gezin*, 155–56.

40. Haks, *Huwelijk en gezin*, 196; Joor, "Echtscheiding," 197–230.

41. Heijden, *Huwelijk in Holland*, 227–29.

42. Heijden, "Women as Victims," 107.

43. GAD, church council notes 276, 30 June, 2–25 August, 5 September 1664, fol. 119.

44. GAD, church council notes 3, 4 December 1600.

45. GAR, church council notes 5, 7 February 1661.

46. Roodenburg, *Onder censuur*, 21–23.

47. For instance: Roeck, "Neighbourhoods and the Public," 193–209.

48. Roodenburg, *Onder censuur,* 23.

49. Ibid., 17–27, 244–54; Haks, *Huwelijk en gezin,* 61–62.

50. Heijden, *Huwelijk in Holland,* 101, 120.

51. Ingram, "'Scolding Women Cucked or Washed,'" 48–80. Roodenburg, "Naar een etnogafie," 219–43. Leuker, "Smaad en belediging," 331–32.

52. Dinges, "Weiblichkeit," 71–98; Burke, *The Historical Anthropology,* 95–110; Garrioch, *Neighbourhood and Community;* Garriorch, "Verbal Insults," 104–19.

53. Roodenburg, "Naar een etnografie," 241–42; Roodenburg, *Onder Censuur,* 250–54; Leuker, "Smaad en belediging," 332.

54. Dinges, *Der Maurermeister,* 140–98.

55. GAD, sentence books 46, 1562, fol. 35–36.

56. Heijden, *Huwelijk in Holland,* 119–20.

CHAPTER 4

Ordering Discourse and Society: Moral Politics, Marriage, and Fornication during the Reformation and the Confessionalization Process in Germany and Switzerland

Susanna Burghartz

Introduction

In 1540 the Zürich Reformer and successor to Zwingli, Heinrich Bullinger, complained vehemently of the "grave sins and shameless vices that have alas multiplied greatly and grown rampant among many in this recent and most perilous time." In what followed, he specifically mentioned adultery, fornication (*Hurerei*), and all manner of impurities such as vile language and unchaste deeds. According to him, the cause of the terrible state of society must be sought in the fundamental semantic disorder of his age: "The reason for all this is that the vices no longer bear their proper names and therefore no one judges them properly as they are upon themselves and before God."[1] The Reformers saw this sorry state of affairs reflected not least in gender relations, whose ambiguity and disorderly nature they regarded as a central threat to their world. These were the roots of the struggle against sexual misconduct that was to become so typical of both the Protestant and Catholic Reform movements. This struggle, so vigorously propagated by Reformers, reveals the fundamental significance that they accorded to the power of naming and definition, particularly in the area of morality and sin. For the Reformers, moral politics was no mere secondary arena, but rather a central means of attaining social power and control.[2] The clerical discussions surrounding (clerical) marriage and fornication thus led to a fundamental reorientation of the theology of matrimony,[3] which put "the entire social order to the test."[4]

78

With their rhetoric of *Un-Zucht* (lewdness or fornication, but literally "un-discipline"), the Reformers succeeded in establishing their polemical speech about the immorality of their age as a description of reality. In so doing, they set up as absolute their own dividing line between marriage and illicit sexuality, with no room left for transitions or intermediate forms, let alone a third option like chastity. At the same time, they created a yardstick that has largely been adopted by historians to assess behavior in the areas of marriage and sexuality and that implicitly remains alive and well in the concept of social discipline. The history of the social control and disciplining of gender relations, marriage, and sexuality thus becomes a history not just of behaviors and their changes, but equally of perceptions and standards of judgment and demarcation, including their inherent powers of definition. Mary Douglas has drawn our attention to the important function of notions of purity as social boundaries and taboos.[5] Social order is established with their help and maintained by means of their permanent reformulation. Accordingly, talk about pure, undefiled sexuality within marriage and its strict separation from all possible forms of illegitimate, "indecent," and thus impure sexuality outside marriage assumed an important function in Reformed debates about a new social order and its realization. As Douglas shows elsewhere, the "purity principle" has played a key role in conflicts between the center and periphery of society in various historical configurations.[6]

Such conflicts are often fought out as struggles between orthodoxy and heterodoxy. The struggles between Reformers and the Catholic Church were also often pursued with the weapons of the purity discourse. In this fight there was, however, no obvious victor, since in the course of the Reformation no clear new center emerged. Instead, after the establishment of the Reformation, various confessional centers spent centuries competing to embody orthodoxy. This permanent competition unleashed a discursive dynamism of its own that became historically effective, if not always in the ways intended by those involved. Against this conceptual background, we can analyze moral politics, its developments and booms, during the reformation period and the confessionalization process—that is, from the early fifteenth century to the beginning of the eighteenth century—simultaneously on the level of discourses, institutions, and actions.[7] The question of control and discipline is then no longer limited to the level of behavior, but rather incorporates perceptions and judgments as well. The history of structures and discourses can thus be applied to the arena of marriage, sexuality, and gender relations. Order, like *dis*order, is revealed to be the result of permanent historical effort. Both are thus the consequence of historical processes of construction. In this way, the alleged moral *dis*order of the Reformation period is interpreted not simply as an absence of order, as "immorality," but rather as an interested ascription within the framework of major processes of reordering. The intersection of confessionalization, state development, and purity discourse reveals once again that questions of purity are questions of power.

Late Medieval Reform Discussions:
The Inception of Official Moral Politics

Beginning in the late Middle Ages, the area of matrimony, the regulation of sexual conduct, and the control competence of kin groups came to be discussed in new ways and, above all in the efforts of late medieval cities to maintain order, were newly regulated. This long-term process, which stretched from the thirteenth to the sixteenth or even seventeenth century, has been described by Michael Schröter as part of the civilizing process with corresponding consequences for psychogenesis and sociogenesis.[8] In the course of this process, the secular authorities established new claims to power by shifting marriage more and more exclusively out of the area of competence of kin groups and into the sphere of the Church, while at the same time massively extending the control of the Church over this legal field.[9] Municipal authorities did not just claim control over the legality of marriages, however. As Beate Schuster has shown for Konstanz and Basel, encouraged by a new Christian self-understanding, they also began to develop their own morality laws and policies against "living in sin" (*zur Unehe sitzen*), with the objective of establishing the sole validity of marriage within urban society. A further consequence of this policy was, ultimately, the municipal campaign against prostitutes in the late-fifteenth and early-sixteenth centuries, which culminated in the closure of the municipal brothels.

In this social climate, reformed theological writings such as the *Reformatio Sigismundi* discussed the negative consequences of compulsory celibacy for the sexual order and called for priests to marry.[10] The issue of clerical marriage and thus also of marital sexuality, and sexuality more generally, was by no means new. Repeated reform movements from the tenth century onward led to the introduction of compulsory celibacy for priests in the twelfth century at the First and Second Lateran Councils. Nevertheless, priestly celibacy was no means completely established in practice by the end of the Middle Ages.[11] In their struggle for a pure society, criticisms of the allegedly immoral state of the clergy became a key point for the reformers of the fifteenth century, and above all for proponents of the Reformation in the early sixteenth century, in their conflicts with the Roman Catholic Church and the papacy.[12] In a reformed polemical pamphlet, for example, Sebastian Meyer and Berchtold Haller attacked the income earned by the bishop of Konstanz from clerical concubinage and the newborn children of priests, whose numbers they estimated at fifteen hundred annually.[13] The Reformation and its discussions of compulsory celibacy and clerical marriage thus did not introduce any wholly novel substantive issues into the discursive field of marriage, but it did accelerate and reshape discursive positions, a process that Bernd Hamm has referred to as "normative centering" (*normative Zentrierung*).[14]

The Reformation Period: Calls for Moral Renewal

In this situation of escalation and intensification, Martin Luther launched an attack against clerical celibacy, among other things, in his 1520 "To the Christian Nobility of the German Nation" and declared the papal law on celibacy to be a diabolical invention.[15] Like other reformers before him (including Erasmus), on several occasions Luther expressed his views on celibacy, clerical marriage, chastity, and logically enough on marriage in general. He declared marriage to be the only estate pleasing to God and distinguished it with severity from all forms of fornication and sexual misconduct. Following Luther, Zwingli also inveighed against compulsory celibacy and in 1522 directly combined the postulate of free preaching based on the Scriptures with his demand that priests be permitted to marry. The new theology of matrimony also contained a new gender anthropology, which declared sexuality, as part of divine creation, to be an inevitable element of human life. For the leading Reformers marriage, not celibacy, now became the site and guarantor of social purity. Outside of matrimony, the option of chastity was rejected as anthropologically impossible. This theological turn was to have far reaching discursive and rhetorical consequences. The nuanced and differentiated late Medieval discussion of different forms of sexuality was replaced by a discourse about sexuality that was clearly binary in structure, recognizing only pure marriage and its opposite. All nonmarital sexuality was declared without distinction to be lewdness (*Unzucht,* an opaque catch-all term) or fornication (*Hurerei*). The boom in polarizing "un" words (such as *Unehe,* adultery or concubinage, literally unmarriage; *Unzucht,* undiscipline, illicit sexuality, lewdness, fornication; *Unreinheit,* impurity; etc.) led to the establishment of a rhetoric characterized by sexual vagueness that could be used in correspondingly broad ways[16]. As a paradoxical result of the fight against the indecent and impure world, the discursive reshaping thus brought with it an increasing sexualization of the whole area of matrimony. In the long run, this sexualization, combined with a clearly negative polarization, had substantial mental and practical effects. Its first and foremost effect in the Protestant world was an enormous boost in the status of marriage as the only guarantor of social purity. The need to separate marital sexuality clearly and unambiguously from all other sexuality (*Unzucht*), and thus to secure the new site of social purity, rose accordingly.

The long-term effects of this reshaping depended not only on theological and thus discursive changes, however, but also on developments in the institutional arena of early modern state building. The Zürich Reformer Zwingli took up the efforts of his municipal authorities to obtain a judicial monopoly and fought the influence of the officiality at Konstanz, among other courts. In 1525 Zwingli and the municipal council in Zürich established the marriage court, which quickly became a model for other cities in southern Germany and Switzerland.[17] The Reformed marriage court became a new discursive site characterized by a specific combination of circumstances: the municipal Reformed marriage courts represented the practical application of the new teachings on matrimony, but in many respects, they also adopted traditions from canon law.[18] In practical terms the courts had to mediate between the various societal demands for order, an economically motivated social order and a theologically and morally motivated sexual order, and their complex interactions. Where the emphasis was placed apparently differed from city to city.

In Zürich, as in Basel or Augsburg, the activities of the marriage courts at first centered on clarifying the validity of promises of marriage and questions of divorce. The prosecution of illicit sexual behavior was initially delegated to special morals courts, as in Zürich, or to the *Unzüchter* (the municipal office responsible for maintaining public order and morals), as in Basel or Augsburg, which mainly issued warnings and reprimands. The relationship between the marriage courts and the morals courts was closer in some cities than others. In Zürich, the two courts were practically synonymous,[19] while in Basel the Reformer Johannes Oecolampadius insisted on a strict separation between secular prosecution and the moral control of the Church.[20] The actual criminalization of all nonmarital sexuality occurred only gradually in the second half of the sixteenth century, parallel to the successful establishment of the Church's exclusive competence in matrimonial marriage.

In the early phase of Protestant moral politics, the new higher status of matrimony and of marital sexuality inextricably linked with it went hand in hand with a sharp separation from prostitution and its traditional acceptance within Catholic teaching as a lesser evil. Demands that brothels be abolished as sites of illicit sexuality in the urban community and as symbols of unacceptable official tolerance or ambiguity in moral matters had their place in the discussion surrounding a purer society. Accordingly, the Reform-oriented authorities devoted their attention to prostitution quite early on. Luther had called for the closure of the brothels in his above-mentioned text "To the Christian Nobility of the German Nation" in 1520. Subsequently, various cities actually closed their brothels.[21] The arguments and justifications invoked by municipal authorities and preachers differed from place to place. In 1532 Basel's Reformed clergy, for example, explicitly formulated their interest in abolition in terms of confessional politics, since they feared disadvantages for Basel's doctrine and church ordinance after Anabaptists and Lutherans took the existence of a municipal brothel as the occasion for insults.[22] Confessional competition was probably a significant factor in the persistence of brothel abolition as a topic of moral politics in both Reformed and Catholic cities throughout the sixteenth century.[23] It not only played a role as an argument in discussions surrounding the abolition of bordellos but also accompanied the later history of moral politics during the confessionalization process.

From the beginning, the Reformers' discussion of celibacy, clerical marriage, and the necessary redefinition of matrimony was orchestrated as a discussion about social order.[24] The new Reformation and morals ordinances aimed accordingly at renewing communal life more generally and putting an end to all abuses and vices.[25] Alongside questions of preaching, ritual, and church organization, the new regulation of the married estate, as a way of life that was now universally binding, became a central aim of these efforts at establishing order.

The Reformed discussion of the necessity of clerical marriage, the impossibility of maintaining celibacy, the omnipresence of illicit sexuality in society, and the revaluation of marriage as the new, and now sole, site of social purity, by no means led to a simply repressive and disciplinal practice in the newly established marriage courts, but to integrative positions as well. The goal was to preserve and establish as many marriages as possible. This orientation is particularly evident in the first years of the Basel marriage court, which was set up at the same time as the Reformation in the city in 1529. In the 1530s the court's main task was to decide whether promises of marriage were valid and thus whether a marriage existed or not. The chances for plaintiffs, whether male or female, to assert their interests in court were still quite good. The second most common group of cases was suits for divorce, mainly because of adultery or "malicious abandonment." It is remarkable that the Basel marriage court issued practically no convictions for fornication in the first half of the sixteenth century.[26] The Augsburg marriage court presents a similar picture for the years 1537–1546. Here, too, plaintiffs who came to court to enforce promises of marriage, as well as women seeking compensation for the loss of their virginity or their childbed expenses, or both, had a good chance of winning their cases. Considerations of social utility, which according to Lyndal Roper were in the foreground in the municipal court, meant not least that in most cases the new marriage court (unlike the ecclesiastical court previously responsible in this area) ordered that women be paid compensation.[27] In Augsburg, too, fornication trials did not yet play a role in the new Reformed marriage court at this period. In Zürich, however, the functions of the marriage and morals courts were combined early, although even here decisions were often in favor of the plaintiffs.[28]

With the new institutions of moral discipline, the first phase of Reformed moral politics sought, particularly in the field of marriage and sexuality, to discipline and sanction. At the same time, however, it also pursued an integrative matrimonial policy before the newly established secular marriage courts, and here, at least, in the first half of the sixteenth century the criminalization of all nonmarital sexuality remained incomplete even in the Protestant world. The orientation and effects of Reformed teachings on marriage and moral politics were and remained quite ambiguous. Only in the course of the long-term confessionalization of Europe did the contents and meaning of Reformed matrimonial doctrine and politics become clearer theoretically and above all practically. The new moral politics and the accompanying efforts at discipline in the fields of marriage and sexuality were the consequences not merely of new Reformed theological positions on these questions. More decisive was the close intersection of this moral theology with new forms of institutionalization and, as a consequence, with institutional judicial practice, which in turn clarified, developed, or reformulated theory in specific ways. Thus began a long-term process in which Protestant reform, Catholic reform, and confessionalization were all involved. The Council of Trent and its confessional political confrontations over clerical marriage, vows of chastity, and matrimonial law led to a structural parallel development of Catholic doctrine and practice in the field of moral policy.[29] This parallelism was intensified by the marked traditionalism of Protestant matrimonial law and legal practice.

The example of Geneva, however, shows quite clearly that despite all the structural parallels in long-term developments in western and central Europe, these processes could take on very different rhythms, tempos, and forms in different places. Even before the actual breakthrough of the Reformation in Geneva, in May 1536, efforts were underway to institute stronger moral control. Examples are the 1534 municipal laws against fornication and adultery and regulating the bathhouses and the 1536 prohibition of prostitution. According to Kingdon, systematic moral politics was only introduced in practice after Calvin's return to the city in 1541, which was soon followed by the establishment of the consistory. This created an instrument that expanded into a genuine moral reign of terror beginning in the mid-1550s.[30] This politics was apparently so successful ideologically and discursively that during his visit to Geneva in 1556 the Scottish theologian John Knox could note approvingly that, although the true faith might be preached in other cities, "in no other city had he seen such good behavior."[31] Despite this positive assessment, the Geneva consistory further extended its control activities in the years that followed. Thus, in the 1560s the regulation of marital conflicts and condemnation of extramarital sexuality—and with it the enforcement of a central aim of the consistory, the absolute regard for marriage—were among its central if by no means only duties, while the establishment of the true faith had already retreated into the background.[32] At the same time, according to E.W. Monter, it was evident by the late 1560s that the exaggerated system of moral surveillance had already passed its zenith, even if it was to persist for another four hundred years.[33] Thus, while Reformed moral politics was introduced later in Geneva than in other Protestant cities in southern Germany and Switzerland, it began earlier there to take on a repressive orientation that reached an extraordinary intensity. The socially dysfunctional consequences of exaggerated moral politics became visible in Geneva correspondingly early without, however, the policies being wholly abandoned.

Confessionalization: The Second Phase of the Morals Campaign

Despite all the Reformers' efforts at establishing a genuinely Christian—that is, pure—society, people continued to complain incessantly about the immoral state of affairs throughout the sixteenth century. Beginning in the 1560s, we can see a new wave of moral politics from above, which now drew its dynamism from the ongoing process of confessionalization and its inherent confessional competition, a competition that did not, however, lead to distinct confessional forms of moral politics, but rather to a tendency to parallels. Confessional interactions are already evident in the results of the Council of Trent, which also formalized and heightened the Church's exclusive competence in matrimonial matters for the Catholic realm and in so doing created the preconditions for the reinterpretation of premarital sexuality as fornication. Toward the end of the century, new, more repressive efforts in various places of differing confessional persuasions became evident not only in the fields of theology and canon law but also in that of practical moral politics.

In Basel, for example, in the second half of the sixteenth century, public prosecutions came to predominate over suits brought by private individuals. The recognition of suits involving promises of marriage and thus the creation of new marriage ties had retreated into the background as had divorces of marriages that no longer functioned and thus threatened the social order. Instead, the courts began in the 1580s to embed the concerns of opposing parties in an increasingly dominant discourse on fornication, which changed perceptions and patterns of argumentation before the court.[34] The marriage court became primarily a site for the prosecution of lewdness and fornication. In Basel, this shift occurred at the same time as conflicts over the confessional orientation of the city, in which the Reformed supporters of Zwingli and Calvin gained the upper hand in the late 1570s. With this change the conflicts surrounding social purity gained new relevance, as statements made by the Calvinist François Hotman, who came to Basel in 1578, show. He criticized circumstances in the city and wrote to Zürich that the reasons for the doctrinal disunity and imperiled harmony among Swiss Protestants must be sought in the lack of effective church discipline. He ended his remarks with the complaint that "*Doctrina reformata est, vita deformatissima,*" a claim typical of the confessionalization phase, in which the reformation of doctrine had been replaced by the reformation of life.[35] The change in the perception and valuation of previously noncriminalized sexual behaviors, despite the persistence of the old normative framework, by no means ended with developments in the late sixteenth century but rather continued with renewed intensity into the seventeenth century. A significant factor in this change was the continuing purity discourse and its inherent dynamism.[36]

Thus, in the initial years after the Reformation, marriage was an instrument in the fight against lewdness and fornication. After all, the recognition of a promise of marriage was tantamount to marriage itself, so that illicit sexuality could be transformed into legitimate, marital sexuality. This function was visible as a paradigm in the marriages of the Reformers themselves, who by marrying transformed the otherwise inevitable fornication into marital sexuality. Accordingly, during the early years of its existence, the marriage court laid great stress on a concept of marriage that made it possible to integrate sexuality into a godly, secular matrimonial order. Beginning in the 1580s, in contrast, the fight against fornication was no longer pursued through integration but rather through delimitation and exclusion, that is, the punishment of all nonmarital sexuality. As a consequence, conflicts over the validity of promises of marriage could no longer be simply settled; the decision not to recognize a promise of marriage as binding now inevitably entailed the punishment of tower imprisonment or a monetary fine for "nullity." Parallel to this development, toward the end of the sixteenth century the courts decided far more frequently that the unmarried people who appeared before them were involved in relationships of lewdness or fornication, and the numbers rose even more sharply in the seventeenth century. As the example of Basel clearly shows, an increase in repressiveness did not always express itself quantitatively, since the number of cases brought before the courts did not rise in relation to population. Instead, a striking, mainly qualitative change occurred: from private suits to ex officio proceedings and thus from decisions about contested promises of marriage to convictions for fornication or "disregard for marriage."

This qualitative change from a more integrative to a more repressive moral politics is confirmed by studies of other regions of varying denominations during the same period. Uwe Sibeth, for example, has noted a shift in church discipline in the field of marriage and sexuality in Hesse-Kassel, which increasingly moved from the idea of Christian admonition aimed at reconciliation with the congregation to church punishments with the character of criminal sanctions.[37] For the bishopric of Speyer, Andreas Blauert has found that from the end of the sixteenth century on, in the course of the Counter-Reformation, the bishops devoted particular attention to the moral reform of their subjects. This interest is documented above all in adultery cases recorded in the aulic council minutes.[38] Blauert does not attribute the clustering of relevant offenses about 1630 to processes of territorialization, confessionalization, or disciplining, however. Instead, he views this phenomenon as the expression of social crises, the fears they produced and the attempts to master them. Joel Harrington for his part considers a rise in the intensity of prosecution by both Protestant and Catholic authorities in Speyer and Rhineland-Palatinate to have been likely, although gaps in the sources do not permit precise figures.[39] Frank Konersmann also paints an ambivalent picture for Palatinate-Zweibrücken. Depending on the ecclesiastical or secular court and the district, he reaches different conclusions about the repressiveness of the authorities in dealing with marital and sexual offenses. While the normative level appears to have been clearly subject to an increasing density of regulation, the divergent and often small numbers of cases permit no uniform interpretation.[40]

The results of the study of so-called serious criminality in Electoral Bavaria undertaken by Wolfgang Behringer are less ambiguous. Morals offenses—chief among them fornication and adultery—underwent a genuine boom at the end of the sixteenth and the beginning of the seventeenth century.[41] At 30 percent, they led the list of offenses prosecuted by the aulic council in the first half of the seventeenth century. The growing repression in this field also meant a massive criminalization of women. According to Behringer, the radicalization of the religious world order in the "confessional age," in Bavaria more specifically a result of the Jesuit-influenced Counter-Reformation, was instrumental in "elevating" misdemeanors to crimes. These criminalization efforts reached their high point in the morality decree of 1635. The quantitative rise in general criminality that followed led to simple morals offenses being delegated to the lower authorities and to the proportion of morals offenses falling substantially to 14 percent in the late-seventeenth century. The offenses studied by Behringer were pursued as serious crimes and thus are not directly comparable to the cases that came before the marriage courts and ecclesiastical morals courts. Ulrike Strasser's study on Munich, however, shows that comparable developments in official moral politics can be found even on this subordinate level.[42]

The Seventeenth Century: The High Point of Christian Moral Politics

In the second half of the sixteenth century, long-term confessional competition, with its interest in purity, on the one hand, and the close interaction of the religious and secular authorities under the conditions of an increasingly strong state (which was typical of confessionalization), on the other hand, led to moral politics becoming a new field of activity for Christian, secular authorities of all denominations. This development was intensified and further consolidated in the seventeenth century, as we can see from the example of Electoral Bavaria and its morality decree.

Accordingly, even one hundred years after the establishment of the Reformation and fifty years after Hotman's complaint, the struggle for a "new purity of life" was as relevant as ever, as the example of Basel shows. Here, after a long conflict between the town council and the clergy, the *antistes* (the first minister of the Church of Basel) Theodor Zwinger pushed through the introduction of a new, stricter Reformation ordinance whose programmatic significance the theology professor Johann Rudolf Wettstein emphasized in the following terms: "so that the Evangelical chosen people may be easily recognized."[43] Particularly in the struggle against sin, clerics and magistrates could prove themselves as truly Christian authorities. Thus, in the new Reformation ordinance of

1637, all nonmarital sexuality between men and women was clothed in metaphors of defilement and pollution, which also implied disorder, defined as lewdness, penalized and thus implicitly diametrically opposed to pure (because marital) sexuality.[44] Through explicit references to Pauline Bible passages, the theological purity discourse entered into the juridical text. The Reformation purity discourse was thus continued in the confessionalization process and extended into the judicial arena, while at the same time the "new" moral politics remained a central factor in the formation of confessional identity. In its basic characteristics, it led—at once logically and paradoxically—to the same results among the different confessions and served the respective Christian authorities as a means of self-representation. This moral logic, as well as its social limits, is visible in paradigmatic form in the newly invented offense of "premature carnal knowledge" (*früher Beischlaf*).

"Premature carnal knowledge" was probably made a punishable offense for the first time in 1534 in Zürich in an undated decree.[45] With this law, premarital intercourse was criminalized as fornication even when the couple subsequently married, thus punishing a behavior that had previously been common, legitimate, and recognized by canon law. This penal provision was, however, apparently not yet enforced in judicial practice. In the second half of the sixteenth century, similar decrees were issued in various other cities and territories. Thus, in Hesse-Kassel the synod imposed a church penance for premarital intercourse (*anticipatio*) beginning in 1556, and the Hessian Reformation ordinance of 1572 also stipulated that the bride could not wear a wreath at her wedding and that the wedding celebration had to occur in private; "premature" childbirth (*partus septimestris*) was also punished with a sentence for fornication.[46] In contrast to Zürich, Hesse-Kassel, or neighboring Württemberg, this stage in the criminalization process occurred relatively late in Basel, with the introduction of the offense of "premature carnal knowledge" in 1637.[47] Practical enforcement seems to have begun in various places about the same time—the mid-seventeenth century— representing a new high point in policies against fornication. Convictions for so-called premature carnal knowledge represented one-third of convictions for fornication in Basel at the end of the seventeenth century. More than ever before, the fight against fornication now became the chief activity of the marriage courts. Accordingly, this new form of combat led to more rather than fewer cases of fornication being heard by the courts.

At the same time, with the introduction of this new offense, the limits of moral politics and its discursive dynamism became visible. Under the new statutory definition, even valid marriages could be affected by accusations of fornication, and illicit sexuality could extend into marriage without there being any question of adultery. Although sentences were regularly reduced beginning shortly after the introduction of the new offense and the trials were highly standardized, when it came to their own wives, the citizens of Basel found this criminalization untenable in the long run. In 1718, in order to spare their wives the disgrace of appearing personally in court, they were still arguing in petitions that a trial would be deleterious to the health of mother and child. The routine treatment of cases, as well as the persistent resistance from local citizens to the shame of appearing in court, emphasizes that sexual order and social order clearly collided in this field. The threat to functioning marriages from a conviction and the reactions to this threat show that the expansion of the fornication discourse had reached a limit whose overstepping could prove problematic. In their studies on the Basel countryside in the eighteenth century, Simon and Schnyder found that the authorities did not really succeed in enforcing their idea that marriage began with the church ceremony and thus failed in their attempts to penalize common rural practice, which approved of sexual intercourse once a promise of marriage had been made.[48] The example of Hesse-Kassel points to a similarly tense competition between sexual and social order as that in Basel. The punishment of premarital intercourse was introduced relatively early here, but the penalization of *anticipatio* aroused controversy from the beginning. In Hesse-Kassel, too, the punishment of legally married couples who posed no threat to the social order revealed the limits of Christian moral politics.[49]

In principle, however, official moral politics underwent a boom not just in Bavaria and Basel but also in other (imperial) cities and territories. Ulinka Rublack has described the heightened "moralism" that prevailed in Württemberg, which found its expression in the expansion of morals decrees and a strict prosecution of "sexual immorality" beginning in the second half of the sixteenth century.[50] Legislation aimed at punishing "carnal crimes" (*Fleischesverbrechen*), as a decree of 1630 called them, reached its apex during the course of the seventeenth century, with regionally distinct temporal emphases.[51] While this process was complete by the mid-seventeenth century in Württemberg, the first, relatively mild decrees were introduced in Hall in 1643. In contrast to those in Württemberg, these laws imposed equal penalties for men and women found guilty of fornication. They were followed in the final third of the century by a campaign of criminalization directed largely against servants. Taking the vehement attacks on servants in Hall as an example, we can describe a shift in the early modern discourse on order.

The stereotype of the disorderly and debauched servant intensified an ominous scenario for an early modern (mainly urban) society characterized by growing social differentiation. The stereotype at once aimed at cementing social distinctions and functioned as part of a distinctive discourse of domination. Here, too, purification and sanctification through admonition and reconciliation were replaced by criminalization and exclusion. Renate Dürr's work on the imperial city of Hall underlines very clearly the meaning and dynamism of this increasingly obsessive early modern discourse of order.[52] In Hall both the penalties for fornication, which could affect women of all social ranks but were presumably imposed disproportionately on maidservants, and the discursive attribution of lewdness to the social group of servants reached a high point in the second half of the seventeenth century. This occurred at a period characterized by especially low rates of illegitimacy.[53] The social intensification of the discourse on illicit sexuality thus in no way corresponded to a worsening social problem that might have expressed itself in high rates of illegitimacy, impoverishment, and subsequent burdens on municipal poor relief. Instead, developments in Hall, too, revealed themselves as another wave of a dynamic and increasingly repressive discourse on order, with all its fears and rigors.

The figures for illegitimate births in Hall correspond to those obtained by Rainer Beck for Upper Bavaria (Unterfinning) between the final third of the seventeenth century and the end of the eighteenth century. Beck explains the extremely low rates of illegitimacy in terms of a traditional culture of honor, in which young people's sexual behavior was marked by "chastity." In this culture, sexuality and the economy were closely linked. The code of honor ultimately guaranteed the close connection between pregnancy and weddings.[54] In his study of so-called wantonness offenses (*Leichtfertigkeitsdelikte*) in seventeenth- and eighteenth-century Bavaria, Stefan Breit modifies this connection and emphasizes that "honor or virginity became a decisive capital" when women possessed no other property, that is, for women of the lower classes.[55] Taking a long overview, he too concludes that even in late seventeenth-century Bavaria, moral and religious aspects remained in the foreground of state sanctions against illicit sexuality, which were displaced at the end of the eighteenth century by social aspects. In the long term, this shift led to the abolition of penalties for "wantonness" in 1808, but also to the perfecting of restrictive state policies on marriage.[56] Both Breit and Beck stress the acceptance of premarital sexuality in early modern Bavarian rural society. Beck regards the connection he finds between low rates of illegitimacy and a high proportion of premarital pregnancies as an important argument against the efficiency of the repressive intentions of church and secular authorities.[57]

Heinrich R. Schmidt reaches similar conclusions for the Bernese communes of Vechingen and Stettlen. According to him, the mid-seventeenth century and above all the eighteenth century witnessed "an intensification of the situation in the area of premarital sexuality—from a raising of the age of majority, punishments for fornication and adultery, the combating of bridal pregnancies, prohibitions on marriages among the poor to compulsory celibacy and a rise in infanticide."[58] At this time Berne, too, criminalized bridal pregnancies ("premature" births); they were penalized from 1686 until about 1770, a remarkably short period of time compared with other regions. The offense of *Hurerei* (fornication, whoring) as well as paternity suits increased in the villages studied. Until about 1735 the Church court (*Chorgericht*) sought to forbid sexual contacts between unmarried persons even if the woman had not become pregnant. After that date, the courts pursued only those cases of fornication that had led to pregnancy.[59]

At the same time the quantitative relationship between marriages and out-of-wedlock pregnancies changed fundamentally. While in the seventeenth century there had been ten marriages for every pregnancy out of wedlock, in the eighteenth century the ratio was two to one. Particularly in the eighteenth century, then, there is no evidence of a successful policing of morals that succeeded in diminishing the number of illicit sexual relationships.[60]

Thus, while Schmidt rejects the thesis that social discipline was successful in the long-term in the area of nonmarital sexuality, for the regulation of marital conflicts he follows the coalition thesis, which claims that women and the authorities pursued parallel interests.[61] According to Schmidt, the "paterfamilias ideology" was aimed programmatically at "a moral reform of its main pillar, the man" and "for that reason represented a weapon in women's hands for domesticating men." Although this thesis may have a certain plausibility for the regulation of marital disputes by the Church court in the Bernese villages studied by Schmidt, in light of the growing repressiveness of the marriage and morals courts in the sixteenth century, and more particularly the seventeenth century, it cannot be generalized to posit a rapprochement between vertical domestication by the authorities and horizontal domestication by wives. Thus, we should reject Safley's thesis according to which "the Reformation not only centralized institutional control of marriage but inspired greater sensitivity, as revealed in court verdicts, to the needs of the petitioners," since from the second half of the sixteenth century, women and men were equally unsuccessful in pressing their claims in suits involving marriage or divorce.[62] Instead, they saw themselves confronted with an increasingly repressive practice of sanctions as part of an ever more rigid moral politics.[63]

This interpretation is also substantiated by Watt's studies of Neuchâtel. The Calvinist city of Neuchâtel also witnessed a clear, long-term criminalization of pre- and nonmarital sexuality.[64] Parallel to the massive rise in fornication trials in the seventeenth century, the number of women's suits to enforce promises of marriage, which now had scarcely any chance of success any more, fell drastically.[65] While in the seventeenth century during the consistory's struggle against sexual impurity and for a pure, Christian way of life, almost equal numbers of men and women were punished for fornication, in the eighteenth century the number of women sentenced rose sharply, by 51 percent, while the number of men convicted dropped by 150 percent during the same period.[66] Watt proposes a direct connection between the court's interest in illegitimate children and the poor relief burdens that were associated with them. Heinz Schilling has noted an intensification of sexual discipline, which was largely directed against lewdness and fornication offenses (*Unzucht, Hurerei*) and thus primarily against unmarried women and mothers, for the city of Emden as well. There, however, harsher repression only began in the mid-seventeenth century, particularly under the Pietist Church Council in the 1690s.[67] In Emden, the stigmatizaton of *anticipatio* also began only in the 1740s, far later than elsewhere.[68]

The Early-Eighteenth Century:
From Morality to "Welfare"

Places such as Neuchâtel arriving at a new discursive configuration in the eighteenth century can be found about the same time, 1730, in the legislation of various regions. It was characterized by the linking of moral with economic arguments, which were directed at the "temporal welfare" of subjects and the community and had substantial consequences in the long term for the status of unmarried mothers and their children. For Palatinate-Zweibrücken, for example, Frank Konersmann speaks of a program of moral and economic discipline on the part of the welfare-oriented church regime.[69] For Hesse-Kassel, Uwe Sibeth notes that in the course of the eighteenth century, in conjunction with the secularization of marriage legislation, an increasing social differentiation and fiscalization of matrimonial law was established with an increasingly complex system of impediments to marriage, which rendered it a social privilege.[70]

At this time, economic arguments were by no means wholly novel in marriage legislation. Thus, for example, in seventeenth-century Zürich proof of sufficient material means was part of the examination of the couple carried out by pastors and a precondition for marriage.[71] In the early-eighteenth century, however, the whole discursive structure of official moral politics shifted. In her historical overview of moral politics in the German states in the early modern period, Isabel Hull notes that in eighteenth-century legislation religious motivations were supplemented or even supplanted by economic and social arguments.[72] Morality and order remained inextricably linked, but morality was no longer grounded exclusively in the religious arguments of a vengeful God, but increasingly also in secular welfare. Hull stresses at the same time that seventeenth-century efforts at establishing and maintaining order were characterized by futility. In the preambles to ever new decrees, the disillusioned authorities expressed, and at the same time perceived, the hopelessness of their efforts. This insight into their failure led the eighteenth-century authorities to withdraw from total responsibility for the Christian moral state of their subjects with all its transcendental implications, while intensifying the efficiency of bureaucratic control over those subjects at the same time.[73]

This makes it easier to understand why the eighteenth century witnessed two contradictory developments: while the draconian punishment of certain forms of nonmarital sexuality (e.g., adultery) abated in some regions of Europe, there was a strong quantitative increase in the penalization of less serious sexual offenses, including out-of-wedlock pregnancy.[74] Despite secularization, however, the moral political discourse of the eighteenth century, with its new sexual policy regime, remained rooted in the religiously motivated moral political tradition of the Christian absolutist authorities. It thus appears problematic to conclude from the *vanitas* rhetoric of these authorities that their efforts in the field of moral politics were especially unsuccessful in the seventeenth century, since these repeated moral offensives led, also and particularly in the seventeenth century, to an increasingly intense criminalization of previously legitimate behaviors. Regardless of developments in the behavior of the population at large, the seventeenth-century theology of the vengeful God depended for its intrinsic functioning on claims of moral decline and decay. Ultimately, the Christianity of the authorities could be demonstrated precisely in a moral politics that was constantly being dramatized and intensified. This was a Christianity whose legitimacy was constantly under threat, at least in comparisons, from ongoing confessionalization, which produced no clear, new orthodox center and which required reassurance to assert its distinction from that of other (less truly Christian) authorities.

Conclusion

Bullinger's complaints about semantic disorder were typical of his time, but they have also remained extremely influential up to the present day. Numerous recent studies of the fifteenth to seventeenth centuries continue to lament the immorality of the period in question and to note either a lack of order or development toward a higher degree of order. This applies to the theses of legalization and social discipline and, to some extent at least, to the domestication thesis, as well as to the closely related coalition thesis. Implicitly, all of these explanations proceed from deficient regulation or order. Thus, an unspoken continuity arises between the Reformed discourse of order and later historiography. In contrast, studies that enquire into social control functions and codes that directed behavior can note long-term and quite fundamental changes on the level of discursive configurations—and thus also in the fields of perception, judgment, and rhetoric—without having to draw direct conclusions about the deficient structures of patterns of action and behavior. Criminalization and increasing repression in the arena of official moral politics thus need not be interpreted as the success or failure of an officially intended fundamental disciplining of behavior. Instead, reordering becomes a concept with its own discursive logic and dynamics.

   In this view, the reorientation of the discourse on marriage in the course of Catholic and Protestant Reform movements led, in conjunction with the emergence of the early modern state, to a lasting change in the frame of reference of those appearing before the marriage courts. This altered frame of reference contained a significant element of discipline. The Church's exclusive competence in matrimonial matters imposed a new boundary between pure and impure and marital and nonmarital to which everyone would henceforth have to refer. On the level of the conduct of the men and women involved, the code of honor was by no means directly replaced by the new sexual morality. In the courtroom, however, those actors, both male and female, who followed the laws of honor were compelled to insert themselves ever more clearly into the framework defined by the new morality. The Church's exclusive competence in matrimonial matters by no means led from a situation of disorder to one of greater order, as the Reformers claimed, but rather above all to a sexualization of gender relations in the relevant court proceedings. Moral politics thus became a vehicle for a specific form of the construction of gender in the early modern period, but at the same time, and far more consciously, also a vehicle for the dramatization of Christian rule and its power to define. This is where the question of the effects of all these efforts at discipline should come in—in a stronger emphasis on the history of discourse and perceptions. We need more than just the mediation between the micro- and macrolevels called for by recent scholars. Equally central is a more complex model of social reality, one more strongly oriented toward the interaction of discourses and practices that also breaks down the simple dichotomy between norms and behavior underlying the classic concept of fundamental or social discipline.

Notes

1. Bullinger, *Der Christlich Eestand,* fol. 2.

2. Lyndal Roper makes a similar argument for different reasons in *The Holy Household,* 5.

3. See Burghartz, *Zeiten der Reinheit,* chap. 2; with a different assessment, see the earlier account by Ozment, *When Fathers Ruled,* chap. 1. On clerical marriage see Buckwalter, *Die Priesterehe in Flugschriften der frühen Reformation.*

4. Puff, "ein schul darinn wir allerlay Christliche tugend vnd zucht lernen," 59.

5. Douglas, *Purity and Danger,* 4–5.

6. Douglas, "Das Prinzip Reinheit und Verschmutzung."

7. For a more detailed account, see Burghartz, *Zeiten der Reinheit,* passim.

8. Schröter, "Staatsbildung und Triebkontrolle"; and *Wo zwei zusammenkommen in rechter Ehe.*

9. For western Europe more generally see Burgière and Lebrun, "Priest, Prince and Family"; for Italy see *Storia del Matrimonio.*

10. *Reformation Kaiser Sigismunds,* 152. On the discussion more generally, see Harrington, *Reordering Marriage and Society,* part I.

11. On the history of priestly celibacy, see Denzler, *Päpste und Papsttum,* vol. 5, I and II.

12. Walter, *Unkeuschheit und Werk der Liebe,* esp. chap. 1.

13. The title of Meyer and Haller's text was, characteristically, "Ernstliche Ermahnung Hugo von Landenbergs . . . zu Frieden und christlicher Einigkeit mit schöner Auslegung und Erklärung [samt] Summarium der schädlichen, tödlichen Gifte, so in diesem Mandat inbegriffen, gedruckt zu Augsburg 1522/23," (Hugo of Landenberg's

earnest admonition "to peace and Christian unity, with a pretty interpretation and explanation [including] a summary of the pernicious, deadly poisons contained in this decree, printed at Augsburg in 1522–1523), in Otto Clemen, ed., *Flugschriften aus den ersten Jahren der Reformation,* vol. 4, no. 5.

14. Hamm, "Von der spätmittelalterlichen reformatio zur Reformation."

15. Luther, "An den christlichen Adel deutscher Nation von des christlichen Standes Besserung," *Werkausgabe,* vol. 6, 405–69.

16. Puff, *Sodomy in Reformation Germany and Switzerland,* 174.

17. On the introduction of the Zurich marriage court and its spread down to the introduction of the Geneva consistory, see Walther Köhler's still fundamental study, *Zürcher Ehegericht und Genfer Consistorium.*

18. See Harrington, *Reordering Marriage and Society;* Safley, "Canon Law and Swiss Reform."

19. Köhler, *Zürcher Ehegericht,* vol. 1, 142 ff.

20. Kuhr, *Die Macht des Bannes und der Buße.*

21. This occurred in Zwickau und Konstanz in 1526 (which according to Beate Schuster represented a genuine breakthrough of the Reformed position), in Berne in 1531, in Augsburg in 1533, and in Basel in 1534, but also in 1530 and 1534, respectively, in the Catholic towns of Überlingen and Solothurn. See Beate Schuster, *Die freien Frauen,* 450–51 and Peter Schuster, *Das Frauenhaus,* 182–84.

22. *Aktensammlung zur Geschichte der Basler Reformation,* vol. 6, no. 170, 136.

23. See Beate Schuster, *Freie Frauen,* 451; and above all Strasser, *State of Virginity,* esp. chap. 2, with interesting observations on the parallels between the abolition of the convents and of the municipal brothel in Munich.

24. See Wunder, "Normen und Institutionen der Geschlechterordnung am Beginn der Frühen Neuzeit," 70; or Harrington, *Reordering Marriage and Society,* chap.1.

25. See the 1529 Reformation Ordinances in Basel, *Aktensammlung zur Geschichte der Basler Reformation,* vol. 3, no. 473, 383; or Augsburg (see Roper, *Holy Household*).

26. Burghartz, *Zeiten der Reinheit,* 118 et seq.

27. Roper, *Holy Household,* 158–62.

28. Köhler, *Zürcher Ehegericht,* vol. 1, 73 et seq., esp. 87 et seq.

29. On the growing tendency toward social control over marriage among both Protestants and Catholics, see Harrington, *Reordering Marriage and Society,* 97 et seq.: "To portray Protestant and Catholic doctrinal responses as ideologically opposed clearly misrepresents the very nature of all sixteenth-century reform. . . . Perhaps the most persuasive evidence of this common continuity is the striking similarity, by the end of the sixteenth century, between Protestant and Catholic marriage codes" (98). For a general account see also Wiesner, *Christianity and Sexuality in the Early Modern World,* 259.

30. Kingdon, "The Control of Morals in Calvin's Geneva," 12.

31. Letter of 9 December 1556 from John Knox to Mrs. Locke, in David Laing, ed, *The Work of John Knox,* vol. 4, 240.

32. Monter, "The Consistory of Geneva, 1559–1569," 473–74: "In general, however,

they were preoccupied with seeing that as many people as possible were satisfactorily married, and stayed that way; Geneva limited parental authority over marriage far more than most sixteenth-century governments dared to try, and its consistory mediated quarrels after marriage more successfully than most other sixteenth-century institutions."

33. Ibid., 484.

34. Burghartz, *Zeiten der Reinheit,* 111 et seq. and 170 et seq.

35. Quoted in: Geiger, *Die Basler Kirche und Theologie im Zeitalter der Hochorthodoxie,* 37.

36. While Safley, *Let No Man Put Asunder,* 162 believes that the causes of the shift he sees from lawsuits between private individuals to ex officio proceedings cannot be fully explained on the basis of a substantive study of the relevant court records, I regard the altered perception and assessment of certain behaviors as the reason for this shift. See Burghartz, *Zeiten der Reinheit,* 114 ff.

37. Sibeth, *Eherecht und Staatsbildung,* 145–46. For the normative level of marriage legislation, however, Sibeth concludes "that the marriage court was not subject to confessionalisation as a fundamental process of social history" (185), which he uses to explain co-operation beyond confessional boundaries. If, unlike Sibeth, one regards confessionalization as a fundamental process that pushed the societies subject to it in the same structural direction, this co-operation is not at all surprising, however.

38. Blauert, "Kriminaljustiz und Sittenreform als Krisenmanagement?" 129

39. Harrington, *Reordering Marriage and Society,* 248–49.

40. Konersmann, *Kirchenregiment und Kirchenzucht im frühneuzeitlichen Kleinstaat,* 339–40.

41. Behringer, "Mörder, Diebe, Ehebrecher," 99.

42. Strasser, *State of Virginity,* chap. 1.

43. "ut ex ea populus evangelicus facile internosci posset." *Memoria Benedicta Dn. D. Theodori Zvingeri à Joh. Rodolpho Wetstenio S.S. Theol. Doct. & Professore,* Basel 1655, 29–30. On the development of the Church in Basel in this period more generally: Geiger, *Die Basler Kirche.*

44. Basel largely took over this Reformation ordinance from Zürich, which had also instituted a new Reformation ordinance the year before. Unlike Zürich, in Basel explicit references to Pauline Bible passages were inserted into the legal text. See Burghartz, *Zeiten der Reinheit,* 98.

45. Köhler, *Zürcher Ehegericht,* vol. 1, 104 et seq.; and for the seventeenth century, Bänninger, *Untersuchungen über den Einfluss des Polizeistaates,* 42 et seq.

46. Sibeth, *Eherecht und Staatsbildung,* 156–57.

47. Berne followed a good deal later, in 1686. Schmidt, *Dorf und Religion,* 200.

48. Simon, *Untertanenverhalten und obrigkeitliche Moralpolitik,* 124 et seq.; and Schnyder-Burghartz, *Alltag und Lebensformen auf der Basler Landschaft,* 262 et seq.

49. Sibeth, *Eherecht und Staatsbildung,* 217 et seq.

50. Rublack, *Magd, Metz' oder Mörderin,* 10 et seq., 199 et seq., and esp. 203 et seq.

51. In conclusion, Rublack emphasizes that "the specific form assumed by patterns

of prosecution resulted from the local interplay between socio-economic, administrative, institutional and denominational structures": *Magd, Metz' oder Mörderin*, 327.

52. Dürr, *Mägde in der Stadt*, chap. 6.

53. Ibid., 229–30.

54. Beck, "Illegitimität und voreheliche Sexualität," 122, 135, 138.

55. Breit, *Leichtfertigkeit und ländliche Gesellschaft*, 109.

56. Ibid., 290–92.

57. Beck, "Illegitimität und voreheliche Sexualität," 131.

58. Schmidt, *Dorf und Religion*, 202.

59. Ibid., 220.

60. Ibid., 236.

61. See Safley on Basel, *Let No Man Put Asunder*, 176 et seq.

62. Ibid., 180.

63. At least in the long run, this practice also had quite different consequences for men and women, if we think of the history of "unwed mothers" and the relinquishing of the paternity principle. See Burghartz, *Zeiten der Reinheit*, chap. 7; and Schmidt, *Dorf und Religion*, 230 et seq.

64. Watt, *The Making of Modern Marriage*, 107.

65. "In any event, the low number of female plaintiffs to contract disputes and the high number of women punished for fornication together show that women did not view the consistories, the new judicial organs that enforced morals and upheld domestic stability, as the defenders of their rights;" Watt, *The Making of Modern Marriage*, 112.

66. Ibid., 181 et seq.

67. Schilling, "Sündenzucht und Frühneuzeitliche Sozialdisziplinierung," 292–93.

68. Ibid., 299.

69. Konersmann, *Kirchenregiment und Kirchenzucht im frühneuzeitlichen Kleinstaat*, chap. 6, passim.

70. Sibeth, *Eherecht und Staatsbildung*, 221, 232 et seq. As rising illegitimacy rates show, this development further intensified in the late-eighteenth and early-nineteenth century. For a general account, see Michael Mitterauer, *Ledige Mütter;* for further examples, see Kaschuba and Lipp for Württemberg, *Dörfliches Überleben;* Sutter for Zurich, *"Ein Act des Leichtsinns und der Sünde";* and Ryter for the Basel countryside, *Als Weibsbild bevogtet.*

71. Bänninger, *Untersuchungen über den Einfluss des Polizeistaates*, 42 et seq.

72. Hull, *Sexuality, State, and Civil Society in Germany*, 67, 94–95.

73. Ibid., 104 et seq.

74. The development in Piedmont is also interesting. See Cavallo and Cerutti, "Female Honor and the Social Control of Reproduction in Piedmont between 1600 and 1800." Cavallo and Cerutti have studied the marital cases that came before the ecclesiastical court in Turin between 1600 and 1800 and explain the early cases, particularly those for breaches of promise to marry, within the framework of the culture of honor. They

observe a slow change in this culture, which led in the long term to a lasting transformation of gender relations that becomes clearly apparent in the mid-eighteenth century. At that period the repression of pre- and extramarital sexuality became
particularly intense, responsibility for sexual relations was increasingly concentrated
on women alone, illegitimate children were no longer considered the "natural children"
of their fathers, and "unwed mothers" had to bear the consequences on their own. Cavallo
and Cerutti conclude that this "dynamic appears reducible to a larger process of iso-
lating the individual from the protective context of broader relationships; this was one
of the principal effects of the penetration of ecclesiastical institutions into the social
fabric," ibid., 100.

CHAPTER 5

Church Discipline in a Biconfessional Country: Ireland in a European Context

UTE LOTZ-HEUMANN

Introduction: The Historiographical Background

In recent German-speaking historiography, one of the major controversies regarding the early modern period has been concerned with the validity of such macrohistorical concepts as "social disciplining" by Gerhard Oestreich, "the process of civilization" by Norbert Elias, "discipline and power" by Michel Foucault, "acculturation" by Robert Muchembled, and last but not least "confessionalization" by Wolfgang Reinhard and Heinz Schilling.[1] With regard to church discipline (*Kirchenzucht*), there has recently been a particularly intensive debate about the application of such concepts, in particular "social disciplining" (*Sozialdisziplinierung*) and "confessionalization" (*Konfessionalisierung*). This discussion is part of a larger controversy about the relationship between macro- and microhistory: In recent years, the question of the relation between history from above and history from below, between societal history (*Gesellschaftsgeschichte*) and cultural history (*Kulturgeschichte*), has found expression in a very lively debate in German-speaking historiography.[2]

From a macrohistorical point of view, church discipline as a field of research and social disciplining and confessionalization as theoretical concepts about historical processes have come to be seen as connected: While church discipline is regarded as an important "method" in the process of confessionalization, that is, the early modern confessional churches' drive toward a confessionally unified population, Wolfgang Reinhard has defined confessionalization as the first phase of the process of social disciplining.[3] Church discipline is thus identified as part of the long-term process of social disciplining from above in early modern Europe, although the original definition of the concept by Gerhard Oestreich had been political and secular.[4]

From a microhistorical point of view and also from the point of view of the concept of "communalism,"[5] this connection between church discipline, confessionalization, and social disciplining has recently been criticized. Drawing on the results of his research on church courts (*Chorgerichte*) in the rural communities of the Reformed territory of Berne in the early modern period, Heinrich Richard Schmidt has come to the conclusion that successful church discipline—if it existed at all—was not due to pressure from above but was based on mechanisms of self-regulation and self-disciplining of the village communities.[6] Schmidt denies the validity of the concept of social disciplining while calling for an end of "etatism" in the research on confessionalization and church discipline. In his opinion, confessionalization and church discipline were communal processes. They could have an effect only because there was a need for regulation within society: within the rural communities, certain gender and social groups took up guidelines and instructions from above (from clergymen and state authorities) and put them into practice because they fitted in with their particular interests. Schmidt does not deny that there were impulses, regulations, and even pressures exerted by confessional churches and governments. However, he sees the communities as the foundation of society and thus as the decisive body responsible for church discipline and confessionalization.

Both possibilities, the macrohistorical "top-down" perspective as well as the microhistorical perspective from the communities, are alone not sufficient to serve as explanatory models—a fact to which Gérald Chaix, Heinz Schilling, and recently Ulrich Behrens have drawn attention.[7] Rather, these authors are arguing for a combination of the view from above and from below, of macro- and microhistorical approaches in order to provide us with the best possible research instruments to analyze the many different forms of social control in early modern Europe.[8] In addition to this, I would argue that we do not yet have enough case studies from the different regions and confessional churches of early modern Europe. This is obvious because the study of ecclesiastical social control has so far concentrated on Calvinist church discipline on the Continent and on the Church courts of the Anglican state church in England.[9]

Ireland As a Case Study in European Perspective

In this article I will therefore try to provide an overview of church discipline in one area of early modern Europe that lay at its periphery and may, because of its political and ecclesiastical makeup, be regarded as exceptional: Ireland. However, Ireland provides an interesting test case because it was a biconfessional country, in which the majority of the population remained Catholic while the state church was Protestant and ministered to a tiny, mostly colonial, minority.[10] In spite of its sometimes rather scarce sources, Ireland provides us with a considerable spectrum of forms of social control and church discipline—formal and informal, in the household, and in the community, as well as state- and church-sponsored social control "from above." And because of the existence of two confessions in one territory, Ireland offers intriguing insights into the question of success and failure of social control and church discipline in a situation where the majority confession is illegal and the members of the established church are in the minority.

Regarding the aims of church discipline, which are embodied in the Protestant canons of 1634 and the Catholic synodal decrees of the early-seventeenth century, the two confessional churches formulated remarkably parallel objectives. For example, both confessional churches laid particular stress on the reform of their clergy. The disciplining efforts directed at the clergy comprised everything from proper qualification for the office and a restriction of preaching to licensed preachers, to the proper furniture for the Mass and Eucharist. The clergy's private life and public conduct and dress were also regulated in detail because they were meant to be examples of discipline to the people.[11] In general, the churches wanted to concentrate religious activities in the parishes, and in order to control their flocks and their attendance at rites, both churches stipulated that parish clergy keep registers of baptisms, marriages, and burials.[12] In addition, the churches required their flocks to acquire a minimal amount of Christian knowledge.[13] They were also careful to regulate sex and marriage, stressing the prohibited degrees, parental consent, and a public ceremony in the parish church.[14] These parallel objectives are not surprising because the above-mentioned measures—providing a well-educated clergy, controlling membership of churches and church attendance, regulating marriage, and catechizing the laity—were part and parcel of early modern confession building and confessionalization.[15]

However, in contrast to other bi- or multiconfessional countries in early modern Europe that, by the end of the sixteenth century, had found some formal arrangement to accommodate two or more churches in one territory—the Edict of Nantes in France, the status of "public church" for the Calvinist church in the Netherlands, the *cuius regio, eius religio* principle in the Holy Roman Empire—the Protestant state and church in Ireland did not acknowledge the presence of a large Catholic population and a functioning Catholic church. Rather, the Church of Ireland clung tenaciously to its status as state church, and particularly to its claim of having a confessional monopoly in Ireland. Although this was modeled on the Church of England, the English situation in the late-sixteenth and early-seventeenth centuries was different. While the English state church embraced the majority of the population, the Irish state church was a minority confession.

The implementation of Protestant church discipline in Ireland was determined by the fact that the Church of Ireland directed its church discipline toward the entire population of the island, not only toward Protestants. As a consequence, the instruments of discipline of the established church developed in a peculiar way, which eventually transformed them from instruments of church discipline into instruments of confessional antagonization: unwittingly, they ended up antagonizing Catholics, causing deep frictions within society and thus widening the confessional gap. In contrast, the illegal Catholic church was—as far as is revealed by the existing sources—remarkably effective in implementing its own system of church discipline, relying on social consensus within the Catholic community. Let me explain this with regard to different instruments of church discipline.

Instruments of Protestant Church Discipline in Ireland

The most important instruments of Protestant church discipline in the established churches of England and Ireland were the ecclesiastical courts.[16] Recent research on the Church courts in England has shown that these courts were generally accepted by society because they performed a useful function as arbitrators, for example, in marital conflicts and disputes between neighbors. The massive criticism that Puritans leveled at the ecclesiastical courts must therefore be regarded as exaggerated.[17] However, although even the Puritan Bishop Bedell admitted that the Protestant church courts in Ireland were not more deficient than the Church courts in England,[18] the shortcomings of the courts in Ireland had different consequences in this biconfessional society. Instead of serving certain needs in society, the Protestant church courts imposed themselves upon an unwilling Catholic population: they antagonized Catholics by prosecuting them for "clandestine marriages," that is, marriages performed by a Catholic priest, and by the imposition of fines.[19]

In order to stress the function of the Church courts as spiritual institutions, it was repeatedly stipulated that they should impose public penance instead of fines and that, when fines were imposed, they should be provided for "pious uses."[20] Archbishop Ussher defended the imposition of fines in the Church courts, arguing that "if men stood not more in fear of the fees of the court, than of standing in a white sheet, we should have here among us another Sodom and Gomorrah."[21] But Bishop Bedell, the only truly perceptive bishop of the Church of Ireland in the early-seventeenth century, understood the consequences of these fines in the atmosphere of confessional rivalry in Ireland: "Contrary causes must needs produce contrary effects. Wherefore let us preach never so painfully and piously; I say more, let us live never so blamelessly ourselves, so long as the officers in our courts prey upon them, they esteem us no better than publicans and worldlings: . . . And if the honestest and best of our own protestants be thus scandalized, what may we think of papists, such as are all in a manner that we live among?"[22]

Another important instrument of church discipline—excommunication—had similarly problematic effects in Ireland. In a confessionally unified group or society, excommunication, especially a greater excommunication that meant not only exclusion from the Eucharist but also from the secular community, can be considered an effective measure of discipline. This has, for example, been shown with regard to Geneva and the French Reformed churches.[23] In order to realize the Church of Ireland's confessional monopoly, excommunication was widely recommended and used as an instrument of church discipline.[24] This was, however, a truly self-defeating measure when used against the Catholic majority in Ireland because a lesser excommunication, that is, the exclusion from Protestant communion, was no threat to Catholics, who were provided with a full-fledged confessional church of their own. But even a greater excommunication did not have the desired effect of disciplining a person through social exclusion. In most locations in Ireland, the overwhelming majority of the secular community was Catholic, and that secular community would not follow the Protestant bishop in excluding the excommunicated person. Whereas most bishops did not fully understand this self-defeating character of excommunication, Bishop Bedell remarked: "To excommunicate them [the Catholics] for not appearing or obeying, they being already none of our body, and a multitude, it is no profit, nay, rather makes the exacerbation worse."[25] Here, Bedell touches all aspects that transformed Protestant instruments of church discipline into instruments of confessional antagonization. Catholics were "a multitude" and "none of our body," that is, they belonged to another, fully developed confessional church and their being targeted by Protestant measures of discipline served only to antagonize them further, rather than induce them to conform.

The Protestant Church of Ireland, in its turn, was not willing to accept defeat, that is, its minority status, and the bishops tried to overcome the ineffectiveness of their sentences of excommunication by having recourse to the secular arm. They applied for a writ *de excommunicato capiendo* with the aim of having the offender imprisoned and sentenced to pay a fine.[26] This could be an effective measure against individual intractable offenders in a society like England in which the Protestant state church could claim the loyalty of the majority of the population.[27] In Ireland, however, where the majority of the population and even many of the secular officials who were expected to execute the writs were Catholic, the effect was reversed. Once again, the original idea and intention of Protestant church discipline directed at Catholics—to include them in the state church—could not be achieved. Consequently, Protestant bishops often expressed bitter frustration since they were unable to impose their will on the community because Catholic secular officials did not proceed against their fellow Catholics.[28]

In contrast, recusancy fines, that is, the fines imposed for nonattendance at the services of the state church, were a measure of church discipline actually directed at Catholics. Whereas in England recusancy fines targeted a small minority of the population, their being directed at a large majority of the population in Ireland clearly shows their problematic nature and their polarizing effect. During the reign of Elizabeth I, recusancy fines were levied only sporadically because the political situation of the country made a systematic enforcement of the fines impossible.[29] In the early-seventeenth century, however, recusancy fines were used more often and more intensively as a measure of church discipline. But instead of achieving their goal of forcing Catholics to attend the services of the Church of Ireland, they had the opposite effect: they strengthened the Catholic resolve to resist the disciplinary measure of church and state.

One of the most prominent examples of this is the so-called mandates that were issued against Catholic aldermen in Dublin in 1605. These mandates ordered the aldermen to attend Church of Ireland services. When the aldermen did not comply with the mandates, they were arrested and sentenced to heavy recusancy fines by the Court of Castle Chamber.[30] In this context, the government explicitly stressed its intention of enforcing conformity with the established church rather than filling the public purse: "and in order that they might perceive that not their goods but their conformity was sought, [Lord Deputy Chichester and the Council] allotted the greatest part of their fines to the repairing of such churches in that city [i.e., Dublin] as remained ruinous since the great blast of gunpowder [1597], to the relieving of poor scholars in the college, and to such other necessary and charitable uses."[31] However, the aldermen and their families refused to pay the fines, pleading their faith and stressing that attendance at the services of the state church was against their consciences. The aldermen stayed in prison for six months, but eventually the Dublin government was directed by London to give in.

The mandates are only the tip of the iceberg in terms of a general policy regarding recusancy fines that had the opposite effect of its intentions. In particular, it was ordered repeatedly that the fines be used to repair the churches—so that after a renovation of its church buildings the Church of Ireland would be ready to minister to the entire population of Ireland.[32] This was, however, a serious misapprehension: for Catholics in early-seventeenth-century Ireland, this use of their recusancy fines only confirmed their resentment against the established church and strengthened their resolve not to go to churches that had been renovated with their fines. At the same time, Catholics in Ireland succeeded in "undermining" the prosecution of recusants and the imposition of recusancy fines in many parishes "from within." In the Church of Ireland, as in the Church of England, the churchwardens were responsible for reporting recusancy. Consequently, the system relied on the cooperation of the churchwardens. In the parishes of the Church of Ireland, the situation was often different, as the commissioners of the regal visitation of 1622 reported: "Churchwardens in most places there are none, but such as are recusants themselves, and being parties in the cause [i.e., recusancy], the service [of presenting recusants] is not well performed by them, ..."[33] As in the case of Catholic secular officials who were expected to execute writs *de excommunicato capiendo* against fellow Catholics, Catholic churchwardens decisively weakened the Protestant system of church discipline "from within."

Poor relief was another area of social control that reflected the situation of confessional rivalry in Irish society.[34] According to the example of the English state church, the Irish Act of Uniformity of 1560 stipulated that recusancy fines be used for poor relief.[35] This was no problem in a church that, like the Church of England, encompassed the great majority of the population. The Irish state church also stipulated that poor relief be given only to persons attending the Protestant services. This was in itself also hardly an unusual measure. On the contrary, it was commonplace to control the distribution of poor relief in this way in multiconfessional societies.[36] However, the two things did not go together. The Irish state church did not intend confessional exclusion by this measure, but confessional inclusion, the realization of its confessional monopoly. Accordingly, the commissioners of the 1622 regal visitation ordered that "such poor may be relieved as duly and constantly frequent divine service" in order to encourage other poor people "to do the like."[37] By assuming that the Protestant church and state had a monopoly on poor relief in Ireland, the Church of Ireland hoped to realize its confessional monopoly. Once again this proved to be a self-defeating measure because the Catholic community in Ireland, as will be described in more detail later, created its own informal system of poor relief, thus making poor relief a blunt instrument of church discipline in the hands of the established church.

Visitations as a measure of disciplining and controlling the flock are another example of an instrument of church discipline that, from the point of view of the Church of Ireland, failed to produce the desired results. In this context, it was not the Catholic community that actively undermined Protestant church discipline. Rather, the biconfessional situation of Ireland and the presence of a Catholic majority in the country were in themselves sufficient to change the nature of the Protestant visitations completely. Because there were so few Protestant clergy and laity to report on in Ireland, visitations increasingly gathered information on Catholic activities and thus became an instrument to watch and control the Church of Ireland's confessional opponent. Consequently, visitations were transformed from instruments of church government and church discipline into instruments of "spying," of recording the activities of the confessional rival, the Catholic Church, as well as the Catholic laity. Unwittingly, they ended up as did all other instruments of Protestant church discipline in Ireland: they antagonized Catholics and widened the confessional gap.[38]

Instruments of Catholic Church Discipline in Ireland

The Catholic Church as an illegal church without state support, which was nevertheless very visible in Ireland, could not rely on formal instruments of church discipline as the established church did. In this context, the Catholic Church's most important asset proved to be its laity. On the one hand, the sheer fact that the majority of the population of Ireland professed the Catholic faith gave its church a lot of room to maneuver vis-à-vis the Church of Ireland. In addition, the urban elites constituted a closely knit social network. Within this network, which was constantly strengthened by intermarriage, the lay elite hid priests from the authorities and provided chapels for Catholic congregations. These social networks, which Protestants tried to break up or penetrate, actually grew tighter and stronger when state and church threatened them with their disciplining measures.[39] On the other hand, the Catholic clergy found that their exercise of church discipline was generally accepted—and sometimes reinforced—by the laity. Therefore, the most interesting aspect of Catholic Church discipline in Ireland is that it relied only on social consensus and informal ways of social control within the families, neighborhoods, and communities.

One of the major achievements in terms of Catholic Church discipline in Ireland was that a system of ecclesiastical jurisdiction could be established on the Catholic side that confronted and competed with the Protestant church courts. While this Catholic system was functioning remarkably well and was frequented by the Catholic population, Protestant bishops accused it of corruption. One of the points of conflict between the two systems of ecclesiastical jurisdiction was marriage. George Downham, the Protestant Bishop of Derry, complained in 1622: "Besides the Jurisdiction exercised by my Chancellor and official there is a Jurisdiction usurped by Authority from Rome, to the great dishonour of god, hindrance of religion and shame of the government."[40] In his diocese of Kilmore, the Protestant Bishop Bedell realized that the Catholic clergy not only exercised their own ecclesiastical jurisdiction but actually tried to obstruct his: "[The Catholic clergy are] more numerous by far than we, and in full exercise of all jurisdiction ecclesiastical, by their vicar-generals and officials, who are so confident as they excommunicate those who come to our courts, even in matrimonial causes, which affront hath been offered myself by the Popish Primate's Vicar-General . . . ."[41]

Excommunication was clearly a much more powerful instrument in the hands of the Catholic clergy than in those of the Protestant clergy: In a letter to Archbishop Ussher, Bedell related a case in which a woman had charged her husband in a Protestant church court, for which she had been "put out of the church, and denounced excommunicate" by the Catholic vicar general.[42] We don't know how this case was resolved, but the general impression one gains from the sources is that excommunication by Catholic clergymen was an effective instrument of church discipline in the Catholic community. Although this instrument of discipline was illegal, operated on an informal basis, and had no means of enforcement other than social consensus, it worked. For example, it was reported that Catholic wives "would neither eat nor lie with their husbands" when their husbands had been excommunicated by a Catholic priest.[43] And in the synodal decrees, the Catholic clergy were warned to make only sparing use of excommunication and public penance so as not to draw the attention of the state upon the Catholic community.[44] It is obvious that such instruments of church discipline could only draw the attention of the state if, as was clearly the case, the Catholic laity acted according to their clergy's judgments.

Poor relief was, as we have seen above, another important area of church discipline in that the Catholic Church responded to Protestant pressure by breaking the Protestant monopoly on poor relief and establishing a system of its own—based on social networks and social consensus. For example, the Marian congregations founded by the Jesuits in the towns saw the relief of the poor as a major part of their activities.[45] Because the Catholic urban elites also staffed the town councils, there even existed Catholic poor relief initiatives that were implemented by local governments: in Limerick a Jesuit prevailed upon the urban magistrates and the citizens to build a hospital for the poor and other destitute persons. And when the initiative was interfered with by persecution initiated by the state authorities, the Catholic citizens voluntarily provided alms for the poor at intervals recommended by the Jesuit father.[46] What a stark contrast with the poor relief measures taken by the president of Munster, Sir Henry Brouncker, in 1606, who levied heavy recusancy fines and used them to build a hospital for the poor in Cork![47]

Jesuit efforts at social control and church discipline succeeded not only with regard to poor relief; they used spiritual means in order to further the pacification and a general reform of Irish society. For example, the Jesuits preached against cattle raiding and acted as independent arbitrators in conflicts between noblemen. They also addressed individual lords and encouraged them to reform the territories under their control in order to establish a peaceful and ordered commonwealth. One nobleman is recorded to have hanged robbers in his territory and made his peace with neighboring lords in response to Jesuit pressure.[48] When addressing the elites in their efforts at social control, the Jesuits indirectly also reached the lower orders: there were social pressures in the family, household, and estate that worked in their favor.

In terms of church discipline, the Jesuits clearly saw the urban elites as a model for the lower orders. For example, they regarded the Marian congregations as institutions where the social elite could give an example of piety to the rest of society.[49] In addition, the elites were also able to exercise social control over, or at least set examples of behavior for, lower social groups. As rich landowners and merchants, their Catholicism became "seigneurial Catholicism"[50] or "household Catholicism," centering not only on their immediate families and relatives but also their households and their dependents. This had vital consequences for their ability to use informal social control in favor of Catholicism. For example, the Protestant Bishop Ram of Ferns and Leighlin reported in 1612 that the poor people excused themselves from not attending the services of the state church by saying "that if they shuld be of our religion, no popish marchant wold employ them being sailors;—no popish landlord wold lett them any lands being husbandmen, nor sett them houses in tenantry being artificers, and therefore they must either starve or doe as they doe."[51] And the Jesuit Holywood reported similar social pressures in a letter of 1606: "At Dungarvan the [provincial] President forced a crowd of peasants to the Protestant temple; but their landlord refused to let them live any longer under him until they were reconciled to the Church."[52]

Conclusion

All in all, we have seen that only an integrative approach that looks at forms of social control and church discipline from above as well as from below brings to light the many different forms of church discipline in early modern Irish society as well as their consequences. The Irish example with its situation of extreme confessional rivalry certainly makes clear that church discipline from above could not function, let alone implement disciplining measures, all on its own: it was dependent on a fundamental consensus within society about the legitimacy of the authority of ecclesiastical and secular officials and institutions. This is obvious by the contrast between the Church of England and the Church of Ireland. While the instruments of church discipline—the Church courts, excommunication, recusancy fines, and visitations—were all generally accepted and reasonably effective measures of church discipline in England (even if we always have to take into account a good measure of negotiation and opposition from the laity), they clutched at thin air in Ireland. There was no consensus about the legitimacy of the Church of Ireland's instruments and institutions because the Catholic majority of the population rejected the state church's claims to a confessional monopoly.

However, the Catholic population in Ireland clearly had a need for self-regulation within the community, which—and this should be stressed in order to avoid all romanticization—was in itself a top-to-bottom process. Catholic Church discipline in Ireland rested, and this is indeed remarkable, upon a consensus within the lay community about the legitimacy of an illegal Catholic Church and its clergy. Based on this fundamental consensus, Catholic measures of church discipline—ecclesiastical jurisdiction, excommunication, and poor relief—could function within the community without the backing of the state or an established church. In addition, we could observe how social control and church discipline remained a process from above even in these circumstances: proceeding from the clergy, the lay elites played an important role in disseminating social control and church discipline throughout society and in particular in their own families, households, and estates.

Notes

Abbreviations for manuscript sources:

BL Add. MS = British Library, Additional Manuscript

TCD= Trinity College, Dublin

1. See Oestreich, *Geist und Gestalt,* 179–97; Schulze, "Gerhard Oestreichs Begriff"; Elias, *Über den Prozeß der Zivilisation;* Foucault, *Überwachen und Strafen;* Muchembled, *Culture populaire;* Reinhard, "Zwang zur Konfessionalisierung?"; Schilling, "Die Konfessionalisierung von Kirche, Staat und Gesellschaft." For the criticism of these concepts, see, e.g., Lottes, "Disziplin und Emanzipation"; Dinges, "Frühneuzeitliche Armenfürsorge"; Schmidt, *Dorf und Religion.*

2. For the general controversy see, e.g., Hardtwig and Wehler, eds., *Kulturgeschichte heute;* Mergel and Welskopp, eds., *Geschichte zwischen Kultur und Gesellschaft.*

3. See Reinhard, "Zwang zur Konfessionalisierung?" 268.

4. See note 1 above.

5. The concept of "communalism" emphasizes the communities as the basis of early modern society. See Blickle, *Kommunalismus.*

6. See Schmidt, *Dorf und Religion;* Schmidt, "Gemeinde und Sittenzucht"; Schmidt, "Sozialdisziplinierung?"

7. See Chaix, "Die schwierige Schule der Sitten," 199–217; Schilling, "Disziplinierung"; Schilling, "Profil und Perspektiven einer interdisziplinären," 3–36; Behrens, "Sozialdisziplinierung."

8. "Social control" is here understood as an overarching and integrative concept, comprising all forms of social control, from formal to informal, from secular to religious, etc. See the introduction to this volume.

9. For a general overview see Schilling, "Die Kirchenzucht im frühneuzeitlichen Europa," 11–40; Schmidt, "Gemeinde und Sittenzucht."

10. For an analysis of the confessional situation in Ireland in the sixteenth and seventeenth centuries see Lotz-Heumann, *Die doppelte Konfessionalisierung in Irland;* Bottigheimer and Lotz-Heumann, "The Irish Reformation."

11. See articles 31, 39, 42, 95 of the canons of the Church of Ireland of 1634, in *Constitutions,* 22–23, 27–29, 56–57; and, e.g., decrees of the provincial synod of Dublin at Kilkenny, 1614, in Moran, *History,* 439–63; decrees of the provincial synod of Armagh, 1614, in McCarthy, ed., *Collections,* 116–46; decrees of the provincial synod of Tuam, 1632, in Moran, ed., *Memoirs,* 386–89.

12. See article 46 of the canons of the Church of Ireland of 1634, in *Constitutions,* 30–31; and, e.g., decrees of the provincial synod of Armagh, 1614, in McCarthy, ed., *Collections,* 122, 128.

13. See article 11 of the canons of the Church of Ireland of 1634, in *Constitutions,* 12; and, e.g., decrees of the provincial synod of Dublin at Kilkenny, 1614, in Moran, *History,* 449–50.

14. See articles 47–52 of the canons of the Church of Ireland of 1634, in *Constitutions*, 32–34; and, e.g., decrees of the provincial synod of Dublin at Kilkenny, 1614, in Moran, *History*, 451–54.

15. See Zeeden, "Grundlagen und Wege"; Reinhard, "Zwang zur Konfessionalisierung?"

16. For an overview of ecclesiastical law and the Protestant church courts in Ireland, see Osborough, "Ecclesiastical Law."

17. See Ingram, *Church Courts*.

18. Letter CLX: Bedell to Ussher, 1629, in Elrington and Todd, eds., *Works*, vol. 15: *Letters*, 468.

19. See, e.g., "Matters of Grace and Bounty . . . , 1626," in McNeill, ed., *Tanner Letters*, 69; Letter CCCCXXVII: Ussher to Irish bishops, 1636, in Elrington and Todd, eds., *Works*, vol. 16: *Letters*, 532.

20. Hand and Treadwell, eds., "His Majesty's Directions," 210, see also 211–12; see also TCD MS 808, "Orders and Directions Concerning the State of the Church of Ireland, 1623," fol. 36.

21. Letter CLXI: Ussher to Bedell, 1629, in Elrington and Todd, eds., *Works*, vol. 15: *Letters*, 474–75.

22. Letter CLX: Bedell to Ussher, 1629, in Elrington and Todd, eds., *Works*, vol. 15: *Letters*, 468. On Bedell see Bottigheimer, "The Hagiography of William Bedell"; Clarke, "Bishop William Bedell."

23. See, e.g., Kingdon, "Social Control"; Mentzer, "Marking the Taboo," 97–128.

24. See, e.g., TCD MS 808, "Orders and Directions Concerning the State of the Church of Ireland, 1623," fol. 38; Abstract of the State of the Church of Ireland, 1622, fol. 45.

25. Letter CLX: Bedell to Ussher, 1629, in Elrington and Todd, eds., *Works*, vol. 15: *Letters*, 471. This situation had not changed in the early-eighteenth century. See Connolly, *Religion*, 177–78.

26. See, e.g., Jones, ed., *A True Relation*, 39–40; for the late-seventeenth and eighteenth centuries, see Connolly, *Religion*, 177–78.

27. See, e.g., Ingram, *Church Courts*, 14, 365–66.

28. See, e.g., the bitter complaints by John Rider, the Protestant Bishop of Killaloe, in the 1622 royal visitation, in Dwyer, *Diocese of Killaloe*, 143; and TCD MS 550, State of Armagh Province, 1622, visitation of Derry by George Downham, fol. 206.

29. See Ford, "Protestant Reformation in Ireland," 52.

30. See MacCavitt, "Lord Deputy Chichester"; Lennon, *Lords of Dublin*, 178–81; "Mandates to the Citizens of Dublin to Attend Church, 3 November 1605," in Hogan, ed., *Words of Comfort*, 124; "Ruling of the Star Chamber, 20 November 1605," in Hogan, ed., *Words of Comfort*, 126–27.

31. "Lord Deputy [Chichester] and Council to the Lords, 5 December 1605," in *Calendar of the State Papers Relating to Ireland, of the Reign of James I*, 356.

32. See TCD MS 806, "Remembrances to the Commissioners of the Regal Visitation, 1615," fol. 119r; TCD MS 582, "His Majesty's Instructions Concerning

the Church of Ireland, Brought Over by Bishop Andrew Knox about 1620," fol. 136r; Bishop Buckworth's "Report of the Diocese, 1622," in Atkinson, *Dromore,* 127; "The State of the Diocese of Killaloe, Presented to His Majesties Commissioners at Dublin . . . per Johannem [John Rider] Laonensem Episcopum, 1622," in Dwyer, *Diocese of Killaloe,* 130.

33. BL Add. MS 4756, "Entry Book of Reports of the Commissioners for Ireland, 1662," fol. 62v.

34. On poor relief in sixteenth-century Ireland in general see Lennon, "Dives and Lazarus."

35. See Curtis and McDowell, eds., *Irish Historical Documents,* 124–25. For the English Act of Uniformity, see Smith, *Emergence of a Nation State,* 421.

36. Compare the Dutch system in which either poor relief was organized by the urban authorities without any confessional considerations or—where poor relief was provided by the Calvinist church and the urban authorities—Calvinist poor relief was restricted to members of the Reformed confession because alternative poor relief was available from the secular authorities. See, e.g., Prak, "The Carrot and the Stick," 149–66; Grell and Cunningham, "Reformation," 4–16.

37. BL Add. MS 4756, "Entry Book of Reports of the Commissioners for Ireland, 1622," fol. 23r.

38. This is described in more detail in Lotz-Heumann, *Die doppelte Konfessionalisierung in Irland,* 408–9.

39. Colm Lennon has described this in detail with regard to the Dublin patriciate. See Lennon, *Lords of Dublin.*

40. TCD MS 550, "State of Armagh Province, 1622, Visitation of Derry by George Downham," fol. 205.

41. Letter from Bedell to Bishop Laud, 1630, in Jones, ed., *A True Relation,* 149–50.

42. Letter CLX: Bedell to Ussher, 1629, in Elrington and Todd, eds., *Works,* vol. 15: *Letters,* 471.

43. Cited in Gillespie, *Devoted People,* 30.

44. See decrees of the provincial synod of Dublin, 1614, in Moran, *History,* 450.

45. See MacErlean, *Sodality,* 14, 16.

46. See the letter from Christopher Holywood to General Aquaviva, 1605, in Hogan, ed., *Ibernia Ignatiana,* 157, see also 150.

47. See "Court of Exchequer, [1606], Munster.—Certain Fines Imposed by the Lord President . . . ," in Hogan, ed., *Words of Comfort,* 139.

48. See the letter from Christopher Holywood, 1605, in Hogan, *Distinguished Irishmen,* 433, see also 426–28; Christopher Holywood to General Aquaviva, 29 January 1605, in Hogan, ed., *Ibernia Ignatiana,* 156–57, see also 431–33.

49. See, e.g., MacErlean, *Sodality,* 15–16. On the role of the Marian congregations in Catholic Europe, see Châtellier, *The Europe of the Devout.*

50. For England see Bossy, "Elizabethan Catholicism"; Bossy, *English Catholic Community.*

51. Cited in Brady, *Essays on the English State Church in Ireland,* 15; see also the letter from William Lyon, Protestant Bishop of Cork and Ross, to Lord Hunsdon, 1596, in *Calendar of the State Papers Relating to Ireland, of the Reign of Elizabeth,* 13, 15.

52. Letter from Father Holywood to General Aquaviva, 1606, translated in Hogan, ed., *Words of Comfort,* 156; the Latin original is in Hogan, ed., *Ibernia Ignatiana,* 201.

CHAPTER 6

Early Modern Discipline and the Visual Arts

Michael Scholz-Hänsel

Until now, there have been no systematic studies investigating the visual arts of the early modern period from the macroperspective of disciplining, a perspective now largely established in general history.[1] This essay, therefore, has an exploratory character. Just to demonstrate the usefulness of the disciplinary perspective for interpreting historical works of art already means a considerable achievement. The enterprise is made difficult because of the great variety in the source material and the heterogeneous character of existing publications, so the main emphasis here must be on my own field of expertise.[2]

When studying the visual arts in relation to early modern discipline, we must distinguish two categories among the works to be considered. One, a series of works originated in the service of early modern discipline. Some of them merely documented corresponding activities, whereas others literally functioned as propaganda instruments for the institutions of social control. Two, a number of works were subjected to censorship and hence the object of social control. This may have been because they unwittingly disregarded existing regulations or because they called for resistance against the agents of early modern discipline.

We can identify examples of both categories within all Christian denominations, but most of the works discussed in this essay originate from Catholic areas and the Hispanic world in particular. Although this selection cannot be considered representative for Europe as a whole, it must be emphasized that until about 1640 Madrid had supremacy in Europe and that the Hispanic world included extensive territories in Italy and the Netherlands.[3]

This article is divided into four sections. The first contains a short research overview of investigations into early modern discipline and the history of art in the Catholic world, highlighting special problems for research in the process. The second introduces the Inquisition as the most important institution of control in the Hispanic world, giving some examples of its influence on the arts. Here, works in the service of the Inquisition and those works censored by it will be differentiated in the way mentioned earlier. The artistic assessors of the Inquisition are ascribed an important role. This role will be discussed in greater detail using the example of Francisco Pacheco in Seville.

The third section asks to what extent artists were able to negotiate within the Inquisition system.[4] In the sixteenth and seventeenth centuries, they seem to have practiced primarily a strategy of surrendering and avoiding. By the eighteenth century, however, we can observe individual cases of resistance. The last section attempts to demonstrate once again—against the persistent criticism of art historians—how important the subject of discipline is for an understanding of the visual arts in early modern Europe. In this case, too, it is primarily a matter of identifying an important topic for future research.

General Fundamentals

There is considerable common ground between questions of early modern discipline and a history of art of the early modern age. In fact, the spectrum of themes has hardly expanded substantially since Emile Mâle's *L'art religieux en France après le Concile de Trente* (1932).[5] The key question remains that of the influence of the Picture Decree passed at the last meeting of the Council of Trent.[6]

The discussion concentrated very clearly on artistic theory. Definite examples were raised only rarely. This had two main reasons. On the one hand, there was extensive secondary literature about authors who tried, in the wake of the Council of Trent, to get their own writings into a canon of correct depictions comparable with the Index of Forbidden Books.[7] The most famous texts here included the *Discorso delle imagine sacre e profane* (1582) from Cardinal Gabriele Paleotti (1522–1597) of Bologna.[8] On the other hand, we find that the same examples are discussed over and over again when it comes to church censorship, namely the painting over of Michelangelo's (1475–1564) *The Last Judgement* (1536–41) in the Sistine Chapel ordered by Pope Pius IV (1559–65) and the Inquisition trial in 1573 against Paolo Veronese (1528–1588) because of his supposedly overly luxurious *Feast in the House of Levi* arranged with genre subjects (figure 1).[9] David Freedberg and the historian Roberto Zapperi have collected some further examples from this context, Freedberg in his book *The Power of Images* (1989) and Zapperi primarily connected with his research into Annibale Carracci.[10]

Until now, early modern discipline in a broad sense did not interest art historians. For this reason, there is research from a historical point of view, but hardly any from that of art history. Consequently, such research merely documents the forms of early modern discipline.[11] There are some publications on works that either served the purposes of propaganda for early modern discipline or belong to the category of censored works. These, though, are not explicitly written from an early modern discipline perspective and, as was already mentioned, generally just relate to the influence of the Council of Trent.[12]

Figure 1 Paolo Veronese, *Feast in the House of Levi,* 1573, Venice, Galleria Dell'Accademia. With permission of the Minister of Cultural Activities, Venice.

Two circumstances help explain why the discussion is advancing so slowly in the field of early modern discipline and the history of art. First, research into Italy dominates the history of art of the early modern era. Second, the archives of the Roman Inquisition were not precisely accessible for scholarly investigation.[13]

Fortunately, with documents on the work of the Spanish Inquisition it is a completely different story. That is why I will be primarily interested in its controlling influence on the arts in the following section. The *Consejo de la Inquisición* worked extensively, independently from the Vatican, and was primarily an instrument of censorship on the part of the Spanish monarchy. Its archives have been open for the scientific public for a considerable time. Moreover, there are standard publications on the Spanish Inquisition, which enable art historians to investigate the rather heterogeneous material on a sound footing.

The Role of the Spanish Inquisition

The original Inquisition arose at the beginning of the thirteenth century in order to fight heretic movements in southern France and northern Italy.[14] The Spanish Dominican monk Domingo de Guzmán (1170–1221) is considered its founder. His work was legalized by the popes and initially Emperor Frederick II (1212–1250). The Spanish Inquisition, by contrast, was not founded until 1483. The background to this was the wish of the Catholic kings to use a joint authority to unite Spain. The country had just been newly united following the royal marriage in 1469. It was precisely this state idea that caused a series of unusual features distinguishing the modern Spanish Inquisition from the old one.

Only a few persons fell victim to the Spanish Inquisition, if measured in the

Figure 2 El Greco, *Portrait of a Cardinal* (Fernando Niño de Guevara), about 1600, The Metropolitan Museum of Art, New York

number of burned heretics. There was also much criticism of its work in the Hispanic world at the time of its founding and even some hidden forms of resistance. For this reason, its disciplining effect on the population was more decisive than the punishments it meted out. In this way, a special form of self-censorship can be seen in many areas of social life on the Iberian Peninsula from the fifteenth century onward because of the "pedagogy of fear" (*pedagogía del miedo*), in the words of Bartolomé Bennassar or, as the historian Angel Alcalá described it, the "inquisitorial mentality" (*mentalidad inquisitorial*) .[15]

Pictures serving the Inquisition included portraits of its representatives, scenic documentations of trials of heretics, and works composed either with the purpose of justifying the disciplinary measures of the court or ostracizing particular population groups. Inquisitors could be art patrons demonstrating not just aesthetic taste but also their interest in new ideas regarding the process of awarding portrait orders. This is shown by El Greco's (1541–1614) portrait of Cardinal Fernando Niño de Guevara (figure 2) from around 1600.[16] Completely contrary to the ideas

Figure 3 Pedro Berruguete, *Burning of the Heretics (Auto da fé)*, 1490–96, Madrid, Museo del Prado

of some twentieth-century interpreters, the artist is not trying to ridicule the Great Inquisitor with the prominent glasses. It is much more the case that he is trying to demonstrate the cardinal's modernity. This is because the thread glasses depicted were the latest fashion in the Hispanic world at the time, and visual aids were considered a status symbol anyway.

Pedro Berruguete's *Burning of the Heretics* was painted 1490–1496 as part of a larger picture program for the Santo Tomás Monastery in Avila, the first

Figure 4 Bartolomé Esteban Murillo, *Martyrium of St. Pedro Arbués,* 1664, Hermitage Museum, St. Petersburg, Russia.

official seat of the Inquisition (figure 3). The painter probably received inspiration through a trial that preoccupied all of Spain at the time and may have made a decisive contribution to the decision to expel the Jews in 1492. In this trial, diverse Jews and their already converted coreligionists (*conversos*) were charged with kidnapping a Christian child in La Guardia near Toledo and killing it in an act of ritual murder.[17] The autos-da-fé were important events, documented in extensive descriptions as well as pictorial portrayals.[18] It can be assumed that the Inquisition's propagandist intentions lay behind the exemplary series painted by Berruguete. The picture program was probably intended to win the King's support for permanent institutionalization of the Inquisition.[19] That the King stayed in Avila several times makes this supposition plausible. Moreover, the institutionalization of the Inquisition still was hotly debated at the time.

The attempt to justify the heretic court is behind the frequent depiction of St. Pedro Arbués. He was inquisitor in Aragon before being murdered by a group of conspirators in 1485 (figure 4). Although the perpetrators also included some Old Christians (those who belonged to families who had always been

Figure 5 Francisco Ribalta, *The Vision of Father Simon,* 1612, London, National Gallery

Christians, not converted Jews), who feared they might lose certain privileges, the murder was blamed solely on the *conversos.*[20]

Also well documented is a series of censored pictures, which became victims of the Inquisition. Two groups of works were under special control here: first, works that broke the *decoro* or completely contradicted official church teachings; second, all forms of nude painting, even in profane areas. An example of the first group was supplied by *The Vision of Father Simon* (figure 5) from Francisco Ribalta (1565–1628). Here, the central figure was painted over, probably on the orders of the Inquisition. This was because the saint, who was so admired by the people, was considered a malingerer by the Church.[21]

The relatively small number of nude paintings in the Hispanic world in comparison with other regions of Europe resulted from early modern discipline through the Inquisition. Rosa López Torrijos proved this in her extensive research *La mitología en la pintura española del Siglo de Oro* (1985).[22] A large number of people will

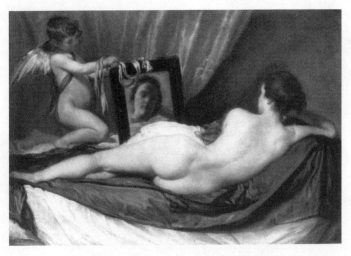

Figure 6 Diego Velázquez, *The Toilet of Venus*, before 1651, London, National Gallery

already be familiar with examples, primarily from the eighteenth century, which show that the heretic court proceeded against both painters and collectors of nudes. Also mentioned is the well-documented case of the paintings of the *Nude Maja* (around 1796) and the *Dressed Maja* (around 1805), painted by Francisco de Goya (1746–1828) for the First Minister Manuel Godoy. For a while, the latter also owned the famous picture *The Toilet of Venus* (before 1651) from Diego Velázquez (1599–1660) (figure 6).[23]

Interestingly, we have personal statements from several artists, in which they ascribe to themselves the function of assessor of the Inquisition. In all cases, the sources are artistic tracts. Thus, in 1693 the painter and author José García Hidalgo (1645–1717) described himself as *Corrector y Calificador* of painting on behalf of the Tribunal.[24] Similarly, in 1724 Antonio Palomino de Castro y Velasco (1655–1726), a biographer of artists of eminent importance for the Hispanic world, reported that the Great Inquisitor had made him *Censor y Veedor de las pinturas.*[25]

However, the case of Francisco Pacheco (1564–1644) deserves special attention because this artist and art theoretician had a pivotal role in all the art of the *Siglo de Oro.*[26] He, too, reports in his major work, *Arte de la Pintura* (1649), that the control of picture works was assigned to him on March 7, 1618, by the Inquisition.[27] Referring to this passage, Palomino concluded that, from this moment on, Pacheco held the function of *Censor y Veedor de las pinturas,* just as he himself did.[28]

Now, so far we still have no sources for active censorship activity on the part of Pacheco. However, it should give us food for thought that he printed the reference to his link to the Inquisition practically as an introduction to the *Adiciones.* It is precisely in that part of his art tract that he gives artists very exact instructions about how they should represent particular religious themes. Isn't

Figure 7 Francisco Pacheco, *Christ on the Cross,* 1614, Madrid, Collection of Gómez-Moreno

a "pedagogy of fear" being deployed here, completely in the meaning of the Tribunal? What could an artist expect who did not adhere to Pacheco's rules?

Actually, Pacheco possessed astonishing authority in Seville, which can hardly have been based on his rather stiff art. When he supported reintroducing depictions of Christ on the cross using the older four-nail type rather than the three-nail variety in vogue in those days (figure 7), he was followed by a whole series of artists, including Alonso Cano and Diego Velázquez. Was it his close relationship to the Inquisition that ensured him this influence?

Possibilities for Negotiating

If we ask about forms of resistance to this early modern disciplining of the arts, then we must emphasize from the start that none of the art theory writings mentioned

Figure 8 El Greco, *Disrobing of Christ*, 1577–79, Toledo Cathedral

manage to assert themselves as a generally accepted set of rules for assessing aesthetic works. Not even those from Paleotti and Pacheco manage this. However, the reason for taking up resistance is not to be found in the protests of the artists. What was decisive, though, was rejection by important patrons and customers of artists, the nobility and propertied bourgeoisie. These social groups were not interested in having their artistic collections examined by church inquisitors, and their power represented a risk that was difficult to calculate for the Inquisition as well. Jaime Contreras is able to demonstrate this most recently using the example of successful resistance against the heretic court in the Spanish town of Murcia.[29] One unusual attempt to still place pressure on patrons of depictions of nudity was represented by a survey on the matter among university professors and its subsequent publication.[30]

The artists themselves appear, as a rule, to have avoided possible censorship measures and to have carried out the desired corrections. El Greco, however, constituted a definite exception in Spain. His pugnacious spirit, in dealing with excessively narrow-minded customers, already drew the attention of his

Figure 9 Caravaggio, *St. Matthew with the Angel,* Berlin, Kaiser Friedrich Museum (destroyed)

contemporaries, and in the eighteenth century Palomino, the artist's biographer, devoted some critical comments to him.[31] However, for Greco it was probably much less a matter of defending his at times very self-willed iconography for its own sake and much more a matter of preventing his deviations from tradition from being misused to force down the negotiated prices.[32] His example showed that you could succeed with legal protest in Spain after all. Moreover, in the case of the depiction criticized, the *Disrobing of Christ* painted for the Toledo Cathedral (1577–1579), it can be shown that he did not carry out the changes demanded by the customers (figure 8).

Caravaggio (1573–1610) was always characterized as being independent, but it is particularly noticeable in comparison with El Greco that he fulfilled all correction wishes only too willingly.[33] There is an idea that the painter repeatedly provoked his patrons, so as to be able to sell two pictures in the end, as in the case of *St. Matthew with the Angel,* where he sold the picture found objectionable to a private art collector (figure 9) and the second version to the location planned. However, this appears to me to overrate his intellectual capacity and to underrate the general social conditions.[34] The latest theory about Caravaggio's death—that he was murdered in a joint plot between the Maltese Orders and the pope—is certainly too far-fetched.[35] It should not be forgotten

Figure 10 Giovanni Volpato, *The Gallery Farnese with the Paintings of Annibale Carracci,* engraving

that he was probably allowed to experiment so freely only because it was known that he operated as a lone wolf and with an artistic interest and not from within a circle of ideologically like-minded people.

The reverse was true with Annibale Carracci (1560–1609). In his case, the political power of his patron, Odoardo Farnese, allowed him to create a highly erotic program in the deeply "puritanical" Rome of Clement VIII (1592–1605) for the Palazzo Farnese (figure 10). Was it really a case here of the artist seeking to push through his ideas against the trend? Or was it much more the customer, who understood how to use this concept to show who had the power in Rome to his adversary on the Papal Throne, Pope Aldobrandini, a man known for his rigid censorship policy against the arts?[36]

We really have to wait until the eighteenth century again for the first artist who can be said to have made a conscious act of resistance against early modern discipline from above. Also, with Goya the conflict took place more in the media of graphic reproduction and drawing than painting.[37]

Figure 11 Jusepe de Ribera, *Scene of Execution,* Haarlem, Teylers Museum

Over all it would be worth asking whether the art of drawing had already provided an important field for strategies of evasion in earlier centuries. At least, it appears that artists like Jusepe de Ribera (1591–1652) and Carracci, to name just two examples, picked out things as central themes in this medium whose depiction in oil painting was prohibited for reasons of necessary self-censorship.[38] I am thinking here equally of depictions of nudity and examples of everyday violence. One execution scene from Ribera supplies an especially extreme example of the latter (figure 11).[39]

Goya, after all, was able to paint his *Nude Maja* contrary to the Rules of the Royal House and the Inquisition only because the customer, Manuel Godoy, was the queen's favorite.[40] With the critical depiction of the *Caprichos* (1799), however, he knew that he had the support of the Spanish Enlightenment. Logically, as this support crumbled, he immediately had problems with the censor. By contrast, drawings that clearly spoke out against early modern discipline, such as those showing the artist Pietro Torrigiani (1472–1528) in jail (figure 12), arose solely for private use, as in the case of Carracci and Ribera.[41]

New Fields of Research

Until now, art historians have had difficulties in seeing examples of the influence of early modern discipline on artistic objects as relevant.[42] Art historians seldom make direct statements and are satisfied with ignoring corresponding research.[43] They willingly argue that in the case of the Spanish Inquisition, in the known trials, most of the artists were not persecuted because of their art, but because of their change in way of life.

In this process, critics of Inquisition research also never really question whether Inquisitional discipline exercised a lasting influence on early modern Spanish

Figure 12 Francisco de Goya, "No comas celebre Torrigiano," 1814–24, drawing, Madrid, Museo del Prado

society. The debate centering on the term "social control" focuses on contradictions between the normative level and actual conditions and so cannot be applied to the heretic court.[44]

The considerable number of Inquisitional persecutions of individual artists that have been traced in the Hispanic world alone show how much this social group must have learned to fear early modern discipline. No major show trials were needed in order to exercise artistic censorship. The smallest punitive actions rapidly led to the desired self-censorship against a pedagogy of fear. In addition, as a rule, the existence of assessors of the Inquisition influenced artistic development to such an extent that those who were close to the censors probably experienced more possibilities for expanding than those who did not enjoy this privilege.

There is one case documented of an inquisitor confiscating public pictures with depictions of the Archangel from one of Madrid's most important streets, the Calle Mayor, because he considered them unusual.[45] The works might possibly have been returned later because the assessor considered them acceptable after all. Even so, it is easy to imagine that afterward the many other picture sellers resident in this street checked very precisely what they were offering.[46]

Velázquez, on the other hand, was able to provide so many innovative contributions to Spanish art precisely because he had less to fear than others from the grip of the Inquisition. After all, his teacher and father-in-law was an assessor of the Inquisition and author of an art tract providing artists with very exact instructions when creating certain religious works. In the secular area, Velázquez himself exercised control functions through his position as court painter. For this reason, we can tell from documents that in October 1633 he assessed portraits of the royal family together with the painter Vicente Carducho (1576–1638). These had been confiscated at various locations in the city on behalf of the court administration.[47] Only a handful of the eighty-four paintings was found to be admissible. In most of the others, the heads had to be removed because they disfigured the royal family. With one whole-figure portrait, it was also demanded that a more decent tone be used instead of the green color chosen for the clothing. The measure was intended to more strongly control or improve the quality of the portraits of the royal family circulating in the city. We do not know if the action was repeated. However, that the poet Lope de Vega (1562–1635) picked out portrait control as a central theme not once, but twice in his work seems to speak against its being a one-time event.[48]

The viceroyalty of Naples interestingly illustrates how strong the influence of an inquisitional mentality was even in places where the Inquisition did not exist as an institution, but where men who had been molded through its presence exercised power. The city's art collection had a very different character from that of the neighboring Vatican State but showed many parallels to developments on the Iberian Peninsula.[49] For example, Naples has a much smaller share of pictures with mythological contents and far more with religious themes in the confessional period compared with Rome.

However, we should not pretend that censorship simply limited the development of arts. It could also have a thoroughly innovative effect. This is probably best illustrated by the example of Bartolomé Esteban Murillo (1618–1685), although he was in a special situation in Seville. The port was frequented by many foreign merchants and sailors, so economic interests forced Madrid to allow far greater tolerance to prevail than on the Castilian Plateau.[50]

It has been rightly pointed out that some of Murillo's pictures contain a hidden eroticization of genre pictures that only appear to be harmless. In fact, the artist has probably very consciously violated the most rigidly controlled ban of the Inquisition in the Hispanic world, that of erotic portraits.[51] One example of this is the work *Two Women at a Window* (figure 13). The way the figures look at the viewer was unusually direct for the time; something makes them stand out.[52] In an eighteenth-century reproduction graphic, the painting was described as *Las Gallegas*. It is worth noting that Galician women had a general

Figure 13 Bartolomé Esteban Murillo, *Two Women at a Window,* about 1655/60, Washington, National Gallery of Art

reputation for working as prostitutes and that in the seventeenth century there were already sayings indicating that women at windows in Spain rapidly provoked sexual connotations. Murillo may have been animated to the theme by Dutch examples, as in other cases of his work. However, by making it less obvious, Murillo converted the indecent aspect, making it acceptable for the underlying situation in Spain. In doing so, he created a personal iconography that is charming precisely because of the greater ambivalence. This shows that early modern discipline could partly lead also to very definite comprehensible modernization in the history of art. Similarly, in the early modern era it is possible to find innovative working adaptation processes by artists under state control in almost all countries. However, here we must limit ourselves to these examples for the reasons identified in the introduction.

One period outside my present analysis that still needs bearing in mind is that of the Franco dictatorship. There are several reasons for this. First, there is now a whole series of important investigations dealing with the discipline of the arts.[53] Furthermore, this research shows that censorship was an important factor in the development of a distinctly "Spanish" picture language. This was because it was often precisely those works that were especially controlled at the time—films by Carlos Saura, pictures from Antoni Tàpies, and so forth—that seem to us today to be particularly valuable examples of a "national" contribution to the history of art.[54]

It is possible only to a limited extent to extrapolate from the structures of the control of art in the twentieth century to similar structures in the early modern era. Nevertheless, this example illustrates once more just how important this new macroperspective is. In fact, anyone taking context research in the history of art seriously will have to adopt this approach in the future, along with everyone else interested in artistic "modernization" factors and the reasons lying behind special developments in individual "art landscapes."

Notes

1. On the terms "social control," "social discipline," "discipline," and "early modern discipline," cf.: Spierenburg, *The Spectacle of Suffering;* Dülmen, ed., *Erfindung des Menschen;* Schilling, ed., *Institutionen.* My own choice of terms is based extensively on the introductory text from Heinz Schilling: "Profil und Perspektiven einer interdisziplinären und komparatistischen Disziplinierung (early modern discipline) jenseits einer Dichotomie von Gesellschafts—und Kulturgeschichte," in *Institutionen ,* 3–35.

2. Here I summarize some results from my unpublished thesis *Kunst und Inquisition,* submitted for the Certificate of Habilitation to the Philipps Universität Marburg in 1995. Another summary of this work can also be found in my following publication: "Pictorial Propaganda against the Others."

3. On the term "Hispanic world," cf.: Elliott, ed., *Hispanic World;* Bennassar, *Spanien. 16. und 17. Jahrhundert.* I have based my work here on an even broader concept of the Hispanic world, covering all territory ruled from Madrid in the seventeenth century.

4. On the term "negotiate," cf.: Dinges, "Aushandeln von Armut in der Frühen Neuzeit."

5. Mâle, *L'art religieux en France aprés la Concile de Trente.*

6. For a history of the Council of Trent and on the importance of the picture decrees, cf.: Jedin, *Geschichte des Konzils von Trient;* Belting, *Bild und Kult;* O'Malley, *Trent and All That.*

7. For the most recent publication on this, cf.: Hecht, *Katholische Bildertheologie im Zeitalter von Gegenreformation und Barock.*

8. On "Discorso" in particular, cf.: Boschloo, *Annibale Carracci in Bologna.*

9. For the most recent research on the Inquisition trial against Veronese, cf.: Warnke, "Praxisfelder der Kunsttheorie;" Priever, "Paolo Veronese's Banquet in the House of the Levi."

10. Freedberg, *The Power of Images;* Zapperi, "La corporation des peintres et la censure des images à Bologne au temp des Carrache."

11. On this, cf. the contributions in chap. 3, Die Bemächtigung des Menschen," 221–322.

12. Publications about the "iconoclasm" form an important exception here, though these can only be partly subsumed under the aspect of early modern discipline. A congress was

held in the University of Berne (Historisches Institut) on this theme in January 2000 entitled *Macht und Ohnmacht der Bilder.*

13. The recent release of the corresponding documents is a further argument for taking greater account of the macroperspective of early modern discipline as demanded here.

14. The authoritative work on the history of the Spanish Inquisition was last published in a revised edition, ref. Kamen, *La Inquisicón española.* Secondary literature on the Inquisition expanded to such an extent that it became hard to survey. The following are interesting for their new methodical approaches: Villanueva, ed., *Historia de la Inquisición en España y América;* Alcalá, ed., *Inquisición española y mentalidad inquisitorial;* Contreras, *Sotos contra Riquelmes; Los Inquisidores,* exhibition catalog (in his article, José Martínez Millán uses the term "confesionalización"). For a recommended introduction to the subject, ref. Peters, *Inquisition.*

15. Alcalá, *Inquisición española.*

16. Scholz-Hänsel, *El Greco "Der Großinquisitor."*

17. Scholz-Hänsel, "El Santo Niño de La Guardia."

18. Maqueda Abreu, *El auto de fe.*

19. Scholz-Hänsel, "El Santo Niño de La Guardia."

20. Martínez Ripoll, "Control inquisitorial y figuración artística: Villafranca mejorado por Murillo."

21. Karge, ed., *Vision oder Wirklichkeit.*

22. López Torrijos, *La mitología en la pintura española del Siglo de Oro.*

23. Tomlinson, "Burn It, Hide It, Flaunt It."

24. García Hidalgo, *Principios para estudiar el nobilísimo y real arte de la pintura.*

25. Palomino de Castro y Velasco, *El museo pictórico y escala óptica,* vol. 2, 94–95.

26. On Pacheco, cf. i.a.: Brown, *Images and Ideas in Seventeenth-Century Spanish Painting.*

27. Pacheco, *Arte de la pintura,* 561.

28. Palomino, *El museo pictórico,* 94–95.

29. Contreras, *Sotos contra Riquelmes.*

30. *Copia de los pareceres y censuras de los reverendísimos padres, maestros y señores catedráticos de las insignes Universidades de Salamanca y Alcalá.* For an early assessment of this text, cf.: Octavio Picón, *Observaciones acerca del desnudo y su excasez en el arte español.*

31. Palomino, *Vidas,* 101.

32. On this, cf. the chapter "Los pleitos del Greco," in Gallego, *El pintor de artesano a artista,* 101–18.

33. For Caravaggio's relationship to contemporary church politics, cf.: Held, *Caravaggio: Politik und Martyrium der Körper; Saints and Sinners: Caravaggio and the Baroque Image,* exhibition catalog.

34. John Varriano, in *Saints and Sinners,* exhibition catalog, 203, correctly certifies Caravaggio as having rather limited understanding of the religious debates of his day. This runs completely contrary to many other perspectives.

35. On this theory, cf. the contribution from Vincenzo Pacelli, "Reconsideraciones sobre las vicisitudes artísticas y biográficas del último Caravaggio," in *Caravaggio,* exhibition catalog, 49–62.

36. Zapperi represents this perspective, *Eros e Controriforma.* 37. Cf. the Master's Paper from Anna Reuter on Goya and the Inquisition (Marburg 1996).

37. Cf. "The Master's Papers" from Anna Reuter, *On Goya and the Inquisition* (Marbury, 1996).

38. Both Carracci and Jusepe de Ribera depicted many things in their drawings, including observations of everyday life, for which there are no equivalents in their oil paintings.

39. On the positional value of this drawing and other depictions of violence in the oeuvre of Jusepe de Ribera, cf. my monograph on the artist published in Cologne in January 2001.

40. Rose Wagner, *Manuel Godoy*

41. On this, cf.: López-Rey, "Goya's Drawing of Pietro Torrigiano"; Scholz-Hänsel, *Künstler als Gastarbeiter in Spanien,* 74.

42. This recently happened again to Zapperi. Research into Carracci cannot be imagined without him, but he is frequently accused of overinterpretation. On this, cf. the assessment of him in the research report: De Grazia, "Carracci Drawings in Britain and the State of Carracci Studies," 302, note 13.

43. Agustín Bustamante García supplied one exception recently with an unusually polemic stance, providing considerable food for thought bearing in mind the documents he found: "El Santo Oficio de Valladolid y los artistas." Clearly, some art historians still believe that their task consists solely in publishing their material and not in its further reaching iconological interpretation.

44. Cf. ibid.

45. Archivo Histórico Nacional, *Legajo 4456, Expediente 14.* I am grateful to Felix Scheffler for pointing out this file.

46. Unfortunately, the documents do not make it clear what happened with the pictures after the valuators had testified their harmlessness.

47. Herrero-García, "Un dictamen pericial de Velázquez y una escena de Lope de Vega."

48. Ibid., 66.

49. Labrot, *Etudes Napolitaines.*

50. There are examples in Kamen, *La Inquisición española,* of tolerance for economic reasons.

51. Brown, "Murillo, pintor de temas eróticos"

52. Brown, *Spanish Paintings of the Fifteenth through Nineteenth Centuries,* 105–9.

53. Neuschäfer, *Macht und Ohmmacht der Zensur.* 54. On this most recently, cf.: Llorens, "Zwei Anmerkungen über die spanische Kunst." In contrast, the influence of discipline in the Franco Era is seen more critically in: García Felguera, "Saura, Millares und die 'Leyenda negra.'"

54. On this most recently, cf. Llorens, "Zwei Anmerkungen über die spanische Kunst." In contrast, the influence of discipline in the Franco Era is seen more critically in García Felguera, "Saura, Millares und die 'Leyenda negra.'"

CHAPTER 7

Early Modern Architecture: Conditioning, Disciplining, and Social Control

Bernd Roeck

Architecture and Social Disciplining

The interrelationships between art and discipline constitute a vast subject matter for research, most of it still awaiting investigation. Yet, its significance is clear: paintings and sculptures, for example, inform and enlighten us; they mediate imaginations and indirectly convey "appropriate" patterns of behavior. They inform us about religious beliefs, and they reinforce concepts of state order and justice.[1] Art affects the social space in many ways. We can often deduce its effect from the intentions of the patron.[2] If the sources remain silent about these intentions, we may assume that particular artistic expressions are very likely to be in conformity with the patron's intention.[3]

As far as their social and political meaning is concerned, works of art can develop a life of their own. This is especially the case when there is a considerable temporal gap between producing and admiring them. As sign systems—as they may be partially, but not entirely, considered—works of art depend on their context; their meaning and effect can only be determined in the broader context of space and time. They depend on their positioning within a specific social system. An obelisk in Luxor or Heliopolis signifies something else than the same obelisk standing on St. Peter's Square in Rome, or in Paris, or in New York. The *Sacra Conversazione* conveys different meanings depending on whether the painting is situated in a church, in a palace, or in a museum.

For the premodern age, it is hardly possible to underestimate these effects of architecture and the visual arts.[4] Works of art had little competition from other media. They existed in a world that was relatively scarce with images compared to modern society, and people were unfamiliar yet with the representation of space as a perspective image. Certain strategies of artists, such as the depiction of the supernatural in "real" space, might have had a marked effect. It simultaneously made religious paintings lose their magic. Conversely, it enabled the spectator to relate to the visionary realm, in which miracles became a direct experience of the viewer.[5]

Many of these observations on paintings also apply to architecture. Its peculiarity lay in the fact that early modern observers were relatively immobile, so that they generally used to see fewer images than the modern observer.[6] Consequently, remarkable, huge buildings were relatively rare, which made them into effective media for communication, often of a disciplinary character.

Finally, we should realize that the language of images, which often appears cryptic to the modern reader and therefore needs to be deciphered, was intended for people familiar with it, who perceived any inconspicuous detail that is difficult to grasp for the modern observer. Occasionally, even the "fine differences" might have been properly perceived. It is important though to distinguish precisely between the various social positions of the observers. The perception of iconography of the learned humanist differed from that of ordinary people. Unfortunately, we hardly know anything about the latter's perception, so that we are left with hypotheses and speculation.

Disciplining and Conditioning

Next to customary terms such as "social control" and "disciplining,"[7] it appears to me that another concept is eminently suitable for describing the effect of art within social space: conditioning. By "conditioning" I mean the process of acquisition of norms, patterns of thought and behavior—including norms and patterns concerning the political order and the religious system—all the way until their internalization. When internalized, they are regarded as a matter of course, no longer reflected upon, and they may become part of the habitus of an individual or even of a whole social group, by which they increase in social relevance. We become aware of the consequences by analyzing the sources. However, mental conditioning can also occur without any visible consequences. Hence, conditioning refers to "being inclined to" or "being disposed to" something.

Art, then, is a symbolic representation of part of the habitus, of the owner or patron for example, but in addition it has a conditioning function, for the observer or user. The practice of this conditioning can involve passive or unconscious processes of internalization as well as conscious changes in thought and behavior caused by media and discursive or physical force.[8] As a last resort, people do not think any more about what they are doing. Conditioning, therefore, can be regarded as one aspect of the larger process of social disciplining; the former is a psychological process, preceding the visible changes of behavior to which the latter concept refers. Both processes are interrelated in a complex manner. Hence, conditioning supposedly is an object of study within the history of mentalities.

Works of art, "texts without letters," can only be looked at; they influence through the eyes. This term is eminently suitable to describe the effect of art. Conditioning implies not so much the use of force, but rather a subtle strategy of regulation of behavior that is a precondition for the interaction of individuals. Every form of coexistence is only possible when people are conditioned by rules. The process of civilization, as analyzed by Norbert Elias, might also be described as the dialectics of conditioning.

Magnificentia and Architecture

The representative architecture of secular as well as religious buildings may condition the onlooker's way of thinking and acting, so they are both involved in the disciplinary process. Because of the paucity of literature on the subject,[9] I will focus on a few examples. I intend to demonstrate that one can use early modern architecture as a source for the study of discipline and the conditioning paradigm generally. Buildings with a clear function in the system of governmental control and discipline, such as fortresses[10] or prisons, will not be discussed here. It is evident, from the "language" of their architecture, that their purpose is to intimidate, deter, and discipline.

From an early date, contemporaries were well aware of the political and social effect of great and splendid architecture. One might find the idea of architecture's disciplinary function in Machiavelli's *Il principe,* especially in chapter 20, where the author discusses the usefulness of fortifications. However, Machiavelli does not explicitly mention the significance of architecture as such. This subject has to be considered especially in connection with the theory that identified *magnificentia* as the ruler's outstanding characteristic.[11] That concept was clearly associated with patronage in architecture. Theories of architecture from the fifteenth and sixteenth centuries, such as the treatises by Alberti, Scamozzi, and Palladio, use a variant of the term magnificentia to characterize great and splendid buildings.[12] They call such a building *magnifico.* The idea of "appropriateness," of the right mixture between mediocrity and display, belongs to the tradition of the theory of magnificentia, and it can be traced from Aristotle until the economic literature of the eighteenth century.

A few centuries after Aristotle, Vitruvius, dedicating his book on architecture to the emperor Augustus, stated that the *princeps* should care for public buildings that served the common good, "so that the dignity of the realm possesses excellent buildings which increase its reputation."[13] The thought that the ruler's magnificentia serves the common good recurs in the work of Aristotle, Vitruvius, and several Medieval authors. Already the *Fürstenspiegel* of Aegidius Romanus (c. 1277–1279) expresses the idea that outward splendor is related to the social status of a person.[14] Shortly after Aegidius Romanus, Piero de

Crecenzi wrote in his treatise on agriculture (c. 1300): "If the nobility and the power of Gentlemen is such that they find it disgusting to live together with their workers in the same courtyard, they could very easily settle at the afore-mentioned and very well layed-out place adorned with palaces and towers and gardens, just as it is appropriate for their nobility and power."[15]

Similar opinions were repeatedly expressed in the period immediately following. The idea of "appropriateness" remained important. The rise of the modern state, embodied in particular by the prince, reinforced the idea that only the man who rules deserves the splendor, which is associated with the notion of magnificen-tia. Aegidius already discussed questions of competition and outward splendor, of status and prestige; the idea that the prince was practically forced to use the power of art in order to express his status symbolically is implicitly present in his work. In the seventeenth century, the Jesuit and educator of the prince of Savoy, Emanuele Tesauro, expressed this idea explicitly: "Someone who is not a prince can therefore not possess magnificentia; or, to put it in a different light, who does not possess it, can never be a prince."[16] In the Europe of early abso-lutism, this attribute became an essential element of the ruler's habitus. The same applies to the gentry and patricians. In an anonymous dialogue about economic life in Genoa, the author assures that the patricians would behave sadistically if they invested more than the necessary amount in splendor, "in order to give pain and to hurt the hearts of those people who can't [afford to] do the same."[17]

At the same time, the patronage of architecture was linked to the Creation. Worldly rulers, wrote Roberto Bellarmin in 1619, followed God's example when, without even caring for the expenses, they constructed buildings that served the common good.[18] Thus, the relationship with the commonwealth and the allegory of the Creation legitimized the patronage of architecture in two respects.[19] The magnificentia, as described above, had a stabilizing effect on society, an idea that is implicit in all these texts. This notion became even stronger in the eighteenth century. Franz Philipp Florin wrote in his *oeconomicus prudens* (1719): "as God regards princes and mas-ters as superior over ordinary people, he may easily accept that powerful people demonstrate their higher social status through outward appearance, in order to gain the respect and honor of their subjects. It seems as if they stand on a stage, where they can be seen by everyone, so that they have to take care that there is nothing about them or in their court which lacks dignity."[20]

It was Christian Wolff who most clearly emphasized the relation between the magnificentia of a building and its stabilizing function in society. In 1736 he wrote that beautiful buildings pleased human beings and increased their bliss-ful happiness. However, they struck people with awe, especially ordinary peo-ple and those who made their judgments according to outward appearance.[21] In the commonwealth, Wolff continued, reputation is important to people, partly because they have to engage in commercial and social transactions, partly because they give orders to others. The economic historian Roberto S. Lopez echoes Wolff's statement by stressing that the palaces of the Florentine Renaissance were a kind of "credit-card of the elite." [22] More important is the observation, made by Wolff and by others such as Johann Christian Lünig, that representation was well suited to impress ordinary people and to legitimize and consolidate power.[23]

Such ideas were expressed not only with respect to the palaces of the princes. Andrea Spinola, who—according to Peter Burke—made biting comments on the "madness of our luxury," nevertheless thought it appropriate to furnish the *Palazzo Pubblico* in Genoa splendidly, because this promoted the republic's stately majesty.[24]

Means of Conditioning: The Language of Buildings

Buildings were effective in conditioning and disciplining—for example in making the political order or a religious system accepted—through a complex semantic, of which only a few examples will be given. First, it was the mere size of a building that impressed the public, since in their own environment people were used to small and narrow spaces.[25] For modern people, the contrast between "large" and "small" might be difficult to grasp, due to a different psychology of perception, which was noted by contemporaries. Today's sky-high architecture often reduces the effect of a historic building right next to it. Furthermore, large squares and boulevards, which were constructed above all in the nineteenth and twentieth centuries, have made the sharp contrast between narrow alleys with small houses and large buildings fall into oblivion. This applies to most gothic cathedrals and town halls.[26] It also applies to St. Peter's Square in Rome, the development of which stretched from the seventeenth through the twentieth centuries, beginning with Bernini's design of the square itself and ending with the construction of the *Via della Conciliazione*. Early modern theorists were aware of the dialectics between large and small. Leonhard Christoph Sturm, for example, recommended arranging the buildings next to the landlord's estate (*herrschaftlicher Gutshof*) beautifully and symmetrically, but primarily they needed to increase the "magnitude of the palace" through their appropriate and modest beauty.[27] Inside the great palaces this strategy can be observed in the order of rooms and space, from which the size of the throne room and the audience room can be deduced. Even in the late Middle Ages, it was well known that size symbolizes power, indeed that it might be power itself. Italian building regulations placed restrictions on the height of clan towers, for example, in Viterbo, Bologna, Lucca, and other towns, or they forbade destroying the tower of the *comune* in order to diminish its height.

The building material was also an important factor. Early modern travel books are rich sources that confirm that building materials played an important role in people's perception. Marble, copper, gold plates, and timber were rated as signs of rank and power, even more than formal qualities or the artists who had been involved in construction.[28] These observations are confirmed in the economic history of architecture. It appears that the cost of building materials and transport accounted for the majority of expenses for architecture.[29]

The contrast between "upstairs" and "downstairs" was equally important. One went up to the throne room, the council chamber and the princely rooms; the *piano nobile* was the second floor, rather than the ground floor or basement. It appears that this development toward a vertical organization of architectural space goes back to the time of Charlemagne. During the Ottonian period, the "exclusive upper storey," first observed in the ruler's gallery in religious spaces, had been developed.[30] The elevated position of the ruler was self-evident then, so that it hardly needed any comment or explanation. The requirement that the manor house should be built high up became a topos of the northern Italian *villegiatura* literature. Alberti already expressed the opinion that the dignity of a place is more important than its utility. Scamozzi instructed that a villa had to be built above the "common land," the *campagna comune,* so he suggested building on hills or other elevated sites. He went on to explain, quoting Averroes, that higher and lower sites were to each other as forms and materials with greater dignity were to those with lower dignity.[31]

Thus, while the landlord could keep his domain under surveillance from his villa, the farmers and workmen literally had to climb up to him. The location of the villa or manor house might serve as a social metaphor; it also brought social reality home to contemporaries and contributed to the acceptance of authority. Similar considerations may have led several proprietors of country estates to preserve elements of the architecture of castles and palaces. Elements of fortification were no longer of military use in the seventeenth century; they were maintained because of their iconographic value, which mirrored the social status of the patron.[32] In an urban context, too, the location of a building was of prime significance. The center of rule usually coincided with the geographic center, its pivotal position marked through outward architectural signs.[33]

Finally, we have to consider elements like coats of arms, emblems, and other subtle signs whose messages are difficult to grasp.[34] At least at first glance, they cannot readily be understood as tools of political and social conditioning. This also applies to obelisks, pillars, and the like. Theorists such as Sturm knew exactly the appropriate architectural forms matching each specific social status, just as he recommended the right stately robes and the seating order at weddings.[35] To what extent his advice and that of his colleagues was followed remains unknown.

The City As Home and Utopia

Contemporaries were aware that "beautiful buildings" might impress onlookers and acquire a reputation of fame. Pierre Grégoire wrote in 1609: "To the extent that cities become more beautiful and more heavily ornamented, they are also perceived as more distinct and attract more people who wish to visit them; and the greater are the honors bestowed upon their rulers, even from foreign nations."[36] Among the various criteria for beauty, one in particular became central for the architects of castles and later also for urban builders: symmetry, or at least clear geometrical patterns.[37] The architecture following this principle had a disciplining or conditioning effect in so far as it was recognized as the product of the ruler's intention.[38] It made all the principal streets lead to the palace or to a church, hence to the very place where power was legitimized. In this way, architecture was a symbol for the ideal order of the state, to be read like a treatise or an allegory.

The straight line displayed power; it had a similar conditioning effect as an arranged unit of soldiers in exercise.[39] The well-ordered architecture of the planned city illustrated the ability of the state or prince to rule. The *gute Policey* was visually demonstrated by architecture as a means of communication. Simultaneously, the ideal city might be regarded as a monument to its founder, visible in paintings, sculptures, or emblems around the town. Sometimes, cities were named after their founder, Pienza and Richelieu, for example.[40] This kind of propaganda obviously strengthened the authority of the prince or patron, even after his death. It stood for the splendor of his lineage.

Work As a Means of Disciplining

Architecture in general, and the planned city of the early modern period in particular, served as a complex metaphor within political theory.[41] The patriarchal model of government, prevalent during the sixteenth and seventeenth centuries, caused theories of architecture to take the family as the model for the state and the city. The whole city was viewed, as it were, as the house of one family.[42] Although this had no great effect on architectural forms, it caused the expenditure for architecture to be heavily discussed, especially the "conspicuous consumption" inherent to representative architecture. The principal consideration was that such buildings expressed rank and reputation and that they constituted, in Johann Christoph Sturm's words, "a primary part of political wisdom."[43]

Quite another argument also pointed at the utility of representative architecture. Expensive buildings, such as residences, baroque churches, fortresses, and Renaissance palaces, provided work and income for many people. To construct them, not only architects, painters, and sculptors were needed, but bricklayers, masons, and all sorts of casual workers as well. In addition, during the early modern period, able-bodied vagrants and paupers or prisoners were set to work on these projects.[44] Turkish prisoners of war, for example, were reported to have contributed to the construction of the canals of the Nymphenburg palace near Munich. As early as the fifteenth century, Cosimo de Medici had set poor people to work on public building projects, as his biographer, Vespasiano da Bisticci, reports.[45] Socio-political considerations may have been the reason for the decision to extend the Palazzo Pitti in Florence; it constituted an attempt to attenuate the effects of the depression of 1629–1630.[46] Well documented is the sociopolitical background of the building of Augsburg's town hall during the years 1615–1620.[47] We know that all patrons of baroque architecture in southern Germany in the seventeenth and eighteenth centuries justified their building projects with the argument that they would provide numerous unemployed people with work.

To conclude, it is undeniable that rulers and other powerful persons consciously used architecture for purposes of social policy and social discipline. This is most strikingly revealed in a letter that the abbot Marianus wrote to the Elector of Bavaria concerning the construction of the *Wieskirche* near Steingaden (Upper Bavaria), a church still famous today.[48] Admittedly, his words were not written for publication, but they prove that he expected positive reactions to the labor-intensive construction of the church. This was clearly meant to increase the abbot's reputation and to ensure that the peasants of the region would consider him their great benefactor. Indeed, the peasants were said to have been quite satisfied with the construction of the cloister and the generous amount of money they received for helping to build it. All masons, bricklayers, and carpenters praised the building that had provided employment and daily bread. The abbot advised the Elector to select a worthy representative who would place the first stone in his name. In that case, the common people would also recognize the Elector's benevolent intentions toward them.[49] This mid-eighteenth-century example shows very clearly to what extent architecture functioned as a means of discipline.

Notes

1. Rosenberg, *Art and Politics in Late Medieval and Early Renaissance Italy.* Further examples in: Roeck, "Visual turn?"

2. Roeck, *Kunstpatronage in der Frühen Neuzeit,* 11–34.

3. Vocelka, *Die politische Propaganda Kaiser Rudolfs II.*

4. I do not differentiate between classical antiquity, the Middle Ages, and the early modern period, because many of the following considerations refer to the age before the "flood of the media" and before increasing communication and traffic relations, hence, before the middle of the nineteenth century.

5. Panofsky, "Die Perspektive als symbolische Form," 258–330. Idem, *Grundfragen der Kunstwissenschaft,* 126.

6. On this aspect, see Roeck, "Macht und Ohnmacht der Bilder."

7. On terminology and for further literature, see Schilling, "Profil und Perspektiven," 3–36.

8. Some examples of conditioning as it is commonly understood are elaborated in

the research on confessionalization. Some behavior patterns, such as reproductive behavior, might be regarded as results of the conditioning effect of specific religious doctrines.

9. Some examples can be found in Hipp and Warnke, *Architektur als politische Kultur.* Compare also Bentmann and Müller, *Die Villa als Herrschaftsarchitektur;* Warnke, ed., *Politische Architektur in Europa vom Mittelalter bis heute;* Roeck, "Stadtgestalt und Macht in der europäischen Renaissance," 109–126.

10. Compare the interesting article by Eichberg, "Geometrie als barocke Verhaltensnorm," 17–50.

11. Fraser Jenkins, "Cosimo de Medici's Patronage of Architecture and the Theory of Magnificence," 162–70. And Oberli, *Magnificentia Principis.*

12. Oberli, *Magnificentia Principis,* 22–23.

13. Vitruvius, *De architectura libri decem, 21.*

14. Compare the following considerations: Oberli, *Magnificentia Principis,* 27–33; on Aegidius: Oberli, *Magnificentia Principis,* 29; and Berges, *Die Fürstenspiegel des hohen und späten Mittelalters,* 211–28.

15. "Ma se la nobilità de signori et la potentia è tanta, che schiffino d'abitare con suoi lavoratori in una medesima corte, potranno agiatamente nel predecto luogo così disposto fare dimorare il loro luogo ordinato di palagi et di torri et di giardini secondo che alloro nobiltà et possanza si converra." Quoted in Bentmann and Müller, *Die Villa als Herrschaftsarchitektur,* 110.

16. "Non può adunque posseder Magnificenza chi non è Prencipe; dirò cosa nuova, che non può essere Prencipe chi non la possiede." Quoted in Oberli, *Magnificentia Principis,* 32.

17. "per dar pena e dolore di cuore a chi non può fare il medesimo." Quoted in Burke, *The Historical Anthropology of Early Modern Italy,* 135.

18. Oberli, *Magnificentia Principis,* 31–32: "Iam vero soli inter homines, Principes magni, in his omnibus rebus, magnificentiam Dei, Regis Regum, imitare aliquo modo possunt. Ipse enim soli aedifica publica & maxima ad usum totius populi, quae sumptus maximos requirunt, erigere solunt. Eiusmodi erant olim apud Romanos Thermae, Theatra, Basilicae, Templa, quorum adhuc vestigia cernimus; & nunc quoque Principes magni Palatia, Fora, Ecclesias, Xenodochia, Scholas publicas & alia sumptuosa aedificia erigunt, quae profecto erigere possunt."

19. The theoretician Paul Decker wrote that the character of the prince, coming from and authorized by God, shall be visible through the outward magnificence of his state and representation. See Decker, *Fürstlicher Baumeister.* Preface to part I: Schütte, "Die Lehre von den Gebäudetypen," 193.

20. Florin, *Oeconomus prudens et legalis,* 60. Schütte, "Die Lehre von den Gebäudetypen," 192: "den gleich wie Gott Fürsten und Herren weit über andere erhöhet"; also "mag Er auch wohl leiden daß Sie den Unterschied zwischen sich und andern auch in dem äusserlichen Apparatu zeigen mithin von den Ihrigen destomehr respectirt und Verehret werden indem sie gleichsam auf einer Schaubühne stehen da sie von jeder-

mann können gesehen werden einfolglich auch sich nothwendig in acht nehmen müssen daß nicht irgend etwas an Ihnen oder an Ihren Höffen gesehen werde das kein Ansehen habe noch Ihrer Hoheit gemäß seie."

21. Wolff, *Vernünftige Gedanken von dem gesellschaftlichen Leben,* 377–78. Schütte, "Die Lehre von den Gebäudetypen," 193: "Ansehen bey anderen (Menschen), sonderlich bey gemeinen Leuten und denen, die nach dem äusserlichen Scheine zu urtheilen gewohnet."

22. Lopez, "Hard Times and Investment in Culture," 29–54.

23. Warnke, "Politische Ikonographie," 23–24.

24. "servono alla conservazione della maestà pubblica": Burke, *Historical Anthropology,* 136.

25. Martin Warnke, "Einführung," 14.

26. The place in front of the town hall in Augsburg, the biggest construction of a town hall in central Europe, was not cleared until World War II.

27. Sturm, *Vollständige Anweisung,* 39. Cf. also Zdekauer and Sella, eds., *Statuti di Ascoli,* 367.

28. Raff, *Die Sprache der Materialien,* 51–53 (about marble); some evidence also in Roeck, "Die Ohnmacht des Dogen," 87 and footnotes 45 and 46.

29. The costs of architecture were relatively low compared to other expenditures of the early modern budget, but often, compared to the great result, extremely low; cf. Oberli, *Magnificentia Principis;* and Roeck, "Augsburger Baukunst," 119–38. Roeck, *Kunstpatronage in der frühen Neuzeit,* 111.

30. Meckseper, "Oben und Unten in der Architektur," 45–46.

31. Scamozzi, *Idea dell'architettura universale,* 119; Bentmann and Müller, *Die Villa als Herrschaftsarchitektur,* 101.

32. Schütte, "Die Lehre von den Gebäudetypen," 242.

33. Geertz, "Centres, Kings and Charisma," 152; Lopez, "The Crossroads within the Wall," 28.

34. Gand, "De la signification," 263–77.

35. According to some theoreticians, decoration with pillars was reserved for the noble buildings ("publiquen Gebäude oder Herren-Häusern"); details in Schütte, "Die Lehre von den Gebäudetypen," 213–16.

36. Hipp, "Aristotelische Politik," 104: "quo enim pulcriores sunt, et ornatiores civitates, eo magis nobilitate censentur, et suo nomine plures ad eas invisendas alliciunt, principem dominum honorabiliorem inter exteras reddunt nationes."

37. Kruft, *Städte in Utopia.*

38. Aristotle, though, from a military point of view, found a "tangle of houses" more secure than a "geometrically ordered" town. See *The Politics,* VII, 11.

39. On the relation of architecture and geometrical spirit, see Eichberg, "Geometrie als barocke Verhaltensnorm"; with subtle differences also: Dinges, "Residenzstadt als Sozialdisziplinierung?"

40. On these towns, see Kruft, *Städte in Utopia.*

41. Hipp, "Aristotelische Politik," 103–4.

42. Palladio, *I quattro libri dell'architettura*, 12 and 46: "La città non sia altro che una certa casa grande, e per lo contrario la casa una Città picciola."

43. Schütte, "Die Lehre von den Gebäudetypen," 193.

44. Stekl, "Labore et fame," 126–27.

45. Bisticci, *Le Vite*, 190.

46. Cochrane, *Florence in the Forgotten Centuries*, 195–96.

47. Roeck, *Wirtschaftliche und soziale Voraussetzungen*. As Zückert shows in his Grundlagen der Barockkultur, the imposition of building taxes (Baufronen) considered too high sometimes caused protests by the subjects.

48. Stutzer and Fink, *Die irdische und die himmlische Wies*, 33–35.

49. "Eben diese Pauren bekundeten ihre vollste Zufriedenheit über das Bauwerk ihres Closters und das schöne Stück Geld, welches sie sich auf diesem Wege erwerben. Auch war zu erfahren, daß die Baugewerker, alß Maurer, Mörtelträger, Zimmerleuth, in Hinkunft auch Stukkateure, voll des Lobes über diesen Bau sind, welcher ihnen viel Geschäft beschert und sie in das sicherste Brod setzt. Bei soviel Wohlbehagen, welches dieses Bauwerk unter dem gemainen Volk verbreitet, dürfte es rätlich seyn, wenn Ihro Churfürstliche Durchlaucht einen würdigen Vertreter bestimme, welcher in Ihro Namen die Legung des ersten Steines fürnimmt. Dem dasigen Volke wird dadurch sichtbar werden, wie sehr Ihro Durchlaucht an seyner Wohlfahrt und besserem Verdienste gelegen ist." Stutzer and Fink, *Die irdische und die himmlische Wies*, 33–34.

Part Two

COMMUNITIES: PERSPECTIVES FROM BELOW

CHAPTER 8

Social Control Viewed from Below: New Perspectives

Herman Roodenburg

Who actually controlled the law in early modern Europe? Was the law merely an instrument in the hands of state, church, or ruling class? Was it all or primarily a matter of control to bottom? Or were the middle and lower classes involved as well? And did the state evolve at the expense of society or was it perhaps the other way round? Was it rather society itself, in its growing demand for regulation, that created the state? And if we prefer this far more complex history, how exactly was this social demand complied with? Was the law the primary institution that people would turn to or were there many other, informal or quasi-formal, institutions that were more or less admitted or even encouraged and supported by the state? Indeed, did people switch from one institution to the other? Over the last twenty years these questions have dominated the exchanges among criminal historians, and they are still debated today. Offering a new understanding of the issues at stake, the chapters collected in this part of the volume all present a perspective "from below." They focus on the lower criminal courts and on the civil courts; on church and consistory courts; on related institutions such as the guilds, the confraternities, and the urban neighborhoods; and on the family. What the authors share is a common interest in the concrete, multifaceted uses of the law. The perspective presented is, above all, a perspective of accommodation and negotiation.

At present the legitimacy of this alternative view has been widely acknowledged. But the debates have been fierce, especially in Germany, where they became part of a wide ranging school controversy between, on the one hand, the defenders of a *historische Sozialwissenschaft,* taking their cue from the works of Karl Marx and Max Weber, and on the other hand, the protagonists of a *historische Anthropologie,* drawing most of their inspiration from cultural anthropology, modern folklore studies, and related disciplines.

To many continental historians, using broad conceptualizations such as "acculturation" or "social disciplining," it was primarily the state or an alliance of state and church that controlled the law. The advocacy of Robert

Muchembled and Heinz Schilling has been influential in this regard. A similar view has been ascribed to Norbert Elias and his notion of a western European "process of civilization." To other mainly English historians, it was not so much the state as the governing class that ruled the law. As the Marxist historian Douglas Hay argued, the law of eighteenth-century England was first and foremost an instrument of class oppression. It was there to discipline the lower classes, and it did so through an imposing mixture of terror, mercy, and ceremony.[1]

Muchembled formulated his thoughts in the late 1970s, Schilling some ten years later. In the meantime they have both modified their positions, making room within their top-to-bottom approaches for dimensions of reception and appropriation.[2] Elias's is a somewhat different case, as he has been treated somewhat unfairly by his critics. For instance, he defined his "civilizing process" as basically blind, as a long-term process generated by a growing and overall intensification of social and psychological interdependence. To reduce these blind developments to a set of active interventions from above clearly misses the deeper message of his work. In addition to this, Elias allowed for civilizing effects independent of court and state, pointing for instance to the social and psychological restraints implied in the world of trading relationships and commerce.[3] Recently, this idea of civilizing pressures not imposed by court and state but, as it were, welling up from below, has been advanced by some historians working on seventeenth- and eighteenth-century England. But they contrast their views with those of Elias, who is identified once more with a one-sided perspective from above.[4]

The masterful narratives of Muchembled, Schilling, Hay, and Elias came to prominence in the 1970s and 1980s. In 1974, however, the French historian Yves Castan proposed a very different approach. Though acknowledging the terror of the law, he was one of the first historians to look beyond the institutions of formal social control and trace the countless practices of informal mediation, including the structuring role of honor and reputation. Confronted with large numbers of "infrajudicial" settlements in the eighteenth-century Languedoc, Castan concluded that discipline and punishment had always come second to the law, that indeed its primary role, by its presence and threat alone, was to enforce a *compensation convenable,* a formal or informal settlement that would satisfy the plaintiff.[5]

In the 1980s and 1990s scholarly interest in this mysterious world of the infrajudiciary quickly increased. In 1980 the historians Bruce Lenman and Geoffrey Parker situated the phenomenon within a long-term transition from the "private law" of the Middle Ages to the "state law" of present-day society. A few years later, the church historian John Bossy described a more open and nuanced transition from "feud" and "charity" (in its Medieval sense of amity and peace) to "law."[6]

Since then numerous studies have revealed the ubiquity of infrajudicial procedures and the social significance both in these and in the formal, judicial procedures of notions of "honor" and "peace." As a consequence, the prevailing notions of acculturation, social discipline, and civilization (in its narrow sense of civilizing from above) were put into perspective. As these new studies argued, to understand fully the workings of social control in early modern Europe, one should also look at the lower and civil courts, at the related church and consistory courts, and at the multitude of sanctioning systems, informal or quasi-formal, maintained by family and kin and by neighbors, guilds, and local authorities. As Michael Ignatieff already observed in 1983, early modern society was "a densely woven fabric of permissions, prohibitions, obligations and rules, sustained and enforced at a thousand points."[7]

Clearly, such a fragmenting of social control requires a broad and quite open definition. A now widely accepted definition (see also Pieter Spierenburg's introduction to this volume) is provided by Martin Dinges who, following the sociologist Donald Black, speaks of "all forms by which people define deviant behavior and react on it by taking steps."[8] In this view, shared by most of the authors here, social control encompasses a myriad of forms, from unofficial forms such as neighborhood gossip, charivari, or infrajudicial settlements, all the way up to the well-known types of formal conviction, imprisonment, and public execution. It also encompasses verbal and physical violence. In early modern Europe, as Martin Ingram and especially Gerd Schwerhoff remind us, violence was both an object and a medium of social control.[9]

Recently, the concept of the infrajudiciary has been specified as well. It has been stressed that judicial and infrajudicial settlements did not oppose each other, that in many cases plaintiffs and even officials could and did switch from one option to the other. Indeed, to define such practices as *infra*judicial, as practices somewhere "underneath" the official court system, tells us more about our own views on the judiciary than about those held by the men and women actually under study. Additionally, to distinguish responses to deviant behavior that come neither under the judicial nor under the infrajudicial system, Benoît Garnot has proposed the categories of *parajustice* and *extrajustice*. The first deals with responses such as vengeance or the duel; the second, with forms of simply tolerating or putting up with deviant behavior, basically forms of nonresponse.[10]

The aim of this introduction is to reflect on some of the issues involved in the new perspectives, in this spectrum from below. These issues have been primarily discussed by German and English historians, though their points of departure, especially their ideas concerning the presence and significance of the early modern state, were very different indeed. I will therefore confine myself to the debates in England and Germany, but I will occasionally refer to similar discussions in France, Switzerland, and the Low Countries. Most of the exchange took place in the last fifteen years or so, as it was only in the 1990s that the ideas of various historians developed into this impressive and exciting avenue of research.

Issues of State Formation

Comparing the exchanges in Germany and England, it is not so much their scope, span, or rhetoric that stand out; what primarily catches the eye are the different directions of the two debates, their opposite points of departure and ensuing line of arguments. In the German controversy over the concept of *Sozialdisziplinierung* (as originally coined by Gerhard Oestreich and reformulated in social terms by Heinz Schilling and Wolfgang Reinhardt), it was first and foremost the implied "etatism," the state's supposed ubiquity and all-pervasiveness, that came to be challenged. Over the last fifteen years, a succession of studies on the administration of justice, church discipline, poor relief, and the functioning of urban neighborhoods, both in Germany and elsewhere, has convincingly demonstrated that the states of early modern Europe were far too weak to meet the disciplinary intentions foisted upon them by twentieth-century historians. Even a cursory glance at the large numbers of criminal or civil cases dropped before a formal sentence was passed suggests a different, far more complicated story.[11] In practice the state had to negotiate with a host of other, mainly local, agencies; it was a matter of reciprocity and relationships based upon negotiation. Indeed, instead of the state's pervading society at all regional and local levels, it was rather the other way round: much of the impetus to state formation came from below. To quote Heinrich Richard Schmidt, in a forceful argument against the etatism of the concept, it was "through its demand for regulation that society created the modern state."[12]

In England (where interestingly the top-to-bottom constructs of acculturation, social discipline, or civilization have hardly caught on among historians), it was not so much the dominance of the state as that of the ruling class that came to be questioned. While one group of historians interpreted the eighteenth-century law above all as an instrument of class oppression and another group argued that much of the early modern English state, including its social and geographical depth, had already evolved in the Middle Ages, a third group followed the historian Keith Wrightson, who was among the first to reflect on the effective presence of the Tudor and early Stuart state in the localities and to elucidate the role of the "middling groups" in the local administration of the law. He distinguished a "reformation of manners" in this period, a cluster of governmental and religious campaigns aimed at the "manners" of the poor.[13] At present, as Robert von Friedeburg reminds us, Wrightson's model has been modified in several respects. One of these, elaborated here by Von Friedeburg in an interesting comparison of Essex and the German region of Hesse-Cassel, concerns the degree to which such campaigns initiated from above were still rooted in the local mechanisms of social control.

Inspired by Wrightson and his seminal ideas, a couple of younger historians have eventually brought the state back into the argument. Michael Braddick and

Steve Hindle, amongst others, have analyzed the participatory nature of "what we are learning to call 'state formation,'" as Wrightson put it in 1996.[14] They stress the growing infrastructural reach of the early modern English state and the intensifying interaction between the state and local societies.[15] To quote Hindle, "State authority was manifested not only in initiatives of control by central agencies, but also as a popular resource for the peaceful ordering of society, which might be employed and promoted at highly localised levels." Indeed, the state "did not become more active at the expense of society; rather, it did so as a consequence of social need." There is a clear resemblance here with Schmidt's observation quoted above.[16]

Both the English and the German debates, then, have focused on the state, though in the German case it was and is its supposed pervasiveness, in the English case its supposed weakness or lack of growth, that has been queried. Ironically, both the enlarging and the reducing of the state's significance led to an undervaluation of the social and geographical depth of early modern state formation, of the many interactive and negotiating relations between central and local authorities. Recently, in a promising convergence of perspectives these relations have come to the fore in both the English and the German controversies.[17] Focusing on this convergence, I will discuss some of the central issues that have dominated the most recent historical writings on social control and that also dominate the chapters in this part of the volume.

Issues of Honor and Reputation

In her impressive analysis of the late-fourteenth-century Zürcher *Ratsgericht,* one of the first studies to actually query the concept of social discipline, Susanna Burghartz contends that the primary function of this institution was not to discipline or criminalize. By imposing sanctions, mostly fines, it aimed to settle all sorts of disputes among the Zürich inhabitants and thus, in the interest of the entire community, to guarantee the urban peace. Zürich, as so many late Medieval towns, witnessed an honor culture in which the victims of verbal and physical violence, by addressing the *Ratsgericht,* sought to restore their blemished reputations. As Burghartz points out, theories viewing the violence dealt with by the Zürich magistracy as deviant behavior to be repressed, or as illustrating an earlier stage in Elias's civilizing process, would miss the social significance of honor and the ensuing demand for both formal and informal dispute settlement.[18] A very similar point of view, building upon a wealth of new research, is developed by Gerd Schwerhoff in this volume.

Comparable conclusions, pointing to the contemporary meanings of honor and assessing the lower secular or religious courts as instruments for the restoring of "friendship" and local peace, have been presented by other Continental historians, among them Martin Dinges, Michael Frank, Schmidt, and Schwerhoff.[19] Following on his definition of social control, Dinges approached honor as a form of "symbolic capital," a complex and potent set of rules for defending one's reputation in public (where it was constantly assessed and reassessed). The rules determined the duty to defend one's honor and its forms and contents, including the appeal to a third party. As symbolic capital, honor acted as a special type of social control. It allowed people to define deviant behavior and to take proper steps, including the strategic redefinition of different (for instance, economic) disputes in terms of honor.[20]

Dinges's conceptual distinctions have found fertile soil among historians as has the notion of *agonale Kommunikation,* coined by Rainer Walz. Village culture, so Walz writes, was strongly "agonal": it was determined by the daily competition for scarce goods and even more so by the nature of this struggle, by the constant attempts to tarnish the reputations of others, by the ever present insults, threats, and other violence. In anchoring the consensual notions of friendship, reconciliation, and peace (so often appealed to in the settling of honor disputes), in a social reality that was far from harmonious, Walz's insights have been very important indeed.[21] In the last decade the historical anthropology of honor and reputation has become a well-researched subject in Germany, with a prominent role for gender history[22] and a growing interest (as represented here by Ingram and especially, in a European overview, by Carl Hoffmann) in the functioning of urban neighborhoods.[23] Many of these studies have taken a critical stance toward the notion of social discipline. As Dinges observes, by studying honor and the many institutions of local governance that men and women appealed to in defending their reputations, one may examine the assumption, implicit both in the concepts of social discipline and Elias's civilizing process, of the undisciplined nature of those to be disciplined.[24]

In England research into honor and reputation has flourished equally. As Ingram put it, defamation cases were "peculiarly characteristic of early modern English society."[25] Much of this work has focused on church court and quarter sessions material, with again a striking contribution from gender history[26] and also from neighborhood studies.[27] As in Germany, the high number of cases dropped was quickly noticed; the availability of arbitration both in the courts and elsewhere, so Jim Sharpe observes, was the litigants' main motive for doing so.[28] However, issues of state formation are hardly discussed in this research. An interesting exception is Robert Shoemaker. Finding a remarkable decline of public insult in eighteenth-century London, he argues, against Elias, that this decline was more related to a civilizing process coming from below than to any civilizing pressures from above.[29]

Recently, the duel in early modern England has been reassessed as well. Inspired by some recent work on Italy[30], Markku Peltonen has convincingly demonstrated that the early modern duel originated in the Renaissance ideology of courtesy and civility, thus rejecting the widely held view (whether or not informed by Elias) that a lingering Medieval culture of honor and violence came to be replaced with this new culture of civility. To put it differently, contemporaries saw the duel not only as an object but also as a medium of social control—and a refined and even conciliatory one at that. Confronted with the meticulous rules of civility, dueling became one of the chief means to the English gentleman of restoring his honor, once the rules were breached. Of course, dueling also had its opponents and its relationship with the law and official attitudes was, to say the least, an ambivalent one.[31] A less refined medium, involving a more "plebeian" notion of honor, was the "ridings" or "skimmington rides" (the English variant of charivari), in this volume discussed by Martin Ingram. Though rather situated at the other end of the social spectrum, this jocular form of folk justice was considered, at least in the sixteenth and seventeenth centuries, as no less a supplement to state justice (cf. Garnot's *parajustice*) as the aristocratic—and far from jocular—duel of honor.[32]

Issues of Enmity and Amity

In discussing the etatism implied in the notion of social discipline, Schmidt offers an extensive overview of what he calls the "communal" side of moral discipline (*Sittenzucht*).[33] Focusing primarily on the Protestant churches, he concludes that the widespread processes of "confessionalization" (defined by Reinhardt and Schilling as the first phase in the long-term process of social discipline) were invariably locally committed and motivated. The Calvinist and Zwinglian churches, with their well-known presbyterial structures, are a case in point, but the same may be said for the other Protestant churches. Crucial to this communal rooting were the widespread practices of precommunion peacemaking. As Schmidt explains, these rituals were not only central to the Calvinist and Zwinglian notions of communion but also to those of the Lutheran, the Anglican, and the Counter Reformation Church. All over Europe, particularly in the Protestant churches of Switzerland, Germany, France, the Netherlands, England, Scotland, and Scandinavia, enmity was perceived as an impediment to receiving the sacrament. Neighbors bearing ill will toward one another should first have their disputes settled. Indeed, as David Sabean puts it in his fine study on the county of Württemberg, to abstain from communion was "the formal, public recognition of a quarrel."[34]

Building upon the work of Peter Blickle and on recent research into petitioning, resistance, and the uses of justice, Schmidt goes on to argue that there was no such thing as an already fully grown state steamrollering society.[35] The state evolved only as a response to the social needs of its subjects and the communal forms of local government. To grasp that process, says Schmidt, one might turn to the sociologist Anthony Giddens and his concept of the "locally embedded society."[36]

Somewhat surprisingly, neither Schmidt nor his German colleagues seem to have assimilated the work of John Bossy on "peace" and "charity." To Bossy the Christianity of the Middle Ages ("traditional Christianity," as he calls it), was strongly geared to the notion of charity, meaning not an act of benevolence (such as almsgiving to the poor), but a state of Christian harmony "which one was in or out of regarding one's fellows." The latter encompassed both the dead and the living and both one's enemies and friends. Central to the liturgy of the Mass were the "kiss of peace" and the commemoration of the living and the dead. The same message of love and amity, of "fictive kinship," was disseminated in the rites of baptism and holy matrimony, in the late Medieval confraternities and guild organizations, and in such paraliturgical rituals as the popular Corpus Christi processions. By the end of the fifteenth century, it was deeply embedded in the Church and Christianity at large.[37]

Recently, Bossy has returned to the subject, examining how this traditional idea of charity may have survived both the Reformation and the Counter-Reformation. He now speaks of a "moral tradition" in which three notions converge: "the notion or practical instinct that to be a Christian means to love your neighbour, and in particular your enemy; the fact that in these times and places it was very likely that people might be in a state of enmity towards others, which would call for arrangements of peacemaking if it was to be resolved; and the historic or perhaps archaic connection between these arrangements and the sites, rites and persons of the church."[38] He has traced the tradition, in particular its arrangements for precommunion peacemaking, in Italy, France, Germany, and England, often using the findings of criminal historians of church courts and similar institutions. His conclusions, allowing for the various and often contradictory trends in both the Catholic Church and the Protestant churches, are surprisingly positive. Apparently, the moral tradition was not waning but waxing during the post-Reformation. It was repressed by Catholic and Protestant Reformers alike but the effect of their campaigns seems to have been only temporary. The tradition simply returned, if it had even been halted at all. Indeed, as Bossy concludes, both churches may have "secured or retained the loyalty of their populations by proving themselves fit vessels of the moral tradition"—another instance of negotiatory relations. Depending for its persuasiveness "on the force of personal, face-to-face, eyeball-to-eyeball enmity," the tradition would only decline with the rise of civility and civil society.[39]

Clearly, Bossy's positive view on the Christianity of the Middle Ages and his argument on the continuity of the moral tradition run counter to any notions of acculturation or social discipline.[40] Important is his emphasis on the indissolubility of amity and enmity—of the ideals of peace and friendship on the one hand and the daily realities of social strife and conflict on the other hand. In this respect his understanding of the sixteenth and seventeenth centuries is very different from, for instance, the idealizing consensual society portrayed by Cynthia

Herrup.[41] There is a striking resemblance here with the later focus among German historians on notions of *Feindschaft* and *agonale Kommunikation.*

As both Schmidt and Bossy suggest, it should be easy to trace more instances of the moral tradition. As Hoffmann shows, it was still alive in the urban neighborhoods of the seventeenth and eighteenth centuries; nor did it suddenly disappear from institutions such as guilds and confraternities. Tomás Mantecón describes how the Spanish guilds and confraternities (with their "peacemakers") were perceived as complementary to the social regulation offered by families and neighborhoods, and he traces their consensual notions and practices until the last decades of the ancien régime. Katherine Lynch has presented a similar argument. Writing on western Europe as a whole, she also characterizes the confraternities as complementary to the primary bonds of the nuclear family. And she goes on to trace the continuities, including the consensual notions of peace and harmony, between the late Medieval confraternities and the new, no less communally rooted institutions of poor relief founded by Lutheran, Calvinist, and Roman Catholic townspeople alike. She concludes, "To see the imposition of behavioral regulations on individuals and families as nothing more than 'top down' social policy imposed by urban elites would be a mistake." Finally, Maarten Prak examines the craft guilds of western Europe and the strategies used by these institutions to make their regulations stick. Though they failed in controlling the journeymen (who often started their own brotherhoods or *compagnonnages*), in other economic, religious, and moral respects the guild regulations proved reasonably effective, including the maintenance of ideals of fictive kinship.[42]

The ideals of amity, then, did not disappear after the Reformation and the Counter-Reformation, but they certainly acquired new meanings in the process. Ian Archer, for instance, perceives an already "changing conception of brotherhood" in the companies of Elizabethan London. The communal bond was still there, but it had become "a more hierarchically articulated one."[43] In the sixteenth century *charity* also took on a new meaning, from a state of Christian harmony to an act of benevolence. But Bossy cautions against taking this semantic change as anything more than a hint of how social reality may have changed; taking it too literally would imply that the moral tradition had already disappeared in the turmoil of the sixteenth century. According to Bossy, it was only the rise of civility and civil society that ended the tradition. As a consequence of this "current of civility"—was it "welling up from below"?—the enmity that the moral tradition had always tried to contain would gradually decrease.[44] Other, mainly German, historians have pointed to the long-term process of *Verrechtlichung,* the steady rise in judicial jurisdiction, to account for the waning of communal ideals. Due to this increase the neighborhoods, guilds, and confraternities were slowly hedged in. But others have pointed to the simultaneous instances of *Entrechtlichung* (see also Hoffmann). Clearly, the waning of the moral tradition was a multilayered phenomenon; we still need further research to complete the picture.

The Uses of Justice

So far we have been looking at issues of state formation, of honor and reputation, and of enmity and amity. But questions regarding the "experience of authority" or, more precisely, the "uses of justice" (who used the law, for what purposes, and with what effects?) have hitherto been discussed only in a cursory manner.

The term uses of justice (*Justiznutzung*) was introduced by Martin Dinges in his stimulating analysis of the defamation charges filed before the police commissioners in eighteenth-century Paris. According to Dinges, going to court was just one option to pursue one's interests. It was often the last step in quite a history of steps or it was a "last warning," a conscious strategy to boost the pressure on one's opponent to accept a settlement out of court. Even pending the official procedure, the plaintiffs could always withdraw and opt for an informal or quasi-formal arrangement.[45]

In his contribution to this volume, Dinges has considerably developed this idea, taking his examples from Germany and various other countries, including England—another indication of how the English and the German debates now seem to converge. Important to his argument, for instance, is Robert Shoemaker's study of the prosecution of misdemeanors in London and rural Middlesex. Misdemeanors are interesting, because in deciding to prosecute and in choosing a method of prosecution, victims and officials enjoyed far greater discretion than in the case of felonies. Shoemaker discusses these discretionary choices, in particular as exercised by the justices of the peace, but we are also informed about the choices of both plaintiffs and defendants. Generally, they could choose from three procedures: informal mediation by a justice of the peace; binding over by recognizance; or summary jurisdiction. In the last case the defendant could be fined or committed to a house of correction. The system proved a flexible and successful one.[46]

Recognizances have been studied by Hindle as well. Magistrates could bind people over for a fixed sum (or "recognizance") and for a fixed period to keep the peace and be of good behavior. Hindle relates this procedure to Bossy's discussion of amity and enmity. As he explains, binding over "acted as a non-aggression pact, initially precluding any further physical self-assertion, and subsequently allowing a cooling-off period during which negotiation, either 'informally'" (through mediation) or 'quasi-formally' (through arbitration), might restore disputing parties to the condition of charity." In fact, the immense popularity of the procedure depended exactly on its curtailing head-on conflict, while avoiding or at least postponing the much more consequential procedure of summary jurisdiction.[47]

A third English illustration of the uses of justice is Peter King's study on justice and discretion in the years 1740 to 1820. King calls the period covered by his study the "golden age" of discretionary justice in England. Focusing on theft as prosecuted in the courts of Essex, he shows how the judicial system offered countless opportunities for discretion, from the pretrial phase to that of formal conviction and punishment. Indeed, though the law forbade felonies to be settled informally, a substantial number of cases were dropped before a trial could take place. Important is King's assessment of the social groups involved. Contrary to Hay's conclusions, it was not a matter of class oppression. The middling sort, the broad group of farmers, tradesmen, and artisans, exercised the most discretionary power, in particular in their capacity as jurors or parish officers, but even the laboring poor knew surprisingly well how to use the law. As King concludes, the law was an arena of struggle, negotiation, and accommodation: having different meanings for different people at different stages of the process, it was used intensively by all social classes.[48]

Conclusion

Although the debates in England and Germany began from very different positions, they now gradually seem to converge in their orientation on the social and geographical depth of the early modern state, on its interactive and negotiatory involvement with local governance. In the process one-sided conceptualizations such as acculturation, social discipline, and civilizing process (in its limited sense of interventions from above) have proved inadequate. As Hindle and Schmidt point out, the state was primarily created as a consequence of social need, as a response to society's (especially the middle and lower classes') demand for regulation. In addition to this, they and other historians have indicated that this demand did not prevent the state from injecting its public authority into the process, that there was also, for instance in the popular practice of binding over, a "symbolically edging forward" of its boundaries.[49]

Recently, a similar conclusion has been drawn by Karl Härter, an expert on German police ordinances (*Policeyordnungen*). Though he discards the notion of social discipline, acknowledging how numerous social groups through conventions (*Landtage*), gravamina, or petitions could directly or indirectly influence legislation, he also emphasizes how the state, in its response to society's demand for regulation, gradually expanded its range and instrumentarium.[50] Perhaps we should reserve the notions of acculturation, social discipline, and civilization (again in its limited sense) to the authorities' intentions and reserve other, more flexible and less anachronistic notions for the complex, negotiatory relationships involved.[51] The coming years will tell us whether such ideas will hold. One conclusion stands out: the new perspectives on the nature of early modern state formation have definitely moved the debate forward on social control in early modern Europe. The chapters that follow all bear witness to this.

Notes

1. Hay, "Property, Authority and the Criminal Law," 17–63; cf. Thompson, *Whigs and Hunters,* 259–69.

2. See for instance Muchembled, *L'invention de l'homme moderne;* Schilling, "Disziplinierung oder 'Selbstreguliering der Untertanen.'"

3. Elias, *The Civilizing Process,* 295n.; of course, Elias has never developed this notion of a noncourtly line of civilization.

4. Hindle, "The Keeping of the Public Peace," 237–38; Shoemaker, "The Decline of Public Insult," 130–31; for a balanced summary of Elias's theory and also for some trenchant criticisms, see Schwerhoff, "Zivilisationsprozess und Geschichtswissenschaft"; cf. Pieter Spierenburg, "Violence and the Civilizing Process."

5. Castan, *Honnêteté et relations sociales,* 70.

6. Lenman and Parker, "The State, the Community and the Criminal Law in Early Modern Europe"; Bossy, "Postscript."

7. Ignatieff, "State, Civil Society and Total Institutions," 75–105.

8. Dinges, *Der Maurermeister und der Finanzrichter,* 169 ("alle Arten, in denen Personen abweichendes Verhalten definieren und darauf . . . durch eine Maßnahme reagieren").

9. See also Schwerhoff, *Aktenkundig und Gerichtsnotorisch,* 126.

10. Garnot, "Justice, infrajustice, parajustice et extrajustice"; for both the complexity and the fruitfulness of the concept, see Loetz, "L'infrajudiciaire," 545–62. See also Garnot, ed., *L'infrajudiciaire.*

11. Dinges, "Frühneuzeitliche Armenfürsorge als Sozialdisziplinierung?"; Schmidt, *Dorf und Religion;* Schwerhoff, *Köln im Kreuzverhör;* cf. for the Dutch Republic: Roodenburg, "Reformierte Kirchenzucht und Ehrenhandel."

12. Schmidt, "Sozialdisziplinierung?" 680.

13. Wrightson, *English Society,* chaps. 6–7. For a helpful discussion of the phrase "reformation of manners," see Ingram, "Reformation of Manners"; the author discusses the term's complex relationship with "civility" (but see also Bryson, *From Courtesy to Civility*), points to similar active campaigns in the fifteenth and early-sixteenth centuries (but see also Mcintosh, *A Community Transformed*), and cautions (like Von Friedeburg) that all such campaigns were always based on a routine system of regulating behavior.

14. Wrightson, "The Politics of the Parish in Early Modern England," 25.

15. Braddick, "State Formation and Social Change in Early Modern England"; idem, *State Formation in Early Modern England;* Hindle, *The State and Social Change in Early Modern England.*

16. Hindle, *The State and Social Change in Early Modern England,* 16.

17. In distinguishing a growing convergence, I do not mean to say that England and Germany have never been compared in their respective systems of social control. An interesting exception is the work of Robert von Friedeburg,; see for instance his contribution to this volume and his recent *Self Defence and Religious Strife.*

18. Burghartz, "Disziplinierung oder Konfliktregelung?"

19. Dinges, *Der Maurermeister und der Finanzrichter;* Frank, *Dörfliche Gesellschaft und Kriminalität;* Schmidt, *Dorf und Religion;* Schwerhoff, *Köln im Kreuzverhör.*

20. Dinges, *Der Maurermeister und der Finanzrichter,* 172; to avoid the economic determinism still implicit in Bourdieu's notion of "symbolic capital" and to avoid the association that honor could be accumulated, the author prefers to speak of *symbolisches Vermögen* ("symbolic capacity" or "power").

21. Walz, "Agonale Kommunikation," 221; cf. Schwerhoff in this volume.

22. Dinges, "Die Ehre als Thema der Stadtgeschichte"; idem, "'Weiblichkeit' in 'Männlichkeitsritualen'"? idem, "Ehrenhändel als kommunikative Gattungen"; idem, *Der Maurermeister und der Finanzrichter;* Bock, "Frauenräume und Frauenehre"; Burghartz, "Rechte Jungfrauen oder unverschämte Töchter?"; Schwerhoff, *Köln im Kreuzverhor,* 312–22; Schreiner and Schwerhoff, eds., *Verletzte Ehre;* Backmann et al., eds., *Ehrkonzepte in der frühen Neuzeit.*

23. Dinges, "Die Ehre als Thema der Stadtgeschichte"; idem, *Der Maurermeister und der Finanzrichter,* 173–215; Garrioch, *Neighborhood and Community in Paris;* Roeck, "Neighbourhoods and the Public"; Hoffmann, "Nachbarschaften als Akteure," 187–202; cf. for the Netherlands: Roodenburg, "'Freundschaft,' 'Brüderlichkeit' und 'Einigkeit'"; idem, "Naar een etnografie van de vroegmoderne stad"; idem, "Reformierte Kirchenzucht," 129–52; Dorren, *Eenheid en verscheidenheid;* for a general overview: Lis and Soly, "Neighborhood Social Change."

24. Dinges, "Die Ehre als Thema der historischen Anthropologie," 61–62; for a similar perspective on the Netherlands and referring to Calvinist church discipline, neighborhood control, and honor conflicts, see Roodenburg, "Reformierte Kirchenzucht."

25. Ingram, *Church Courts, Sex and Marriage,* 319.

26. Sharpe, *Defamation and Sexual Slander;* idem, "Such Disagreement betwyx Neighbours"; Ingram, *Church Courts, Sex and Marriage,* 292–319; Hindle, "The Shaming of Margaret Knowsley"; Meldrum, "A Women's Court in London"; Gowing, *Domestic Dangers;* Foyster, *Manhood in Early Modern England;* Turner, "'Nothing Is So Secret But Shall Be Revealed'"; Shoemaker, "The Decline of Public Insult"; on Scotland: Leneman, "Defamation in Scotland"; Todd, *The Culture of Protestantism.*

27. Garrioch, *Neighbourhood and Community;* Boulton, *Neighbourhood and Society;* and see note 30.

28. Sharpe, "Such Disagreement betwyx Neighbours," 175; similar conclusions in Gowing and Ingram.

29. Shoemaker, "Decline," 130–31; for a more nuanced interpretation of Elias, see above.

30. See for example Muir, *Mad Blood Stirring,* 247–72; idem, "The Double Binds of Manly Revenge in Renaissance Italy," 65–82; Weinstein, "Fighting or Flyting?"; Quint, "Duelling and Civility," 231–78.

31. Peltonen, *The Duel in Early Modern England.*

32. On charivari, see also Hoffmann in this volume.

33. Schmidt, "Sozialdisziplinierung?"

34. David Sabean, *Power in the Blood,* 47.

35. For Blickle and petitioning, see for instance *Resistance, Representation and Community.*

36. Schmidt, "Sozialdisziplinierung?" 680.

37. Bossy, *Christianity in the West;* see also his "Blood and Baptism," "Holiness and Society," and "Postscript."

38. Bossy, *Peace in the Post-Reformation,* 2.

39. Ibid., 96–100.

40. Cf. O'Maley, *Trent and All That,* 10: "Bossy's view of the Christianity of the Middle Ages tends to be as positive as Delumeau's is negative."

41. Herrup, *The Common Peace;* for this discussion see also Hindle, "The Keeping of the Public Peace," 215–16.

42. For guilds and confraternities in England, see also Brigden, "Religion and Social Obligation"; McRee, "Religious Guilds and Regulations of Behavior." Idem, "Religious Guilds and Civic Order"; for the Dutch Republic, see Palmen, "De gilden en hun sociale betekenis,"221—33; on the Dutch urban militia guilds, see Knevel, *Burgers in het geweer,* 53–62, 161–76.

43. Archer, *The Pursuit of Stability,* 120, 124; see also Heal, *Hospitality,* 392–93, 402.

44. Bossy, *Peace in the Post-Reformation,* 97.

45. Dinges, *Der Maurermeister und der Finanzrichter,* 177–82; cf. for the French countryside: Fontaine, "Les villageois dans et hors du village."

46. Shoemaker, *Persecution and Punishment.*

47. Hindle, "The Keeping of the Public Peace," 217.

48. King, *Crime, Justice and Discretion.*

49. Hindle, "The Keeping of the Public Peace," 237.

50. Härter, "Soziale Disziplinierung durch Strafe?" 365–79.

51. Cf. Dinges, "Policeyforschung statt 'Sozialdisziplinierung'"? 344.

CHAPTER 9

The Uses of Justice As a Form of Social Control in Early Modern Europe

Martin Dinges

Introduction

As many studies of the history of criminal justice in early modern Europe testify, the number of indictments dropped before a final verdict was reached was surprisingly high.[1] They far surpassed the number of procedures resulting in formal convictions. Apparently, there was a great discrepancy between the number of accusations taken as cases into court and those actually tried. One explanation for the courts' behavior might be that they considered the issues raised in the accusations irrelevant and wished to unburden themselves of such trifling controversies. This institutional filtering of unwelcome affairs is then construed as a successful example of judicial policies. In keeping with these policies, the courts prosecuted only those cases deemed important by the authorities, the alleged controllers of the institutions of justice. This interpretation has been offered for the French judicial policies of the 1760s, when the prosecution of violence was toned down in favor of the prosecution of theft. Similar spurts in the criminalization and decriminalization of certain offenses have been observed elsewhere. In this view the institutions of justice were merely instruments in the hands of the authorities; it was a question of "top-down" social control.

However, when viewed from a different perspective, that of the actual plaintiffs, the large number of dropped cases may be explained in another way. It might equally be argued that having recourse to justice was never intended to institute and conclude proceedings. Rather, lodging a complaint was merely one of a myriad of possibilities for making oneself heard in a conflict out of court.[2] Submitting a case to court was simply an instrument for advancing the settlement of a personal conflict by taking it to a higher—mostly a government—authority. To put it differently, the many cases dropped could indicate that people used the institutions of justice merely as an additional instrument of everyday social control, not dissimilar to an admonition or a form, even a violent form, of self-help. Lodging a complaint, then, was merely a judicial step. Whether that procedure also led to a formal conviction was totally inconsequential to the parties involved. Adopting this perspective, namely the plaintiffs' motivations, we must first examine the demand for justice.

The concept of the "uses of justice" is interpreted as referring to the many ways in which contemporary individuals have dealt with the courts. It denotes both the recourse to justice and the forms this took. The courts are understood as an institution of the authorities, whose activities were only partially determined by those in charge. In general, the role of the courts was equally determined by the people. In the long term, such processes of appropriation can alter the institution's nature as much as any reforms of the judicial system initiated from above. Clearly, the uses of justice can tell us much about how early modern Europeans perceived the functions of the criminal courts.

In taking this position, we are confronted with a range of theoretical and empirical perspectives, in the first place with the widespread assumption that in supplying justice the authorities also determined its demand. Writing about some long-term changes in Castilian justice in the Spanish Golden Age, the historian Richard Kagan argued how a first phase of intensive recourse to justice and of institutional development was succeeded by a second one, in which a deliberate establishing of thresholds only widened the gulf between the royal courts and the population. Considering the national and later the urban interests as the driving force behind this development, Kagan considered the plaintiffs' behavior as merely a dependent factor.[3]

A similar bias may be found in Wolfgang Schmale's comparison of the judicial cultures in early modern Saxony and Burgundy.[4] Though he takes the demand for justice as his point of departure, his overall perspective is that of a modernization theory centering on the gradual differentiation of our present-day separation of powers between the judicial and the executive. Compared to Burgundy, Saxony experienced more disputes around its judicial system, but these are discussed simply as "system errors." The author does not acknowledge that people could negotiate the organization of the courts by proceeding more frequently against their functioning. To find out how people maintained their judicial interests, it may be useful to examine concepts other than their legal acculturation or the "professionalization" of the courts.

Again, in relating peaks in the lodging of complaints to the concrete interests of the groups involved (for instance the promoting of stricter morals regarding premarital sex or of stricter poor relief), scholars have already reconstructed collective uses of justice for a variety of issues. The plaintiffs determined a government's chances of having its policies realized, particularly with respect to moral campaigns. Adopting Keith Wrightson's notion of the "two concepts of order," justice might be said to have functioned well in terms of what the authorities envisaged when the government's concepts of order and those of the population agreed. However, the authorities could hardly realize their own concept when the most prominent sections of the population pursued different interests.

Looking solely at the meaning of the uses of justice for the two concepts of order would already reduce the analysis of how people confronted the courts to the issue of social order in general. We learn nothing about the social effects of those uses of justice that do not agree with the mainstream of a particular phase. Individual strategies for extrajudicial conflict settlement, the lion's share of all activities to generate social order, are left aside.

Finally, I mention Robert Shoemaker's study of misdemeanors in London and Middlesex in 1660–1725, approximately, and his analysis of cycles in the recourse to justice.[5] His comparison of town and country and his sustained quantification provide a precise assessment of its structure. He argues how phases during which the population relied less on the judicial institutions alternated with other phases—sometimes short-lived—during which the population displayed greater confidence in the courts. Examining some recent comparisons of Germany and the Netherlands, one is even tempted to dismiss the notion of a long-term acculturation of the institutions of justice. The Netherlands still cherishes its tradition of extrajudicial settlement within small social entities, such as neighborhoods or local and church communities.[6] Certain forms of legal council underscore this trend. As Dutch public order does not function less than, for instance, that in Nordrhein-Westfalen, it may be inferred that an expansion of justice is in no way identical to an analogous increase in public order. Looking at the past, we can no longer accept assessments that more often than not adopt this very premise.

What these and other findings suggest is that closer inspection of justice from the perspective of its uses is in order. We are confronted with a history of constant change, not only of the institutions and their supply but also of the population, thus supporting the basic assumption of a permanently variable relationship between the judicial and nonjudicial settlement of conflicts. This would apply particularly for those periods in which a balanced legal system and a well-regulated court system had yet to materialize. Clearly, in analyzing the role of justice in the generation of social order, a more careful look should be taken at the importance of the nonjudicial forms of conflict settlement.

The concept of social control that I propose here encompasses both a horizontal and a vertical dimension of control.[7] As such, it accords better with an anthropologically informed notion of history than with the concept—well known in Germany—of "social discipline" (*Sozialdisziplinierung*). Social control in its narrow sense is understood as "all forms by which historical agents define deviant behavior and react to it by taking measures."[8] Society is seen as a permanent process of mutual social control in which norms compete with one another and are constantly being contested. Accordingly, one should always allow for multiple instruments of social control and integrate the supply of judicial institutions into a continuum of everyday strategies. My definition also implies the reversibility of moral campaigns and their sanctions. Crucial to my definition's view of society is, of course, the unequal distribution of power resources and spheres of influence among the agents of social control. Starting from here, this chapter aims to clarify the significance of justice as but one of the instruments of mutual social control and so widen the field for a more encompassing analysis of social control.

Helping Oneself or Using Justice?

Basically, it is far from natural to exert social control by appealing to an institution of justice. Most people first try to react directly to deviant behavior or call in a third party as arbitrator. And, there was always the possibility of a partly tolerated, violent form of self-help, which could even take the form of a strongly ritualized and therefore regulated reaction to deviancy. If necessary, people could mobilize arbiters from, for instance, their families, local dignitaries, or the lower clergy. The settlements reached—even in conflicts of a criminal nature—could be registered with a notary in countries where notaries were generally available. With regard to the English justices of the peace, the importance of such settlements may now be assessed numerically. In up to two-thirds of the conflicts examined, the plaintiffs preferred an informal to a formal settlement, and this was the case even with crimes strictly falling under the jurisdiction of the courts.[9]

In England around 1700 it was far from obvious to crime victims that they should inform a criminal court. Instead, they opted for procedures (mostly extrajudicial) that would result in compensation. Accordingly, most plaintiffs had an instrumental attitude to justice, preferring indemnity of their material interests. Such uses of the judicial institutions tell us little about the people actually endorsing the authorities' claims in criminal procedures. The plaintiffs often appealed to the courts simply to improve their own chances in the extrajudicial settlements, which they fundamentally preferred.

If informal settlements prospered even in the metropolises of Paris, London, or Cologne, these observations may be expected to apply in particular to the countryside. Shoemaker forwards four arguments to buttress this conclusion. First, the countryside with its notables had more generally acknowledged arbiters available. Second, because there was less mobility, the word of one's opponent could be more readily trusted. Third, the pressure exerted by the higher legal institutions to conduct a criminal case at the proper court may have been higher in the towns, as professional judges and lawyers competed for their market share. Finally, the less-well-to-do, both in the towns and in the countryside, probably far preferred the cheaper extrajudicial settlements or simplified procedures.[10]

In London, the lower classes' demand for informal settlements introduced a new procedure. For a nominal fee the justices of the peace could be asked to issue "recognizances," which in case of good behavior would not result in forfeiture. These low-priced threats were intended to achieve the same results as the more expensive formal pleas of guilt. This institutional support is a fine instance of the interplay between the dealings of the legal system and out-of-court procedures. Justices of the peace and judges perceived their role as arbiters as being more prestigious than their role as judges. A negotiated peace enjoyed higher esteem than a formal sentence. As the powers of the lower courts in England were only vaguely demarcated, all parties often preferred a settlement even in criminal matters. These as well as the higher courts worked much longer for negotiating peace than for disciplining. Clearly, by bringing gentle pressure to bear on the parties, the lower-court judges often underscored their readiness for reconciliation. By not accepting all accusations, the legal institutions themselves also encouraged informal settlements.

These findings bring us back to the question whether the courts' criminal prosecution should be interpreted as justice's overriding interest or merely as a primary one in cases of strongly deviant behavior. We should try to establish more clearly whether the criminal courts, in their massive everyday practice as a machine of justice, really aimed at imposing norms, or whether the courts, more than has been realized until now, simply felt obliged to inculcate a form of social control. In that case, justice would have considered itself a secondary institution.

Which Court to Use?

Initiating prosecution always pushes social control to a higher, more formal level, especially in criminal justice. To avoid the complex issue of the early modern courts' confusion of civil and criminal jurisdictions, in the next pages I will discuss only "criminal justice," meaning (resisting any technical criteria) those legal institutions that at least also had a kind of criminal jurisdiction. The definition thus encompasses marital courts and those institutions exercising moral discipline in the territories of the German Empire boasting an established church. All these institutions had a quasi-criminal procedure. Important to the uses of justice is that there were overlaps, both in the supply of regulations and sanctions, and that contemporaries knew perfectly well how to exploit the situation. They were quite aware of the functionally equivalent role of criminal justice and church discipline. Of course, this can only be assessed historically by taking seriously the daily practices of contemporaries in our attempt to understand historical processes.

Options for appealing to one or the other court and its sanctions were always available when various institutions competed for similar cases. Such competition is found between church courts on the one hand and criminal or similar courts, such as the village and higher governmental courts, on the other hand. People seem to have preferred the institutions directly within reach or the courts not presided over by any persons with a legal training.

Contemporaries understood the particular role of criminal justice. Benoît Garnot, for instance, concludes that the French were quite willing to use alternative courts.[11] The civil courts were more profitable for the judges and consequently more accessible than the coarser network of the criminal courts. The French also avoided the criminal courts because they feared their sometimes unfathomable brutality and the system's incalculable machinery. Around 1700, hoping to keep the damage under control, the English preferred courts that did not sentence the guilty to houses of correction but rather imposed lesser penalties.[12] The people pragmatically selected those courts that did not drastically contradict their own views of justice and kept open the options for possible reconciliation. In the southwest of France, the fear that justice would penalize crime even more severely led to an increase in extrajudicial settlements.[13] The accordance of the two concepts of order cherished by the population and the authorities held only as long as the court-imposed sanctions were considered suitable.

Since the criminal courts exercised such superior power over the defendants, Garnot's argument that it was criminal matters that the people preferred to settle out of court seems plausible.[14] In analyzing social control, the greatest insight will probably be gained from studying the uses of justice in the realm of criminal justice. However, care should be taken not to exaggerate the orientation of past societies to consensus. The criminal courts were generally consciously appealed to for a merely civil objective: fearing the nearing execution of a civil sentence, many plaintiffs risked a highly unpredictable ruling.

Even allowing for regional differences, the criminal courts were not particularly accessible, creating conditions in the countryside quite different from those in the towns. Despite the gradual unification of criminal justice in this period, a situation of legal pluralism persisted. It is precisely the longtime underutilization of the institutions that allows us to attempt a reconstruction of the choices either for the courts or for the other institutions and to seek additional clues as to what people preferred.

The Significance of Offenses for the Uses of Justice

Let us look more closely at Shoemaker's study of London and the south of England, as it perfectly illustrates what has been discussed so far. He first distinguishes two types of offenses: felonies and misdemeanors. Felonies afforded the users of justice less latitude because the interests of public prosecution prevailed. The more serious the offense (looking at the criteria of criminal law), the less elbow room there was for the people. However, crucial to the intensity of prosecution was the presence of judges who were personally involved. Individuals eager to prosecute looked for active judges, thus demonstrating the importance of "lay networks" for the exchange of information about which judges would be best for initiating prosecutions. Shoemaker rejects older hypotheses positing a direct relationship between demographic and economic trends on the one hand and patterns of prosecution on the other. Statistically, the cultural notions of plaintiffs and justices of the peace came first. Even allowing for a constellation with cooperative justices, the determining factor in criminal proceedings was the people's handling of accusations, and that was determined by three other factors: the nature of the offense, the person of the plaintiff, and that of the offender.[15]

The first factor is the clearest when taking the example of violence. After all, murder was not always murder. Its meaning changed, depending on whether it was committed in sixteenth-century Rome, the eighteenth-century Massif Central in France, or eighteenth-century Paris. In the sixteenth century the level of violence in southern Europe was double that of Europe north of the Alps, a gap that seems to have widened in the eighteenth and nineteenth centuries with the divergent development of the two areas, though north of the Alps we also note different trends in the violence registered for town and country. Underlying these changes in criminal statistics are also changes in the perception of violence. In France's Massif Central it was far from natural to report a murder even in the nineteenth century. To defend their honor, the inhabitants traditionally chose to take the law into their own hands. People acting on notions of honor perceive violence very differently from those geared to a public order guaranteed by the state. Depending on the amount of violence involved, the nonreporting of murder thus reveals a general restraint with respect to the courts.[16]

Violence was also differently perceived by its victims, meaning that even identical offenses may have been reported differently. Crucial to this are the limits of tolerance in the plaintiff's social environment and objectives, not the seriousness of a violent act as established in a legal text. In the area of sexual offenses, a woman's extramarital pregnancy and the bearing of an illegitimate child could generally go unreported, if she was protected by her environment—for instance, because she was reputed to be a good worker. Such cases were decided out of court, by local public opinion following its own views of what was socially acceptable. It might merely pass a provisional sentence or initiate prosecution for a formal conviction. In the early modern perception of things, the plaintiffs and offenders as people were more important than the offenses themselves.

The Plaintiff's Significance for the Uses of Justice: Who Uses Justice Actively?

Societies appear to allow for a certain degree of social deviance, although such tolerance may diminish when societies come under duress. We should therefore look beyond individual offenses and presume levels of tolerance that could vary in time and place and move in several directions simultaneously. For instance, it may well be that at the end of the eighteenth century an increasing tolerance for violence and extramarital sex went hand in hand with a decreasing tolerance for property crimes.

However, times of tolerance alternated with times of anxiety about personal safety, public morals, or one's socioeconomic position, making people more inclined to file charges. When societies feel insecure because serious crimes remained unsolved, as happened for instance in Paris after the Cartouche case or in London in times of demobilization, brief bursts of lodging complaints take place.[17] This heightened readiness to report offenses reveals that at such moments people looked upon one another with greater suspicion and used justice mainly to reassure themselves.

Religious groups involved in moral campaigns have somewhat different motivations. These "virtuosos," to quote Max Weber, tried to impose a more "Christian" life on their environment, believing this to be the only way of securing their own salvation and that of society as a whole. Relatively independently of any particular confession, though more widespread in Calvinist than in Anglican, Lutheran, or Roman Catholic contexts, for some years they would report offenses they saw as particularly dangerous, such as idleness, public games, drinking, dancing, and so on. Often coming from the middle classes, these religious crusaders deliberately searched for active justices of the peace to exploit the judicial system for their own purposes. Occasionally they succeeded in heightening the intensity of prosecution. They could also address consistory and church courts in territories dominated by the Calvinist and Anglican churches. In these campaigns it was exclusively the person of the plaintiff and his orthodox belief that determined the uses of justice.

A third type of accusation wave had a slightly different structure, arising mostly from socioeconomic tensions, for instance, from changeover crises in the country. In these cases the more affluent smallholders—who usually reported offenses—were the ones opposing a new emphasis on socially accepted relationships and the guaranteeing of hereditary succession. The charges particularly affected widows, single women, and the local youth. Illegitimate offspring should not become a public charge any more than needy strangers. Here justice is pragmatically exploited by the local upper classes and occasionally also by the middle classes precisely to ensure the unequal distribution of wealth. As the village of Terling reveals, such an increase in prosecuting offenses could easily be reversed following a community's economic recovery.

Besides these waves in the lodging of complaints, other motives related to the person of the plaintiff that favored or curbed the uses of justice may be distinguished. In all rural societies, so it seems, strangers hardly ever lodged complaints, confirming the notion that people only appealed to criminal justice as a last resort. Obviously, there had to be a long previous history and the insight that people had to get along with each other before an offense would be prosecuted. Still, this did not prevent the local population from being disturbed by strangers and prosecuting them to protect their local concepts of order from any deviancy. It is difficult to say whether this model also holds for the towns, where establishing just who was or was not a stranger was even more of a problem. The perception of otherness may tell us more about the uses of justice in the countryside than in the towns.

More important is that most of the plaintiffs at the criminal courts—and also most of the defendants—were men. Those disturbances of the peace that the gendered public considered important enough to be tried formally were committed and also caused by men. In the next pages I will modify this assumption somewhat, but it should be borne in mind that women more than men adhered to other agents of social control, such as the nuclear family, the neighborhood, or the wider family. From the perspective of gender history, the analysis of these other forms of social control exerted by and on women even becomes paramount.

Though numerical comparisons of the uses of justice may be biased by circumstances of gender, they provide interesting findings on the opportunities and obstacles women encountered defending their interests before the courts. These findings also allow us to examine more precisely how formal and less formal types of social control interlocked. Unfortunately, as they have hardly been examined, we have few statistical data on the gender of plaintiffs at our disposal. This notwithstanding, women seem to have been most active as such in the field of so-called petty crime. Naturally, such crime and its impact on everyday life were of far greater significance to contemporaries than is suggested by the legal term with its epithet "petty." Data on eighteenth-century Paris suggest that women disturbed the peace in only one of every four defamation cases. As plaintiffs they figured in every third case and as witnesses even in every two out of five cases.[18] Other studies will have to decide whether these findings may be generalized into a hypothesis of women's uses of justice. As one would expect, women figure most often as plaintiffs in cases exclusively (for instance, in the case of rape) or mainly (in cases such as marital violence) related to themselves. Yet recent research on such offenses discloses that the women themselves often became violent. Men did not prosecute, they just hit harder. Had they not, given prevailing ideas of masculinity, they might have advertised themselves within the community as a "softie" (*Waschlappen*, as it was called in Neckarhausen). At the same time, women could exploit their socially desirable self-image by reporting the offense with floods of tears.

Several factors, which could be described as gendered impediments to the uses of justice, may explain why women figured less frequently as plaintiffs before the courts. In a series of offenses, instead of lodging a complaint herself, the woman was represented by her husband. This is also found at the civil courts. A more decisive factor was women's dependent economic position. A battered wife or a wife swindled out of her inheritance would think twice before she brought her husband, the head of the family business, to court. Still, those who did prosecute a rabid husband were generally protected by the courts.

Such dependency surfaces particularly in cases of sexual aggression, an offense that did not much interest the courts. Because of their dependency, housewives often used the complaints as a warning shot. As women did not have equal access to the labor market, they were not interested in having the main provider of the household confined for any length of time. This and the fact that women rarely had large amounts of money may also explain why they preferred the simpler and cheaper procedures. In England, however, there is a vast difference between women in the country, who rarely lodged complaints, and those in town. Sometimes having a profession or living of their own, the latter were economically less dependent and used the courts and similar institutions with greater frequency. They primarily prosecuted by recognizance, which Shoemaker relates to their shortage of money. Working women used the judicial system more frequently and preferred its tougher procedures.[19]

Despite these findings for a European metropolis, having recourse to justice remained an option favored less by women than by men. On the whole these data do not allow any broader conclusions on the actual readiness of women to fight unwelcome behavior in a formal procedure, but they do reveal a range of specific impediments and inform us about the different options for men and women in similar situations.

To have access to justice, the plaintiff's class situation or socioeconomic position hardly mattered: plaintiffs and defendants often came from the same class. An important threshold was the expenses already referred to. Tariff reductions sometimes tripled the number of accusations, giving us an idea of how the uses of justice in the past were hampered by economic considerations. Judges in England—and they may have been typical—advised their poorer plaintiffs to invest their money in clothes for the family rather than in trying to obtain expensive indictments. In this way these plaintiffs were dissuaded from having recourse to justice because of the costs involved as well as the disdain of many a judge. As a consequence, they had to develop other forms of social control.

The Significance of the Offender for Lodging Complaints: Against Whom Is Justice Being Used?

In the last twenty years or so, historians have written extensively on the social profile of those subjected to criminal justice. Some tolerance thresholds held for all offenders: only crimes perceived as serious or committed repeatedly were reported to the courts. A premise of the tolerance of local societies is their ability to maintain the social order even when confronted with a certain degree of deviancy. But this is possible only when a code of conduct guarantees a fair and independent regulation of deviancy. This would not work without equal opportunity for the settling of disputes. Accordingly, an attack by ambush, as a particularly condemned

act, was reported to the courts. Even a local person who obstructed a fair conflict settlement within his or her community could expect to be summoned before
an outside institution of justice. Tolerance thresholds reveal both the central importance of informal settlements in early modern societies and the limitations of
their integrating capacities. The self-regulating qualities of the countryside seem
to display, no less than in the larger cities of the time, a striking boundary vis-
à-vis strangers; people were more inclined to use justice against them.

Similarly, in moral campaigns the lower classes, immigrants, and young single
women who had recently moved to town were singled out for prosecution, even
for minor offenses. In the case of older single women, the combination of age and
sex led people to assess their chances of defending themselves as low and so they
were particularly prosecuted against. In England the less severe procedures were more
frequently instituted against women and the sentences were generally milder.

The socioeconomic position of one's opponent had other consequences for
the uses of justice. For instance, it was more efficient and easier to negotiate extrajudicial settlements with people of property, because they could be expected to
effectively find sureties. In England, therefore, the poor were more readily indicted
or committed to a house of correction. This was done more easily as they could
not afford professional legal assistance, and they were exposed to harsher proceedings. If committed to a house of correction with all its various costs, they
incurred higher expenses than the people of property with their sureties.

How Were the Procedures for Prosecution Used?

Because popular views of the law were basically instrumental, its users may be expected
to have acted strategically. Examining the way the complaints were recorded, it appears
that the victims could submit their charges orally to a clerk, possibly legally trained.
If courts were not within reach, complaints could be submitted in writing, drawn
up by the plaintiff himself, or if he could not write by a third party. It is difficult
to say how in the sphere of criminal justice the professional or nonprofessional phras-
ing of the complaint affected the argumentation and the plaintiff's chances before
the court and how this changed in the course of the sixteenth to the eighteenth
century. Discourse analysis may be helpful at this point, because at courts with both
a civil and a criminal jurisdiction the skillful composing of the events could decide
which procedure would be followed. Even conflicts entailing bloodshed could be
filed as civil cases, although the victims of serious crimes seem to have preferred a
criminal procedure to bring the conflict to a higher, more official level.

Important to a successful staging in behalf of one's interests was the exact moment
when the history of the conflict with the defendant began. It allowed the plaintiff to determine the nature of the investigation to a substantial degree and to
keep the court in the dark about the actual background to the complaint. It was

advisable to represent oneself as a peace loving man or as a helpless woman, just as it was prudent to present oneself as having acted on impulse or under the influence of alcohol. Another way of rhetorically enhancing one's peacefulness was similarly used by plaintiffs in Paris, who emphasized that they felt compelled to come forward. They merely intended to employ the nonofficial instruments for keeping the peace, not to appeal to a court.[20]

Since only the written complaints have come down to us, we must bear in mind that this process of recording altered the original complaint: it was smoothed out and regimented by the clerk's questions and the discussion of the events. Crucial was the inclusion of the criminally significant features of the events, as these produced the legally relevant narratives that could win the case. The necessary cooperation between the clerk, with his specific legal expertise, and the plaintiffs makes these sources cultural hybrids. They inform us about the plaintiffs' agility, but the idea that popular culture would manifest itself here does not generally hold true. Instead, it is more useful to establish the plaintiff's linguistic latitude for each institution and each type of complaint. As such these texts constitute a nearly classic example of discourse analysis. As a discourse formation the judiciary only allowed for certain truths, although it also provided opportunities for saying things that otherwise would have been left unsaid.

People had many options for how to proceed with the judiciary. Probably the most important strategy, at least for the defendants, was simply to duck the courts. Considering early modern judicial organization, this was relatively easy, though it was more readily available to the floating groups among the population and to individuals repeatedly accused. Those who stayed could be prosecuted in case they did not show up. Another strategy was to deny the act. If the procedures were based on a defendant's confession, this could considerably affect the establishing of the truth. In a society characterized by elementary solidarities, the manipulating of witnesses played another prominent role. Although we only hear about such practices when detected, they were probably widespread.

Finally, at various phases of the proceedings, people asked for grace. At the moment of apprehension, authorized individuals, such as the offender's relatives, local priests, and local notables, could act to thwart the arrest. The notables could also influence the procedure at the hearing of witnesses. Asking for grace may be seen as another important aspect of the uses of justice. Widely practiced up to the end of the early modern period, it was even continued in the form of petitions. A last example of such practices is the special procedures, originally based on the king's right to pardon and submitted in letters bearing his seal (lettres de cachet).[21] In France they offered a noteworthy alternative to criminal proceedings. A convict's last chance was to negotiate to have the penalty changed. This is another aspect that has hardly been investigated for the early modern period. However, a relevant study of the later Middle Ages suggests that there may have been similar chances in the uses of justice in later periods. All these aspects reveal that the courts supplied numerous options for an active appropriation of justice in one's own interest. Justice, then, emerges more as an arena of divergent interests than as a locus of acculturation or social discipline.

How Did the Uses of Justice Work and What Do They Mean for the Original Conflicts?

Socially, recourse to criminal justice bespeaks a rift and—regardless of what traditional legal historians may say—should therefore not automatically be assessed as a means of pacification. On the contrary, appealing to a court initially intensified the conflict. At the same time, the rift was never so great that it could not be healed by the parties involved, as indicated by the huge discrepancy between the number of accusations and formal convictions. By nevertheless arriving at an agreement, plaintiffs withdrew numerous conflicts from the judicial system; they usually preferred to return to the less expensive forms of dispute settlement. It is exactly this massive, purely instrumental use of justice in order to enhance one's settlement chances that reveals how people chose to exert social control as autonomously as possible. A pacifying function of justice would then, paradoxically, come down to the fact that it was merely exploited additionally. Only in a minority of the cases leading to a conviction could it permanently end or intensify a conflict.

Nor should justice's pacifying effects in other constellations be overestimated. For instance, cases in which the filing of criminal charges was meant to prevent the execution of a civil sentence reveal that one legal option was chosen in order to thwart the arbitral effects of another one. Trials lost constituted the background of one-seventh of the Parisian honor conflicts I examined.[22] Such switching from legal proceedings to often violent behavior has been observed elsewhere. Obviously, the courts could broaden the social rift. For some who lost a trial, then, the recourse to justice could increase the need for other forms of social control. The uses of justice were only a part of a continuum of such tools and were not perceived by contemporaries as superior in any way. The specific impediments encountered by women and the poor also had their secondary power effects on informal mediation. Since these groups could not successfully threaten to take people to trial, they had a lesser chance of succeeding by settling out of court.

What Do the Uses of Justice Contribute to the Realization of Local Peace and State Building?

Asking what the uses of justice meant for the role of criminal justice in early modern state building, we may look first at the context in which the government institutions were appropriated. The clearly discernible practice of a self-reliant recourse to justice confirms what we know from other fields in the administration of justice, such as the prosecuting of witches. Walter Rummel, for instance, demonstrated how in filing charges people greatly appropriated the government-inspired discourse on witchcraft while simultaneously pursuing their own interests in the unmasking of other witches.[23] Similar inversions have been described for postrevolutionary France.[24] The history of denouncing demonstrates the misuse of special courts and special police forces. Again, in peasants' revolts the conscious uses of justice alternate with violence just to dodge an institutional order that was perceived as unjust. And, in Saxony, the peasants and the authorities fought a long battle over the institutions of justice.[25]

Such influencing from below is found already in an earlier period in the representation of the estates. Recently, studies on the filing of petitions demonstrated the degree to which subjects cooperated in the enforcement of law and indirectly even in the process of legislation. In seventeenth-century England women petitioned for and eventually succeeded in obtaining pensions for soldiers' widows, though this was not what the legislator originally had in mind.[26] Under the ancien régime, petitions deciding individual cases were as typical for the legislation as the *Policey-* or *Landes-* ordinances, meant to guide such decisions. Subjects, then, could contribute considerably to the realization of public order and in this way were not subjected (*subiecti*) at all.

The self-reliant use of criminal justice was part of a continuum of options, open to early modern subjects, of negotiating political relations. The important and powerful party of the state was a natural quantity in this negotiation process. Surprisingly, issues of crime and prosecution have so dominated the study of criminal justice that scholars have hardly queried the motivations and practices of its users.

The example of the procedures for prosecution invites us to interpret the judicial culture of the ancien régime more strongly from an enculturation paradigm and to focus in particular on the learning processes between criminal courts and the people. The acculturation paradigm centers too much on a perspective from above and underestimates the people's contribution in changing this culture. Similarly, the concept of *Verrechtlichung* overemphasizes the systemic aspects in a history omitting the people, and it overlooks that the historical agents, whether authorities or subjects, first had to learn how to handle the developing institutions. Enculturation stresses the mutuality of the learning processes and through its inclusion of culture the systemic changes as well. Seen from this perspective, the question of the uses of justice serves primarily as a heuristic device to trace those fields that should be examined first for this different understanding of criminal justice and its social effects: the people's daily practices and perceptions, which develop under restrictive conditions, generally also have a structuring effect because of their massive nature. Of course, the uses of justice interact with the two other analytic approaches to justice, the logic of the institutions and the interests of those who run the courts. Here we have merely examined the least analyzed approach to date. Another significant theme, that of popular attitudes to the law, had to be omitted.

Conclusion

My empirical findings disclose the structural restraints of justice's pacifying functions. Because of the central significance of other agents of social control, scholars should study not only the criminal courts, including the moral courts and other institutions of justice, but also the family, the neighborhood, guilds, fraternities, and so forth, from a microhistorical perspective and as analogous to one another. Explanations perceiving the supply of justice as the driving force in the development of judicial culture should be modified, just like the functionalist explanations that construe the uses of justice as determined by socioeconomic changes. Similarly, the notion of concepts of order overlooks the central significance of informal mediation in deciding whether to use justice or not. Though the supply of justice logically comes first, the nature of its uses depends primarily on how people assess their other options of social control. Taking into account aspects of gender, age, and social status, as well as the offenses and offenders involved, they carefully judge their uses of justice in relation to the availability of other, preferable forms of social control.

Clearly, we cannot grasp the long-term changes in social control on the basis of theories emphasizing exclusively the institutional supply and its internal developments. Instead, empirical findings from various countries may prompt us to examine more closely the uses of justice. Only this perspective will allow us to understand the judicial system in its social contexts. The development of justice and its uses varied from place to place.

Taking a long-term view, the outstanding feature of the early modern period—that it did not yet have an extended system of justice with all its institutions—now appears less exotic. Although the choice of various institutions still allowed for wilder uses of justice than in the nineteenth century, present-day discussions on the reform of criminal justice reveal that the forms of social control are still changing. Campaigns of criminalization and decriminalization, often discussed in terms of a higher institutional efficiency, alternate with one another. Expanding the police forces; delegating criminal cases to civil jurisdiction, social workers, psychiatry; and the inclusion of neighborhood control in police strategies are the institutional alternatives of today.

In the early modern period, one notices trends of *Verrechtlichung*, for instance, an increase in the uses of judicial institutions. However, taking stock of the many insignificant frictions fought before the courts, one wonders whether in many areas perhaps more matters were taken to court than today.

Crucial is that in most criminal cases people did not intend to use the institution until a formal conviction was passed. Therefore, a term such as *Verrechtlichung,* which merely calculates the number of formal uses, is too vague. Moreover, longtime trends in *Verrechtlichung,* if they occurred, often alternated with phases of deinstitutionalization. Nevertheless—and this is even more important for the prospects of criminal history—the functional alternative between the uses of justice and other forms of social control obviously remains and if needed is revived time and again, partly by the users, partly by the institutions.

The view of the uses of justice as only one form of social control may stimulate us to combine studies of a quantitative and qualitative nature from a new perspective. It may provide us with a new classification of societies from the perspective of social control and show us how the significance of the uses of justice has changed over a long time. German historiography is not alone in cherishing a state-building history that has taken hardly any notice of the popular demand for social control. In itself, the supply of legal institutions does not produce public order. Nor is such order dependent on socioeconomic or demographic pressure, driving the groups involved to file accusations. Rather, it is the outcome of a complex interplay of all these factors as they are assessed by historical subjects, deciding whether they will use justice in the first place or opt for a settlement of their own making. Findings on present practices in the Federal Republic of Germany reveal the actuality of such considerations to the uses of justice in the early modern period.[27]

Notes

This essay is based on my German article "Justiznutzungen als soziale Kontrolle" in Blauert and Schwerhoff, eds., *Kriminalitätsgeschichte,* 503–44. See that article for a more extensive annotation and bibliography (as of 2000).

1. See, for example, Sharpe, "Disagreement," 173; Shoemaker, *Prosecution,* 134–36; Lenman and Parker, "State," 21; Christelle, "Les délits," 148.

2. Compare Dinges, *Maurermeister,* 177; see also Claverie and Lamaison, *L'impossible mariage;* Spittler, "Streitregelung," 23, 27; Krug-Richter, "Konfliktregulierung"; Sälter, "Ordnung."

3. Kagan, *Lawsuits,* 223, 227; Kagan, "Golden," 160 et seq. See also Heras Santos, *Justicia.*

4. Schmale, *Archäologie,* 189 et seq.

5. Shoemaker, *Prosecution,* 62 et seq., 317.

6. This tradition continues to the present in the form of pre-judicial offers. Cf. Blankenburg and Verwoerd, "Prozeßhäufigkeiten," 322. For the social control function of neigh-

borhoods in the Netherlands: Jacobs, "Sociaal kapitaal"; Roodenburg, "Freundschaft," 17.

7. Compare Sack, "Kontrolle." For a recent overview of the discussion about social control: Scheerer and Hess, "Control." See also the literature mentioned in Dinges, *Maurermeister,* 174.

8. For an explanation of this definition, see Dinges, *Maurermeister,* 169–74. There must be a precise and empirically verifiable definition if the concept is of any use. For another opinion: Scheerer and Hess, "Control," 103.

9. Shoemaker, *Prosecution,* 55.

10. Ibid., 90–92.

11. Garnot, "L'ampleur," 70.

12. Shoemaker, *Prosecution,* 317. This holds true in particular for women: ibid., 210.

13. Castan, "Autorité"; Castan, "Criminalisation," 54 (even with respect to serious violence).

14. Garnot, "L'ampleur," 70.

15. Shoemaker, *Prosecution,* 76–79; see also Beattie, "Crime," 62 et seq.; Schnabel-Schüle, *Überwachen,* 170; Schwerhoff, *Köln,* 88; Rousseaux, "Inititative."

16. Rousseaux, "Ordre"; Blastenbrei, *Kriminalität,* 282; Garnot, "L'ampleur," 75; Castan, *Honnêteté;* Spierenburg, "Lange-termijn trends"; Spierenburg, "Faces," 710–16; Dinges, "Formenwandel"; Claverie and Lamaison, *Mariage;* Rossi, "Writer," 167.

17. Peveri, "Cette ville"; Shoemaker, *Prosecution,* 250; Blastenbrei, *Kriminalität,* 53 et seq.

18. Dinges, *Maurermeister,* 183 et seq.

19. Shoemaker, *Prosecution,* 211. On early modern labor relations, see Wunder, *Er ist die Sonn,* esp. 89–154; Wiesner, *Women;* Lorenz-Schmidt, *Vom Wert;* Simon-Muscheid, *Was nutzt die Schusterin.*

20. Dinges, *Maurermeister,* 181.

21. Farge and Foucault, *Familiäre Konflikte;* Spierenburg, *Prison Experience,* 223 et seq.

22. Dinges, *Maurermeister,* 178.

23. Rummel, "Ausrottung."

24. Gwynn, "La terreur blanche."

25. Schmale, *Archäologie,* 189 et seq.

26. Hudson, "Negotiating."

27. Hanak et al., eds., *Ärgernisse.*

CHAPTER 10

Moral Order in the World of Work: Social Control and the Guilds in Europe

Maarten Prak

I n urban communities guilds exercised a wide ranging, if incomplete, social control during the early modern period. This social control encompassed both members and nonmembers and mainly touched on their economic lives but was also extended to such social issues as marriage and burial and the gendered division of labor, and to cultural aspects like common meals, celebrations, and rituals, or a shared religion among the membership, as well as exclusion of other religions, notably the Jewish.

In developing this argument, the chapter will, at one and the same time, claim that social control was very important in the early modern guild system but that it was also circumscribed in various ways. One of these is that the guild system was basically an urban phenomenon—and townspeople were a small minority compared to the huge numbers of villagers. If we consider 10,000 inhabitants the standard to call a community urban, a mere 10 percent of Europeans lived in towns by 1800 and only half that percentage in 1500.[1] Even if we consider this standard excessive, there is no way in which the figures can be fundamentally redressed in favor of the towns.

In the towns, moreover, the guilds' control in areas it claimed to supervise, such as training, or the production of many privileged goods, was not necessarily complete. In fact, the assessment of this particular aspect of the guild system has shifted significantly in recent years. For a very long time guilds were seen as bulwarks of conservatism, holding the urban economies of early modern Europe to ransom with their outdated monopolies. Guilds were portrayed as Gothic relics, carried over from the Middle Ages into a time that would have been better off without them.[2] Significantly, their demise happened to coincide with the industrial revolution, strongly suggesting that progress had been hampered by their grip on the economy. The point was hammered home by Adam Smith, who observed in his *Wealth of Nations*:

> People of the same trade seldom meet together, even for merriment and diversion, but the conversation ends in a conspiracy against the public, or in some conversation to raise prices. It is impossible to prevent such meetings, by any law which either could be executed, or would be consistent with liberty and justice. But though the law cannot hinder people of the same trade from sometimes assembling together, it ought to do nothing to facilitate such assemblies, much less to render them necessary.[3]

Smith died just before his proposals were enacted by the French revolutionaries in 1791, when the guilds were abolished.

The essence of Smith's remarks is that incorporated artisans not merely conspired against the public but were actually capable of enforcing their control of labor and product markets. This is strongly doubted in the more recent literature. Much of that recent literature explores how the rules of the guilds translated into practice, and the general opinion seems to be that there were serious gaps between what the statute books said ought to happen and what was in fact happening on the work shop floor.[4] "Flexibility" has become the new buzzword when it comes to characterizing the activities of the guilds and explaining how they were able to survive across seven centuries and against the odds of major changes in the structure of the economy and the general society.[5] The new orthodoxy, however, creates a dilemma that is conveniently passed over by most authors. If the guilds were so easily adaptable to any new circumstance confronting them and gave in to any serious challenge to their monopolies, what was the point of continuing them in the first place? That question is in order, because guilds were ubiquitous in early modern Europe and were charging people to join them. Some authors claim that people continued to pay admittance fees simply to avoid the hassle of confrontation.[6] However, to see millions of people over several hundreds of years paying often substantial amounts of money, all for the relatively minor pleasure of being left alone, seems to beg the question of how these guilds were able to instill such fear. Certainly not by being merely "flexible"!

The debate about the guilds' regulations and their enforcement thus strikes at the very heart of social control. On one side we find sets of fairly strict regulations, on the other side presumably flexible practices. In the light of modern research, it will not do merely to insist that the regulations mattered. The guilds had to come to terms with the fact that many of their privileges were very difficult to monitor and to enforce. At the same time, there can be no question that substantial efforts were nonetheless made to enforce them. This chapter deals with the strategies used by craft guilds to make their regulations stick.[7] Guilds in all western European countries tended to underline a dichotomy between insiders and outsiders, that is, between those who were members of the guild, or otherwise belonged to the guild community, and those who did not.[8] We will be looking at the guilds' attitudes toward their own recruitment and membership and at their attempts to regulate the workforce, as well as at the ways guilds were dealing with nonincorporated competitors, especially females.

Apprentices: Learning the Rules of the Game

It was possible to enter the guild system through alternative routes, mainly that of matrimony (marrying a master's widow or daughter), but by far the most common point of entry was apprenticeship.[9] So whatever control guilds could exercise, it had to start here. And indeed, most guilds cared deeply about apprenticeship and tried to regulate it in great detail. Extensive lists of registered apprentices also suggest that guilds tried their best to keep track of the people in the system.

Initially, apprenticeship may have fallen outside the scope of guild regulations.[10] After 1300, however, it is mentioned routinely in guild statutes. The primary goal of apprenticeship was, of course, learning the skills of a trade. Indeed, S. R. Epstein has recently claimed that transmitting skills was, in the absence of state-sponsored schools, the main economic function of guilds. It allowed guilds to continue playing a key role in the transmission and distribution of technological innovation, and tacit knowledge more generally. It was, Epstein claims, also the main reason for their survival over an impressive period of time.

Apprenticeship usually took place during a child's teens and took several years. Two or three years seem to have been a minimum, but apprenticeships of seven, eight, or even ten years are recorded, and they may not even be exceptional. In eighteenth-century Paris an apprentice stayed with his master for an average of four years and ten months.[11] In England, the Statute of Artificers of 1563, which regulated apprenticeship across trades and across the country, stipulated a general term of seven years for all apprenticeships.[12] Dutch tailors' guilds usually required two years of training, but in actual practice an apprentice served three to four years in the service of a master.[13]

Remarkably, the statutes have very little to say about what the training actually entailed.[14] But obviously, it must have been more than just skills.[15] The varying lengths of apprenticeships already suggest this: if Dutch tailors were supposed to learn their trade in two years, why should the English need seven?[16] One possible explanation is that masters had to recoup their initial investment in a child's training, by employing him (or her) at substandard wages for an additional period of time. This might explain why Dutch orphanages had to agree to three- or four-year contracts to apprentice their orphans. Part of the answer, however, seems to be that the apprentice was supposed to learn other things as well, besides the "mystery" of the trade. In actual fact, the statutes are more concerned with these aspects than they are with the technical education of the apprentice.

In Paris, the guilds insisted that the apprentice be of legitimate birth and come from a Catholic family. He should under all circumstances behave respectfully toward the master and the master's family.[17] Likewise, the master and his wife should look upon their young ward benevolently. Daniel Defoe has a fictional master exclaim that he is "a parent to the boy tho not a father, and that the duty of taking care of him, both soul and body, was mine."[18] Although this is not written down, it seems evident that the guilds themselves conveyed a strong moral framework of Christian charity, as well as middle-class honesty. It thus provided an introduction into "a more general bourgeois culture."[19] In seventeenth-century England, cheap manuals instructed apprentices on how to conduct themselves. These manuals emphasized such values as "honesty, sobriety, sexual abstinence and, above all, diligent attention to the master's interests."[20]

In London, City regulations stipulated that apprentices could wear only the clothes provided by their masters.[21] The tin-plate workers' guild also required the apprentices to wear a special badge, and the vintners' apprentices had a cap badge. The dress code for apprentices required modesty and precluded wearing colorful outfits or precious tissues like silk.[22] English apprenticeship regulations could even extend to the youngster's hairstyle: it should be cropped. In 1626 the London butchers hired a barber to give the apprentices a haircut.[23] And in July 1640 the London Court of Aldermen insisted that an apprentice who wanted to receive the freedom of the city "shall first present himself at that time with the hair of his head cut in a decent and comely manner."[24] Beards were out of the question, of course. Apprentices should not dress above their status. The masters, who were supposed to provide a chest in which the apprentice's clothes were kept, had the right to inspect the contents of that chest.[25]

Apprentices' behavior was also regulated outside the workplace. In numerous Parisian apprenticeship contracts, it was expressly stated that the apprentices should not go into bars or hang out with the wrong sort of people.[26] In London apprentices could not participate in dances or masquerades, nor could they go to tennis courts or bowling alleys, not to mention brothels or cock fights. Apprentices could not get married.[27] It is important to keep in mind that the apprentices were mostly teenage males and for this reason alone guilds, parents, and public authorities were keen to oversee their comings and goings.[28] When, in eighteenth-century France, apprenticeship came under fire as part of the guild monopolies, those in favor of the institution defended apprenticeship as a pillar of the biological and moral order, concerned as it was with the socialization of males during puberty, as much as with the economic (learning a trade) and sociopolitical (introduction into the corporate world) orders of society.[29]

Apprenticeship was regulated in three distinct ways in early modern Europe. England was the only country where national law provided the framework for apprenticeship, from its introduction in the Statute of Artificers in 1563 until the repeal of the apprenticeship clauses in 1814.[30] However, its enforcement was not provided for, and it was mainly the guilds who undertook this. As a result, the statute's clauses were monitored much more closely in incorporated towns than they were in the countryside.[31] In France apprenticeship was regulated by private contract, usually notarized. Guilds, however, were very often cosignatories to the contract.[32] In the Low Countries and the German-speaking territories, apprenticeship was directly overseen by the guild, which laid down the rules and took care of registration and enforcement wherever deviation from the rules was suspected.[33] It is as yet too early to explain these variations, but we have good reasons to assume that in all three types the guilds played a crucial role. Were they also successful in making the rules stick?

In general, that is difficult to say. We have no systematic information on enforcement of apprenticeship rules. The best information relates to time aspects of the apprenticeship contract. As was discussed above, it is quite likely that most trades could be learned in a relatively short span of time. Long terms of apprenticeship, like the seven years required in England, therefore were not necessarily in the interest of the apprentice, who might be tempted to run away before the expiration of his term. To persuade the apprentice to stay on, he might be offered a small wage during the later stages of the apprenticeship.[34] But that diminished the master's return on the time and effort invested in the apprenticeship. The great majority (almost 90 percent in Bristol during the seventeenth century) finished the full apprenticeship anyway, and some stayed on even longer.[35] In sixteenth-century London the drop-out rate was substantially higher than in Bristol, or in the small towns of England. No more than forty percent of apprentices actually stayed the full seven years. However, among a sample of 250 apprentices entering seven different London companies, only seven had not completed a seven-year apprenticeship, and as much as sixty percent in this group had done more than the required seven years of training.[36]

So, even if not all apprentices served the full term—and it seems a great many did take the whole course—guilds were successful at enforcing the requirement for their own members. One possible explanation is the check, afterward, of their record as an apprentice. Many guilds, not just in England, requested a candidate member to produce not only a masterpiece but also proof of his apprenticeship record.[37] In sixteenth- and seventeenth-century London, however, about half of the apprentices failed to become masters. In Bristol as many as two-thirds did not become masters after finishing an apprenticeship. Part of this is explained by early deaths; teenagers were still a vulnerable age group. Some were discharged early by their masters because they were good-for-nothings, or for some other reason. But the great majority simply drifted away.[38] Detailed research in seventeenth-century Bristol strongly suggests that the town–countryside relationship was crucial here. Although apprenticeships in the countryside were quite possible,[39] the urban guilds probably provided better training facilities for many crafts. It may have contributed also to one's reputation as a craftsman to have been trained in a town.[40] Bristol apprentices may have found the financial obstacles of setting up a shop in town simply too expensive, or the prospects too unattractive. When the local economy improved later in the seventeenth century, the number of apprentices recruited into the local guilds increased significantly, as opportunities opened up again.[41] The Bristol data thus strongly suggest that even where there were no formal exams, as in the countryside, apprentices would tend to take the full course.

If necessary, masters would force runaway apprentices to finish their terms. Cases brought to trial under the 1563 Statute of Artificers usually concerned runaways. Most were apprehended with the help of informers, hoping for a reward. Already in the Middle Ages guilds had employed such informers. But the authorities were not very active in this area, and the number of court-cases—ten to fifteen per annum—was completely insignificant if we consider that in London alone the companies admitted four to five thousand apprentices annually in the early-seventeenth century.[42] So, even if we do not underestimate the impact of the negative incentives, it seems that at least for the term of apprenticeship (and by European standards it was unusually long in England) the positive incentives persuaded most apprentices to abide by the rules.

Journeymen: An Unruly Workforce

Perhaps no single publication has done more to shatter the image of the corporate world as one of peace and harmony than Robert Darnton's account of the "great cat massacre," that occurred in Paris in the 1730s. Although the circumstances are only vaguely known, because the story was committed to paper long after the event, the essential details are telling. In his autobiography the printer Nicolas Contat recounts how, as an apprentice, he and the other journeymen decided to take revenge for all the unpaid hours and abuse they had suffered while working for the presumably draconian master printer Jacques Vincent. Vincent's wife, who must have been an equally unpleasant character, was very fond of cats, particularly *le gris,* the grey one. By mimicking a bunch of love-sick cats underneath the Vincents' bedroom window for several nights in a row, the workers managed to provoke their employer into ordering a clearing of the cats from the neighborhood—but not *le gris,* of course. The journeymen went after the cats straightaway. The first to be battered to death was *le gris.* By the time Vincent and his wife realized what had happened, a great many cats had been butchered. The implied message of their dreadful fate could not be lost on anyone involved.[43]

If the mutual feelings between Vincent and his workforce were less than cordial, the way his journeymen taunted him also tells us something about the potential power of the workforce. The apprentice was bound by contract to his master and needed a certificate or letter of recommendation to establish himself in the trade. But the journeymen were proud of their skills, and if Vincent did not like them any longer, they were confident of finding another employer. One of the most remarkable results of recent scholarship on the world of work in early modern Europe is the exposure of the fluidity of labor relations and hence the dynamic of the labor market. Wherever one looks, the figures are staggering. Among the wigmakers in Rouen, between March 1783 and August 1791, no less than 5,320 job placements are recorded, relating to 3,274 individual journeymen. On average, a journeyman wigmaker worked a mere 118 days for the same *patron*. Among the journeymen tailors in the same city, the turnover rate was equally impressive: between mid-July 1778 and mid-November 1781 there were 4,903 registrations by 1,859 individuals. The tailors' guild of Rouen was not small by any means, but its membership of 274 in 1775 is dwarfed by the number of journeymen passing through their workshops.[44] Among cabinetmakers in Vienna the numbers were less impressive, but they suggest the same substantial turnover. While the guild's 142 masters employed about 200 journeymen at any given time, as many as 600 journeyman cabinetmakers were registered every year. This figure again suggests an average term of employment of about four months.[45]

The journeymen were recruited from a very wide area. Among four Viennese guilds—bookbinders, cabinetmakers, bag makers, and silk weavers—the number of journeymen who were recruited locally was between 6 and 16 percent in the eighteenth century.[46] Of the journeyman tailors registered in Rouen, only 5 percent were natives, while another 35 percent came from the direct hinterland or adjoining areas. That leaves over half of them originating from farther afield.[47] And this was not at all a recent phenomenon. Of the journeyman lock makers registered in Frankfurt, Germany, in the fifteenth and sixteenth centuries, more than half came from towns situated over 500 kilometers away from Frankfurt.[48] This combination of high turnover and long-distance travels is possibly related to the custom, in both France and the German-speaking parts of Europe, of journeyman touring, known as *wandern* in Germany, the *tour de France* in France, or tramping in England.[49]

To facilitate the combination of supply and demand in this very dynamic labor market, tramping journeymen would usually meet at specific addresses in towns. In Rouen, around 1780, almost 60 percent of journeyman tailors gave an inn as their address. It was at *Au Chat Qui Dort, Aux Trois Images,* and two or three other such places that master tailors could expect to find their workers.[50] In Dijon in the 1670s, the journeyman joiners stayed with Bénigne Simonnet, who was designated as their *père*. Besides lodgings, Simonnet provided a meeting room for the journeymen's organization. Each new arrival was greeted with an elaborate ritual, which included a washing of the hands of those present by the newly arrived *compagnon* and his paying for a pint of wine, a loaf of bread, and a piece of meat, which would then be consumed. Only after he had gone through this ritual, could the initiated expect to find work in the city.[51] In German towns, journeymen likewise had fixed premises, where they would meet and drink. Early references go back to the fourteenth century.[52] Obviously, these would be the first places of call for itinerant journeymen.

Although there may not be a direct connection between tramping and formalized organization by journeymen, the existence of meeting places and their role in local labor markets must have contributed to the success of the institutionalized journeymen's organizations. In most countries journeymen were not in any formal sense part of the corporate order. Only in English craft guilds were journeymen accepted as members and, if the situation in London can be taken as indicative, they were even there allowed a certain amount of autonomy. The London yeomanry, the humblest subsection of the companies, did include independent craftsmen (so-called householders) but the majority seem to have been journeymen.[53] In Germany, journeymen were organized in what was variously known as "guilds," or "brotherhoods," or "confraternities." In France they were known as *compagnonnages*.[54] Their origins are closely related to the existence of craft guilds, as is demonstrated, for instance, by the claim of journeyman wool weavers in 1331 in Zürich that they wanted to establish a box to pay for the burial of their members and felt they were entitled to have such a benefit, because it already existed "in all towns along the river Rhine where there are guilds."[55]

Such welfare boxes could easily develop into union-type organizations. There is a strong correlation between the incidence of strikes and other labor unrest and the presence of journeymen's organizations.[56] In some trades, for instance hat making in the southern Netherlands, journeymen succeeded in integrating their organizations into regional networks, so as to be even more effective in protecting their members' interests.[57] Everywhere, they were concerned with regulation, under their own supervision, of the labor market. They tried to control supply, by supervising the hiring mechanism. They sought the exclusion of cheap competitors, especially women. They organized strikes against specific workshops and, if necessary, walk-outs, which deprived a complete trade of its workforce by moving to an adjacent town. Interestingly, from the point of view of social control, they also tried to uphold guild legislation, once the rules had been changed to their satisfaction. And journeymen organizations tried to improve the quality of labor, by trying to suppress drinking on the job and other abuses.

Obviously, both guilds and civic authorities had mixed feelings about these journeymen's associations. They may have contributed to the disciplining of the workforce, but at the same time they were a source of strife, if not worse. In general, however, attempts at suppression met with little success. The organizations might go underground, but would reemerge at some later stage. The fluidity of the labor-force, in combination with the fact that they had their own autonomous organizations, enabled journeymen to escape, at least to some extent, from the supervision of their masters.[58] Instead, they nurtured a culture of independence, complete with nicknames such as Liberty, or Without Respect,[59] and ridiculing their masters, if necessary with the loss of some cats' lives.

Masters: The Price of Community

Although it has become fashionable these days to emphasize the social and cultural sides of the corporate system, the core business of early modern guilds was economic. Almost invariably, guilds were organized on the basis of one or more professions shared by their members. The guilds' privileges gave those members exclusive access to the production and retail sale of specified goods, which might range from the humble, routinely produced, but also vital daily bread, through more complex clothing, to expensive, unique, and luxurious works of art in paint or precious metals.[60] To enforce their monopoly, the guilds had to ensure that attempts at infringement by outsiders would be rebuked, their members would refrain from trying to reap the potential benefits of bending the rules, and the craftsmen would deliver the professed advantages of the corporate system for customers, mainly the stamp of quality.

Most guilds saw the monopoly as the single most important justification of their existence, at least insofar as the members themselves were concerned.[61] They spent huge amounts of effort, and if necessary money, on enforcing this monopoly. Take the example of Willem Swinderswijck, a minor painter in the town of Haarlem, in Holland. Haarlem boasted the oldest guild of St. Luke, the patron of painters, in the Dutch Republic. Its records went back to the early-sixteenth century. Moreover, the guild was the proud owner of a relic, a small piece of bone, of its patron saint, a Catholic memento that was still revered after the introduction of the Reformation in Haarlem during the 1580s. Willem Swinderswijck was selling paintings in Haarlem, even though he was not a member of the guild, which therefore summoned him to come and explain himself in its meeting of March 1642. But Swinderswijck did not show up. In April he was summoned again, to no avail. In May the guild explicitly excluded Swinderswijck from further exercising his trade, but in June it was reported that the culprit had only laughed at the guild official who had come to serve him the writ. In August it was reported on two separate occasions that, despite the injunction, Swinderswijck had sold works of art. In early September there was another such report. On each occasion a three-guilder fine was imposed, which if collected would more than wipe out any profits Swinderswijck had made on his no-doubt modest work. It seems that the fines, in combination with the perseverance of the guild, finally did the trick, because on September 15, Swinderswijck gave in: he told the guild he would pay the usual fee and join the guild. The guild itself, having achieved its goal, was prepared to drop charges and abstain from collecting the fines.[62] Swinderswijck had been transformed from an outsider who had to be coerced into complying with the guild rules, into an insider to whom the *violence douce* of community was applied.

Enforcing the monopoly was the single most important issue in the seventeenth-century records of Haarlem's guild of St. Luke. From those records we learn that the guild must have had numerous "eyes and ears" in the city, although it is not entirely clear who exactly was spying on illegal production and sales. In London, a city perhaps ten times as big as Haarlem, guilds at times employed paid informers, to help them smoke out the "ground rabbits" (interlopers).[63] But even in London, we can safely assume that interested parties, not least the members themselves and their relatives, were looking for offenders and informing the guild wardens about them. The wardens themselves, moreover, were vigilant too. The London companies held regular "searches" that took them to specific districts, where they invaded workshops and stalls to look for illicit products or journeymen and apprentices who had not been properly registered.[64] In Paris, the *jurés* of the guilds "launched investigations that included spying on suspects; they conducted 'visits,' usually in the company of police officials, that involved searches and seizures, they participated in the issuing of summonses, in arrests and in trials."[65] Members whose products were found to be shoddy were fined and, if necessary, the product was publicly destroyed. The gold- and silversmiths' guild in Amsterdam, which was also responsible for maintaining the standards of precious metals, routinely destroyed work by its members that was found to contain less than the minimum amount of gold or silver.[66] Such measures involved members as much as outsiders.

To what extent was all of this effective? That really seems very difficult to say. James Farr, for instance, who is one of the most important modern historians of the artisans' world, thinks that the searches by the London companies were a ritual more than anything else. Their route was known beforehand and the cortege so loud and large, it was no problem at all to hide illicit journeymen and their work, or so he claims.[67] Nonetheless, offenders were captured and fines were imposed. And as the Swinderswijck case suggests, the harassment at times could be effective enough to persuade an outsider to join the guild. Generally, of course, the problem was of the guilds' own making. The monopoly was designed to create rent streams and it was only natural that free riders would try to tap into them. Even the guild members themselves might consider playing it both ways, going by the corporate rules and also trying to get around them.[68]

However, some unique data on the sales of Dutch paintings suggest that, after all, the guilds were not completely powerless in the face of outside competition. Because paintings were signed and sometimes listed in probate inventories, their origins and whereabouts can be traced. Painstaking research by Michael Montias in the notarial records of seventeenth-century Amsterdam has revealed that about half the paintings sold in that town were of local origin, with *local origin* defined as masters registered with the guild of St. Luke. Similar research in Delft and Haarlem produced percentages that were even higher, 66 and 79 respectively.[69] The inhabitants of Delft and Haarlem accounted for 6 and 11 percent respectively of the total urban population in the province of Holland, where most Dutch art of the period was produced.[70] So it is safe to say that, especially in these towns, the guild dominated the local market, and even in Amsterdam, with its very busy port and manifest flows of imports and exports, as well as migration, the guild members were substantially overrepresented in the market. But obviously, that domination was incomplete, as it must have been in many other trades. In her book on Dutch tailors' guilds, which found it equally impossible to maintain their monopoly in full, Bibi Panhuysen suggests, and rightly so to my mind, that it is of little help to think in terms of either a monopoly or a free market. Instead, guilds devised a variety of strategies to deal with these problems, ranging from attempts to suppress competition, to incorporation of the competitors into the guild itself. However, these strategies, as Panhuysen states, were always designed to give the master tailors control over the most profitable parts of the trade, while they were willing to compromise in what was seen as the peripheral activities.[71]

One reason why guilds seem to have been at least moderately successful in maintaining their economic privileges was that they could often count on the active support of the civic authorities. The bakers' guild in Paris and the local police were working closely together in regulating the bread market in the French capital. The rules were laid down in the statutes of the guild, as well as in the municipal ordinances, and violating them was thus an offense against both the corporate and the civic law.[72] In Antwerp, the municipal authorities encouraged individuals to accept the mediation of the guild and applied extra penalties if they failed to do so.[73] In London, the companies' courts of assistants played an equally vital role in resolving disputes and dealing with crimes against the community. These courts, meeting as often as twice a week, were usually composed of the past and present wardens of the company and could apply fines, close down shops, and expulse members from the trade if the offense was very serious. They dealt with any issue, trade related or not, as long as the defendant was a member of the company.[74]

Guilds also had privileged access to municipal authorities. When the Haarlem guild of St. Luke considered filing a petition in 1642 that should put an end to the lotteries that were supposed to be spoiling the market for paintings, they prepared the ground during an informal visit to one of the town's mayors.[75] In Antwerp, guilds filed on average twice as many petitions as individual citizens during the seventeenth century.[76] In France, guilds took their complaints to the courts. By combining the limited resources of modest individuals, guilds could mobilize expensive legal aid. When, for example, the linen drapers' guild of Paris, an all-female corporation, came into conflict with the powerful *merciers,* they ensured that their case was presented by Maître Belin, a lawyer with a twenty-year track record.[77] An appeal to the courts was, in France, such an obvious route to take for the guilds that, as Michael Sonenscher reminds us, they tended to phrase any conflict in their ranks in "words and phrases . . . not drawn from the experience of particular trades, [but] derived, instead, from eighteenth century civil jurisprudence and the vocabulary of natural law."[78] In some regions of Europe guilds were themselves directly represented in local government. It is a subject that awaits more systematic investigation, but generally we find this to be the case in many German and some Swiss towns, in the southern Netherlands, and in the eastern parts of the Dutch Republic.[79] There, of course, they could expect an especially sympathetic court hearing.

While the supervision of the production and marketing of urban industry was uppermost in the minds of many corporate officials, it was by no means their exclusive concern. In many places they saw it as their duty to supervise the morals of their members or prospective members. Two areas seem to have given particular concern: the family and religion. During the Middle Ages, there had been an intimate relation between the guilds and the Church.[80] Guilds maintained altars and religious services, either directly or through religious confraternities that were really satellite organizations. In Protestant areas the guilds' religious impact was redirected in the course of the sixteenth century but not necessarily lost. In regions that were officially declared to be religiously homogeneous, it was more or less taken for granted that guild members belonged to the official church. This seems to have been the case in London, for instance. Where the community was religiously mixed, two patterns might emerge, as the Dutch Republic demonstrated. In the west, where a patriciate of merchants and rentiers ruled the towns and cities, religion was not an issue, except for Jews. Even in tolerant Amsterdam, Jews were excluded from the guild trades.[81] For other religions, including Catholics and Anabaptists, there were no obstacles, although the only publicly tolerated religion in the Netherlands at the time was Calvinism. In the eastern towns of the Dutch Republic, however, another pattern prevailed. Although there were no formal religious bars preventing candidates to join a guild, citizenship was open only to Calvinists. And citizenship was a prerequisite for guild membership. In these towns guildsmen, directly or indirectly, had a significant influence in local government, and it was they who insisted on the religious purity of the citizen community. In some towns artisans were kicked out of their guild, and out of their jobs, when it was discovered that they were participating in Catholic rites.[82]

In Germany, we find a similar situation. According to a survey undertaken by Etienne François, this resulted in three patterns.[83] In a very limited number of cases, all in southern Germany and with Augsburg as the most notable example, a system of power sharing was developed. In Augsburg the guilds' political power was taken away by Charles V in 1548, and this effectively ended attempts to impose religious views, one way or another, on the citizenry.[84] In small towns, dominated by middle-class guildsmen, there was no room for compromise. Here, religion was seen as one of the foundations of the community and the community's preservation as depending on religious unity. In newly established towns and capital cities, however, religious minorities were protected by absolutist princes and enjoyed a reasonable degree of toleration.[85] Thus, in towns where guilds were politically influential, they were able to impose religious uniformity on their membership.

Already in their very early stages, guilds tended to define their community in terms of "artificial families."[86] They referred to the membership as "brothers" and "sisters." In some Dutch towns guilds had common graves, where deceased members would be buried together. In the town of Dordrecht, in Holland, the guilds of the carpenters, the cabinetmakers, the bakers, and the shoemakers between them buried on average ten masters, masters' wives or widows, and masters' children annually during the eighteenth century in the guilds' own crypts.[87] In many parts of Europe it was common practice to provide a guild burial for deceased members, with a required presence of the complete membership.

The importance attached to the guild's involvement at the end of a member's life was matched by its supervision over the earlier stages. Especially in the German territories, guilds were obsessed with the propriety of their members' marriages and the legitimacy of their offspring. In many, perhaps most, of the small towns of the Holy Roman Empire, guilds would admit only candidates who could prove four legitimate grandparents. In his famous description of these "home towns," Mack Walker demonstrates how one German artisan, the tinsmith Flegel from Hildesheim, was ostracized by his guild after marrying a woman whose father had been born out of wedlock but was later legitimated by the national court, a verdict that was, however, not accepted by the Hildesheim guild.[88] Such intransigence was not the privilege of small-town guilds, as Walker suggested. In Augsburg, a city of 45,000 in the middle of the sixteenth century, the guilds also required their members to be of legitimate birth. Engagements and weddings were celebrated in the guild house. During a brief interlude, in the 1560s, anyone wanting to contract a marriage in Augsburg had to be both a citizen and a member of a guild![89] In Dijon, France, the authorities expressed similar concerns over the descent and marital state of prospective guild masters. It seems that they preferred candidates to be marrried, and depositions mention the parents' marital state at the time the candidate was born, so as to testify of his legitimacy.[90] And although there is no evidence about its enforcement, the Parisian guilds also insisted that their members be of legitimate birth.[91] Even if there were no official rules relating to these issues, as in eighteenth-century Amsterdam, guild rhetoric routinely assumed that their members were family men, with responsibilities for wives and children, inhabiting family homes, in contrast with journeymen, for instance, who were pictured as celibate and inhabiting single rooms.[92] This insistence on connecting guild membership with traditional family arrangements would

have highly significant implications for the ways in which guilds looked upon
the issue of gender.

Women: Social Control within and outside the Corporate System

One area in which the guilds exercised significant social control during the early
modern era was the division of gender roles. The guilds' attitudes toward females
changed dramatically, especially in the sixteenth century. Whereas females had
been pictured as at least potentially equal to male masters in the Middle Ages,
guild statutes started to exclude women from the guilds' ranks after the
Reformation. Changing religious attitudes may have been one of the reasons why
this happened,[93] but the changes are better documented than explained and alternative interpretations cannot be ruled out at this point.

Many Medieval guild statutes routinely assumed that a candidate for membership could be of either sex. The statutes of the tailors' guild in The Hague,
Holland, for example, stated in 1505 that the aspiring master had to demonstrate his skill "as a man or woman" before the guild's examiners; the masterpiece could be either a man's or a woman's garment.[94] Two centuries earlier, in
1304, a general ordinance concerning the trades in the city of Utrecht stated that
"those who want to exercise an incorporated trade, be they man or woman, have
to become members."[95] It is difficult to assess the role of women in the Medieval
urban economy on the basis of this evidence alone. Many guild statutes remain
completely silent on the subject. That women were acceptable as members does
not mean that they were numerous, or influential within the guild. Some evidence suggests that females were already relegated to the margins. It was highly
unusual, for instance, for women to take up guild offices.[96]

Nonetheless, there is every reason to assume that things were taking a turn
for the worse during the sixteenth century. Thus, in 1524, the tailors' guild of
Haarlem introduced a prohibition against women cutting new cloth, thus effectively barring them from the trade. The female members of the guild were allowed
to continue, but "they will die out, and no new female members shall be accepted
into the guild."[97] The same thing happened in London, where the weavers' company stipulated in 1578 that "no manner of person or persons exercising [their
trade] shall keep, teach, instruct, or bring up in the use, exercise, or knowledge
of [weaving] any maid, damsel, or other woman whatsoever."[98] Around the same
time, the Nuremberg ring makers decided that "from now on, no maid is to be
used for any kind of work in this craft."[99] It was a trend that could be observed
all over Europe.[100]

This dramatic deterioration in women's positions in the corporate world has
been explained in different ways.[101] Martha Howell, one of the most influential

among modern scholars addressing the issue, sees the marginalization of women as the result of shifts in the economy and the political role of guilds. Women's economic positions, Howell argues, had always been defined in the family sphere. Women's work was additional to their husbands' and never seen as the mainstay of the household. As artisanal production moved away from household production into a more commercial mode (defined by Howell as "small commodity"), women lost their traditional foothold. Because they had never won political influence within the guilds, they were now unable to counter this development by an appeal to the urban authorities. When the linen weavers' guild in Leyden, Holland, was established in 1563, it welcomed women who, of course, were long active in the trade. But only a few years later, it seems, females were barred from the guild and thus banned from the independent exercise of the trade, or at best relegated to its margins.[102]

Merry Wiesner also sees the guilds as a key factor in engineering these changes and the state of the economy as an important structural condition but blames the journeymen. During the sixteenth century they found it more difficult to set up shop as an independent master. Instead, journeymen were forced to live in hostels much longer, sometimes all their lives. The hostels were all-male communities, where the symbolism of male honor became much more important than it had been before. These values were transferred to the guilds, as journeymen's associations clamored for the exclusion of women from the trade, or when the journeymen finally managed to win membership and brought their gendered identities into the guilds.[103] Others also see the guilds' negative attitude toward women as primarily defensive: under threat from shrinking markets, male masters sought to break the weaker links in the chain of the trade. Thus, in the course of the eighteenth century, when rural protoindustry was making headway in Prussia, urban guilds there tried to redefine "real" work as a male preserve, while the sloppy products of rural industry, and women's work, were labeled together as inferior.[104]

In the process, women's roles in relation to work were recast in much more narrow ways. One telling example is the Berlin tailors' guild's exclamation, in 1803, that married women must be maintained by their husbands, know housekeeping, and care for and educate their children. The unmarried may work as domestics or engage in other feminine occupations outside regular manufacture.[105] This opinion reflects a long tradition of discourse, which was not necessarily new even in the sixteenth century but much reinforced during that age. As we saw earlier, the guilds of Augsburg, with the help of the Reformed town council, were able to set up a regime of moral righteousness centered around family values. In this scheme of things, Lyndal Roper tells us, the "master's wife was . . . guarantor of her husband's achieved adult masculinity: she proved his masterhood, while at the same time being responsible for the food, light, bedding, heat, water and other domestic needs of the shop's small labor force."[106]

The exclusion of women was not just a matter of guild discourse and ideology; it also translated into practice. Females were still apprenticed in large numbers in eighteenth-century England. But the great majority were trained either in husbandry or in housewifery.[107] Already in the first half of the sixteenth century, two-thirds of female apprentices in Bristol were destined for specifically female occupations, such as seamstress and, again, housewife. And even though their social backgrounds were similar to those of male apprentices, they found it increasingly difficult to establish themselves as independent producers. By 1600 it was all but impossible for women to enter Bristol's incorporated trades.[108] In Germany there was a general rollback of women from all but a small number of crafts.[109]

In the eyes of the guilds, the exclusion of women from the incorporated trades may have rid them of some serious competition, but at the same time it created new problems. One was that cheap female labor could be profitable for the guild masters too, under specific circumstances. According to regulations going back to the mid-sixteenth century, female silk weavers in Lyon, France, could work in the industry alongside their husbands. During the 1730s, when more and more master silk weavers were in danger of losing their independence at the hands of the merchants, they clamored for the right to allow their wives to go to work in another master's workshop. By extending the idea of patrimony, they hoped to preserve the household's economic integrity. The merchants, in retaliation, managed to get the labor market for silk weavers declared open to all women, whatever their relations with the master weavers. The market was thus flooded with cheap labor, to the horror of the guild. Interestingly, the guild itself had considered promoting this step sometime earlier, during a period of acute labor shortage. Its plans, however, had included only a limited access for women, instead of the open-door policy adopted by the town council, a policy that threatened male job opportunities and their remuneration. Both masters and journeymen therefore protested vociferously, but to no avail. As a result, journeymen's wages came under pressure and masters were forced to cut costs, for example by employing the same female labor they had so recently opposed.[110]

Another problem resulted from the creation of competition from outside the guilds' own jurisdiction. This was recognized by the London weavers' company, which had so emphatically excluded all females and foreigners from its ranks in 1578. In 1630 the guild's bailiffs, wardens, and assistants pleaded with the city's aldermen to allow them to admit foreigners again into the guild, because only then would they be able to keep control of the trade in the sprawling metropolis that was seventeenth-century London.[111] For the very same reason, if no other, the guilds found it impossible to completely suppress female labor. In their attempts to control female labor, various strategies were employed. Dutch tailors' guilds tried to come to terms with female labor in at least four different ways. First, in Amsterdam, by far the largest among Dutch towns, the seamstresses were organized into a separate guild in 1579, in the context of a general reorganization of the town's guild system immediately after Amsterdam had joined the Dutch Revolt and had become a Protestant town. Like everywhere else, the Amsterdam seamstresses had to limit themselves to the production of clothing for females and children. In nearby Haarlem, the seamstresses were in a state of permanent conflict with the tailors throughout the seventeenth century, until 1707 when they were organized into a subdivision of the tailors' guild. This happened after the tailors complained that their trade was being ruined by the large numbers of seamstresses and that as a result they found it impossible to provide assistance to their members in need. The seamstresses were brought under guild control as much to boost the guild's finances, as to allow the latter to keep a closer eye on female competition. Like the men, women were entitled to benefits, but they could not hold office in the Haarlem guild. In the city of Den Bosch (or Bois-le-Duc), the seamstresses were also forced to pay an annual contribution, and a substantial one at that, but basically they received nothing in return, except the right to exercise their trade. In the small town of Zutphen, a former Hansa town in the eastern part of the Netherlands, women could enter the tailors' guild, but only with special permission of the town council. In 1755 the council decided to introduce a very tight limit on the number of seamstresses in Zutphen. Henceforth, no more than five could work at any one time in this town of seven thousand inhabitants. Obviously, the market for women's and children's clothing was still very much a male preserve in Zutphen.[112]

Flexibility, if that is what we want to call these variegated responses to the challenges of the gender division of labor,[113] was required especially in areas where the guilds had little political clout. In Den Bosch the guilds for a long time had appointed the members to one of the three tiers of the local government. Even though they lost that right in 1629, they were still a powerful force in the community. In Zutphen, the citizenry, and hence guild members, could directly influence the composition of the town council. Significantly, in the southern Netherlands, where guilds held seats in urban representative institutions and had to approve of, for instance, new taxation, they found it relatively easy to push women to the margins of the clothing industry. The available data suggest that in the Flemish towns seamstresses were much less numerous than in the Holland towns.[114] Thus, where local elites had greater autonomy, as in Amsterdam and Haarlem for example, they were more likely to grant a hearing to women's complaints and balance their interests with those of the male-dominated guilds, than in towns where the guilds themselves could call the shots.[115]

All-female guilds were not completely unknown before the seventeenth century,[116] but they acquired a new meaning after the guilds' two centuries of attempts to force female labor into the framework of the artisanal family model. Significantly, the new seamstresses' guilds, established almost simultaneously in Paris and in Rouen in 1675, swiftly developed a new language and social ideal, which was diametrically opposed to the patriarchy of the traditional corporations. These newly created guilds were designed to cater specifically to female customers. In Paris women were, in so many words, excluded from the tailoring business, except when they were the wife or daughter of an established master. The seamstresses as a result had few connections with the tailors, and they were able to establish themselves as an independent corporation thanks only to a financial crisis of the French crown. In contrast with the tailors' guild, where entry was mainly through family connection (60 percent entered that way), the seamstresses were free from family intervention, with only 8 percent of the members entering through that channel. Whereas the tailors propounded a world view that emphasized family values and women subject to male authority, the seamstresses underlined the individuality of the members. While the tailors, during the 1776 crisis when Turgot had abolished the guilds in France, depicted the future as one of total anarchy, now that both guilds and families were threatened, the seamstresses pictured themselves as vulnerable individuals, who needed the guild to protect them against undesired contacts with men.[117]

So family values came home to roost. In Den Bosch the seamstresses took their critique one step further still and fundamentally questioned the whole of the corporate system that sustained patriarchy. Triumphantly they announced the "Liberty, Equality, or the Needle Struggle" in 1795, shortly after the town had been "liberated" by the French revolutionary armies. They demanded complete freedom of production, even—and this was previously unheard of—the right to make men's clothes if the opportunity presented itself. This they did not get, but the six guilders annual payment to the tailors' guild was scrapped by the *Municipalité*. The tailors retaliated in the usual way: they entered the seamstresses' shops and confiscated all illegal produce. But the seamstresses of Den Bosch, who condemned the guild's appeal to ancient custom and privilege as completely outdated, won the day: they were relieved from the annual payments because "it was unfair to have to contribute to a fund from which one could not profit."[118] Their attacks, ostensibly on a financial arrangement imposed on the seamstresses, but in actual fact casting doubt on the guild order as such, tell us something about the depth of the crisis of the ancien régime. But at the same time it should serve as a reminder of the potency of that very same guild order, and the social and economic constraints it had so cunningly imposed on female labor, and women's lives more generally, through a wide array of containment strategies.

Conclusion

The trouble with social control is that we know it is happening all the time but will find it incredibly difficult to put a finger on the precise mechanisms that translated prescriptive discourse into social practice. As far as the guilds are concerned, this problem has become all the more acute since recent scholarship has shattered the naive assumption that the rules, laid down in guild statutes, were straightforwardly applied in practice. As many scholars have emphasized during the last fifteen years or so, guilds had to employ a variety of strategies to achieve any success in making their rules stick.

In this chapter we have looked at a broad set of rules that the guilds hoped to impose on various groups of people within the orbit of the corporative system. These groups included adolescent apprentices, journeyman wage laborers, male masters, and female, usually nonincorporated, artisans. In each section of the chapter, I have attempted to establish at least one standard that might indicate the success, or lack of it, and the extent of corporate social control. It proved impossible to find even one such indicator for the journeymen, and this seems to confirm a more general impression that guild authority was weakest when it came to controlling the labor force. Journeymen, moreover, were the only group in the corporate system that managed to establish its own organizations, more or less independently from the guilds.

With other groups the guilds seem to have been more successful. They managed to force apprentices to stay the full length of their term, or at least require this from candidates who wanted to join the corporate system. To judge by the distribution of Dutch paintings in the seventeenth century, guilds were quite, if not completely, successful in protecting local markets against outside competition. In towns with a mixed-religion population, guilds managed to impose religious constraints on their members whenever they were politically represented, either directly or indirectly, in the town's governing institutions. In such towns they were also relatively successful in suppressing female competition, as is demonstrated by the lower number of seamstresses in areas where guilds held political power.

All of this does not amount to conclusive proof, if that were ever possible with a topic like social control. Further research, moreover, should make this picture more detailed. We need more systematic information on local and regional variation and have only a limited understanding of the ways in which the system changed in the course of the seventeenth and eighteenth centuries. It would be interesting to analyze what happened in the wake of the abolition of the guilds during the French Revolution. But for the time being, and in the light of the repeated insistence that guilds were merely "flexible," it is important to note that they could be effective, if only partially, in imposing their rules in important areas of their jurisdiction and that the strategies employed in dealing with the inevitable fact that the rules could not be enforced completely helped protect significant benefits for, but also imposed significant constraints on, substantial sections of the urban populations in early modern Europe.

Notes

1. De Vries, *European Urbanization,* 39.

2. This critique goes back to the eighteenth-century Enlightenment. For a discussion of the French *discours* against the corporations, see Kaplan, *La fin des corporations,* 7–49; a Dutch seventeenth-century critique of the guilds is discussed in Lucassen, "Het welvaren van Leiden (1659–1662)," 13–22. See also Davids, "From de la Court to Vreede." For the nineteenth-century evaluation of guilds, especially among German scholars, see Ehmer, "Traditionelles Denken und neue Fragestellungen," 19–29.

3. Smith, *The Wealth of Nations,* 232–33 (bk. 1, chap. 9, pt. 2).

4. The tone for this argument was set by the brilliant and highly influential work of Sonenscher, *Work and Wages.* See also the slightly earlier, very outspoken Swanson, "The Illusion of Economic Structure," 29–48.

5. See, e.g., Deceulaer, "Guilds and Litigation," 207; Farr, "On the Shop Floor," 25, 54; idem, *Artisans in Europe,* 88, 91; Ward, *Metropolitan Communities,* 146; Woodward, *Men at Work,* 28. Likewise, Rosser recently emphasized "the remarkable diversity and adaptability of organizations of working people in medieval European towns": "Crafts, Guilds and the Negotiation of Work," 30.

6. Schwarz, *London in the Age of Industrialisation,* 215.

7. For guild strategies, see Cerutti, *La ville et les métiers;* idem, "Group Strategies and Trade Strategies"; Poni, "Local Market Rules and Practices"; and Panhuysen, *Maatwerk.*

8. See, e.g., Prak, "Individual, Corporation and Society," 272–76.

9. This section has profited from the discussions at a conference on Apprenticeship (Middle Ages–2000), organized in Alden Biesen, Belgium, by the FWO Research Network on Labor, December 8–9, 2000, where the program included papers by Peter Stabel (Ghent), Karel Davids (Amsterdam), Bert De Munck (Brussels), Reinhold Reith (Augsburg), Clare Crowston (Urbana, Illinois), Gilles Postel-Vinay (Paris), and Jeroen Onstenk ('s-Hertogenbosch) that proved helpful for this chapter.

10. Dunlop and Dunman, *English Apprenticeship and Child Labour,* 31–33; Epstein, *Wage Labor and Guilds,* 239–40.

11. Kaplan, "l'Apprentisage," 450–51.

12. Snell, *Annals of the Labouring Poor,* 228.

13. Panhuysen, *Maatwerk,* 140.

14. Ibid., 139; Epstein, "Craft Guilds," 694–743; Davids, "Apprenticeship and Guild Control," paper presented at the conference Apprenticeship (Middle Ages–2000), Alden Biesen, Belgium, December 8–9, 2000.

15. This is borne out by the fact that in early modern London a former apprentice could enter any trade, no matter if it coincided with his training or not (Schwarz, *London in the Age of Industrialisation,* 216–18). This, however, was unusual, probably even in England. In most towns an applicant had to be apprenticed in the trade he hoped to enter.

16. By common consent, however, three to four years was enough to acquire the skills, also in England: Krausman Ben-Amos, *Adolescence and Youth,* 123.

17. Kaplan, "l'Apprentisage," 442. Dunlop, *English Apprenticeship*, 44 refers to the exclusion of bastards and foreigners, or even people from neighboring districts.

18. Lane, *Apprenticeship in England*, 213–14.

19. Brooks, "Apprenticeship, Social Mobility," 77; see also Kaplan, "l'Apprentisage," 436.

20. Lane, *Apprenticeship in England*, 188.

21. Smith, "London Apprentices," 150.

22. Lane, *Apprenticeship in England*, 206–7.

23. Brooks, "Apprenticeship, Social Mobility," 80.

24. Smith, "London Apprentices," 151.

25. Lane, *Apprenticeship in England*, 208–9.

26. Kaplan, "l'Apprentisage," 441–42.

27. Smith, "London Apprentices," 150–51. Lane, *Apprenticeship in England*, 191, 196; Brooks, "Apprenticeship, Social Mobility," 78.

28. Smith, "London Apprentices," 157; Brooks, "Apprenticeship, Social Mobility," 53–54; Lane, *Apprenticeship in England*, 187.

29. Kaplan, "l'Apprentisage," 468.

30. Snell, *Annals*, 228. The statute's regulations were inspired in many ways by those already in force among the London guilds.

31. Dunlop, *English Apprenticeship*, 73–75, 83; Brooks, "Apprenticeship, Social Mobility," 54.

32. Kaplan, "l'Apprentisage," 437; Kaplan, *The Bakers of Paris*, 198.

33. Unfortunately, the only systematic study of apprenticeship in the early modern Low Countries is not yet in print: Bert De Munck, *Leerpraktijken*. For the tailors, see Panhuysen, *Maatwerk*, 137–42; Deceulaer, *Pluriforme patronen*, 261–90.

34. Reith, "Apprentices in the German Crafts in Early Modern Times."

35. Krausman Ben-Amos, "Failure to Become Freemen," 166. See also Snell, *Annals*, 235–40 for evidence that most apprentices in England, in rural as well as urban areas, served the full term, at least until the middle of the eighteenth century.

36. Rappaport, *Worlds within Worlds*, 311, 320.

37. In France this document was generally introduced in 1781 and called the *livret*: Kaplan, "Réflexions sur la police," 56–57; idem, *Bakers of Paris*, 215–16.

38. Krausman Ben-Amos, "Failure to Become Freemen," 155.

39. See Snell, *Annals*, chap. 5, which deals mainly with rural apprentices.

40. The importance of the master's reputation for the apprentice is briefly discussed by Brooks, "Apprenticeship, Social Mobility," 60.

41. Krausman Ben-Amos, "Failure to Become Freemen," 163–65.

42. Davies, *The Enforcement of English Apprenticeship*, 17–19, 25, 83; the number of London apprentices is provided by Brooks, "Apprenticeship, Social Mobility," 55.

43. Darnton, "Workers Revolt." The original source for the story is Contat, *Anecdotes typographiques*.

44. Sonenscher, *Work and Wages*, 153–54, 159–60; also Sonenscher, "Journeymen's

Migrations," 74–96.

45. Ehmer, "Worlds of Mobility," 187.

46. Ibid.

47. Sonenscher, "Journeymen's Migrations," 82–83.

48. Wesoly, *Lehrlinge und Handwerksgesellen,* 276.

49. On German *wandern*: Reininghaus, "Migrationen von Handwerkern," 194–212; Elkar, *Walz;* on tramping: Leeson, *Travelling Brothers.* Regional variations in tramping are discussed in Epstein, "Journeymen Mobility."

50. Sonenscher, "Journeymen's Migrations," 89.

51. Truant, *Rites of Labor,* 96–97.

52. Wesoly, *Lehrlinge und Handwerksgesellen,* 336.

53. Rappaport, *Worlds within Worlds,* 220–22.

54. About the London yeomanry: Rappaport, *Worlds within Worlds;* and Schulte Beerbühl, *Vom Gesellenverein;* on the German organizations: Reininghaus, *Die Entstehung der Gesellengilden;* and Schulz, *Handwerksgesellen;* and on French *companonnages*: Truant, *Rites of Labor.*

55. Quoted in Wesoly, *Lehrlinge und Handwerksgesellen,* 306–7. The only book length study of these boxes, to my knowledge, is Bos, *"'Uyt liefde tot malcander.'"*

56. This paragraph closely follows the argument in the masterful survey by Lis and Soly, "An 'Irresistible Phalanx,'" 11–52.

57. Lis and Soly, "De macht van 'vrije arbeiders,'" 30–32.

58. This is ironic in the light of some claims that guilds had originally been created with the specific goal in mind of controlling the workforce and the labor market: Epstein, *Wage Labor and Guilds,* 259.

59. Truant, "Independent and Insolent," 170.

60. For the bakers, see Kaplan, *Bakers of Paris.* The tailors are discussed by Deceulaer, *Pluriforme patroner;* Panhuysen, *Maatwerk;* and Crowston, *Fabricating Women.* The painters and their guild are discussed in Montias, *Artists and Artisans in Delft.* For the gold and silversmiths, see Bimbenet-Privat, *Les orfèvres Parisiens;* and Mitchell, ed., *Goldsmiths, Silversmiths and Bankers.*

61. In some branches, like hat making, the major workshops were so powerful, they did not need the guild to help bolster their market position. As a result, these guilds were notably more relaxed about the enforcement of the monopoly: Sonenscher, *The Hatters,* 49.

62. *Archiefbescheiden,* edited by Miedema, vol. 2, 514, 518, 525, 526, 539, 541, 546, 550. The history of the Dutch guilds of St. Luke is the subject of Hoogewerff, *De geschiedenis van de St. Lucasgilden in Nederland.* The Haarlem guild is discussed in Taverne, "Salomon de Bray." For the delicate balance between punishment and consensus: Berlin, "'Broken All in Pieces,'" 83; Kaplan, *Bakers of Paris,* 491.

63. Archer, *The Pursuit of Stability,* 138–39. The word 'ground rabbit' was used in Germany, and also in the Low Countries, for illegal, i.e. nonmember, workers: Walker, *German Home Towns,* 86.

64. Berlin, "'Broken All in Pieces,'" 79–80.

65. Kaplan, *Bakers of Paris,* 165.

66. Hesselink, "Goud-en zilversmeden," 143–44; see also Berlin, "'Broken All in Pieces,'" 80.

67. Farr, *Artisans in Europe,* 89.

68. See the seminal article by Kaplan, "Les corporations, les 'faux ouvriers' et le faubourg Saint-Antoine," 353–78.

69. Montias, "Art Dealers," 248–49.

70. Percentages calculated for 1622 on the basis of de Vries and van der Woude, *The First Modern Economy,* 64 (table 3.10). Amsterdam's share in the urban population of Holland in 1622 was 29 percent.

71. Panhuysen, *Maatwerk,* 276–79; cf. also Deceulaer, "Guilds and Litigation," 205–6.

72. Kaplan, *Bakers of Paris,* 481.

73. Deceulaer, "Guilds and Litigation," 182.

74. Rappaport, *Worlds within Worlds,* 201–5, 212.

75. Miedema, *Archiefbescheiden,* vol. 2, 522, 532; cf. Friedrichs, *Urban Politics,* 39–40.

76. Deceulaer, "Guilds and Litigation," 190. On the contents of such petitions, also Prak, "Individual, Corporation."

77. Truant, "Parisian Guildswomen," 53.

78. Sonenscher, *Work and Wages,* 246.

79. Farr, *Artisans in Europe,* 164–69; also Bossenga, *The Politics of Privilege;* Lis and Soly, "Entrepreneurs, corporations et autorités publiques," 725–44; Prak, "Corporate Politics."

80. For a survey, see MacKenney, *Tradesmen and Traders,* chap. 2.

81. Lourens and Lucassen, "Ambachtsgilden binnen een handelskapitalistische stad," 134–39, 152.

82. This argument is further developed and illustrated in Prak, "The Politics of Intolerance."

83. François, "De l'uniformité à la tolérance," 783–800.

84. More details on this arrangement in François, *Protestants et catholiques en Allemagne.*

85. Interestingly, in Dublin, a city with a mixed Catholic and Anglican population, the guilds also managed to use their political influence to impose religious uniformity. The result here, however, was that guilds lost control over parts of the local economy: Hill, *From Patriots to Unionists,* 32–41.

86. Black, *Guilds and Civil Society,* 4. Significantly, this situation among the guild masters was mirrored by that of the journeymen. The French *compagnonnage* system also created 'fictive families,' with the innkeeper and his wife called "father" and "mother": Truant, *Rites of Labor,* 190–91 (quotation on 191).

87. Palmen, "De gilden en hun sociale betekenis," 229–31; for Utrecht: Bos, *"Uyt liefde tot malcander,"* 147; Prak, "Politik, Kultur, und politische Kultur," 78–79.

88. Walker, *German Home Towns,* 73–76; see also Farr, *Artisans in Europe,* 222–23.

89. Roper, *The Holy Household,* 38, 136–39.

90. Farr, *Hands of Honor*, 22–23.

91. Significantly, sons born before their fathers had become a member of the guild were treated as outsiders and deprived of the privileges available to "genuine" sons of the masters: Kaplan, *Bakers of Paris*, 273–74.

92. Prak, "Individual, Corporation," 265–66, 273.

93. But certainly not the only one, as this process was already underway before Luther: Herlihy, *Opera Muliebria*, chap. 7.

94. Panhuysen, *Maatwerk*, 206.

95. Quast, "Vrouwen in gilden in Den Bosch, Utrecht en Leiden," 30.

96. Kloek, *Wie hij zij*, 48–77.

97. Panhuysen, *Maatwerk*, 206.

98. Ward, *Metropolitan Communities*, 128.

99. Wiesner, *Working Women*, 166.

100. Howell, *Women, Production, and Patriarchy*, 88–89; Wiesner, *Women and Gender*, 103; Honeyman and Goodman, "Women's Work," 610–12.

101. For a general discussion, see Honeyman and Goodman, "Women's Work."

102. Howell, *Women, Production, and Patriarchy*, 89–90, 133, 137 and *passim;* idem, "Women, the Family Economy and the Structures of Market Production."

103. Wiesner, "Guilds, Male Bonding, and Women's Work," 125–37.

104. Quataert, "The Shaping of Women's Work in Manufacturing," 1122–48.

105. Ibid., 1133.

106. Roper, *Holy Household*, 31.

107. Snell, *Annals of the Labouring Poor*, 279–82.

108. Krausman Ben-Amos, "Women Apprentices," 229–30, 234.

109. Wiesner, *Working Women*, 165–79.

110. Hafter, "Women Who Wove," 48–57.

111. Ward, *Metropolitan Communities*, 131, 142.

112. This paragraph relies entirely on Panhuysen, *Maatwerk*, 209–33.

113. Compare also Musgrave, "Women and the Craft Guilds," 151–71.

114. Deceulaer and Panhuysen, "Schneider oder Näherinnen," 96–98.

115. This complements the observations by Howell, about guilds and political power, in her *Women, Production, and Patriarchy*, 137.

116. See Wensky, "Women's Guilds," 630–50; Coffin, "Gender and the Guild Order," 774.

117. This paragraph closely follows the argument in Crowston, "Engendering the Guilds," 339–71; but see also Coffin, "Gender and the Guild Order"; and Truant, "Parisian Guildswomen," 46–61.

118. Panhuysen, *Maatwerk*, 222–24.

Behavioral Regulation in the City: Families, Religious Associations, and the Role of Poor Relief

KATHERINE A. LYNCH

In this essay, I explore the history of social control in western Europe as it related to the urban household and family. I argue that households and families of the lower and middling ranks of urban society were weakened by the impact of high urban mortality and levels of migration, making the formation of bonds of mutual assistance and control beyond the household particularly vital to the survival of individuals and their families. Beginning in the Medieval period, the search for sources of community and control outside the family often took place within voluntary associations that included men and women from diverse backgrounds. From another direction, I suggest that during the sixteenth century, religious and civic authorities became more active in regulating behavior from within the household itself as part of the confessionalization process. In both cases, evidence suggests that members of religiously based or civic communities accepted or even sought out a certain level of behavioral regulation. This regulation was legitimated in part by the fact that community membership often conferred entitlements to assistance in time of need. The existence of these entitlements, with their attendant requirements of behavioral conformity, led to a higher level of social integration than would have been possible without them.

I address several lines of historical inquiry. The first concerns historical assessments of the treatment of the poor in the early modern period. Social historians in the last twenty years or so, many of them influenced by the work of Michel Foucault or repelled by an earlier, self-congratulatory historiography on charitable institutions, have often judged the effectiveness of poor relief policy by its treatment of the poorest of the poor, those who were increasingly subject to the harshest state and city government repression from the sixteenth century onward—the "sturdy beggars" or homeless vagrants who sometimes terrorized the countryside of Europe in years of high prices, war, or general social disruption. A focus on government policy toward these groups must necessarily yield the grimmest of assessments of the intentions and effectiveness of poor relief, since policy was designed as much to repress as to assist these elements of the poor.[1] However, studies of what the Dutch called the "house poor" or residential poor, who have been known across the centuries as the "respectable" or "deserving" poor, suggest that these sorts of poor people have very often enjoyed fairly dependable entitlements to small amounts of assistance from civic collectivities as well as church sources. In this essay I focus upon the "house poor," members of the urban lower classes who were also among those of modest means most likely to participate in groups that provided for mutual assistance while seeking to regulate the behavior of their members.

From a second historiographical direction, I address the relationship between poor relief and the confessionalization process of the sixteenth century. Historians of the sixteenth and seventeenth centuries have used the notion of "confessionalization" to understand the means that leaders of the three major religious confessions, Lutheran, Calvinist, and Roman Catholic, used to spread their differing versions of Christianity.[2] Confessionalization involved the establishment of theologically well-defined churches with doctrines that church leaders attempted to teach more systematically to the laity. Clergy became more active in teaching and upholding tenets of new or renovated faiths. The confessionalization process was particularly active in urban centers. Towns and cities were critical to the process of Europe's confessional development, serving in many instances as incubators, and later, showcases for newly emerging visions of community that confessionalization brought about. Moreover, urban dwellers were generally the first to experience intensified forms of social regulation during the sixteenth and seventeenth centuries, including efforts by secular as well as religious authorities to exert greater control over domestic and public life. For some scholars, social regulation was in fact the key result of confessionalization, serving as a harbinger of more aggressive forms of social discipline that early modern territorial rulers gradually imposed upon their subjects in the process of modern state building.[3] Although early modern heads of state were doubtless innovators when it came to building institutions for regulating the lives of their subjects more closely, the spirit that informed the idea of regulating the urban order was hardly new.

Third, this study seeks to illuminate interrelationships among household life, poor relief, and social regulation by expanding Peter Laslett's work on the "nuclear hardship hypothesis," which suggests that the nature of a society's household organization is strongly related to the relative dependency of household members upon assistance from others during times of need. Laslett argues that in societies where nuclear households were the norm, people depended upon kin outside the household as well as larger collectivities such as parish groups, confraternal organizations, or other charitable and poor relief institutions for assistance. The practice of "neolocality," which prescribed that newly married young people set up their own households, also contributed to making nuclear households more vulnerable. He writes:

"the more widespread the nuclear family, and the more strictly neo-local rules are applied, the more important collective institutions will be for the security of the individual." In fact, "[t]he collectivity provided just those forms of assistance which might be supposed to belong to the responsibilities of family and kin."[4] According to Laslett, households formed at the time of marriage, and then consisting ordinarily of parents and children, or even one generation, were—ceteris paribus— more vulnerable than complex or extended households to what Michael Anderson termed "critical life situations," including poverty brought on by the death, sickness, underemployment, or old age of key providers living in the household.[5] Thought of in insurance terms, individuals living in smaller households were able to spread the risks associated with life's "critical" situations among fewer adults than was possible for those in large, complex households. Laslett notes that: "The collectivity was normally the only agency other than the immediate family . . . which stood in an insurance relationship to the individual."[6]

The idea that people living in nuclear households would need more assistance from external collective agencies than people whose residential families were larger and more complex makes a great deal of sense. However, the level of security provided to individuals in complex or extended family systems must not be overstated. Even in cities such as Florence where large patrilineal structures predominated among the city's patriciate, there were whole categories of people who remained unprotected by family ties. Not only those without families, orphans or foundlings, but the poorest members of wealthy families often ended their days in charitable institutions sponsored by church or commune, some of which had been endowed by their ancestors.[7] Thus, while those living in northern Europe or other regions where nuclear households and neolocal household formation predominated needed assistance from extrafamilial collectivities, even members of affluent social groups in southern Europe often had recourse to associations that not only helped them preserve their families but also sought to exert some behavioral control over them.

Where did European urbanites look for viable models of mutual support and control that they could use to build organized networks of support for themselves? People cannot create such organizations out of nothing. They need tools and materials to construct such collective organizations including financial resources, values and mentalities, and even inspiration. One of the most fruitful sources of specific models for the construction of extrafamilial forms of assistance and control available was provided by the Church. Because of their viability and moral prestige, religious or religiously inspired organizations became models that urban laymen and laywomen could use to address insecurities both they and their households might experience in the normal course of life. However, these urbanites did not simply accept ready-made organizations or institutions handed to them by the Church. Rather, men and women tried to adapt certain elements of church organizations and fashion them to their own uses as well as they could, seeking to build networks of association that would furnish the sorts of protection and control that in many other societies are provided mainly by extended kin or clan.

Mutual Support and the Regulation of Behavior in Confraternities

The church elite consisted of men and to a much lesser extent women religious who dwelt together in regular communities or collectivities of their own. Monasteries, convents, and brotherhoods of the mendicant orders proved particularly influential as sources of inspiration for those seeking a greater level of security. Interestingly, it was these sorts of organizations that patristic writers thought of when they considered the "family." As the late Michael Sheehan observed, there was relatively little systematic thinking in patristic writing about family relations as we think of them. When canonists discussed families, what they had in mind were organized communities such as monasteries or the households of bishops rather than groups of individuals related by bonds of blood or affiliation.[8] Given the size of their "households" and their mainly adult composition, these organizations were arguably much better sheltered from the "critical life situations" that threatened households of the laity, whether nuclear or extended. The prestige they enjoyed and the collective values they practiced made these religious institutions worthy of emulation, or at least of adaptation, to the needs of lay families and individuals.

Voluntary, self-regulating communities of wide appeal to late Medieval and early modern Europeans sought to build fraternal ties of the "spirit" among their members that would regulate their behavior at home, at church, and in the street. For many men and women of the middling and lower classes, confraternities performed some of the protective functions of extended kin. Beyond behavioral regulation, confraternities often provided men of the urban elite with opportunities for forming ties of association that helped maintain the governments of civic communities.

At the most general level, late Medieval confraternities (or in England, fraternities) were groups of men and women who united for the celebration of religious services, who often provided mutually for the burial of group members, and who looked out for each other in times of individual need by distributing charity and alms from the contributions of living members and the legacies of defunct ones. Beyond these broad general features, lay confraternities developed along several types. There were confraternities devoted exclusively to regular devotions within a confraternal church or chapel. Other confraternities were based in neighborhoods that, while focusing on the distribution of charity among neighbors, gave gifts to strangers as well. In addition, the fourteenth and fifteenth centuries witnessed the emergence of particularly zealous penitential confraternities, usually limited to men, whose members sought to emulate the piety of mendicant religious orders by flagellation and other public demonstrations of self-mortification. Some urban confraternities of the late Medieval and early modern period became increasingly outward looking, organizing more systematic forms of almsgiving and charitable activities outside the confraternal community.[9] These included such efforts as assisting foundlings, prisoners, or the wandering poor, and raising funds to dower poor unmarried women.[10] With the exception of confraternities tied to specific crafts, which were not only exclusive but usually obligatory, urban confraternal membership represented an expression of conscious choice.[11] Indeed, confraternities can be considered among the original voluntary associations of Western society.

The growth in confraternal participation in late Medieval Europe is well documented, though measures are imprecise. The religious sociologist Gabriel Le Bras, one of the fathers of confraternal studies, believed that between the thirteenth and fifteenth centuries, most Christians were members of confraternities, which may have been true of those living in the countryside.[12] Many historians, however, have focused on the growth of confraternities in towns and cities, which have left richer archival sources. Estimates of the numbers and sizes of confraternities are quite approximate. The town of Zamora, in Léon-Castille, for example, saw its first confraternity in 1230. By 1400, there were ten, and by the second half of the sixteenth century when the town's population was approximately 8,600, there were 150 confraternities, most of them numbering 20 or 30 individuals.[13] Elsewhere in Spain, confraternities grew most rapidly in the fifteenth century in territories won back from the Muslims.[14] In the small Tuscan town of San Sepolcro in the mid-thirteenth century, confraternity membership totaled about 1,200 in a population of less than 5,000. At that time, approximately one-third of the town's households were represented by a male confraternity member.[15] The fifteenth-century Norman city of Rouen had confraternities in 88 percent of its parishes.[16] In medium-sized cities of the fourteenth and fifteenth century, the number of confraternities usually ranged from 30 to 40.[17] In fifteenth- and sixteenth-century Bologna, 10 to 20 percent of the adult population belonged to a confraternity, though membership varied by gender and social class, with wealthier men being most likely to join multiple groups.[18] In late sixteenth-century Geneva, there were 60 confraternities in a town of 10,000–12,000.[19]

Many urban confraternities seem to have been remarkably heterogeneous organizations that included both men and women and crossed boundaries of social class and sometimes neighborhood. Confraternal membership generally required evidence of good character and the desire to live in harmony with other members, who might number from fifty to several hundred.[20] Confraternal dues varied, but an average seems to have been a sum approximating several days' wages of a working man.[21] Other costs could include occasional alms, fines for missing confraternal events, and payments in wax for devotional candles. Although the destitute sometimes benefited from confraternal outreach efforts, they were largely unable to join urban confraternities by virtue of their inability to pay annual dues, contributions, and alms.[22] Confraternities, therefore, generally attracted urbanites from the lower and middling ranks of society above the very poor and destitute and below the ranks of the nobility.[23]

Most studies of urban confraternities show not only that women participated in them but that many confraternal companies were nearly evenly balanced by gender.[24] In certain instances, this balance stemmed from the fact that husbands and wives could join the same confraternity.[25] In other settings, however, confraternal records show little tendency for husbands and wives to join together.[26] Companies in which women played the most active role included those with a strong basis in local neighborhoods, devotional confraternities that women wished to restrict to themselves, and those with well-developed charitable goals. By contrast, women were excluded de facto from confraternities composed solely of members practicing the same craft, and gradually from the fourteenth century onward, from the newer penitential confraternities.[27]

Jacques Chiffoleau has done the most to suggest the intimate links among urban patterns of high mortality and migration and the consequent need that attracted many people to the solidarities of confraternal life to help compensate for their lack of blood kin. In wills left by migrants who had come to the city alone, many lamented being cut off from their ancestral roots in the countryside and from the consolation of burial among kin in their places of birth. Migrants' wills reflected a loss of extended ties of kin solidarity both in daily life and in the afterlife, leading some to request burial in their places of birth and others to express a longing for a set of ancestors whom they had known or imagined.[28] Those with few relatives in the city were especially moved to seek out confraternity membership to ensure themselves of proper Christian burial in the here-and-now and security for the care of their souls after death.[29]

The growth of confraternities and the dedication of much of their devotional life to commemorating the deaths of departed "brothers" and "sisters" suggest that confraternities filled a real need for social inclusion and community in the face of unpredictable mortality patterns and an absence of kin members to assist them. Indeed, several observers have suggested that confraternities can best be understood as artificial families. Gabriel Le Bras argues that confraternities served to mitigate certain negative aspects of urban life by facilitating newcomers' relations with more settled people and linking individuals together for mutual assistance.[30] Given the size of most urban confraternities, which appear to have numbered in the hundreds, it is wise not to take the family analogy too literally, though as Chiffoleau suggests, a kin group of this size would have been an extraordinary comfort to a relatively isolated individual. Maurice Agulhon's notion of the confraternity as a sort of artificial extended family is more accurate. Confraternities seem to have served less as a substitute for primary bonds of the nuclear family and more as a complement to them, much in the manner of an extended kin network.[31] As Catherine Vincent argues: "There was no substitution of one structure for another, but rather a prolongation of one into the other. Generally speaking, the confraternal movement was not built on the ruins of family bonds; better, it was nourished by them without ever totally eclipsing them."[32]

The importance of artificial families of spiritual kin varied by social class. For artisans or small merchants who constituted the backbone of confraternal membership in many late Medieval cities, confraternal membership gave "cooperative access to the spiritual resources that [the wealthy] enjoyed by virtue of . . . personal wealth and status: a confessor, indulgences, an honorable funeral, and interment in mendicant robes."[33] For men and women of more modest means, regular attendance at monthly meetings and the security of knowing that one lived in a network of spiritual kin probably helped accomplish what one scholar has identified as many laymen's chief goal amidst the Church's and larger world's disastrous conditions of the fourteenth century: to look "for recovery of a simple relation of love to God and neighbor."[34] Among individuals or couples literally without kin in the city, the extended kinship network that confraternities supplied might well have provided the principal players who mourned their passing.[35] For wealthy men, associations born within large gender-segregated communities could supply useful business contacts.[36]

Joining a confraternity not only meant participating in a shared ritual life and gaining some entitlements to practical assistance in times of penury or death. It also meant agreeing to a code of conduct or set of behaviors toward other members. A membership document from the Gild of the Holy Trinity and St. Leonard in Lancaster attested to this group's concern with chastity and the marriage bond, noting that "the honour of the women of the gild was to be a matter of concern to all the brethren, who were enjoined not only to observe personal purity, but to refuse admission to their homes to those who were known to be adulterers."[37]

Like confraternities on the continent, urban parish fraternities in England tried to ensure peace and harmony among their members at confraternal banquets and in daily life. They forbade lawsuits among members, refused to allow members to stand as guarantors of one another's debts, and excluded quarrelsome individuals from their midst. While confraternities had always attempted to regulate the behavior of their members by accepting only people of good reputation, and by seeing to it that brothers and sisters maintained peaceful relations with one another, evidence suggests that by the fifteenth and sixteenth centuries, this kind of behavioral regulation became increasingly important, especially among confraternities of the urban elite. The lengths to which urban fraternities in such towns and cities as Leicester, Norwich, London, and Canterbury sought to regulate their members' behavior often stemmed from the fact that urban associations more often attracted wealthier members than rural ones, sometimes including those who played a conspicuous role in town or city government. Men of the more fashionable confraternities seem to have become increasingly conscious of the need for discretion and self-control in their behavior in order to preserve their own as well as the group's reputation.[38]

Although the organizational model that inspired the founding of most confraternities was a religious one, and many were, in fact, inspired by clerical example and participation, confraternal life in European cities and towns represented an important example of ways that voluntary associations of laymen, both men and women, sought to regulate and control the behavior of their members. Serving multiple functions of building patterns of sociability, religious observance, and mutual trust, confraternities also increased the level of social integration within the urban setting. In very practical terms, they served as the kind of collectivity that Laslett describes, stepping in to help individuals in their time of need.

Impacts of Humanism and Protestantism

By the sixteenth century, many confraternities' original concern with providing prayers for the care of their members' souls after death seemed to be on the wane. Indeed, by this period, many of the more fashionable groups were becoming objects of criticism for their worldliness and their seeming betrayal of the sort of charitable behavior that had once extended beyond the boundaries of their membership. In the view of some, confraternities now appeared selfish and self-absorbed. Those that still brought together rich and poor men in the same organization were often divided sharply along class lines, with the poor members being essentially the charitable agents of the rich. In the context of such critiques, humanist scholars stressed the need to recapture a purer Pauline sense of charity and community.[39] Martin Luther was only one of many of his generation who criticized confraternities for what they saw as the lapse of charitable activities, criticizing them for their behavior on the occasion of annual feasts, activities that were especially offensive at a time when a growing number of the urban poor needed help.[40]

What concerned humanists and reformers most was not that confraternities were neglecting to care for the itinerant poor or vagrants, but that they apparently felt little concern for those to whom they were most obligated to be in closer bonds of charity—their neighbors, the poor who lived in their towns and whom they passed on the street on a daily basis, those who were themselves members of the urban community. The work of reclaiming a spirit of authentic charity therefore focused upon the domiciled, or house poor.[41] While problems of begging and vagrancy in many sixteenth-century cities loomed large, the task of building confessional or civic communities suggested the more urgent necessity of reaffirming bonds with those individuals and households of the city who had the strongest and most legitimate claims on local relief funds.

Efforts to extend relief to the local poor were important for a variety of reasons. First of all, this kind of assistance was consistent with Medieval notions of charity, which involved ongoing, face-to-face relationships between giver and receiver. Distributions of food, firewood, and other necessities of life to the domiciled poor could be discreet when necessary and redounded more to the credit of civic institutions than to individual donors, thus avoiding charges of private patronage.[42] Furthermore, it was easier to screen domiciled recipients of assistance for their conformity to confessional values or civic norms of behavior.[43] The domiciled poor were easier to assist, and they were also more likely to express the gratitude and humility appropriate to their dependent status.

While reformers such as Zwingli or Bucer struggled to integrate civic and confessional visions of community, in towns where Calvinism won over sizable portions of city populations, Reformed churches were often confronted by the obvious fact that boundaries of confessional and civic communities did not coincide.[44] Although Calvinist authorities hoped to expand their "household of faith" to include the entire population of cities and towns, the sixteenth-century Calvinist definition of confessional community was a very restrictive one. Anyone could attend services, but only those who in the view of the church's leadership conformed to behavioral norms were considered worthy of receiving communion and being considered full church members. The experience of Calvinist churches during the late-sixteenth and seventeenth centuries suggests that only a minority of any town's population where Reformed churches survived was likely to display the religious commitment and behavior required for full membership.

Struggles over family-based poor relief arrangements in areas affected by the Calvinist Reformation became vastly more complicated than in Lutheran or Catholic areas because of the problematic relationship that emerging Reformed churches bore to the states or cities in which they developed. While Calvinism was granted the status of "public" church in a number of localities, enjoying the support of local magistrates, in others it failed to gain the kind of monopoly status that Lutheran or Catholic churches enjoyed in many territorial states and towns of the Empire.[45]

There was no single way that Calvinist church leaders organized poor relief. In many cases, tension developed between their desire to shape a spiritually and behaviorally restrictive confessional community, and local government officials' sometimes competing desire to use poor relief resources to bind together the larger civic community. In the presence of such tension, the best solution that Calvinist authorities sought was freedom to organize poor relief within the confessional community without the intrusion of municipal authorities. In the southern French Calvinist stronghold of Nîmes, for example, Reformed congregations were content to be allowed to limit their poor relief activities to church members, being careful not to give money from legacies, church collections, or alms boxes to Roman Catholics residents, war refugees, or travelers.[46] This sort of arrangement was also possible in certain towns of Holland. In Amsterdam and Dordrecht, where civic authorities were sympathetic to the Calvinist movement, municipal governments granted Calvinist consistories—the governing authority of churches composed of laity and clergy—a high degree of autonomy in organizing relief to the poor, including those who were not members of the congregation. However, in towns such as Leiden or Gouda where leaders of town government were hostile to the growth of a restrictive confessional church, Calvinist deacons—those directly in charge of distributing assistance—were subject to more municipal control.[47]

The development of poor relief in the Calvinist East Frisian city of Emden illustrates many of the problems that the Calvinist movement encountered in adapting an older civic form of poor relief to its own confessional purposes. Like the urban poor in much of Europe, Emden's poor were assisted by income from endowments that pious laymen had willed over the years for their care. Income generated by these foundations was generally left to assist the indigenous, respectable, or "house" poor. With the success of the Calvinist movement during the 1560s and 1570s, church leaders advocated simply combining the offices of church deacon and overseer of the town's poor. An inherent tension nonetheless continued to exist between the older poor relief system that combined Roman Catholic piety and concern for the civic poor, and the Calvinist system that was designed essentially to bind together a newly emerging confessional community. Since the town still contained a large number of Roman Catholic poor, even as the Calvinist church gained in status, what was one to do with them?

To address this problem, Emden's Calvinist leaders created a new way to raise money for deacons to distribute exclusively to the poor of the Calvinist congregation so that they would not be forced to beg. They called it their "Becken" diaconate, so named for the collection plate passed around in Sunday services for this purpose. In this way, the church consecrated monies to the congregation's poor while leaving funds from older endowments for the support of the civic poor without regard to church affiliation. Significantly, Calvinists established this new source of poor assistance "to eliminate criticism from outside the church that the church did not take care of its own members."[48] In the competitive world of confessional rivalries, the charge of failing to support one's own poor was a serious one.

Like confraternal organizations, religious communities formed by the process of confessionalization not only contributed funds to their members in times of need; they sought to shape the domestic and public behavior of their members as well. Records of city governments and certain religious bodies during the sixteenth and early-seventeenth centuries reveal the active role that civic and religious leaders played in the domestic lives of members of both sorts of communities. Although such intervention was not new to Reformation Europe, organizational records suggest that the domestic and public behavior of ordinary citizens during this time became subject to increased scrutiny as confessional and civic authorities worked to teach and enforce standards of acceptable behavior.

Confessional and civic bodies of the period seem to have wished to inculcate the sort of peaceful behavior that late Medieval confraternal groups required of their members, but with an increasing emphasis upon individuals in their family and wider community lives. Church, consistory, and civic marriage courts set up during the Reformation had the task of building or overseeing the confessional community itself. In the course of their duties, Calvinist consistories and civic courts in Lutheran areas dealt with the sins of "aversion" that had long threatened ties of charity and sociability among believers. Nonetheless, with their increasing concern for domestic life, authorities were also increasingly concerned with at least public manifestations of sins of "concupiscence" that threatened marriages and families and the larger civic and confessional order that was built upon them.[49] Although all areas touched by the Protestant Reformation experienced the growth of new courts regulating marriage, regions where the influence of Reformed Protestantism was greatest—whether Zwinglian, Bucerian, or Calvinist—seem to have been especially marked by agencies seeking to reform morals within the family as well as in the larger urban community.[50]

Regulation of marriage and family life was based upon ecclesiastical courts composed of clergy, church bodies comprising clergy and laity, and courts composed only of laymen. Whatever their composition, the identification of these bodies with reinvigorated values of civic or confessional movements seems to have bolstered their sense of legitimate entitlement to intervene into family and neighborhood relations to bring belief and behavior into conformity with civic or new religious norms. The Reformation in the imperial city of Augsburg brought with it the establishment in the 1530s of two lay institutions with jurisdiction over marriage and family life. These included the Discipline Lords who had the power to levy fines, imprisonment, and banishment for transgressions including violent behavior, fornication, and adultery; and the Marriage Court, which adjudicated disputes over promises of marriage, the loss of virginity, child support, and divorce.[51]

Although the Discipline Lords had the power of banishment and imprisonment, they—like members of the Marriage Court—carried out their mission mainly through admonition. In their goal of teaching proper behavior, they had few guides in Medieval canon law, which though focused on marriage, had no real interest in nor remedy for the sort of "disorderly marriages" that the Discipline Lords confronted daily. They therefore had to draw on a mixed repertoire of confessional piety, common sense, and civic values to address the multiple domestic problems they faced.[52] City fathers sitting on the Marriage Court sought to reinforce the city's families with using the values and mores of the households of respectable guild members, including the subordination of wives to husbands and children to parents. They tried to enforce a family ethic that emphasized the virtue of gaining parental permission for marriage. The Marriage Court did not challenge husbands' right to discipline their wives but prohibited excessive violence and affirmed that what went on within the household was very much the business of civic authorities now alert to the enforcement of both civic and confessional values.[53]

There were broad similarities between the concerns of Augsburg's Marriage Court and the concerns of Calvinist consistories elsewhere. In their earliest years, the clergy and lay church officers who composed these local bodies were mainly concerned to inculcate and enforce Calvinist religious practices while eradicating other loyalties, whether Catholic or Lutheran. But beyond trying to enforce the rules of their newly emerging confession, they were also presented with a variety of domestic and community issues ranging from ruling on the validity of certain promises of marriage to problems between wives and husbands, parents and children, and neighbors.

Nîmes' consistory was initially concerned mainly with extirpating lingering signs of Catholic practice, regulating sexual behavior, resolving questions relating to marriage vows, and resolving disputes among members of the community. On the issue of marriage, the consistory here was particularly eager to ensure that parental consent for marriage was given for women under age twenty-five and men under thirty years of age.[54] The consistory used church members to try to effect mutual reconciliation among quarreling neighbors. Minor sins such as card playing and dancing brought on a "tongue-lashing," while more serious offenses led to the consistory's censure, their requirement of public penance, or finally excommunication for fornication, apostasy, and "other outrageous acts."[55]

In Geneva, the supervision of community and family life required the consistory there to become involved in a similar variety of problems that were either referred to them by neighbors or ferreted out by deacons or other officials of the Church and civic community. Errors that included deviations from Calvinist practice, lack of respect for secular officials, conflicts between neighbors, or adulterous behavior that had become public knowledge all qualified as fit subjects for consideration by church consistories. Unlike secular courts, which could and did sentence offenders to mutilation and capital punishments, the consistory mainly cajoled and admonished the errant, meting out severe tongue lashings for recidivists and reserving their harshest penalty of excommunication for the most intransigent.[56] The population of Geneva was subjected to a high level of scrutiny in the 1560s when an estimated 7 percent of the city's population was called in annually by the consistory to answer charges. Excommunication took place in over half of the cases it heard, an atypically high figure in comparative perspective. Those willing to express penitence publicly in church were admitted back into the confessional community. The admonitions of this "remarkably intrusive institution" concerning matters related to marital discord seem to have had some effect, since recidivism rates were quite low.[57]

Confessional Differences?

There has been some disagreement on how and whether Calvinist consistories were more active than other local judicial or police institutions in intervening in domestic life. In his comparative study of Catholic and Calvinist areas of the Rhineland Palatinate, Joel Harrington finds that while there was little difference in the proclivity of civil magistrates living in areas dominated by the three major religious confessions to intervene in family matters, Calvinist consistories were more engaged in regulating domestic life, bringing a "striking sophistication in its approach to marital strife."[58]

It does not seem that overworked consistory members aggressively searched out matters to consider, however.[59] In most cases, consistories summoned church members to appear before them only when neighbors became aware of domestic troubles, conflict or scandal had become public knowledge, or persistent rumors reached the ears of church officials who routinely made home visits to members of the congregation. Similarly, though conversations between those individuals summoned before them and the consistory were themselves private, punishments that they handed down were frequently public, whether between individual men and women, among neighbors, or before the congregation as a whole.

Calvinist consistories' emphasis on public expressions of penitence and atonement seems rather consistent across time and space, especially in cases where those who had been excommunicated were requesting reintegration into the community. Thus, one woman whom the Nîmes consistory had excommunicated and who requested that she be allowed to participate in a ceremony of penitence at a 5 A.M. Sunday religious service rather than the 9 A.M. service was denied her request.[60]

Conversely, though Calvinist consistories saw themselves as fully entitled to summon individuals or couples for domestic behavior that violated confessional norms against fornication or adultery, thus imposing their authority over domestic relations, there were certain areas of privacy that interested them relatively little. For example, Calvinist consistories seem to have been relatively uninterested in probing the inner workings of individuals' consciences, being more concerned with modifying outward behavior. In this respect, an appearance before the Calvinist consistory that was composed largely of laymen seems to have been quite unlike a visit to the Catholic confessional. Thus, consistories' concern to modify domestic behavior that literally spilled out into the public sphere, or that had obvious negative public consequences, contrasted sharply with an increasingly intensive probing of the individual conscience, accompanied by a private, personal, penitential regime that prevailed in the Catholic confessional.[61]

Although Calvinist consistories could, in principle, order disciplinary measures only for church members, in many instances they attempted to exert control over the larger civic community, for example by trying to urge magistrates to enforce restrictions on activities during the Sabbath. Moreover, in areas where the Calvinist church had some claims to public support, with its deacons serving as overseers of the poor, those of the house poor who received poor relief were expected to conform to behavioral norms of congregation members. As in many cities of Holland, in Nîmes the Calvinist consistory supervised distributions of bread to all of the town's resident poor, not just members of the church.[62] Along with their bread, the poor therefore received a "strong dose of moral guidance and social discipline."[63]

Interestingly, though consistorial regulation in Nîmes and other cities often created grumbling and evoked only grudging compliance among people on the margins of Calvinist congregations, it was not necessarily the case that the poor rejected the principle of church discipline itself. Indeed, in towns like Emden, some of those receiving poor relief from the Calvinist congregation criticized the church's consistory because of its relative laxity when compared to more exacting discipline standards of the rival Anabaptist congregation![64]

Resistance to consistorial efforts to correct behavior resulted from a variety of causes ranging from apathy and religious heterodoxy to anger at the violation of personal dignity that a public summoning entailed. In areas of the Holy Roman Empire where Calvinism was instituted or recently reinstituted, as was the case with the Palatinate after 1584, lingering Lutheran sympathies among the common people led to the heckling of Calvinist preachers during sermons, general rowdiness during worship, and a widespread failure to attend the growing number of required prayer and catechetical meetings that took place outside regular worship times.[65]

Huguenots of Languedoc, for their part, had notions of personal honor that meant that consistories often had to summon individuals several times in order to exact their appearance. Skepticism over the authority of the entire consistorial system with its lay elders encouraged reluctant Calvinists here to resist bowing to its efforts to regulate relations inside the family and larger community.[66]

Men at the top of the social hierarchy were particularly difficult to bring to order. In Calvinist Scotland, the Presbyterian kirk sessions (the equivalent of continental consistories), encountered little resistance to their authority of the kind found in the Palatinate. Yet, even they found it difficult to exert their authority over powerful men, particularly in matters of sexual promiscuity that led to public scandal. Kirk sessions were prepared to adjust the requirement of public penance into penalties more in keeping with the gentry's need to save face in the community. One 1585 case of fornication called forth a punishment rather different from the sort imposed upon the lowly. Confessing his sin to the kirk session, the Provost of Elgin nonetheless argued that "repentance consistit not in the external gestoir of the bodie . . . but in the hart." Despite this astonishing theology, he was allowed to contribute to the repair of a church window instead of making a public penitential appearance.[67]

Even at the height of confessional movements, consistories and church courts were not able to enforce compliance in the same manner as secular courts and were hardly able to enforce it at all on the geographically mobile. Yet the threat or reality of excommunication from Calvinist congregations involving expulsion from the celebration of the Eucharist was real and apparently meant a great deal to householders and serious church members. Consistorial power sometimes extended its reach over all households of the city, requiring at least outward conformity to confessional norms among poor households that received assistance from church or civic community. Both the workings of poor relief systems targeting the house poor and the relatively widespread acceptance of church discipline suggest that those who wished to be members of the confessional community or to remain within boundaries of the civic one gradually accepted a tighter scrutiny of their public and domestic lives. Many had no choice if they wished to remain within town walls.

Balance

By the eighteenth century, a combination of circumstances including the growth of a new, more inner-directed piety, a decline in confessional militancy, and the process of secularization occurring in many towns and cities meant that the sorts of organizations I have studied here lost their ability to regulate the behavior of urban dwellers, especially those who lived their lives largely outside the reach of religious organizations. Increasing rates of in- and out-migration associated with this period also further weakened the ability of any urban authorities—secular or religious—to control the behavior of lower-class inhabitants. This does not mean that all sources of regulation were in decline, however. Religious, philanthropic, and civic poor relief systems in many cities continued to favor the house poor and to require that households receiving assistance observe certain behavioral norms.

To see the imposition of behavioral regulations on individuals and families as nothing more than top-down social policy imposed by urban elites would be a mistake. As I have tried to suggest, from the earliest period of Medieval urbanization, city and town dwellers had become used to gathering together and having their lives as individuals or as families regulated by authorities both religious and secular. The acceptance of some of this regulation was explicitly voluntary. At other times, it was part of the price that one had to pay for the higher level of security that might come from numbering among the more entitled members of confessional or civic communities. Erasmus captured best the enduring relevance of an ancient form of collective life to the individuals and families that composed European towns and cities and who depended upon sources external to themselves for support. In a well-known letter of August 14, 1518, he asked: "What, else, I ask you, is a city than a great monastery?"[68]

Notes

The editors thank Cambridge University Press for permission to reproduce excerpts from Katherine A. Lynch's book *Individuals, Families and Communities in Europe, 1200–1800: The Urban Foundations of Western Society.*

1. For generally gloomy considerations of the impact of assistance to the poor see Foucault, *Madness and Civilization;* Hufton, *The Poor of Eighteenth-Century France;* Lis and Soly, *Poverty and Capitalism;* Jütte, *Poverty and Deviance in Early Modern Europe.*

2. Reinhard, "Reformation, Counter-Reformation," 383–404. Reinhard dates this process from the 1520s until the late-seventeenth century, with the Revocation of the Edict of Nantes.

3. "'Social regulation' referred to totally unsystematic and reactive attempts to produce norms of discipline and order: 'Social regulating' wants to help prevail over the negative conditions of the social surroundings through drill and preparation and to order the societal life.' On the other hand, 'social discipline' wants to strengthen, with a view to the state, the ordered life in the society and to discipline human behavior in work and in morals." See Fehler, "Social Welfare in Early Modern Emden," 32–41. Fehler's excellent introduction to this literature considers Schulze, "Gerhard Oestreichs Begriff," 265–302; and Martin Dinges's work on Bordeaux: "Frühneuzeitliche Armenfürsorge," 5–29. See also Schilling, "Confessional Europe." Fehler's study is now published as *Poor Relief and Protestantism.*

4. Laslett, "Family, Kinship," 156, 166.

5. Anderson, *Family Structure,* 136–61.

6. Laslett, "Family, Kinship," 166.

7. Gavitt, *Charity and Children,* 192, 204. For some parents, even the abandonment of their child to a foundling home represented only a temporary measure—designed to relieve the family during a "critical life situation." Nonetheless, given high mortality levels, only a very small percentage of children were eventually reclaimed.

8. Sheehan, "The European Family and Canon Law," 348–49, 356.

9. On the outward looking features of late Medieval confraternities, see Banker, *Death in the Community,* 57–58.

10. Nicholas Terpstra details the different types of confraternities in central Italy. See *Lay Confraternities,* 38–49.

11. Agulhon, *La sociabilité méridionale,* 173, makes this remark concerning confraternities affiliated with different occupational groups.

12. Le Bras, "De la sociologie rurale," 433–34.

13. Flynn, *Sacred Charity,* 15.

14. Vincent, *Les confréries médiévales,* 43.

15. Banker, *Death,* 59, 64. Flynn, *Sacred Charity,* 16–17, supplies data mainly for the sixteenth century, when Valladolid (population 30,000) boasted "at least 100 confraternities," and Toledo (population 60,000), 143. In the province of Cuenca, there was one confraternity for every 48 households, and one for each 100 households in

New Castile. There were 75 confraternities in Florence (population 59,000), 68 in Lyon (population 45,000–65,000), 67 in Lübeck (population 25,000 in 1400), and 99 for Hamburg (population 16,000–18,000) on the eve of the Reformation.

16. Vincent, *Des charités bien ordonnées,* 58–59. She notes that only 13 percent of other deaneries in the diocese had approved confraternities. This finding may stem, however, from the inequality in the record keeping between rural and urban parishes, with the rural parishes producing and preserving fewer of them.

17. The cities include: Nantes, whose population of 12,000 at the end of the fifteenth century contained 30 confraternities, and Dijon, with a similar population and number of confraternities. Ghent, with a population of 64,000 had 40; Florence, whose population shrank two-thirds, from 110,000 to 37,000 in 1440, nonetheless saw the number of confraternities increase from 30 in 1325 to 52 in 1400. See Vincent, *Les confréries médiévales,* 42–43; and Henderson, *Piety and Charity,* 39.

18. Terpstra, *Lay Confraternities,* 83.

19. Binz, "Les confréries . . .," 239.

20. Vincent, *Les confréries médiévales,* 54, 136.

21. Binz, "Les confréries," 250. Two days' wages of a workman, plus the cost of one-half pound of wax for devotional candles, was the entry fee for the fifteenth-century confraternity of Our Lady and the Blessed Sacrament in Liège. See Dietrich, "Brotherhood and Community," 121.

22. Little, *Liberty, Charity, Fraternity,* 71–73.

23. Vincent, *Les confréries médiévales,* 185.

24. Chiffoleau, *La comptabilité de l'au-delà,* 277–78. Gender mixing was the norm in Switzerland, according to Binz, "Les confréries," 247, 250. Banker, *Death,* 54, 59, 111, studying the Italian confraternity of San Bartolomeo, shows a balanced sex ratio from the 1260s to the early-fourteenth century. Beginning in the early-fourteenth century, however, both "praising" and "discipline" confraternities began to exclude women. Hanawalt, "Keepers of the Lights," 25, found women in all but five of the 500-odd confraternities whose memberships were summarized in reports of 1389. When clergy members are excluded, women composed approximately 50 percent of the membership of those groups.

25. Vincent, *Des charités,* 207. She shows that in the Norman confraternities or "charities" that she studied, husbands and wives who joined in couples constituted between 33 and 62 percent of members.

26. Morard, "Une charité bien ordonnée," 278, shows husbands and wives entering devotional confraternities together. See also Vincent, *Les confréries médiévales,* 57; and Westlake, *The Parish Gilds,* 23–24. Dietrich, however, found little evidence of husbands and wives joining the same confraternities. See "Brotherhood," 132, 163. He shows (p. 193) that there were ties of blood linking together confraternity members but notes that confraternities' "lines of spiritual kinship cut across the lines of blood kinship" (231).

27. Banker, *Death,* 149; Terpstra, *Lay Confraternities,* 116–25, on the newer Observant model of confraternal life and the gradual exclusion of women from it.

28. Chiffoleau, *La comptabilité,* 180–1, 199–201.

29. On the lack of family bonds in new areas of the cities, see also de la Roncière, "Les confréries à Florence," 305–6. Henderson, *Piety and Charity,* 29, writing of thirteenth-century Florence, notes that those joining penitential confraternities "were recent immigrants who needed to make contact with people outside their professional circle or immediate neighborhood."

30. Le Bras, "De la sociologie rurale," 423.

31. Agulhon, *La sociabilité méridionale,* 211. Cf. Heers, *Le clan familial,* 259–61, who argues that confraternities may have been artificial substitutes for clan bonds in Genoa and the rest of western Europe.

32. Vincent, *Les confréries médiévales,* 61–62.

33. Terpstra, *Lay Confraternities,* 81.

34. Ibid., 40; Little, *Religious Poverty,* 209, mentions the existence of Benedictine-inspired confraternities in the eleventh century and similar types of organizations within Sufi Islam in the twelfth and thirteenth centuries.

35. Henderson, *Piety and Charity,* 157–60.

36. Weissman, *Ritual Brotherhood,* passim.

37. Cited in Westlake, *The Parish Gilds,* 35. He notes that this clause seems to have been written before the composition of the company's ordinances in 1377 and was unusual.

38. McRee, "Religious Guilds and Regulation of Behavior," 108–16. Remling, *Bruderschaften in Franken,* 268–77, describes the growing appeal of membership in Kitzingen's St. Anne confraternity among city councilors as well as merchants and wealthy craftsmen in the early-sixteenth century.

39. Pullan, *Rich and Poor,* 224–38.

40. Ozment, *The Reformation in the Cities,* 84–85. Pullan, *Rich and Poor,* 126, cites the 1543 decree by Venice's Council of Ten forbidding the city's elite *Scuole Grandi* from their habits of ostentatious banqueting on the same grounds as Luther—because money could better go to the poor.

41. Wandel, *Always among Us,* 128, 151, notes this central concern in the Zurich case.

42. See Allesandro Caravia's criticism of these aspects of the "charity" of the Venetian Scuole Grandi in the mid-sixteenth century in Pullan, *Rich and Poor,* 117–19.

43. Wandel, *Always among Us,* 132, notes the increasing specificity with which Zurich's City Council articulated those behaviors expected among recipients of poor relief according to a new Poor Law in 1520 and that "caritas" was to be exercised within the limits of the community defined by a set of norms including "dress, demeanor, [and] behavior" (162).

44. Reinhard shows that one of the primary goals of confessionalization was to create a homogeneous religious community, based on dissidents' expulsion or emigration. Situations of religious pluralism such as those under discussion here were, therefore, the exception rather than the rule. See "Reformation, Counter-Reformation," 393.

45. In 1572, the States of Holland and Zeeland made the Reformed faith the privileged but not formally established church of the provinces.

46. Mentzer, "Organizational Endeavour," 7–17. The author notes, however, that waves of Protestant refugees from centers of warfare overwhelmed the town's financial resources by the 1580s, resulting in the Church's increasing reluctance to assist outsiders, even their coreligionists.

47. Parker, *The Reformation of Community,* 90–96, 116–22. The accommodation between leaders of urban governments and Calvinist churches in Haarlem and Delft lay between these two ends of the spectrum. In Haarlem, Calvinist deacons were allowed to minister to the poor of the congregation without municipal authority interference. In Delft, the government required Calvinist deacons to care for all of the city's poor, at least until 1614 (van der Vlis, *Leven in armoede*).

48. Fehler, *Poor Relief,* 122–30, 164–77. Keeping assistance for the congregation's poor separate from funds for the rest of the town poor became too difficult to manage, however, so the two funds were merged in 1578.

49. John Bossy, *Christianity in the West,* 35, discusses this distinction between sins of the spirit and sins of the flesh, the former (including pride, envy, and anger) being particularly destructive of bonds of community.

50. Roper, *The Holy Household,* 16–17.

51. Ibid., 61–63.

52. Martin Ingram makes the same point about the work of the Church courts in England in a slightly later period: "Domestic relations were . . . on the border of public and private morality in this period—matters to be influenced by exhortation but not ordinarily by the exercise of formal discipline." See *Church Courts,* 142.

53. Roper, *Holy Household,* 169–71.

54. Legislation requiring parental consent for marriage was a product of the Reformation in many areas, though the age of majority varied. Estèbe and Vogler, "La genèse," 376, imply that the age of majority was twenty-five years for both women and men in the consistories of the Palatinate and Languedoc that they sampled. Safley, "Civic Morality and the Domestic Economy," 176, notes that men under twenty and women under eighteen in Reformation Basel needed parental permission to marry. Van der Heijden reports that the age of majority for marriage was twenty for women and twenty-five for men in seventeenth-century Rotterdam. See "Secular and Ecclesiastical Marriage Control: Rotterdam, 1550–1700," 42, fn. 15. Despite the focus of some historians on sexual matters, data for Nîmes at least show that only 7.5 percent of the consistory's cases there were for violations of sexual morality. As Mentzer notes, a higher proportion of cases involved the sin of dancing. See "*Disciplina nervus ecclesiae,*" 103–4.

55. Mentzer, "*Disciplina nervus ecclesiae,*" 111.

56. Robert M. Kingdon notes that earlier published studies on the consistory of Geneva often focused on exceptional and notorious cases. A more systematic sample yields a portrait of the Geneva Consistory from the 1530s to 1560s as mainly a "compulsory counselling service" (8). See "Calvin and the Family," 5–18; and Monter, "The

Consistory of Geneva," 467–84. In contrast, Martin Ingram saw little "counselling" in the English church court setting. See *Church Courts,* 188.

57. Kingdon, *Adultery and Divorce,* 180.

58. Harrington, *Reordering Marriage,* 263. Unlike Kingdon, Harrington is more skeptical about the definitive nature of the behavioral changes that consistories were able to effect, noting (though not statistically) that many couples were recidivists, especially those for whom domestic violence was the cause of their original summoning.

59. Ibid., 249–51. Harrington suggests that the aggressiveness of Calvinist consistories has been exaggerated. He cites their hesitancy to intervene into household affairs unless constrained by the need to suppress what were public scandals.

60. Mentzer, *"Disciplina nervus ecclesiae,"* 112.

61. Ibid., 113–14. The author notes, "The sacrament of penance within pre-Reformation and more especially Counter-Reformation Catholic circles was a very private, introspective affair. . . . The confessor assisted each penitent in the identification and correction of an entire range of transgressions. He was as attentive to sins of thought as to those of word and deed. Emendation, moreover, was personal, something to be discreetly worked out between the individual sinner and his or her spiritual advisor. Excommunication was infrequent and public reparation reserved for spectacular situations. . . . Calvinist pastors and elders, seated in the consistory, adopted a different approach. Their attention fastened on public failings of word and deed. Secret sin, though admittedly wrong, did not directly concern them." See also his reference to a judicial official summoned before the consistory to answer to charges of sexual misconduct. Having gone through one appearance before the consistory, he refused to return for a second, expressing his preference for auricular confession over the pastor's "harsh admonitions" (95). Roper, *Holy Household,* 64–65, makes the same distinction.

62. Mentzer, "Organizational Endeavour," 28.

63. Ibid., 17–28. The growing popularity of parliamentary legislation designed to regulate the behavior of the lower orders leads Paul Slack to observe: "All this suggests that the machinery of the poor law was not designed as an economic regulator, but as a moral, social and political one." See *Poverty and Policy,* 130.

64. Pettegree, *Emden and the Dutch Revolt,* 236.

65. Estèbe and Vogler, "La genèse d'une société protestante . . .," 371–72.

66. Ibid., 385.

67. Mitchison and Leneman, *Sexuality and Social Control,* 74–75, 203–6, 237. They note, however, that from the 1660s until the latter-eighteenth century, among the ordinary people, two-thirds of men identified as fathers of illegitimate children admitted their paternity quickly and some accompanied the mothers of their children when they were summoned by the kirk session. Ingram, *Church Courts,* 336, suggests that English ecclesiastical courts believed that "it was not necessarily in the interests of public order to expose leading citizens to shame and humiliation" and sometimes permitted punishments to be paid in cash.

68. Letter to Paul Volz, of 14 August 1518, cited in Wandel, *Always among Us,* 14.

CHAPTER 12

Social Control of Violence, Violence As Social Control: The Case of Early Modern Germany

GERD SCHWERHOFF

TRANSLATED BY LUKAS HOFFMANN

The problem of the containment, control, and suppression of violence is inextricably linked with that of its nature. Scholars of present-day violence, as well as historians concerned with the topic, sometimes fail to see this central connection or to discuss it appropriately. Thus, the author of a recent overview of sociological publications dealing with violence complains that a real sociology of violence is almost totally lacking. According to Trutz von Trotha, sociologists—following the classic route from Durkheim and Weber to Simmel and Elias—restrict their analysis to the reasons for violence, instead of developing a real phenomenology of violence. In Trotha's view, a "thick description" (Clifford Geertz), a microhistoric exploration of violence, is needed.[1] My contribution tries to reach this goal, for the field of history rather than sociology. When sociologists discuss violence, they often do so with the opportunities of its prevention in mind, whereas historians are concerned with the shape of violence and its control in the past. The problem at the root of both discussions is the same: without a precise understanding of what violence actually is, one can hardly talk adequately about its prevention, suppression, or changing shape.

There are various ideas about the true nature of violence. The implicit or explicit starting point of many discussions is the assumption of an inborn drive to aggression, which needs to be suppressed and modified by strong sociocultural forces. Among those forces, the emergence of the state in the early modern period has always been credited with a central role. Opinions differ, however, about the question to what extent the control of violence can be regarded as historically successful, or if such a control can be successful at all. Even though it does acknowledge internal ambivalences, the theory of civilization by Norbert Elias can be seen as the optimistic branch of such a viewpoint, according to which the suppression of violence is not only possible but sociologically probable over the long term. Not only could violence thus be suppressed outwardly, but its control could be internalized and thus become a habit. Other, more pessimistic views have gained prominence during the twentieth century with its wars, civil wars, and genocides. The authors concerned see civilization merely as a thin veneer through which the animal within the human being can break out to the surface at any time.[2] In its most radical form such a view not only rejects a discussion of the reasons for violence but also refuses to attribute a social meaning to acts of violence. Thus, according to Wolfgang Sofsky, any attempt to make sense out of incidents that seem senseless at first sight fails to acknowledge the unique character of violence; the understanding resulting from it would suppress the essential truth of violence: namely the sufferings of its victims and the lust for violence of the culprits.[3]

Hence, the following analysis of the social meanings and the context of early modern violence must be considered as one analysis among various possibilities. It is by no means the only legitimate approach to the phenomenon of violence, and it does not exclude alternative interpretations. Nevertheless, to me it seems a necessary and useful perspective, after all, that presents an alternative to a "history of violence" based on Norbert Elias's theory of civilization. Unmistakably, the approach based on this theory is undergoing an astonishing renaissance at the moment, perhaps because its capacities to solve problems are suggestively convincing at first sight. In my view, however, this approach conceals many problems, so that it ultimately results into a problematic distortion. In contrast to Elias's approach, this article tries to view violence from a historical-anthropological perspective, while it also draws inspiration from micro- and gender history.[4] But far from presenting a case study, this article is largely based on scattered research. The empirical base for my remarks is constituted mainly by German research into crime and violence—which has been largely neglected internationally until now. Further, I am going to refer to examples from my own research into the city of Cologne, whenever this seems possible and reasonable.[5]

The initial part of this article (Terms and Definitions) explains what kind of violence is focused on here and which concept of social control will be used in this article. Following this, a first overview is given showing the various forms of violent acts. The evidence of the criminal sources is presented in the traditional language of legal history (Cases). For a proper interpretation of the social meaning and the context of violence, however, I then have to create an analytical framework that centers on the notion of honor (Phenomenology). The next section poses the question whether a more precise classification of early modern violence is possible (Typology). Only then are we able to discuss both sides—Social Control of Violence and Violence As Social Control. Finally, I will give some thought to the problem of the Historical Change of violence during the period dealt with.

Terms and Definitions

"Violence" and "social control": even if these two terms are considered separately, both remain as complex as they are amorphous. Their combination brings the risk of multiplying the initial problems. Would it make things easier for us if I were to name the issues at stake in this article the traditional "crime" and "punishment," until recently a favorite combination in the titles of German books? Or what about "delinquency" and "sanctions"? As we can see, there are some preliminary terminological and conceptual questions to be cleared, even though some readers may consider this a typically German bad habit.

To begin with, the definition of violence seems to be less difficult, at least if I were to focus wisely on "physical violence" in the sense of bodily harm, or damage to the bodily integrity of a human being.[6] But even physical violence constitutes a vast area. From the aim of contextualizing violent acts—a major theme of this article—it follows that there is no such thing as violence per se: we can only discuss its various manifestations. Here, we will only be concerned with those forms of physical violence that can be found in the judicial and criminal records of early modern societies; in other words, the violence that has been criminalized by an authority. Hence, we must deal with all those crimes that primarily included the exercise of violence or in which the exercise of violence formed an integral part. The legitimate use of violence by the authorities is largely excluded from this analysis. The purpose of violent sanctions and punishments as a medium of social control in general is widely accepted, although their history and specific functions in particular are hotly debated.[7] In this article those forms of violence will be discussed that are usually regarded only as targets of social control.

So far, however, some forms of violent crimes have been privileged by scholars. Homicide, for example, was in the center of an international debate because it is supposed to be the only valid quantitative indicator left that could provide us with information on the development of violence. The theory of civilization is often closely connected with such an argument.[8] Although I am going to use this discussion as a starting point in the next section of this article, the emphasis will be on different aspects, according to the research perspective outlined at the beginning.

At this point, my second theme, that of social control, comes in. In order to have a useful and not too broad understanding of the term social control, it is advisable not to include too many forms of reaction or sanctioning. Following a recent suggestion by Martin Dinges for a suitable definition, social control would be any form of social interaction and communication in which persons or groups define deviant behavior and react by taking measures against it.[9] For some sociologists such a definition might be too narrow, but they can be ignored here. For some historians, on the other hand, this definition might be far too broad.[10]

Precisely this broadness and flexibility, however, constitute the advantage of this definition, in contrast to more limited terms such as crime and punishment that are too much determined by the institutions of justice. The range of possible reactions is as broad as the character of the norms according to which deviant behavior is defined and corrected. The range of possible sanctions includes a set of initiatives going from verbal stigmatization, via exclusion from social circles, to material or bodily punishments. The norms can refer to authoritative matters or they can be highly informal norms. They may be shared by the whole community or only by a particular group with a very limited scope. Hence, conflicts about norms can be included very easily into a discussion of social control. In addition, this approach offers the opportunity to sharpen our view of non-authoritative forms of reactions, which would help us to place the role of justice firmly in its social context. Therefore, I am disinclined, generally speaking, to associate the concept of social control with those great narratives that have been subject to such strong criticism recently. Instead, it should be seen as a useful instrument for leaving a top-down model aside for a more complex understanding of the handling of violence in past societies.[11]

Physical violence in premodern times, according to my thesis, had a dual relationship to social control. On the one hand it can be understood as the object of this control: obviously, norms and sanctioning measures at various levels aimed at reducing, or at least coping with, physical violence and at a relative pacifying of society. On the other hand—and this is often neglected—violence is also a medium of social control. Frequently, violence is a reaction to or a sanction on the undesirable behavior of individual persons or groups who act contrary to previously defined norms. As a medium of social control, physical violence enjoyed a certain degree of acceptance in premodern times, even if—as an object—it was viewed as undesirable. The two dimensions are somewhat opposed to each other, and their mutual relationship has changed over time.[12]

Cases

Let us first take a closer look at the various kinds of violence to be found in the criminal records and how they were categorized. There was simple murder to start with, defined as the deliberate act of killing. The Carolina, the Imperial penal code of 1532, distinguishes between intentional, willful murder and without malice or out of revenge, both of which were punishable by death—the former by the wheel, the latter through the honorable execution by the sword.[13] To be put on a wheel was not the only cruel punishment for murder: for the insidious and secret murder by poisoning committed by a woman the penal code stipulated that the woman was to be drowned.[14] In practice, however, intentional murder was mostly connected with the crime of robbery. The drive for personal enrichment represents one of the most common motives for intentional murder. Often, the reader of early modern court records is taken aback by the seemingly unemotional summing up of cruel acts in the confessions of arrested murderers. For example, according to his own statement, Ludwig von Tetz, sentenced to the wheel in Cologne in October 1527, had committed at least seventeen murders together with various accomplices during the previous four years.[15] For several itinerant tradesmen, apprentices, or peasants their encounter with Ludwig meant the loss of their lives; they were killed because of their usually very modest belongings and were left along the streets unburied. Violent burglary in remote farms and casually committed murders were the specialty of Ludwig and his accomplices. Still, this multifaceted case does not suffice to illustrate all kinds of murder.

Most cases of violent death in early modern times—and there is common agreement on this fact within the international research community—were not intentional acts of murder, but rather impulsively aggressive acts arising out of a given situation. Quite typical for an urban context is the situation described by Hermann von Weinsberg, a member of the city council of Cologne: a group of Dutch sailors started a quarrel in an alehouse that developed into a fight. They fought it out in the streets later, and the situation escalated. One of the men participating in this fight hurt his leg and died the following day. The culprit fled across the Rhine.[16] Such an act of homicide in the heat of the moment was not a single isolated act, but the most extreme form of an often rather casual violent conflict whose lethal consequences were usually unintended.

A nocturnal encounter of some men in the center of Cologne in February 1593 could have had lethal consequences very easily, too. At 7 P.M. two groups of people met each other at a street corner: three master tailors who were just coming out of their guild house and three apprentice tailors on their way home from a tavern. The members of the two groups knew and mistrusted each other. The apprentices bumped into master Clais Steffen, who had just said goodbye to his two colleagues, and he noticed that his assailants proceeded to go after his friends. He followed them in his turn and shouted at his fellow masters to warn them that they were in danger and should be careful. Andrieß von Langenberg, the leader of the group of apprentices, shouted back angrily that Clais was lying and that no one was pursuing anyone. Despite this, in no time master Bernd von Dorsten suffered several deep cuts at the upper side of his nose and a still deeper wound above his eye where the knife had remained stuck. The identity of the culprit, however, remained unclear—nothing unusual for a violent encounter at night in which so many people were involved. It was established, though, that Andrieß von Langenberg, who was arrested, could not have done it.[17]

Other acts of violence, such as daily neighborhood quarrels, had a less spectacular character. On January 29, 1569, two carters, Heinrich Büchsenmacher and Contz von Bonn, faced each other in front of the town official. Heinrich filed a regular suit against Contz for recently attacking and wounding him, without any reason, at 10 P.M. in the street where they both lived, as he was coming home with his wife and his servants. Contz told a completely different story. When he was on his way home that evening, he saw Heinrich and his wife and greeted them with a friendly "good evening." Heinrich replied with rude and blasphemous remarks, for example that Contz should do his father's job and love his mother. In an attempt to calm the situation, the wife of Heinrich, who was just about to get completely mad, told Contz that her husband was drunk, so it would be best if he, Contz, went home. She even took the initiative herself by grabbing her neighbor's arm to lead him home. This, however, got Contz's wife into action who yelled at the other woman: "What makes you lead my husband; he is still able to walk on his own!" At the same time, Heinrich hit Contz with his arm, which was wrapped in his coat, while he carried a knife in his other hand. According to Contz, he had to defend himself in order to save himself from being wounded. This then developed into a brawl in which both opponents and their wives slipped on the icy street and fell to the ground. At the end Heinrich claimed he had been wounded seriously and filed a regular suit. When his wounds were inspected by the officials, however, he made a fool of himself because they could not find the slightest scratch.[18] The verbal confrontation seems to have been worse after all than his wounds.

Two further exceptional forms of violent activity are closely connected to the category of gender. One such form of violence is rape, which is often categorized as a sexual offense in modern descriptions, yet has a predominant violent aspect to it. Thus, the Carolina (article 119) defines rape as a criminal offense provided that the act had been forced upon the victim violently and against her will. In practice, however, as has been stressed by all historians, the barriers for prosecuting rape were very high, and it was extremely difficult for a potential plaintiff to prove that a crime had been committed.[19] Hence there are only a few such cases to be found in the criminal records. In the second gender-related form of violence, women were the perpetrators rather than the victims. The Carolina ranked infanticide among the most serious of its list of homicidal acts, defining it as the killing of a living baby, complete with all its limbs, in a secret and mean way (article 131). The case of Merg von Dülpen, an approximately seventeen-year-old unmarried day laborer who became pregnant, can be viewed as a classic example of this offense. After trying to hide her condition, she gave birth to a child in her chamber. She claimed her labors had been precocious, which had caused the child to die. The court, however, regarded it as proven that she had strangled her baby. Its body was found the following day in the toilet, and the mother was denounced by her neighbors, who had been suspicious for quite a while. In December 1591 Merg was drowned in the Rhine for her offense.[20] The determination with which the authorities imposed the officially prescribed punishments, in this case and in many others, shows that infanticide was considered a type of violence that shook the very foundations of the social order.

Phenomenology

The categories of offenses just discussed are only the starting point for a detailed description of violence in its specific shapes.[21] Such a phenomenology of violence cannot do without certain categories. Although it is difficult to be systematically consistent, a possible categorical pattern includes at least the following three aspects:

- The persons involved (by gender, age, social status, and other distinctive features, including perpetrator–victim relations and constellations, such as the question of a single culprit versus a group of perpetrators)
- The motives for violence (reasons and occasions)
- The forms of violence (the scene of the crime, the time at which the incident took place, circumstances surrounding the case, weapons involved, the way the escalation took place, and how fast this escalation happened)[22]

We could take each of the offenses already discussed and examine them in greater detail according to the dimensions listed above. We would then discover that these dimensions exhibit a great variety or a relative homogeneity according to the offense. Infanticide, for example, a well-researched crime, appears very homogeneous. The culprits are mostly young women, often maids, and the victims, as defined by law, their newly born children. In most cases, the women acted on their own without help from others. They had tried to hide their pregnancy. After the equally secret birth in a chamber, a field, or another arbitrarily chosen place, they killed the newborn child by hitting, strangling, or drowning. It is very difficult to make a sensible distinction between the reasons and the occasions in this case: the preservation of the woman's sexual honor, which was decisively curtailed or ruined completely by giving birth to an illegitimate child, suffices in most cases as the motive. So far, this is my attempt to briefly describe this offense with the help of our categorical pattern. However, this very rough description ignores the sophisticated level of discussion about the phenomenon of infanticide. For one thing, the legal conclusion drawn at the time, that concealment of pregnancy implied willful infanticide, is problematic. The women involved might have postponed the problem, hoping that it would be solved in a natural way by miscarriage or, in the last resort, by stillbirth. Even in case of a live birth, they had one more option in the form of abandonment. With respect to the way the offense was committed, finally, it can hardly be concluded from the statements of culprits like Merg von Dülpen whether it was an intentional violent act committed in cold blood, or if it was done out of panic in an extreme situation. Generally speaking, however, there are quite a few arguments that can be advanced in favor of viewing infanticides primarily as indicative of the shame and despair of single mothers rather than of violence and aggression.[23]

The segment making up the largest part of the criminal statistics, which I called affective violent activity and which also may be called agonal violence, is much more differentiated and diverse.[24] In fact, this segment is so diverse that it is questionable if one could describe and analyze it in a general way at all. Yet, I will attempt to do so, discussing some of the problems involved along the way. Let us first examine the protagonists. Their most characteristic feature is their male sex, even though the proportion of women was considerable in less serious forms of violence. The example of the neighborhood quarrel has shown that women had a supporting function in a brawl. Furthermore, the patterns of interaction in those quarrels reveal in the majority of the cases a gender homogeneity, to the extent that men faced men and women opposed women. Tellingly enough, the wife of Contz von Bonn became involved in the quarrel by attacking the wife of his opponent verbally. The age of the protagonists can be estimated only in a minority of the cases.[25] Nevertheless, there are many indications that the proportion of young people was very high among violent criminals.

Despite these differentiations, as far as the social status of the delinquents is concerned, we observe as a characteristic feature that violent activities, far from being marginalized to the social periphery, occurred at all levels of society. In rural areas, well-to-do husbandmen took up violence as often as day laborers. In the village of Heiden (in the County of Lippe) the proportion of violent criminals belonging to the upper classes was higher than that of any other class.[26] Also, in late Medieval and early modern towns, violence originated from the center of the community and not from fringe groups or poor casual laborers. The core group among the perpetrators appears to have been the artisanate, especially apprentices, but also masters. Special groups such as soldiers, sailors, carters, students, even town officials, also stood out from the general population as particularly aggressive. Toward the end of the Middle Ages, town patricians were known to be especially violent. By contrast, Joachim Eibach notes a wide-scale absence of smaller and bigger tradesmen and merchants among violent criminals in eighteenth-century Frankfurt. We will come back to this difference later on.[27]

Moving beyond this crude social positioning of the culprit, we can analyze the perpetrator–victim relationship. Often the people involved in a quarrel knew each other. In an urban context, Cologne for example, they were relatives, neighbors, or fellow professionals. In rural areas it was even more likely that people were ushered into violence with someone they knew. Aggression against strangers usually fell into the special category of xenophobia; in particular it was often a reaction against members of vagrant fringe groups or against soldiers.[28] In comparison, the likelihood was considerably higher that strangers met each other on urban streets and in town alehouses rather than in rural surroundings. In this respect it is also significant that these strangers usually belonged to a sim-

ilar social group; the violent encounter of craftsmen in Cologne is a typical example. Collective violence also was more characteristic of towns. Further, it was more
likely that brawls took place at festivals, such as the parish fair or carnival, than
at any other time of the year, both in the countryside and in towns. Even if individual opponents stood in front of a crowd, they were often surrounded by helpers,
supporters, and sometimes even mediators.

Let us now consider the second analytical dimension—the motives. First, we
can distinguish two ideal types (in Weber's sense): acts of violence that arose out
of the situation, in which no profound reasons seemed to be involved, and in
contrast, those that already had a previous history. Violent encounters arising
out of the situation usually involved people who did not know each other before
the incident. Those conflicts in which friends, relatives, neighbors, or workmates
were involved were bound to have a history of some sort or another. Yet, this
history is not always visible to the historian. Heinrich's attack on his neighbor
Contz, for instance, was described as having happened quite suddenly and without any warning, even though it is highly plausible that this incident was one
in a series of neighborhood quarrels. During encounters among strangers, however, the interaction was influenced by their prior experiences and stereotypes.
Certain preconditions, therefore, always played a part.

Deeper lying reasons for violence usually depend on a specific context; they
can hardly be classified within an abstract, universal system. Rainer Walz's description of the mental background of early modern rural societies has gained widespread acceptance. According to him, the actual shortage of goods caused the
rural imagery to be pervaded by the idea of a limited and constant supply of
goods. Consequently, the increase in wealth and the success of a neighbor were
almost automatically perceived as a personal loss and a personal defeat.[29] This
might explain why any quarrel about pasture rights, the use of common land,
or debts could escalate so easily and lead to years of conflicts. These conflicts
often erupted spontaneously out of the situation, even if the opponents had been
living on seemingly peaceful terms in the meantime. The actual origin of the
conflict, the historic nucleus of the dispute, could thus quickly be overlaid by
numerous secondary and tertiary incidents, which led to insults and disgraceful
deeds, to envy, hatred, and quarrel. The same argument can be applied to disputes over inheritance. In towns, the number of possible reasons for conflicts
and conflict constellations may well have been even more varied than in villages.
Consider again the quarrel between the master tailors and their apprentices in
Cologne. According to his own statement, the apprentice Andrieß von
Langenberg, arrested as one of the main culprits, did not work for a master; instead,
he went to citizens' houses "on his own initiative" in order to do tailoring work
there. He had even hired a couple of apprentices for some time. Without having gone through the usual years of apprenticeship, without having submitted
his masterpiece, he worked on his own, which in the eyes of the guild masters,

was an affront against their legitimate authority. Conversely, it is obvious that apprentices opposed the masters with hostility at times when it was difficult to obtain a master craftsman's diploma. Besides, Andrieß was not punished for the violent act but fined for disobeying the rules of the guild.

Actually, the occasions for violent conflict are situated at the border of our second category, that of motive, and the third, that of forms of violence. The sources hardly ever disclose when exactly the neighborly joking, poking fun at each other, and playing with words turned into a serious confrontation implying a conflict about one's honor, which could end in violence. Alcoholic drinks surely had an important catalyzing effect in this context, but historians fiercely debate whether beer, wine, and brandy merely facilitated violence or actively generated it. Personally, I am inclined toward the first position, and additionally I wish to place stress on the alehouse as an important scene of violent encounters.[30] What the other locations of crime—the streets and squares in a town, the village green and fields in the countryside—had in common was usually their public character. Hence, the insults, threats, and attacks made there were thought of as being exceptionally grave and defamatory.[31] But some quarrelers reacted extraordinarily sensitively, even if they were among themselves. Interactions in premodern times always aimed at preserving and defending one's honor and respect. An especially private sphere of action, in which the strict rules of moral respectability were set aside, could only have existed on an extremely restricted scale.

As already implied by these remarks, forms of violence cannot be analyzed in terms of certain static characteristics. Instead, the causes and the development of violence—and to a certain degree the violent acts themselves as well—should be thought of as a process. Typically, a conflict could start with a verbal confrontation and end with homicide. In between, there are various stages of escalation. Consequently, the distinction between perpetrator and victim can only be made afterward, in view of the rather accidental result of who in the end was wounded or killed. The escalation of violence, at least up to a certain turning point, usually conformed to specific social rules. Therefore, the relevant literature talks about ritualized violence or a liturgy of violence.[32] As mentioned earlier, no fixed script existed for the order of events in a conflict, but there was something like a set of behavioral components. Most of the protagonists shared a common logic of acting—or as Rainer Walz called it, an "agonal communication." Following the sociologist Niklas Luhman, Walz regards the "interaction among those present" and the focus on honor as being most characteristic for a simple social system such as early modern society. Accordingly, the characteristic feature of this form of communication is the continual screening of the acts and utterances of others for potentially defamatory aspects and an urge to react. No one involved wanted to lose face. Retaliation was one way of reacting, which meant to pay back a person's accusations or threats with the same kind.[33] An alternative was to further the escalation by using stronger words or even physical violence.

The essential element of agonal communication consisted of a broad spectrum of insults, defamatory phrases, and threats. Throughout northern Europe
an almost canonical repertoire of insults prevailed: "rogue" and "thief" for men
and "whore" for women recur with an astonishing regularity. Even blasphemies
can be understood as part of that predominantly male, provocative behavior that
was prevalent in the streets of early modern Europe.[34] The suggestion of incest
that Heinrich Contz uttered against his neighbor (he should do his father's job
and love his mother) certainly was among the more serious ones in the spectrum
of that repertoire. The extensive literature on insults and trials for defamatory
speech cannot be discussed in greater detail here. Barbara Krug-Richter's warning remark must suffice; she points out that insults, despite their stereotyped character, have always been used contextually dependent and were thus applicable
quite flexibly.[35]

The line between mere calumnies and unspecified threats on the one hand
and a very concrete threat of violence on the other hand was very thin indeed.
To use the personal pronoun in the second person singular while addressing the
other (*du*), which was only used among friends or by superiors while addressing
subordinates, or to snap one's fingers toward someone ranking higher, were meant
to elevate one's own social status or to degrade the social position of one's opponent, or both.[36] One of the most important gestures of aggression was the so-called
Herausfordern aus dem Haus: to challenge someone to come out of his house. If
the attacker succeeded in this, his opponent had stepped out of a special place of
peace, judicially protected as such; if the opponent did not appear, the attacker
could revile him as a coward. In the latter case, an aggravation could consist of
a violent attack on the house, damaging its fence, smashing the windows, or plung-
ing a knife into the front door. As a substitute for the body of the other, the external frontiers of his possessions were damaged.[37] When the opponents faced each
other directly, specific threatening gestures marked the borderline between verbal and physical violence. When sharp tongues proved ineffective, the use of knives
came in. These were mostly only bread knives, whose distribution could not be
controlled by the authorities for a long time. The drawing of knives was a central threatening gesture in the dramaturgy of a conflict shortly before the use of
physical violence. The first physical attack marks another stage of escalation. Knocking
down the other's hat, for example, was the initial provocative and degrading act
immediately prior to the use of fists. From that point, it was only a small step to
a slap at the ears and thus to the use of direct physical violence.

This is a typical phenomenology of violence in its agonal form. In order to
avoid any misunderstandings: this agonal culture can be found in many early
modern criminal records, but this does not mean that it was absolutely predominant.
Apart from instrumental varieties of violence, such as robbery (whether or not
accompanied by murder), it is also extremely difficult to categorize domestic violence according to this scheme, in particular violence between spouses or

between children and their parents. Ultimately, criminal records provide only a small glimpse through the keyhole into the inside of the house. The punishment of wives by their husbands and the punishment of children by their parents were, according to contemporary understanding, expressions of the legitimate power (*potestas*) that the head of the family or the parents possessed. By no means were these punishments viewed as instances of condemnable *violentia*. Only in cases of abuse, that is in cases of severe, long-term, and continued misuse of this right of punishment—or when physical violence was used excessively—did the authorities intervene. Whether such interventions can be regarded as the beginning of the domestication of men by the authorities or whether marriage was a violent relationship throughout the early modern period has recently been under dispute among historians.[38]

Typology

Is there a still better way to categorize criminalized violence in early modern times, beyond the outlined phenomenology? Can phenomena of violence be reduced to a few concise bipolarities? Pieter Spierenburg and Eva Lacour recently made suggestions leading in that direction. The nucleus of Spierenburg's theoretical model of analysis is a system "of two related but distinct axes." The poles of the first axis are "impulsive violence versus 'rational' violence"; those of the other axis are "ritual or expressive violence versus instrumental violence."[39] With the help of this model, Spierenburg tries to detect a change in violent behavior in Amsterdam. According to his analysis of the court records, impulsive violence had been predominant up to about 1750, whereas its share declined rapidly after the middle of the eighteenth century. With this observation he combines a statement about the perpetrator–victim relationship. Impulsive violence was predominant among strangers and their companions in the shape of sudden eruptions of aggression, taking place mostly in alehouses or in the streets. From about 1720, however, Spierenburg notes an increase in interfamilial violence while the violence against outsiders declined: "a shift from the killing of strangers to the killing of intimates."[40] Furthermore, this interfamilial violence increasingly was an expression of long-term tensions between spouses, for instance—and not, as in previous times, impulsive panic reactions.

Eva Lacour has taken up Spierenburg's suggestion, but she criticizes his typology and modifies it accordingly.[41] In Lacour's view, opposing impulsive and rationally planned violence seems inadequate. Instead, she suggests a three-dimensional analysis: motivation (angry or expressive versus instrumental), form (ritual or willful versus uncontrolled), and planning (planned versus unplanned).[42] At first sight this terminology might be confusing, but it hints at interesting differences in conceptualization between the sociologically inspired historian Spierenburg and the historically oriented psychologist Lacour. According to her, "impulsive aggression" can be found only where there is a reduction in or a complete loss of cognitive control on the culprit's side. Hence, she includes in this category only those cases from the court records in which the culprit attacked his victim but in which there was no preceding verbal conflict.[43] Still, in another sense she classifies two-thirds of the violent cases as being "caused by an impulsive act," as aggressions that were accompanied by anger and rage, serving the purpose of defending one's self-image, taking revenge, or something similar. Based on these criteria, more than 59 percent of all cases were uncontrolled acts, whereas only 15 percent were ritualized sequences of interaction. On the other end of the spectrum, we find almost one-third of the remaining acts being categorized as instrumental ones in which the participants tried to further their interests. Her conclusion that violence in daily life was "filled with anger and often used in an uncontrolled manner" is compatible with a scheme of fast and direct escalation. She draws up a useful scheme of three stages, borrowed from modern sociopsychological research: the first stage, verbal attacks, is followed by a second, more ambivalent stage, which is marked by an increase in the frequency of threatening gestures, a cry for help to people not involved, or sometimes by withdrawal, and the third stage is simple—physical violence. Although Lacour is able to apply this modern scheme to the early modern period, her findings distinctly differ on one point: the middle stage had a much shorter duration and, in many cases, it was even absent. Thus, violence was exercised "in a faster and more direct way."[44]

Both attempts to develop a typology are inspiring in my view, but they have their methodological shortcomings. For one thing, both are problematic to the extent that they attribute single cases to the poles of these models. Let us compare their suggestions with the categories used in the phenomenological outline, especially with the category of motivation. The isolation of a more restricted sphere of instrumental violence seems unproblematic—namely in cases of robbery and murder. But how are the affective and the instrumental aspects to be assessed in those cases of agonal violence that have a discernible or hidden history? Particularly in regard to the forms of violence and the respective sequence of events, these concepts do not fit at all into the phenomenology outlined above. Both authors tend to limit the sphere of physical violence very strictly. Although the history and the cultural context of conflicts are taken into consideration, in the end they are excluded from the analysis of violence as such. If violence is confined to the moment of hitting or stabbing just like that, then its understanding is almost inevitably reduced to naked aggression, to the pure drive. Moreover, Pieter Spierenburg is not consistent in this respect: although he excludes the sphere of verbal conflicts from the field of violence, he notes that affective violence was highly ritualized.[45] Lacour disagrees with him on this point and from her view with good reasons: because the ritual escalation of a conflict, too, refers rather to the history of that conflict than to the violent act itself.

My phenomenology of affective violence, which I have tried to describe systematically above, takes a different route in regard to two decisive points. For one thing, the history of indirect physical violence—insults, threats, and threatening gestures—forms an integral part of a cultural-historical definition of violence. Second, the issue of honor is, in my view, closely connected to this as a key motive of early modern violent acts. To the first point: to include threatening gestures, other kinds of threats, and even words may at first seem strange, viewed from the angle of a modern definition of violence. But this was the perspective of the contemporary protagonists. Although early modern jurisprudence was well able to differentiate between insults and beating to death, terms like *iniuria realia* (real injuries) which could include extremely brutal acts of violence, marked a broadly overlapping zone between physical and verbal violence.[46] Undoubtedly, this was the judicial reflex to social practice. In daily life, insulting words often marked the beginning of a spiral of escalation that could end with homicide. To talk about verbal violence conforms to the view of contemporaries. Insults hurt their honor, which was at least as important as the bodily integrity of their person. One could view this honor almost as being something like a second skin that had to be defended against violent attacks just like one's biological skin.

Different terms and definitions have their consequences. Thus, the differences between the phenomenology outlined above and the results of Eva Lacour's research appear less at the level of empirical data than at the level of categorical interpretations. Her conclusions about a fast and uncontrolled sequence of events in a conflict seem questionable because a large number of insults are excluded from her analysis of violence. With 18.3 percent in the county of Virneburg, for instance, the insults form a larger share than all other violent acts taken together (13.4 percent).[47] It is here that we would find those interactions that potentially could have led to violence but did not, maybe because the second stage of the sequence of events had indeed led not in the direction of an escalation of violence, but in the direction of an avoidance of violence. By no means did entering this second stage necessarily have to result in physical violence, as Lacour suggests. In Medieval Konstanz, to take another example, the 582 cases of violence registered in the criminal statistics had a leading position, with 33.7 percent of total criminal cases. But no fewer than 309 of these cases belonged to the category of armed threats, most of which were cases of knives pulled out. This also means that, although threats to use arms were involved, some 53 percent of all violent acts did not escalate.[48]

The importance of honor, to explain my second point, is essentially undisputed among scholars. But in detail there are important categorical differences that again can be illustrated from the work of Eva Lacour. In her analysis conflicts over honor are ranked at the same level with other types of violence, such as property fights, revenge, and alehouse quarrels.[49] The author herself, however, admits that many violent interactions not classified as conflicts over honor, including those about property, could have a strong aspect of honor. Likewise, many types of conflict could be seen as revengeful aggressions. Let us look at an example of a family feud in the rural area of the Eifel around 1750: after the first round of a brutal brawl between two families, the male aggressor wanted to retreat from the scene of the fight. At that moment, the wife of his opponent cried, "if your wife had not begged for mercy, you would already have received what you deserve!"[50] She referred to the fact that he was a criminal, who had just been saved from a more severe punishment by the mercy of the court. Whatever the story behind that injury was—as usual, we do not learn anything about it—it caused a new wave of violence: the accused turned around and started another fight, this time more vehemently than before.

This story confronts us with the problem of the relation between the motive of honor on the one hand and some different, more subtle motives and reasons on the other. Confronted with the expanding research on the topic of honor in recent years, some scholars have expressed a concern about a possible conceptual imbalance: Is there a danger of seeing quarrels about honor everywhere, or are we fooled by those smart protagonists who used the issue of honor as an excuse to hide their real, often very ordinary, materialistic motives?[51] In my opinion, this inherent danger applies only to those approaches in which conflicts over honor are perceived as one type of conflict among others (such as property quarrels). In contrast, historical-anthropological studies try rather to detect the intertwined relationships between conflicts about material interests and those about honor. Historical anthropologists acknowledge this as a central function of the semantics of honor. People spoke about honor or made use of it in order to elevate their conflicts of interest onto the level of conflicts about fundamental values.[52] Thus, no matter what the occasions or the reasons for most of the agonal violent quarrels were, the rigid code of honor homogenized the heterogeneous motives by translating them into a common language. In other words, no matter what a quarrel was actually all about according to our modern understanding, conflicts fought out violently in the streets of early modern Europe were mostly conflicts about honor, too, according to the social logic of the protagonists. The impending loss of honor constituted the motor of violence. In individual cases, the exact relationship between conflicts over material interests and conflicts over honor can hardly be assessed precisely. Often it is noticeable, however, that the original causes for the conflict paled into insignificance before the quarrels that followed these initial incidences.[53]

Social Control of Violence

Now we can make a better assessment of the place of violence within the system of social control in early modern Europe. Analytically, we can distinguish between three different dimensions of social control: the level of violence prevention; the level of the containment of violence; and the level of sanctions. The late Medieval and early modern town must be regarded as the classic birthplace of measures for violence prevention; the village and the early modern territorial state followed this example later on. Peace was one of the most basic values in urban constitutions (if not the most important one).[54] On a regular basis, statutes and civil oaths made the renunciation of self-help a condition for every inhabitant of a town by referring to the course of the law and thus defining violence as deviant behavior. Various other norms supported the basic value of peace, for example, by prohibiting arms or declaring curfews at night. Not only do these observations apply to the town as a whole, but also to corporations, guilds, and brotherhoods, which again and again impressed on their members the order to behave civilly and peacefully. This order was embodied in their institutions by using harsh words, sometimes even combined with threats, to impose sanctions on acts of violence. Obviously, the most important social groups and the early modern authorities were all in the same boat in this respect.

As far as the containment or the cessation of violent conflicts is concerned, the question of possible coincidences or discrepancies between written laws and informal norms of life has not yet been thoroughly examined. On a regular basis the authorities obliged all office bearers and often even all people to intervene in conflicts and to call for peace. Examples seem to prove that the intervention by another person was of crucial importance in bringing about the end of violent conflicts.[55]

We are best informed about the third level, that of sanctions, due to the richness of the sources. Agonal violent acts not resulting in death were regularly punished with a fine. Until the end of the early modern period, in towns as well as villages, only the notorious violent offenders faced more severe sanctions, like imprisonment or banishment from the country. Quite telling is that nonlethal bodily harm was not dealt with in the Carolina, the penal code of the Emperor Charles V of 1532. As the predominant form of sanction, fines could have two receivers: the authorities, in order to amend the breach of the written norm, and the victim, in order to compensate for the harm suffered or as a compensation for the cost of treating any wounds. Both forms of penance could exist side by side. Often, the harm done to the immaterial body by insults and defamatory speeches was dealt with analogously. Here, too, the reconciliation between the parties, thus reestablishing social peace, was regarded as the most important aim.

The modern spectator may find it strange that there was no fundamental difference between the punishment of homicide and that of bodily harm well into the late Medieval period—more evidence that most cases of violent death were "unintentional cases of escalation."[56] Thus, a case of manslaughter in fourteenth-century Zürich was fined with ten to twenty marks. The simple breach of the peace was fined with ten marks, too. Theoretically, of course, the sin of homicide obliged one to much more punishment than just the payment of a fine. The authorities also expected acts of penance and repentance toward the survivors of the dead, which were supposed to prevent the development of a lethal circle of bloody vendetta. Erecting memorial crosses and donating memorial services took care of the salvation of the deceased's soul, while a pilgrimage might mean the spiritual cleansing of the culprit from sin. Thus, not only did the parties among themselves have to be reconciled, but the killer reconciled with God as well.[57]

When we look at the measures concerning the social control of violence and contrast them with those dealing with nonviolent crimes, the former's exceptional profile appears very prominently. The leading idea was not, as for example with property offenses, the social stigmatization of the culprit and the criminalization of his deed; instead, the aim was the prevention of violence, or if that was unsuccessful, a modest punishment of the deed, followed if possible by a reintegration of the culprit into society. In comparison to modern Western societies, this obviously reflects also a different function and social judgment of violent behavior. The historical discovery that violence originated from the middle of society and was not confined to its margins thus gains additional plausibility. On the basis of these observations, the productive role of violence can be approached more closely, too.

Violence As Social Control

In most descriptions, violence is portrayed implicitly or explicitly as a loss of control. The opposite proposition, that violence could simultaneously be seen as a medium of social control, is not as completely absurd as it may seem at first sight. Thus, the typology of aggression by Eva Lacour also includes a category she calls "social control," which is closely linked to a moral or moralistic norm of acting. In her categorization, revenge and retaliation are viewed as "premoral." Accordingly, only a few cases in Lacour's sample are classified under the heading of social control.[58] By contrast, I suggest a much broader and more technical understanding of social control: each form of social interaction and communication in which deviant behavior of persons or groups is defined and measures are taken against it.

The relation between violence exercised collectively and social control is recognizable much more easily than in cases of individual deviancy. The classic form of violent control actions were the charivaris: young men made a loud noise in front of the house of two women, for example, in a village at the beginning of the eighteenth century, barricaded their front door, fixed a gallows rope above it, and sang defamatory songs about these women in the local alehouse. This was a classic example of "rough music," which aimed at punishing the unconventional behavior of, for instance, beaten husbands, or seemingly indecent (or perhaps also too bashful) virgins.[59] As John Cashmere showed very convincingly with the help of a French example, such rituals can be divided into a benevolent variant, as a means of legitimate social control, and a bad variant of excessive violence.[60] Similarly, expressions of social protest—numerous upheavals in towns and villages, which often escalated into violence—have mostly been seen as political events and not as crimes. In doing so, one ignores that crime is always a construct, the result of an act of labeling, and that political protest was often criminalized in early modern times. A comprehensive discussion of the relation between violence and social control should include public unrest as a central element.[61] It is obvious that in these cases deviant behavior was construed and that measures were taken to correct it. The violent acts of the protesters might be directed against the authorities and their position, which the protesters regarded as unjust, but they might also be directed against fringe groups, such as vagrants, beggars, or ethnic minorities who were perceived as threatening. Sometimes the actions were directed against both the authorities and a fringe group at the same time, as was the case in the *Fettmilch* upheaval in 1614, in which both the Frankfurt patricians and the Jewish community in town were a combined target in the rioters' view.[62]

The phenomenon of witch hunting lies on the borderline between individual and social control. Whereas it was regarded as a predominantly authoritative action in the past, recent studies have emphasized to what extent the accusations of witchcraft originated from the middle of society. The term "witch" belonged to one of the core insults in many early modern disputes about honor, but it could also imply a very specific accusation. In that case, it often meant an attempt to stigmatize nonconformist behavior, especially by women, and hence was an act of social control. The frequent escalation of quarrels over honor into violent confrontations shows the potential of violence inherent in such accusations of witchcraft, which could lead to forms of lynching in extreme cases.[63]

Violence as social control can also be demonstrated in many types of noncollective aggression. First, the corporal punishment of wives, children, and servants, in line with the early modern *patria potestas,* was perceived as a legitimate punishment of deviant behavior within the microcosm of the household. Second, acts of violence nurtured by motives of revenge and retaliation are to be included here. Usually, these acts were a reaction to a breach of a norm. According to the self-image of the protagonists, they had been harmed by this violation. The act of self-help aimed to reestablish this very norm. Third, we have to consider the category of instrumental violence. On the one hand, it could be seen as an obvious break from a generally accepted norm, as for example in the case of robbery. In that case, the aspect of social control is clearly missing. On the other hand, instrumental violence could also be used to support and sanction norms. If, for instance, a peasant hunted a thief, took from him the stolen goods, and gave him a proper whipping thereafter, this was clearly an act of social control on the borderline between revengeful violence and meaningful violence. Fourth, there is a strong element of social control to be found in all the quarrels concerning material motives. Usually, we focus on the individual claims and interests brought forward by both sides in the course of early modern conflicts, not on the commonly shared norms to which all these arguments are referring. However, if we accept that the term social control implies no distinction between general and particular norms and that every institution, group, or individual can be a decisive center of defining nonconforming behavior, physical violence can be described as an act of social control just like an accusation in court or an attempt to influence public opinion about certain persons by gossiping and spreading rumors.

Whereas these background motives and interests are not central to our phenomenology, the predominant agonal character of early modern acts of violence is. Here, the central position of honor was emphasized. And this language of honor always referred to commonly shared values and norms or aimed at suggesting a breach of norms by the opponent. This becomes particularly obvious in soft, verbal forms of violence. The typical insulting words always included a deviation from the ruling norm, such as the alienation of property ("thief") or ignoring decent modes of behavior ("slut"). Very often, the victim described the behavior of the opponent as a break from decent neighborly behavior, as an attack on his integrity or self-image. Hence, it is not by chance that in cases of defamatory insults, justice was used against the opponent: references to previous punishments or sanctions that had been graciously suspended (compare the example from the Eifel region mentioned above) or the use of threats are not confined to eighteenth-century Paris.[64]

So, physical violence can be interpreted as a firm attempt to exercise social control or at least to justify violence in these terms. Simultaneously, agonal violence can be understood as an expression of fears regarding measures of social control. The logic of escalation in these conflicts was influenced by the fear of the participating protagonists—their fear of losing face in the eyes of the virtual public if things turned out badly. There was no authoritative law prescribing virility as a positive norm of behavior. Yet, to the protagonists it was basic knowledge that bodily strength had to be acted out and in cases of emergency even defended in the social drama of daily life. An assumed or actual provocation—whether an insult, a degrading gesture, or a violent attack—had to be answered in some way or, preferably, countered by a more ferocious attack in order not to be regarded as a coward.[65]

When we consider both dimensions of the relationship between social control and violence, their discrepancy is of course striking. Violence was used as a medium of social control and its exercise was expected by the peer group; however, it was—at the same time—not welcomed and hence viewed negatively by both the authorities and the entire community. The call for peace and the code of honor were each other's rivals, as it were. The compromise necessitated by this state of tension gave the system of premodern judicial norms and sanctions regarding violence its special character. In particular, this strained relationship explains why agonal violence was not criminalized for a long time, in contrast to intentional robbery and murder. In her already classic analysis of the magistrates' court in Zürich at the end of the fourteenth century, Susanna Burghartz gives a perceptive characterization of the strained relation just referred to. According to her account, the council court functioned as a possible instance of settlement and reconciliation between the parties. The payment of a fine to the town appeared as an act of balance by which the proper relation between the code of honor precipitating violence and public order, bound for the prevention of violence, was established or reestablished. The measures taken by the court were thus not meant to exclude the culprit from the town community, but to reintegrate him.[66]

Historical Change

In the case of late Medieval Zürich, the balance between the legitimacy and illegitimacy of exercising violence is all too clear. This was about to change in the following centuries, but only very slowly. At the normative level, the increasing criminalization of homicide clearly implied a growing intolerance of violence with lethal consequences. As early as 1501 a preacher in the cathedral of Strasbourg, Geiler von Kayersberg, expressed his outrage that a killer got away with a fine, whereas a thief was executed.[67] Increasingly, violent homicide was described, in the laws and judicial writings of that time, not as bad fortune for the victim, but rather as an awful crime. As a consequence, from the sixteenth century onward, the culprits were increasingly subjected to the severe punishments they had only been threatened with before. In spite of this judicial aggravation, the exculpation of homicide remained in function well into the seventeenth century, and in some regions the practice of pardoning moderated the harsh judgments of the courts.

But even when the authorities and justice remained unmerciful, different standards prevailed among the people. For them it was hardly explainable why accidental homicide had such dramatic consequences, whereas other forms of violence were still viewed as harmless incidents. Most of the killers could escape and were thus not prosecuted by justice, evidently because they received far reaching support from their social environment.[68] Obviously, however, the practice of violence was subject to a process of change in the early modern period, although its dimensions remain controversial. Some historians have noted a long-term containment and suppression of violence from the Middle Ages to the modern period, which they considered an important indicator for the process of civilization. In my view, a decline in registered cases of homicide is plausibly verifiable in the seventeenth and eighteenth centuries only.[69] Nevertheless, these two indicators—the change of norms and the change in practice—suffice to speak of a change

in violence in the early modern period. Although a detailed analysis of this secular process cannot be presented within the framework of this article, my claim
is that any description and interpretation ignoring the double-faced character
of violence remains incomplete. When violence was both an object and a subject of social control, it is implausible to assume that the subsequent suppression of violence was reached merely by a reinforcement of that social
control—no matter if we call it civilization or social disciplining. Undoubtedly,
the state's monopoly of power was a necessary precondition for the marginaliz-
ing and decisive criminalizing of violence, but by no means was this sufficient.

Following my own considerations, I would like to formulate the test question for a sufficient model of social change in this way: What factors did contribute to the change in which the social control of violence became dominant,
while the social control by violence lost its legitimacy? Or, in order to formulate
this question in terms of our well-tried categorical pattern: To what extent were
the changes at the level of motives and reasons for violence, at the level of the
forms of violence, or at the level of the participating persons responsible for the
observed development?

At first sight, an evaluation of the reasons for violence would be easy: If premodern society, pervaded by shortage, indeed witnessed envy and quarrels of its
members as a structural feature, a decrease in violence could be the consequence
of a structural social change in the sense of growth for all. Such an interpretation, which would view a spurt in modernization as the decisive factor for the
transition from a traditional to a modern, bourgeois society, could be questioned
on the basis of chronology alone. In the eighteenth century, the number of conflicts about scarce goods increased again significantly. The judicial conflicts of
that time clearly reflect the problems connected with the pauperization of large
sections of the population.[70]

A more elaborate model of modernization has been proposed by Michael Frank.
The starting point of his interesting case study of a little village in the county of
Lippe was a change in the mechanisms of social control. Influenced by Keith
Wrightson's idea of "two concepts of order," Frank observed two competing models operating in this village: on the one hand an authoritative model codified in
formal laws, on the other hand a local model, not constituted by written norms
but by informal though equally binding rules of the village community. What I
have previously called social control by violence fits into the informal rural set
of norms. For a long time, the efforts of the Lippian authorities to overcome the
informal rural culture and get their own laws accepted remained unsuccessful.
The social diversification of the eighteenth century finally brought about a decisive breakdown of the people's informal network of rules. The lower class grew
in size, which resulted in an intensification of the internal potential for conflict.
Attempts to cope with this new situation within the framework of the local system of order failed, which cleared the way for formalized types of social control,

in particular the courts, to take over. The rural elites felt threatened by the growing number of highly mobile landless persons, which caused them to rely for
their security on the state's system of order. "Hence, the crisis of the rural world
formed a landmark in the process of internal state formation."[71] Further
research is needed in order to tell whether these findings can be generalized.

Frank's analysis also leads us to the second level of our categorical pattern,
the social groups exercising violence. Physical violence belonged to the common
cultural repertoire of most social classes and groups in premodern Europe at the
turn from late Medieval to early modern times, even though the appropriation
of violence could vary significantly. Noble feuds may have differed from the bloody
conflicts of common people in individual cases, but their common structural similarities were more important.[72] Therefore, we can describe the transformation
of violence in terms of a process of distancing by various social classes from the
common culture of violence or, from a different perspective, as the marginalization and stigmatization of classes who still exercised violence. One could also
consider this process a crucial aspect of the "cultural desynchronization" analyzed by Robert Muchembled for France—a distancing of the upper classes from
the norms and modes of behavior that they had shared with other social groups
before.[73]

Although the notion of an antagonistic dichotomy between a popular and
an elite culture has become questionable, the concept of desynchronization can
perhaps be made fruitful for the research into violence. For his part, writing about
eighteenth-century Frankfurt, Joachim Eibach observes that its inhabitants increasingly adopted bourgeois standards of behavior (*Verbürgerlichung*).[74] In his own
way, he takes up Elias's idea that the modes of behavior of the upper classes had
a formative influence on other classes and groups in society, but we have to wait
for a more detailed analysis. It seems plausible for the entire early modern period
that merchants and intellectual elites distanced themselves from the culture of
violence of peasants and craftsmen (as much as they did from the violent culture of the nobility). But did the behavioral standards of this class at some point
become a role model for those social strata identified earlier as the carrier groups
of the agonal culture? And did violence really retreat from the public into the
private sphere of the family and, with this, lose its function as an instrument of
social control?[75]

These questions take us to the third level of our categorical pattern, the forms
of violence. Presumably, the shape of violence did not change fundamentally in
some contexts. Within the family, for example, a change of forms would be difficult to establish. With instrumental violence, such as in cases of robbery, continuities seem to have prevailed, too.[76] After all, the agonal pattern of conflict
can be observed far into modern times. Thus, the proletariat of the early-nineteenth century copied many ritualized rules of conduct for aggressive conflicts
that had previously been adhered to by craftsmen. In this case, too, the code of

honor and a concept of masculinity tolerant of violence prevailed. The social, democratic labor movement, however, ostentatiously distanced itself from such rules of conduct. Instead, it adopted the bourgeois, civic values of order and self-discipline—further evidence for the marginalization of violence.[77]

The history of this process in early modern Europe is largely unexplored yet. One could begin, however, with the interesting development of a growing willingness to settle conflicts in courts (*Verrechtlichung*).[78] It was not the suppression of violence that led to its disappearance, as followers of the theory of civilization would have it; rather, the extension of an attractive and functioning judicial system, which could be used by a broad spectrum of the population, offered an alternative for solving conflicts without violence. And yet, the judicial system, though plausible at first sight, is misleading: to this day informal mechanisms of social control exist alongside their authoritative, judicial counterparts. It is only that, within these informal mechanisms, violence no longer occupies a central position, at least in Western societies. Thus, we should focus our attention on the interplay of the two levels—the formalized social control by justice and informal agents of control within society—and inquire whether and how this interplay has changed over time. In this respect, the concept of the usage of the judicial system (*Justiznutzung*) deals with the question of how historical agents used the old and the new institutions.[79] Relevant studies show the great extent to which the options of an individual user could vary: whether he chose the route of violent self-help, or aimed at an out-of-court settlement, or decided in favor of legal proceedings remained context-dependent for a long time.

Conclusion

This essay has made a modest beginning at analyzing the overall transformation in the social control of violence. It drew the outlines of a research program that is by no means complete yet. For example, religion as a pacifying factor probably deserves more consideration than it has been granted so far within the debate on violence. With the present state of our empirical knowledge we can hardly ask for more. Some of the shortcomings of contemporary research originate from a fateful polarization among the investigators of crime and violence. Most studies of long-term change are based on simplistic macrotheories that underestimate the complexity of historical and contemporary forms of violence. The authors of "thick descriptions" of violence, on the other hand, are often principally skeptical about the possibility of categorizing changes in reasons, forms, and intensity of violence in history. This essay is meant as a contribution to overcoming this polarization. The study and interpretation of historical change belong to the indispensable tasks for the historian, and despite all methodical difficulties we should continue in our efforts, even when or exactly because such a difficult topic as violence is at stake. Such an analysis, however, can only be adequate when we have gained an appropriate understanding of violence in the past and in contemporary society. In order to achieve this, we have to consider not only the destructive character of violence but also its productive and constructive side.

Notes

I am greatly indebted to Pieter Spierenburg for checking and improving the English version of this article—even those parts he disagrees with.

1. Compare Trotha, ed., *Soziologie der Gewalt,* 15, 20–22.

2. Wimmer et al., eds., *Das zivilisierte Tier.*

3. Sofsky, *Traktat.*

4. I have already formulated my initial thoughts about this approach in Schwerhoff, *Aktenkundig,* 112–30. A critical analysis of the "civilization-of-crime-model" is to be found in Schwerhoff, "Criminalized Violence." I suggest reading that article complementarily to this essay.

5. On the cultural-historical alignment of the German research on crime: Schwerhoff, "Historische Kriminalitätsforschung," 21–67; Eibach, "Recht—Kultur—Diskurs." A look at the headlines and content of anthologies published recently—such as Lindenberger and Lüdtke, eds., *Physische Gewalt;* Hugger and Stadler, eds., *Gewalt;* Meumann and Niefanger, eds., *Schauplatz;* Sieferle and Breuninger, eds., *Kulturen der Gewalt;* and Eriksson and Krug-Richter, eds., *Streitkultur(en)*—shows that also the German-speaking discussion of violence is characterized by a cultural-historical perspective that is in itself rather heterogeneous.

6. Compare the definition (following Heinrich Popitz in this respect) in Trotha, ed., *Soziologie der Gewalt,* 14.

7. Compare for the history of capital punishment Evans, *Rituals;* Martschukat, *Inszeniertes Töten.*

8. Compare Schwerhoff, "Criminalized Violence."

9. Dinges, *Maurermeister,* 169–71; Dinges, "Justiznutzungen," 508–9.

10. Very deliberately, such a technical and formal definition of social control distances itself from concepts such as social disciplining, which prefer a top-down view—privileging the perspective of the state's instances of control. Also, a differentiation between horizontal and vertical social disciplining (Schnabel-Schüle, *Überwachen*) still has a considerably narrower focus, in so far as social disciplining always means the extinction of undesirable behavior on the basis of generalized norms (Breuer, "Sozialdisziplinierung," 62). Note also the undoubtedly existing division of power between representatives and subjects: Härter, "Soziale Disziplinierung."

11. For the latest review of this discussion about social control, see Scheerer and Hess, "Social Control."

12. The references in Schwerhoff, *Aktenkundig,* are mentioned only summarily here. Among the recent publications on the theme of violence, the following are particularly important from the perspective of criminal history: Schuster, *Stadt vor Gericht,* 88; Lacour, *Schlägereyen;* Lacour, "Faces of Violence Revisited"; for the issue of insults (*Injurien*), Fuchs, *Um die Ehre,* is important.

13. Radbruch, ed., *Peinliche Gerichtsordnung,* art. 137.

14. Ibid., art. 130. See also Göttsch, "Gattenmord," 313–34; Nolde, *Gattenmord.*

15. Historisches Archiv der Stadt Köln (HAStK), Verf. u. Verw. G 310, fol. 109r–116v. For other cases compare Spicker-Beck, *Räuber.*

16. Höhlbaum, ed., *Buch Weinsberg,* 126. This case is quite representative for the circumstances to be found in Cologne; compare Schwerhoff, *Köln,* 265–67.

17. HAStK G 227/8, February 1593.

18. HAStK G 211, fol. 189v.

19. Schwerhoff, *Köln,* 390–402.

20. Schwerhoff, "Frauen," 456–59. Compare for infanticide in general, Schwerhoff, *Aktenkundig,* 50–58.

21. Moreover, they do not cover the whole spectrum of criminal or criminalized violence. Thus, attempted suicide—also punishable by death according to art. 135 of the Carolina—is left from our analysis. On this subject: Lacour, *Schlägereyen,* 162 et seq.

22. This categorization is partly inspired by the types of offense defined by Eva Lacour. In my view, however, her categories are too heterogeneous, because she uses the reasons and occasions of conflicts, places, culprits, and victims for the characterization of respective types. Thus, a systematic comparison is absent. Lacour, *Schlägereyen,* 111; Lacour, "Faces of Violence Revisited," 659.

23. Spierenburg, "Long-Term Trends," 73.

24. Rexroth, "Gewaltverbrechen," 62–63, distinguishes between agonal and nonagonal acts of killing for fourteenth-century London, in order to avoid the anachronistic differentiation between murder and manslaughter.

25. Compare Schwerhoff, *Köln,* 304–7; Lacour, *Schlägereyen,* 95–97.

26. Frank, "Ehre und Gewalt," 337; compare also Rummel, "Verletzung"; Lacour, *Schlägereyen,* 97–98.

27. Schwerhoff, *Köln,* 182–94, 301–12; Schuster; "Richter," 362; Eibach, "Städtische Gewaltkriminalität," 372–73.

28. Lacour, *Schlägereyen.*

29. Walz, "Agonale Kommunikation," 222.

30. Compare for my own research: Schwerhoff, *Köln,* 294–97. In eighteenth-century Frankfurt in one out of four cases, the scene of the crime was the tavern (Eibach, "Städtische Gewaltkriminalität," 371). The same ratio can be found in the rural society of that time (Lacour, *Schlägereyen,* 112). Compare for the importance of taverns and alehouses: Kümin, "Useful to Have"; for the connection between alcohol and violence: Wettmann-Jungblut, "Gewalt."

31. Frank, "Ehre und Gewalt," 323.

32. Cashmere, "The Social Uses"; Lacour, *Schlägereyen,* 29, talks about "scripts," or cognitive patterns that determine the conditions of acts and their sequence of events.

33. On the concept of retorsion: Walz, "Agonale Kommunikation," 232 et seq. Incidentally, contemporary jurisdiction granted an offended person the right of retorsion: Fuchs, *Um die Ehre,* 56.

34. Compare Schwerhoff, "Starke Worte," 237–63.

35. Krug-Richter, "Von nackten Hummeln."

36. Fuchs, *Um die Ehre,* 138; Loetz, "Zeichen der Männlichkeit?"

37. Schwerhoff, *Köln,* 318; more detailed, Heidrich, "Grenzübergänge."

38. Compare Hohkamp, "Häusliche Gewalt," 276–302; Schmidt, "Hausväter vor Gericht," 213–36.

39. Spierenburg, "Long-Term Trends," 70.

40. Ibid., 94.

41. Incidentally, for her rural research area, the highlands of the Eifel situated in western Germany, she comes to different conclusions than Spierenburg does for Amsterdam: according to her study, between the sixteenth and eighteenth centuries there were "only a few major changes," in particular an increase in interfamilial violent acts.

42. Lacour, *Schlägereyen,* 182–83; Lacour, "Faces of Violence Revisited."

43. Lacour, *Schlägereyen,* 57–58, 177–78.

44. Ibid., 174–78.

45. "Verbal violence" seems to Spierenburg, "How violent were women?" 10, as being virtually "confusing from a linguistic standpoint."

46. Fuchs, *Um die Ehre,* 139–42.

47. Lacour, *Schlägereyen,* 89, 171–73.

48. Schuster, *Eine Stadt vor Gericht,* 71, 95. The judgment made by Loetz, "Zeichen der Männlichkeit," 283, for her area of research is also very telling, according to which squabbles about honor in early modern Zürich were not about the "physical extinction" of the opponent, but about his "symbolic subjection."

49. Lacour, *Schlägereyen,* 120, defines only those cases as conflicts over honor in which honor was the immediate occasion or where its reestablishment was intended.

50. Lacour, *Schlägereyen,* 122.

51. Ulbrich, "Weibliche Delinquenz," 284. As far as the research of the previous years is concerned, only Fuchs, *Um die Ehre;* and the respective articles in Backmann et al., eds., *Ehrkonzepte;* and Schreiner and Schwerhoff, *Verletzte Ehre* are mentioned here; now of central importance, Krug-Richter, "Von nackten Hummeln."

52. Dinges, *Maurermeister,* 414.

53. Walz, "Agonale Kommunikation," 221.

54. Schuster, *Der gelobte Frieden.*

55. Schuster, *Eine Stadt vor Gericht,* 213. According to the observations of Lacour, *Schlägereyen,* 176, third persons did interfere later in early modern times than in escalating conflicts in modern societies.

56. Burghartz, *Leib, Ehre und Gut*, 152.

57. Compare Battenberg, "Seelenheil." Of course, one should not neglect here that many killers were threatened by severe punishments at the end of the Medieval ages; compare for the removal of the compositional system footnote 69 below.

58. Lacour, *Schlägereyen*, 58, 177.

59. For an example, see Lacour, *Schlägereyen*, 116. Compare the classic articles in Le Goff and Schmitt, *Le Charivari*. More recent German research is rare; compare for a similar theme Schindler, *Widerspenstige Leute*, 175–214.

60. Cashmere, "The Social Uses," 292.

61. Würgler, "Diffamierung."

62. Friedrichs, "Politics or Pogrom?"

63. An overview of recently published German research on witchcraft is to be found in Schwerhoff, "Vom Alltagsverdacht zur Massenverfolgung"; for the hypothesis of witchcraft accusations being a means of social control of nonconformists, see Labouvie, *Zauberei*, 182; on witchcraft accusations in general, most recently: Gersmann, "Gehe hin," 237–69.

64. Dinges, "Michel Foucault," 198.

65. Compare Loetz, "Zeichen der Männlichkeit," 264–93; and Schwerhoff, "Starke Worte." To what extent other forms of violence, which are not in the center of our analysis here, could partly be understood as reactions to social control would have to be checked more closely. Infanticide, for example, was obviously an attempt to conceal deviant behavior punished with social sanctions with a renewed, substantially graver break from the norm.

66. Burghartz, *Leib, Ehre und Gut*, 200.

67. Israel, *Johannes Geiler*, 261.

68. Compare also the differentiation between killer and the act of killing in Spierenburg, "Long-Term Trends," 72. More general on this trend, Rousseaux, "From Case to Crime"; and Pohl, "Ehrlicher Totschlag."

69. This is argued in more detail in Schwerhoff, "Criminalized Violence."

70. Frank, *Dörfliche Gesellschaft;* Kottmann, "Gogerichte."

71. Frank, *Dörfliche Gesellschaft*, 352.

72. Peters, "Leute-Fehde."

73. Muchembled, *Erfindung*, 126–29.

74. Eibach, "Städtische Gewaltkriminalität," 381–82.

75. Compare Spierenburg, "Long-Term Trends."

76. Compare Schwerhoff, *Aktenkundig*, 130–49.

77. Jessen, "Gewaltkriminalität," 251.

78. Compare Schulze, *Bäuerlicher Widerstand.*

79. Dinges, "Justiznutzung." See also his contribution to this volume.

CHAPTER 13

The Making of Popular Cultures of Social Control: A Comparison of Essex (England) and Hesse-Cassel (Germany) during the Reformation

Robert von Friedeburg

In 1659, in the Hessian village of Merzhausen, Ziegenhain district, local peasants and day laborers, led by the local squire, stormed the parsonage and burned down the house of the minister to arrest a rioter he had hidden there. Merzhausen was part of the principality of Hesse-Cassel, the major Protestant, and from 1605 Calvinist, power in central Germany.[1] By issuing the Ziegenhain order of discipline in 1539, the Hessian church had introduced the first attempt to organize local church discipline on German land. It had instituted the office of church elders to that end. Minister and elders were meant to enforce a reformation of life that would supplement the reformation of doctrine. In 1656, after the ravages of the Thirty Years' War, the Ziegenhain order was refined and reissued. As Heide Wunder has demonstrated in a seminal article, such orders were meant to provide a guideline for morality in both civil and ecclesiastical life.[2] Throughout this period, the struggle against the custom of premarital pregnancy was one of the core aims of church discipline. However, during the entire first half of the seventeenth century, one out of five first-born children in the county of Ziegenhain was conceived out of wedlock.[3] The peasants and day laborers who stormed the parsonage participated just as much in the exercise of social control as the ministers who had failed to suppress premarital pregnancy. But social control remained embedded in a popular culture that had not abandoned its own older standards of acceptable behavior. Rather, villagers had combined these older standards with the new standards of the Reformation. Because Hessian villagers failed to accuse their neighbors of lacking righteousness as defined by the theologians, the Church had to adapt. In the eighteenth century, and even well into the nineteenth, villagers had amalgamated their older popular culture and the new morality of the Reformation into a new, coherent popular culture.

In 1637, William Allen of Earls Colne, Essex, was charged with "pissing in
the clock chamber so that it ran down and annoyed the church [and] easing himself nearby the chancel door in the churchyard in service time to the great annoy-
ance of the church and churchyard and offence to the parishioners' noses."[4] The
archdeacon of Colchester, in whose jurisdiction Earls Colne lay, had attempted
to eradicate more than just such spectacular practices. The Reformed view held
that God did not only deal with the individual soul but with the entire secular
community as well. The community should be bound to God's moral law, which
the magistrates, both civil and ecclesiastical, had the duty to enforce. Together
with substantial inhabitants of many villages and towns, the archdeacon punished not only recusants but suppressed drinking, swearing, and Sabbath breaking. English historians have addressed this effort as the Reformation of
Manners, similar in scope and intention to the enforcement of morality in Hesse.[5]
But while significant segments of the urban and rural population of Essex participated in this new popular culture of piety and put allegiance to it above loyalty to their neighbors, equally significant elements refused to submit to these
new standards of behavior. In Earls Colne, since the 1590s, these two groups
began to participate in mutually opposing popular cultures, splitting communities all over Essex into hostile factions.[6]

It would be hazardous to push any comparison from just two isolated examples such as that of Merzhausen and Earls Colne too far. But these examples serve
to illustrate two points. First, while the population of neither place had been turned
wholesale into adherents of Reformed theology, it would be the gravest of errors
to conclude that the Reformation church and its moral program had not left its
mark on local popular cultures. Indeed, by the middle of the seventeenth century, significantly different relations between local communities and their
mechanisms of social control, on the one hand, and the Reformation church and
its program of implementing morality, on the other hand, had emerged in Hesse
and Essex. These differences, however, should not primarily be understood in
terms of the suppression or survival of popular culture, for popular cultures had
always been molded by the doctrines of the Church. They had always served as
a sphere of communication about the proper means of social control and had
provided tools for such control. And they had always expressed locally accepted
forms of morality. The relation between social control and popular culture was
thus never simply an adversarial one. At issue here is the specific amalgamation
of local mechanisms of social control, of the new tools of the Reformation church,
and of the various forms and views of morality among the population.[7]

In a seminal article Bruce Lenman and Geoffrey Parker have argued that the
willingness of members of local communities to bring the behavior of their neighbors to the attention of the courts of church and state was crucial for any understanding of the success, or failure, of new forms of social control as imposed by
church and state.[8] In many Essex communities the "hotter sort of protestants"

were willing to participate in the prosecution of their neighbors to purge sin from their communities. Not so in Hesse. Many years ago, Walther Sohm pointed out that the "Christian morality" that the Hessian Reformation attempted to establish had been practiced and desired in particular by one specific group in the region, the Anabaptists. In central Germany, however, the Anabaptists had abandoned their hope for a general reform of the Church early in the Reformation and instead had chosen to separate from their sinful neighbors.[9] While many pious Protestants in many Essex communities also separated from their local church to avoid contagion from their sinful neighbors[10] and the degree of cooperation between this hotter sort of Protestant and the Church of England is a contentious issue,[11] there is little doubt that the hotter sort of Protestants did to a considerable degree attempt to enforce the moral law among their neighbors with the support of church and state.[12] Essex townsmen and villagers did so because they had begun to forge ties with mutually opposing popular cultures with "moral economies" excluding each other and fought each other even if that meant enlisting support from outside.[13] By contrast, Hessian villagers, though asking the representatives of state and church for help against outsiders, still shared a common, though transformed, popular culture.

To be sure, German villages by no means lacked internal conflict and social strife. Indeed, in many villages of Hesse, as in other German regions that have been put to close historical scrutiny, social differentiation increased massively until the Thirty Years' War. In many regions, such change pitted wealthy peasants against poor cottagers. It prompted village elites to ally themselves with the control of marriage by the new Reformation courts.[14] But such strife did not translate into the emergence of mutually hostile popular cultures that were able to realign social relations at the local level along loyalties beyond the local community. In what follows, these different paths of the interaction of the social control of local communities and the social control as enforced by church and state will be pursued with regard to Essex and Hesse.

The Hessian Anabaptists

In 1526, when Prince Philip of Hesse invited noblemen, clergy, and urban representatives to discuss the reformation of the Church in his lands, the Reformation in Germany was well under way. Its message had been spread by broadsheets to the common men, beyond the control of either state or church. By the end of the Peasant War in 1525, most nobles, princes, and town patriciates were convinced that the course of change had to be put into the hands of the magistrates.[15] Against this background, the maintenance of order was of overriding importance to noblemen and urban citizens alike. In 1526, Prince Philip presented to his vassals as well as to his urban subjects a plan for the reformation of the Church, based on the scheme of the French humanist François Lambert from Avignon. According to that scheme, the Church was to become a self-sustained body running its own affairs.[16]

By the 1530s, that scheme had catastrophically failed. With the disciplinary muscle of the state seemingly gone, many parishioners alienated church lands, refused to pay tithes, and ceased to attend services. In particular the pious among the population began to flock to the Anabaptist preachers, who pointed out the very real decay of the official Church. By 1534, when the Anabaptist kingdom of Munster had become a serious menace to the political, social, and religious order, Anabaptism began to be viewed as a real threat to the social and political order in Hesse as well. Whatever Hessian Anabaptists actually wanted or believed, the Hessian state had no option but to prosecute them.

Just as other Anabaptist groups, Hessian Anabaptists had no clear or uniform religious and political program let alone wish to threaten the social or political order. Where possible, they were even willing to push the authorities into a course of pious reform.[17] What Hessian Anabaptism was mainly about was an uncompromising critique of the practices of the visible Hessian church and the behavior of its membership. Unable to press for reform, they were thus ready to separate from their neighbors. While many Anabaptists still cooperated with their neighbors in many respects, they were not willing to share with them their religious life. Whereas some of the aims of Hessian Anabaptists were rooted in general grievances of the population at large,[18] they shared, as Gottfried Seebaß has recently reminded us, a deep dissatisfaction with church reform as it had been accomplished by state and official church.[19]

A typical example is the journeyman Velten Raumeissen. He had helped neighbors build a house during the summer of 1529. One of the other laborers, Otto Haunmöller, told him during this time about the punishment of the Lord that would be inflicted in due course. All would be damned that still adhered to the old faith. In particular those who had been baptized as infants but had failed to renew their covenant with God through adult baptism faced damnation. Raumeissen later explained, when questioned, that these prospects had frightened him and had prompted him to agree to a new christening. After that event Heinmöller warned him to stay away from the worldly pursuits of his neighbors, friends, and kin. He told him he must not attend church service with the rest of the parishioners and not join his friends for drinking parties at infant baptisms but instead had to live in his house on his own and pursue a pious life. Velten objected that he could not earn a living by keeping himself apart from his neighbors, but his teacher told him not to worry, to lead a pious life and avoid the contagion of his damned neighbors. Handed over to the authorities and questioned by them, Velten now begged to be allowed to go back to his family. He wished to return to the true Church and remain an obedient subject ever after. Moreover, he intended to warn others against the dangers of the "devilish sect."[20]

Like other members of the Reformation's "left wing," the Hessian Anabaptists were not content with the reform of doctrine alone but aimed at a reform of life. They blamed the magistrates' Reformation, like the one put into practice by Prince Philip and his advisors, to have reformed at best the doctrine of the Church, not life in the parishes. To them, the life of their neighbors remained unreformed and embedded in sin. In order to establish a true church, these neighbors had to be purged of their sins. Wherever possible, Anabaptists sought to enlist the authorities to that end.[21] Recent research on Anabaptism has shown that the separation of Anabaptists from their neighbors was not part of their original program but only a consequence of the failure of their quest for pious reform.[22]

Without the active support of pious noblemen and gentry, godly minorities in the towns and countryside of England would hardly have been able to enforce the Reformation of Manners on their neighbors. In Germany, however, the Anabaptists had been identified as dangerous to the order of church and state from an early date. Moreover, their refusal to take part in the social activities of the rest of the community, in particular when associated with drinking, met with suspicion from their neighbors.[23] Whereas in many other towns and territories prosecution remained the only response to this perceived threat, Philip summoned support from Martin Bucer to persuade arrested Anabaptists to return to the official Church. In particular during the 1530s, leading Hessian Anabaptists were interrogated in Marburg. While Bucer left no doubt that there was no alternative to reentering the official Church, he did listen to the complaints of Anabaptist leaders.[24] How could the authorities expect pious people to join a church whose members lived their life as unreformed and sinful as the majority of Hessian subjects? The direct result of these negotiations was, first, the return of many Anabaptists into the official Church. Second, a synod assembled at Ziegenhain in 1538 agreed to the Ziegenhain order, which was meant to enforce godly discipline in the parishes. According to that order, the pious of each parish should be recruited as elders. Together with the minister, these elders were to admonish the sinful, remind them of their duties toward the Lord, and make sure that only those who had truly repented of their sins took part in the Lord's supper.[25]

The Ziegenhain order became a source of protracted conflict between various segments of local society. On the whole, a new popular culture emerged that took up some parts of the new faith but also defended older forms of sociability. Most Anabaptists kept resenting this culture as sinful. The minister at Homberg explicitly warned his flock to stay away from that culture.[26] Indeed, most Hessian Anabaptists were pious people who deeply resented the way of life of their neighbors and feared their own damnation, should they fail to separate from them.[27] Adam Angersbach had heard how the Hessian Anabaptist leader Melchior Rinck reminded everyone of Christ's words "from their fruits they will be recognized, those false teachers . . . Since then he had lived a good life and refrained from swearing, gluttony, drinking and other sins, and, according to his best knowledge, baptism was a covenant between Christ and those people who start a new life and intend to abstain from sin."[28] Few of the imprisoned Hessian Anabaptists actually resisted the order of church and state. Some, like Georg Schnabel, actually quoted the standard textbook of the Hessian advisor Johannes Ferrarius on the pious state and stressed their willingness to defend such a godly commonwealth.[29] However, it remained plain to them that church and state had utterly failed to live up to their task of reforming the citizens. For example, Georg Schnabel complained that the state of the Church was worse then among the followers of the pope.[30] In fact, the opinion of these Anabaptists paralleled the impression of the official Hessian clergy, who throughout the sixteenth century deplored the sinfulness among ordinary parishioners.

Sociability and Social Control

The decision of many Anabaptists, such as Adam Angersbach, to withdraw from the life of "feasting, drinking and other sins" of his neighbors also implied a withdrawal from the communal mechanisms of social control and cohesion. Despite church ordinances to the contrary, Hessian local communities vigorously defended their custom of celebrating marriages and baptisms with drinking parties that might last several days. Local town councilors and village headmen refused to prosecute participants. Throughout the 1540s, for example, the Marburg town council obstructed any implementation of the Ziegenhain order of discipline. When questioned by Prince Philip's regional representative, they said they would be willing to act in cases of public vice, but the punishment of drinking, in particular during marriages, was unnecessary and overdone.[31] The town council even sought to protect local beer brewing, and hence local beer consumption, in order to provide employment to the local poor. Similarly, local authorities in Essex defended the practice of brewing against its condemnation by a Puritan preacher with the argument that the poor must have work.[32] As in Essex, the Marburg town council, after considering the pious concerns of hotter Protestants in the community, concluded that piety was good, but that social cohesion and employment for the poor were equally important. The Marburg council explicitly stated that the maintenance of civil unity demanded that Marburg citizens should, in the past as in the future, brew their own beer and sell it on their premises.[33]

Under pressure from the clergy, pious citizens, and the prince's representative, the council finally agreed to limit disorder during weddings and to restrict drinking and dancing strictly to those persons actually invited for the ceremony in question.[34] But as late as 1543 the representative of the prince complained about public disorder, about public drinking, and running and screaming in the streets without any interference from the local council.[35] Again, the town council defended these customs, openly refusing to arrest Marburg citizens for drink-

ing and screaming in taverns and the streets and even trying to persuade their
superior to release some Marburgers who had already been arrested.[36] The council repeatedly attempted to negotiate longer time periods for celebrations at marriages and baptisms than specified in the Ziegenhain order. In sum, it
attempted to prevent the full implementation of that order in Marburg, with its
concomitant effect on the city's popular culture.[37] In 1548, after nearly a decade
of evasive reactions, the town council finally declared the Ziegenhain order to
be repulsive and unacceptable for the town, because it violated local wedding
customs.[38]

Marburg did not stand alone. At least until the 1590s, the town of Hersfeld
defended its local custom of celebrating weddings with meals during several days.[39]
From the 1530s on, this town had been a major center of Anabaptism. The impious behavior of the large majority of the Hersfeld inhabitants made recruitment
among the pious minority particularly successful. The majority, however, retaliated. As late as 1577 some of the inhabitants were handed over to the authorities as Anabaptists.[40]

The resistance of citizens and town councilors in Marburg and Hersfeld cannot simply be interpreted as part of a struggle between local popular culture on
the one hand and the early modern state and its church on the other hand. It
must be understood as a conflict among different segments of local populations
over the meaning of piety and the necessary means to establish good order in
church and state. The majority of Hessian subjects resented any implementation of the Ziegenhain order, and they despised those among their neighbors who
refused to take part in common pastimes. Anabaptists withdrew from a number of common activities that forged community, including services in the local
church and common pastimes during weddings and infant baptisms.[41] Some of
them, like Doll Franck, were explicitly warned by fellow Anabaptists not to participate in the secular and ecclesiastical affairs of their neighbors and to abstain
from swearing and drinking.[42] To be sure, in large towns such as Marburg, some
local citizens were willing to petition on behalf of arrested Anabaptists, arguing
that, after all, they were only pious folk who should not be prosecuted.[43] The
Anabaptist leader Georg Schnabel was allowed to escape from prison in 1538
to enable him to see his family. Likewise, arrested Anabaptists in Wolkersdorf
were released by local officials who shared some of their critical views toward
the visible church.[44]

In general, however, Anabaptists found shelter in their kinship networks, which
provided protection and loyalty.[45] Outside those networks, they had to reckon
with outspoken hostility from their neighbors. Anabaptists even developed secret
signs to communicate with each other in local environments they perceived as
largely hostile.[46] A member of the Oswald family, accused of Anabaptism in 1539,
later recounted how his neighbors had actively urged the authorities to prosecute him; with that accomplished, they had harassed his relatives and robbed

them of their property, so that they had to flee the region.[47] At Neumorschen, ordinary neighbors informed the authorities about anyone who suspiciously avoided the Lord's Supper.[48] In the Sorge area, a center of Anabaptism in East Hesse, local people were ready to actively support prosecution.[49] Although ordinary villagers often were prepared to tolerate the strange ways of their pious neighbors for a while, without sharing their sense of piety, pressures from the local environment, such as the threat of exclusion from communion, forced even these tolerant persons to take sides. In 1575, when it was publicly announced from the pulpit that the intended marriage of the daughter of a Treysa Anabaptist was refused, she declared in the presence of her father, the whole parish, and the minister that she would henceforth abstain from her father's errors.[50]

In particular, the refusal to baptize infants led to an intense hostility among neighbors. Shortly after the wife of the notorious Anabaptist Valentin Merten from Breitsbach had given birth to a child, her neighbors told the local justice at Vacha that the child, who had died, had not been "Christened." Merten, they alleged, had refused to baptize his child. Obviously, the neighbors had tolerated the strange ways of this adult couple, but they insisted on a proper baptism for the newborn child and informed the relevant authorities when the parents themselves failed to make this happen. Villagers thus enforced compliance with their norms, both within the realm of local social control by informal means and through enlisting the apparatus of the state for support. Local popular culture and the state reinforced each other here. The justice first questioned the midwives who had been present during the mother's labors. The midwives reported the birth of twins, one stillborn and the other dead a day later. Merten had been present during labor and had explicitly ruled out the baptism of his children. The midwives further told the justice that the whole community now worried for Merten's wife, who might die as well. Moreover, there was something suspicious, they alleged, about the child who had been born alive. First, it was not so weak or ill at the time of birth to warrant a premature death. Second, it had lost strange liquids from its nose when it died.[51]

Anabaptist Merten had clearly tested the tolerance of his neighbors to breaking point when he refused to baptize his child. While they had allowed him to pursue his own way of piety, midwives and neighbors turned into participants of popular culture of social control once baptism did not take place. They sought at least to protect his wife and attempted to explain the death of the children from the perspective of their own piety, which stressed the utter importance of child baptism. At other occasions, Anabaptists were even denounced to the authorities merely for failing to attend service.[52] In such cases, burgomasters, town council, citizens, and villagers acted together and in accordance with the officials of the prince to detect secret meetings.[53] The defense of certain aspects of local popular culture, such as drinking and swearing, by no means precluded active cooperation with the authorities to defend a godly order.

Given this state of affairs between Anabaptists and their neighbors, it cannot come as a surprise that villagers and townsmen were outraged when Hessian clergymen told them they were worse than the Anabaptists. In one case, the minister of Homberg had criticized the hunting and court life of princes and nobility in a fashion quite typical for sixteenth-century court critique. But more than that, he had vigorously attacked participation in carnival and had accused local participants of allying themselves with the devil. He had even refused to take part in the burial of one town councilor, whom he had accused of an impious life.[54] The Homberg parishioners, led by their councilors, now turned to the supralocal authorities. In their attempt to enlist support from church and state, they portrayed their minister as a dangerous rebel, who tried to induce loyal subjects into rebellion by criticizing court life. When questioned, they had to admit that their minister had only warned them of the seditious behavior of Anabaptists, rather than inciting them toward revolt. But they insisted he had excluded parishioners from the Lord's Supper. According to the Ziegenhain order of discipline, that was one of his tasks indeed.[55] Yet, he had to leave Homberg after a while, because his position had become untenable. The inhabitants of Homberg had successfully defended their new popular culture that included traditional forms of sociability. The state had proved unable to enforce the "true morality" the Ziegenhain order was supposed to maintain, because its attempts at enforcement lacked substantial local support.

English Rural Communities: The Historical Debate

Beggars, the Puritan divine William Perkins wrote, are for the most part a cursed group. "They joyne not themselves to any setled congregation for the obtaining of God's kingdome, and so this promise belongs not to them."[56] Puritan preachers reminded assize juries of their duty to regulate moral behavior.[57] Statements like the one Perkins made led historians, in particular during the 1970s and 1980s, to discuss the Puritan Reformation of Manners in terms of social control.[58] At least since Christopher Hill's *Society and Puritanism in Prerevolutionary England,* research has focused on three related issues: the "cause of preachers, religious publicists and social controllers" during England's Second Reformation; the doubling of England's population from about the mid-sixteenth until the mid-seventeenth century; and the effect this increase in population had on the social structure and on social relations.[59] When considering these developments, in particular, the historiography of the 1970s not only assumed an increase in tensions between rich and poor but also used this assumption to explain changes in piety, church discipline, and lay concerns for order. All developments together were interpreted in terms of a society that increasingly lacked solidarity and became divided into the world of the illiterate poor and that of a literate elite.[60]

Keith Wrightson and David Levine provided empirical evidence for such asser-
tions in a case study of the village of Terling. There, population growth indeed
led to an enormous increase in the number of the local poor, while denunciations of neighbors before the Church courts reflected the desire of some members of local society to regulate the behavior of others. These activities matched
the effort of the Puritan divine Richard Hooker and several of the local yeomen
families to purge the village of sinful behavior. Thus, Wrightson and Levine's
study seemed to confirm the thesis of a cultural conflict between the laboring
poor on the one hand and the better sort, in alliance with local Puritans, on the
other hand.[61]

Three assumptions proved to be vital to this argument. First, piety was understood to have functions beyond the realm of religion. Without doubting the sincerity of each individual's belief, historians assumed that Puritan piety gained
in acceptance because it served to explain a world in disarray and suggested appropriate patterns of behavior. Second, Wrightson and Levine distinguished
between defensive purposes, such as the regulation of sexual behavior by the Church
courts, and offensive purposes, that is, "to promote new standards of behavior"
in using the courts to discipline local inhabitants.[62] They mainly focused on the
offensive purposes, supposedly motivated by the Puritan Reformation of
Manners and consisting of campaigns against alehouses, strict enforcement of
the Sabbath, and attacks on popular customs such as dancing at maypoles and
watching bear baiting. Third, the kind of culture this group of hotter
Protestants was trying to impose on local society leaned heavily toward the literate section of the population. Its strong sense of iconophobia and its reliance
on Scripture necessarily excluded the illiterate.[63] Thus, the affluent within local
society were especially prone to be attracted to the piety of Puritan ministers like
Hooker and Shepard. The faithful few in each community saw themselves as a
minority among their neighbors anyway.[64] For both religious and social reasons,
the exclusion of the poor from their midst convinced the elites that the poor did
not belong to the "invisible church" in the first place, and this stiffened their
attitude toward the "rude multitude," that "many-headed monster."[65]

A debate among historians ensued, which questioned precisely the three assumptions made by Wrightson and Levine. Thus, Margaret Spufford claimed that
Nonconformist piety, including Puritan piety, was widespread across all strata
of the English population, rather than confined to the higher echelons of the
social order. She stressed that, also among the poorer sort, many were able to
read and write, while nonwritten forms of communicating religious beliefs integrated even the semiliterate into pious networks. Communication networks, of
street pedlars and family traditions, for example, accounted for the spread of piety,
not social class.[66] It is disputable, however, whether Spufford's evidence really
points at equal proportions of the pious among all social groups, so that the notion
of the social exclusiveness of certain forms of piety is not as weakened as Spufford

claims.[67] Nevertheless, it is no longer possible to draw a clear line between the pious better sort and an unbelieving poorer sort; this distinction has to be established in each individual case when it can be proven.

Second, both Martin Ingram and Margaret Spufford, while observing a concern for order involving defensive as well as offensive denunciations within the Church courts, note that these were unconnected with piety in general and Puritanism in particular. Spufford compares efforts to control population growth and to suppress customs considered disorderly in the early-fourteenth century with similar campaigns in the late-sixteenth century. Ingram shows that efforts to control population growth and disorder in Wiltshire in the late-sixteenth century were not motivated by a Puritan Reformation of Manners.[68] Moreover, efforts to discipline neighbors in the Essex Hundred of Havering (Administrative Unit near London, County Essex) in the fifteenth and early-sixteenth centuries—a period generally acknowledged to be relatively free of social crisis—cast doubt on the thesis of a connection between the incidence of social crisis, real or perceived, and waves of social control at the local level. Finally, both Spufford and Patrick Collinson remain skeptical about a functional interpretation of piety and insist upon explaining religious beliefs in their own terms.[69]

In a later study of the Hundred of Havering during the years 1500–1620, Marjorie MacIntosh dealt with a whole range of measures by courts and local officials that she summarized under the heading of social control. It reflected the current state of debate on the issue. To her, the regulation of marriage, the enforcement of regular church attendance, and the battle against premarital sexual intercourse, all by the ecclesiastical courts, made up the contemporary effort at social control. None of its three elements was particularly associated with the Puritan Reformation of Manners; they had gradually come into existence since the late-fifteenth century.[70] Moreover, the very institution that exercised this social control tried desperately to keep a Puritan schoolteacher from preaching in his home. Social control and the specific impact of England's Second Reformation and the conflicts stemming from it were clearly separated. The Puritan complaint literature may have attempted to profit from a widespread perception of social crisis to hammer its case home, but neither the Reformation of Manners nor the piety of evangelical Protestantism were the consequence of a crisis.

Social Control and the Poor

The work of Ingram, Houlbrooke, Spufford, and McIntosh leads to a definite conclusion.[71] First, Wrightson and Levine's "defensive motive" was involved in a higher proportion of cases handled by the Church courts than Wrightson and Levine themselves had thought. Second, they overestimated the role of Puritan piety in inducing people to denounce offenders to these courts. Instead, we observe

a traditional concern for establishing order, limiting population growth, enforcing regular church attendance, and suppressing those popular pastimes identified as potential sources of disorder. This traditional concern existed
independently from the cultural impact of the Reformation in England, and it
can be traced back to an earlier period, possibly as early as the fourteenth century.[72] Admittedly, a part of the concern for order was necessarily directed at the
poor: the control of vagrancy, for example, or the prevention of building unauthorized cottages.[73] But this is far from saying that the traditional concern for
order, let alone the Reformation of Manners, was primarily aimed at the poor.

In the village of Earls Colne, which had become polarized between a mass of
landless weavers and laborers and a few yeomen and gentlemen, the relatively
low geographic mobility of the poor allows us to identify the social status of the
villagers appearing in the Church courts.[74] Despite growing problems with poor
immigrants, with wood theft, and the construction of unauthorized dwellings,
the local poor were not overrepresented among any category of offenders these
courts dealt with. Perhaps this comes as no surprise in the case of the group accused
of premarital intercourse. However, also among those accused of absence from
church, drunkenness, swearing, and playing football at Easter, all social strata
were represented. The common element rather was their age group, most of them
being in their early to late twenties. Moreover, evidence on the biography of the
offenders, even of multiple offenders, does not hint at a polarization between
two cultures of personal conduct. Even the small group of recidivists turned into
respectable members of local society when they married, serving as jurymen and
churchwardens. Admittedly, the office of constable was monopolized by local
yeomen families from the early-seventeenth century, but members of yeomen families who had been prosecuted for drunkenness or swearing were excluded from
it.[75] Despite the emergence of a rigid social hierarchy in the village, with little
mobility between classes, the Church courts were primarily concerned with the
young and unmarried, irrespective of class.[76]

Moreover, the Reformation of Manners in the village, championed by the Puritan
divine Thomas Shepard and led by the local squirearchal family, was opposed
primarily by yeomen and husbandmen who had been living there since the early-
sixteenth century. These families had experienced the resident squire's predecessor,
and they viewed the massive increase in entry fines (fines to be allowed to "entry"
possession of a piece of rented land) by the new squires with dismay.[77]

It is perhaps dangerous to make a too sharp distinction between the traditional concern for order and the cultural and disciplinary impact of the
Reformation of Manners. First, the court of the archdeacon of Colchester not
only proceeded against unmarried persons for pregnancy but also prosecuted to
an increasing extent couples already married for premarital pregnancy. In due
course, the number of such cases nearly equaled that of unmarried persons. Most
of the couples involved were relatively well off. There seems to have been no appar-

ent reason to fear that their children would burden local poor law resources. The archdeacon who initiated this change of policy, George Wythers, was a committed partisan of the Puritan Reformation of Manners. He had preached against images on church windows at Cambridge in 1565. In his doctoral thesis, submitted to the theological faculty at Heidelberg in 1568, he emphasized the right of the Presbyterian Church to proceed even against the monarch in matters of church discipline. Then Archbishop Grindal recruited him, making him archdeacon of Colchester in 1570, where he stayed until his death in 1617.[78] By prosecuting married couples, he added a novel element to the traditional concern for population control and premarital intercourse.[79]

Despite these considerations, on the whole a distinction can be made between the impact of the Puritan Reformation of Manners and an older, traditional concern for order.[80] We can draw the line most easily in cases where this concern for order and the Reformation of Manners were in conflict. While Puritan preachers demanded an attack on alehouses, the responsible justices of the peace might grant licenses to serve drinks, in order to provide poor men with a living. Despite their loyalty to the Puritan cause, the Puritan squires of Earls Colne licensed alehouses during a slump in the cloth trade.[81] Some contemporaries even denounced the Reformation of Manners for destroying communal pastimes that had served to unite the local community and increase its internal cohesion.[82] Similarly, urban magistrates in Hesse vigorously defended the brewing of beer as part of the income of the local poor, even if that meant to allow for a certain amount of drinking during pastimes.

Later on, efforts to revive or defend such pastimes were stigmatized as Arminian, in the context of a confrontation that was evolving since the 1570s and 1580s.[83] In the contest over Arminianism we can see the divergence between two types of social control most clearly. The traditional concern for order was broadly shared by the strata responsible for it. They enforced order through the official apparatus of the Tudor and Stuart regimes, and this was no issue of debate in the political arena.[84] To that extent, social control was exercised from the top down. This was quite different from the Puritan Reformation of Manners, whose influence over the English church and population is still an issue of debate.[85]

After the establishment of the Reformation in England and its consolidation from 1559 on, the cause of evangelical Protestants urging for a Second Reformation became less popular.[86] They were only partially successful in enlisting the ordinary sinews of power for their cause, because other, competing strands of Protestant belief existed from the beginning.[87] Despite this lack of a wholehearted or unilateral support from England's leading elite, evangelical Protestantism was able to exert enough influence to cause, as Ronald Hutton concludes, the decline in lay pastimes during the second half of the sixteenth and the beginning of the seventeenth centuries.[88] Either in spite of this one success or due to it, evangelical Protestantism was never accepted by the whole political nation.

Instead, it contributed to the "dynamic and mutual antagonism" with English Protestantism. The social control that evangelical Protestantism attempted to exercise, therefore, never succeeded in becoming fully an instrument of the existing order. Instead, it became involved in the struggle between two "startlingly different moral economies" within the Church of England and between two different popular cultures, each defending its own moral economy against the other.[89] Thus, the struggles within the Church of England and its ministry about the true meaning of church and piety were transmitted, through the Church courts, to local religious factions.[90] These debates among theologians gave religious meaning to factional and social strife in the myriads of local petty conflicts that, since the 1580s, were becoming the "English Wars of Religion."[91]

The lack of consensus limited the effectiveness of social control by the Puritan reformers. Their efforts rather contributed to the destruction of communal life wherever two local factions chose to align themselves with the opposing sides in the religious struggle. The attack on lay pastimes destroyed precisely that part of customary communal life that had, to some degree, helped local society to overcome its many internal divisions.[92] Moreover, the Puritan set of beliefs often put an unprecedented focus on otherwise widely dispersed conflicts, providing opponents an additional reason for quarreling. Many local examples confirm this.

In Earls Colne, for example, part of the Essex-Suffolk cloth belt, some manors were taken by the Harlakenden family from the DeVere family, Earls of Oxford, in 1583. From then until 1592, the DeVeres fought a legal battle to regain what they still considered their property. In order to assert their ownership of the manors and all rights associated with it, including ecclesiastical appointments, the Harlakendens wanted to replace a DeVere vicar. In the Church court, they accused him and his wardens of letting pigs into the churchyard, of administering two cures, and of failing to denounce villagers who had allegedly been playing football at Easter. The archdeacon who handled the case, a committed Calvinist, believed the accusations and replaced the vicar. This was merely the start of a local feud that continued until after the Civil War. Several yeomen families, who had watched with dismay the massive increase in entry fines under the Harlakendens, disturbed the services of the new vicar from the outset and kept on participating in Easter football. In retaliation, the Harlakendens excluded the members of these families from the office of constable. While they successfully banned Sunday drinking from the village center to the periphery of the parish boundaries, neither the Harlakendens nor their pious followers among the leading yeomen could force the local opposition into complete surrender. Members of the very families who had been opposing the Harlakendens, their vicars, and the transformation of local life since the 1590s backed local Quakers in their refusal to pay tithes during the 1650s.[93]

While this feud went on, the archdeacons of Colchester, whether they embraced Puritanism or criticized it, continued to prosecute absence from church, drunkenness, defamation, and above all, premarital intercourse. For their part, the Earls Colne churchwardens and constables chased pigs from the churchyard and drunkards and football players from the village, with or without church support. Since most of the churchwardens and all the constables were substantial local yeomen, while the ordinary drunkard was, like most of his neighbors, poor and landless, the new reformed discipline was indeed exercised by the better sort against the poor. Nevertheless, the main effect of the Puritan Reformation of Manners was an intensification of local factional strife to unprecedented heights. Throughout England, especially in the home counties (the area surrounding London), the shift in the aims and means of social control envisioned by godly people divided local societies. Two mutually hostile popular cultures emerged, with divergent views about the nature of ecclesiastical discipline and the face of social control.

Conclusion

Hesse and Essex constitute two examples of a vigorous campaign for a fundamental reform of doctrine and life, of the Church and individual conduct, and of morality in civil and ecclesiastical affairs. Local societies and local customs changed in both cases. By the later-seventeenth century, local popular cultures had been transformed. However, whereas the Church and local society had found a new equilibrium in Hesse, in Essex two hostile popular cultures had emerged.

During these transformations, who was controlling whom? No doubt, both in Essex and Hesse, local communities attempted to enforce a vigorous social control among neighbors. The more neighbors depended on each other in everyday life, the more social control became inevitable. Thus, the Reformation did not introduce social control into popular cultures from which it had been absent before. The reformed program sought to replace some forms of social control with others. The new forms, like the older ones, were in line with current views of piety and how to achieve salvation. Neither in Essex nor in Hesse, however, did an undisputed consensus prevail among the population on these crucial issues. Indeed, widely diverging ideas concerning them existed even within the emerging Protestant church of Hesse, let alone in the Church of England. The events in Hesse and Essex amounted to local struggles over the meaning of piety, which directly affected the means of social control and were embedded in a specific framework of political and religious change. The outcome of the reformation of doctrine and life, however, was very different in Hesse and Essex. Whereas significant sections of local society in many Essex towns and villages embraced Puritan piety and collaborated with Puritan ministers and gentry to reform the manners of their neighbors, the overwhelming majority of Hessian villagers and townsmen, while accepting the reformation of doctrine, successfully defended a wide array of local customs. Only in the Essex countryside, therefore, did two different popular cultures emerge: the pious one of the hotter sort of Protestants and that of popular pastimes.

In Hesse, zealous villagers were not numerous enough to put pressure on their neighbors, or they had become Anabaptists. For reasons outside the principality, cooperation between these individuals and the institutions of church and state remained impossible. The compromise reached in the later 1530s, which prompted most Anabaptist leaders to return to the official Church and resulted in the Ziegenhain order of discipline, was an exception in Protestant Germany, not the rule. The establishment of a unified church at the territorial level precluded the toleration of pious groups outside it. Consequently, the Church had to be content with the piety of ordinary men and women. It had to accommodate traditional popular culture to some extent. By the later-seventeenth and early-eighteenth centuries, the result of this accommodation was the exercise of ecclesiastical discipline at the local level. As late as the 1730s, however, the disciplinary effort faced drinking, swearing, and popular pastimes as integral parts of a rural popular culture shared by committed Hessian Protestants.[94] The Reformation had finally led to nationally specific pathways concerning the relation of popular culture to the sinews of state and church.

Notes

I would like to thank Patrick Collinson, Martin Brecht, and Pieter Spierenburg for commenting on earlier versions of this article.

1. Repgen, *Ferdinand III,* 319–43.

2. Wunder, "Justitia, Teutonice Fromkeyt," 307–32. On the meaning of civil life and civil order as informed by Lutheran doctrine and laid down in the Confessio Augustana, see Liebig, *Confessio Augustana.*

3. Friedeburg, "Village Strife and the Rhetoric of Communalism," 201–26.

4. Essex Record Office, Court of the Archdeacon D/ACA (Act Books), 50.

5. Ingram, *Puritans and the Church Courts 1560–1640,* 58–91, also see 72–75; idem, "Reformation of Manners in Early Modern England."

6. Lake, "A Charitable Christian Hatred," 145–86; Friedeburg, "Reformation of Manners," 347–85; idem, *Sündenzucht und sozialer Wandel,* 163–77.

7. Scribner, *For the Sake of Simple Folk;* Robisheaux, *Rural Society;* Wrightson and Levine, *Poverty and Piety in an English Village;* Spufford, *Contrasting Communities;* Collinson, *Elizabethan and Jacobean Puritanism,* 32–57; see notes 57–93 for more complete references.

8. Lenman and Parker, "The State, the Community and the Criminal Law in Early Modern Europe," 11–42.

9. Sohm, *Territorium und Kirche in der hessischen Reformation,* 130. See for recent assessments of the Anabaptists, synthesizing research, and also emphasizing the will-

ingness of Anabaptists to enlist lay authorities for the course of pious reform and their separation as a result of their frustration with the official church: Seebaß, *Der "linke Flügel der Reformation,"* 151–64; Goertz, *Die Täufer,* 144–57.

10. Collinson, "The Cohabitation of the Faithful," 51–76.

11. Ingram, "Puritans and the Church Courts," 62–69.

12. Ingram, "Puritans and the Church Courts," 81–82.

13. Collinson, *The Birthpangs of Protestant England,* 143.

14. Robisheaux, *Rural Society,* 68–120; Friedeburg, *Ländliche Gesellschaft und Obrigkeit,* chap. 1; Sabean, "Family and Land Tenure," 1–15; idem, *Power in the Blood.*

15. Rabe, *Reich und Glaubensspaltung,* 210.

16. Heinemeyer, *Das Zeitalter der Reformation,* 225–66, see 238.

17. Stayer, *Anabaptists and the Sword,* 201: "Among the scattered, persecuted, and badly instructed congregations arose expressions of every possible standpoint on Sword and Covenant"; Oyer, *Lutheran Reformers against Anabaptists,* 97: "Clearly [central German] Anabaptism presented no unified set of ideas on the Christian's attitude toward the civil order. The disunity can probably be attributed to insufficient instruction and the all pervasive influence of the Peasant's War among the lower classes from which Anabaptism drew much of its membership."

18. Scribner, "Practical Utopias," 743–74; Stayer, *The German Peasant's War.*

19. Seebaß, *Der "linke Flügel der Reformation,"* 153–54. On the development of debate see Stupperisch, *Melanchthon und die Täufer,* 150–69; Maurer, *Luther und die Schwärmer,* 103–33; Bergsten, *Balthasar Hubmaier,* 13–54; Stayer, *Anabaptists,* xii–xiv; idem, *Luther und die Schwärmer,* 269–88; Goertz, *Die Täufer,* 144–57.

20. Franz, ed., *Urkundliche Quellen zur hessischen Reformationsgeschichte,* vol. 4 (further referred to as Franz 4), 21, 24–25.

21. Seebaß, *Der "linke Flügel der Reformation,"* 158.

22. Stayer, *Anabaptism,* xiii; Goertz, *Die Täufer,* 11–27, 144–57.

23. Kobelt-Groch, *Unter Zechern, Spielern und Häschern,* 111–27.

24. See on Martin Bucer and the Marburg negotiations with Anabaptists, in particular with the Anabaptist leaders Schnabel and Tesch: Greschat, *Martin Bucer,* 164–66; Joisten, *Der Grenzgänger Martin Bucer,* 116; Münch, *Zucht und Ordnung,* 111–13; Stupperich, *Schriften von evangelischer Seite gegen die Täufer,* 5.

25. See Greschat, *Martin Bucer,* 165; Packull, "The Melchiorites and the Ziegenhain Order of Discipline," 11–28; Packull and Tasch, "From Melchiorite to Bancrupt Wine Merchant," 276–95.

26. Franz, ed., *Urkundliche Quellen zur hessischen Reformationsgeschichte,* vol. 2 (abbr. as Franz 2), 226.

27. Franz 4, 3 no. 10 B; see as well 29, no. 11.

28. "an fruchten soll man sie erkennen die falschen Lehrer . . . Daruf habe er sich uf gut begeben und von gotes schwuren, fressen, saufen und andere sunde abgezogen, und eines solches gute gewiessens sei die taufe ein bundtnus mit Christo und den Menschen, die ein gude leben anfangen und von sunde abstehen wollten": Franz 4, 43.

29. Franz 4, 175, no. 63. He used Ferrarius to explain that his attack on usury was lawful. See also Georg Schnabel, "Verantwortung und Widerlegung," in Franz 4, 170. But see his earlier comments 75, no. 30, where he refused to wage war. See on this: Weiß, "Herkunft und Sozialanschauungen," 162–89, in particular 171–86, on the teachings of Tesch and Schnabel.

30. "erger zu dan bei dem babst": Franz 4, 214, no. 77.

31. Küch, ed., *Quellen zur Rechtsgeschichte der Stadt Marburg*, vol. 1 (abbr. Küch), 325, 318.

32. Wrightson and Levine, *Poverty and Piety in an English Village.*

33. "Es ist, um bürgerlich einigkeit zu halten, vor nutz und gut angesehen, dos ein ider sein bier, er habs legen, wo er wolle in seinem huse, da er gesessen, verschenken sol": Küch 1, 330, no. 253. On the struggle of the Marburg council against competition from brewers outside town, see Küch 1, 353, no. 257.

34. Küch 1, 340, no. 262.

35. Ibid.

36. Küch 1, 341, no. 265.

37. Küch 1, 342–44, no. 266.

38. Küch 1, 375, no. 283.

39. Staatsarchiv Marburg (abbr.= StAM) 17 I no. 5119, Beschwerde der Stadt Hersfeld wegen Hochzeitsordnung 1590.

40. StAM 17 I no. 5125; see as well Franz 4, 387, no. 169.

41. Franz 4, 25.

42. He was told "das er zu kainer Gesellschaft solt gehen, dann die Welt wer boss, mit essen, trinken, fluchen, schweren und dergleichen": Franz 4, 23.

43. The petition was written on behalf of Anabaptist leader Hermann Bastian; see Franz 4, 199.

44. See Franz 4, 190, no. 65, report on the flight of Georg Schnabel.

45. Franz 4, 22–24.

46. Becker, "Zur Geschichte der Wiedertäufer in Oberhessen," 66–105, in particular 71–75.

47. Sohm, *Territorium und Reformation,* 191.

48. Franz 4, 49, no. 18a.

49. Sohm, *Territorium und Reformation,* 131.

50. "Hat sie in gegenwertigkeit ihres vatters und der gemeine dem pfarrherrn mit mund und henden zugesagt, sich ihres vatters irrtums genzlichen zu entschlagen," Franz 4, 385, no. 167.

51. "Dan es solt den tag davor nit so schwagge gewesen sein, das man sich seins doets versehen. Item, es solt, da es verstorben sei, ganz warm gewest aein und zuz der nasen ausgeschweist haben, das andere Kindern nit pflecgen zu tun, un mummeln und vomutung haben solten, das durch Valentin, den vater, etwan schaden entpfangen, das ich ine nit draget mog, das teufen zu lassen": Franz 4, 77–78, no. 31.

52. Franz 4, 147, no. 49.

53. See for instance Franz 4, 150, no. 51.

54. He had them "hesslich geschulten, sie seien alle des Teufels" and had said "Es sei kein statt im fürstentum hessen, da mehr leut in seien, die dem evangelio zuwieder sein, als alhier zu Homberg, die von Homberg sind erger dan die Wiedertäufer," Franz 4, 226, 297.

55. Ibid., 228.

56. William Perkins, Works III, 191, quoted in Hill, *William Perkins and the Poor,* 212–33.

57. Wrightson, "Alehouses," 1–27.

58. Wrightson, "Two Concepts of Order."

59. Hill, *Society and Puritanism in Prerevolutionary England,* 507–10; Collinson, *From Iconoclasm to Iconophobia,* 4 (quotation); Wrigley and Schofield, *The Population History of England;* Wrightson, *English Society 1580–1680;* idem, "Aspects of Social Differentiation," 533–47; idem, "The Social Order of Early Modern England," 177–202.

60. See Hutton, *The Rise and Fall of Merry England,* 244–46.

61. Wrightson and Levine, *Poverty and Piety in an English Village.*

62. Ibid., 140.

63. Collinson, *Iconoclasm,* 4–7; Cressy, *Literacy and the Social Order.*

64. Collinson, "The Cohabitation," 51–76; idem, *Iconoclasm,* 4–6; idem, *The Birthpangs of Protestant England,* 143–45.

65. Hill, "The Many Headed Monster," 296–324; Duffy, "The Godly and the Multitude," 31–49.

66. Spufford, *Contrasting Communities;* idem, *Small Books and Pleasant Histories;* idem, *The Importance of Religion.*

67. Spufford, *The Importance of Religion,* 20, claims for instance that 34 percent of 90 Quakers of a Buckinghamshire Meeting were laborers or poor husbandmen. Given that in some regions laborers and poor husbandmen amounted to three-quarters and more of the total number of heads of households, a proportion of only 34 percent might indeed hint toward an underrepresentation of the poorer sort among these dissenters.

68. Spufford, "Puritanism and Social Control," 41–57; Ingram, "The Reform of Popular Culture," 129–65; idem, "Religion, Communities and Moral Discipline," 177–93; idem, "Ridings, Rough Music and the Reform of Popular Culture," 79–113.

69. Spufford, "The Importance of Religion," 78–102; Collinson, *Iconoclasm,* 6–7; McIntosh, "Local Change and Community Control," 219–42. On problems with the concept of "crisis," see Elliott, "Yet Another Crisis," 301–11.

70. McIntosh, *A Community Transformed,* 240–50. See also Houlbrooke, *Church Courts and the People,* 55–75, on the importance of the punishment for incontinence for English ecclesiastical jurisdiction.

71. In addition to the titles already mentioned: Ingram, *Church Courts, Sex and Marriage.*

72. Spufford, "Puritanism and Social Control," 51–53, suggests that even the prosecution of Sabbath breaking, dancing, ales, dice playing, illegitimacy, and incontinency

before marriage could be features of late and high Medieval church discipline. Recently, this argument has been reinforced by McIntosh, *Controlling Misbehavior in England.*

73. Hunt, *The Puritan Moment,* 69–79.

74. Friedeburg, "Reformation of Manners"; idem, "Social and Geographical Mobility," 375–400; idem, *Sündenzucht,* 37–120.

75. Friedeburg, *Sündenzucht,* 163–77.

76. Friedeburg, "Social and Geographical Mobility," 375–400.

77. Sreenivasan, "The Land Family Bond at Earls Colne," 3–37; Friedeburg, *Sündenzucht,* 169–71.

78. LeNeve, *Fasti Ecclesiae Anglicanae,* 197; Collinson, *The Elizabethan Puritan Movement,* 81, 96, 110, 228, 256; Milward, *Religious Controversies,* 48; Parry, *A Protestant Vision,* 153–64.

79. On the importance of the "coitus anticipatus" for Reformed church discipline, see Schilling, "History of Crime or History of Sin," 289–310; idem, "Reformierte Kirchenzucht als Sozialdisziplinierung," 261–327.

80. On this distinction see Wrightson and Levine, *Poverty and Piety in an English Village,* 140.

81. Friedeburg, *Reformation,* 363–65.

82. Wrightson, "Two Concepts of Order," 21–46. See in particular Rowledge, *A Monster Lately Found, Amsterdam 1628,* 13, quoted in Wrightson, "Alehouses," 10–11.

83. Collinson, *The Birthpangs of Protestant England,* 143; Hutton, *Merry England,* 154–97.

84. Penry, *The Tudor Regime;* Hutton, *Merry England,* 72–110. Given the character of the Elizabethan regime, some kind of consensus at least among a comfortable majority of the political nation was in some way inevitable to succeed in politics; see Collinson, *The Monarchical Republic of Queen Elizabeth I,* 394–424.

85. Collinson, "England and International Calvinism," 197–223; Bernard, "The Church of England"; Davis, *The Caroline Captivity of the English Church;* White, *Predestination.*

86. Collinson, *England,* 80–95; idem, *Birthpangs,* 7–16.

87. Collinson, *Iconoclasm,* 4–5; idem, *Birthpangs,* 140–45; White, *Predestination,* 175–202.

88. Hutton, *Merry England,* 146.

89. Collinson, *Birthpangs,* 143.

90. White, *Predestination,* 13–38, 98, on Perkins: "purpose . . . to destroy any accommodation between Lutheran and Reformed doctrines."

91. Collinson, *Birthpangs,* 124.

92. Hutton, *Merry England,* 120–46.

93. Friedeburg, "Reformation of Manners."

94. Friedeburg, "The Public of Confessional Identity."

CHAPTER 14

Social Control from Below: Popular Arbitration of Disputes in Old Regime Spain

Tomás A. Mantecón

S ocial control is a multifaceted concept. As an apparently neutral term, it covers all social processes that induce conformity, from infant socialization down to public execution. Roughly speaking, social control requires that a deviant form of behavior is transformed into tolerable conduct. In its turn, deviant behavior comprises individual or collective immorality, weakness, sickness, and deficient or perverse attitudes, all of which may or may not be categorized as illegal behavior or crime. The reaction to deviant behavior can be punishment, reform, defense, segregation, rehabilitation, prevention, treatment, or even assault. Social control is facilitated (or sometimes inhibited) not only by norms, the law, and social tolerance but also by emotions such as revenge, compassion, and benevolence—passions that were felt equally by specialized controllers such as judges, policemen, teachers, social workers, criminologists, sociologists, psychiatrists, aldermen, the president of a university or country, the national government, as by nonspecialists such as the father of a household, neighbors, and kin. The objects of social control were deviant people, that is, people who were considered social monsters, outsiders, dangerous criminals, rebels, lunatics, beggars, or other individuals disobedient to law, custom, authority, local norms, or family values. Anyone can become a social deviant. The discourse of social control is extremely broad ranging, since it includes labor discipline, schooling, teacher's authority, prisons and imprisonment, police tasks, paternal correction of children, and patriarchal authority in general.

In 1977, Michel Foucault explained that power is constituted neither by individual nor by collective purposes or interests.[1] Although power has links with economics, politics, and culture, it is also self-generating, because political practices are the result of coordinating and giving sense and direction to individuals, social groups, and institutional forces. Social control was part of these power relationships with two basic directions: from above (from the political arena and elite culture) and from below (from social forces and popular culture). I am concentrating here on the settlement of everyday disputes in early modern Spain by informal means or sometimes by semiformal ones, making use of institutions. In fact, as I will explain, more than half of the lawsuits in all courts together ended with an agreement out of court. This occurred most frequently in the Crown tribunals, where about three-fourths of the cases in the lowest courts ended with an extrajudicial settlement. The Church courts, however, left less than a fourth of their cases without a sentence. This difference between Crown and Church courts is due to the types of crime handled by each of them. Church courts might deal with homicide if the victim was a priest or a nun, but a large part of their business concerned sexual affairs. In those cases a sentence usually was the end of the story, because that was the result the parties were after. The judge would decide whether a promise of marriage had been broken and the guilty party had to pay compensation; he granted or denied the request for a couple's separation; he decided whether a case concerned adultery, simple fornication, rape, or homosexuality. In the eyes of the Church, all such affairs had to be solved clearly, and this could be done only by means of a judicial sentence.[2]

Early modern Spaniards were increasingly keen on going to court to negotiate their disputes. In the seventeenth and eighteenth centuries, Castilians increasingly took their everyday disputes to the local judge, instead of bringing them before a higher court as they had usually done before. This process of devolution of jurisdiction from the highest to the lowest courts also had further effects.[3] The highest courts used to resolve every case with a sentence, whereas local judges usually ended a case without a sentence. The rule was discussion in court and resolution out of court. The judge and the judicial procedure were merely the vehicle that every party used to negotiate an acceptable solution. In that sense, there was also a devolution of jurisdiction from judicial administration to social forces, both groups and individuals. That is the reason why I focus this article on popular social control and arbitration of disputes.

In early modern times, every corporate structure of Spanish society and every sphere of sociability was an arena of social control. From the basic community—the household—to the commonwealth, there existed a hierarchy of domains of social control. Viewed from the perspective of several centuries, it is apparent that interaction between all these spheres provoked general changes in social as well as power structures. Both sides of the problem—social control within every social sphere on the one hand, and on the other hand, the more general processes of change—will be discussed in this article. First, I explain that paternalism formed the main base of social control in early modern Spain. The second subject is family discipline. Third, I discuss social control within the neighborhood. I then outline the popular lexicon of social control, and finally I present some ideas on the nature of the dialogue between community intolerance and royal pardon.

Paternalism: An Ideology of Social Control

Anthropologists have found large patriarchal kinship groups in the Mediterranean area, although they also describe the various routes of a common historical process whereby conjugal families took the place of large family groups.[4] Patriarchy refers to a social organization in which authority was concentrated in the hands of male chiefs of a family or kinship group. With a cross-cultural focus, patriarchy can even be seen as a universal category.[5] It had its own peculiar features, however, in Mediterranean Europe.

The major political thinkers of early modern Spain legitimized patriarchal authority as a principle of social order and social control. In their eyes, the basic social sphere was the household, ruled by the father. The art of a good paternal government was the so-called *oeconomica*. The kingdom was viewed as a large household or a great *polis,* where the king was the father of all and ruled according to *politica* or *ars guvernativa.* Even at the end of the eighteenth century, the king frequently asked his provincial and urban chief magistrates to settle judicial cases in conformity with patriarchal principles. According to the philosophers, there were complementary levels of social control in every sphere of sociability: self-control (*etica*), the authority of the *pater familias* at home (*oeconomica*), and the king's government (*politica*). The Spanish judge Castillo Bovadilla explained it clearly at the end of the sixteenth century. His arguments were political but also theological: "there are many levels of legitimate authority and dominion. Every one of them has its own limits: the son has to respect the father, the wife her husband, the citizen his or her urban magistrate and the latter has to obey the prince. . . . The first apostles preached in favor of those principles of legitimate authority."[6] This view was not unique to Spain, nor was it confined to the early modern period. Nevertheless, such ideas underlay all major political affairs in early modern Spain.

As late as 1800 Fr. Miguel de Santander, although associated with the Enlightenment, explained in one of his sermons that "the first obligation of the children to their parents is love and obedience and the second is to help and honor them." Also, his view of the social order self-evidently included "what the obligations of the children towards their parents are, and how married women relate to their husbands, pupils towards their teachers, servants towards their masters, parishioners towards their priest and the subjects towards their king."[7] Reversals of that scheme and order were considered unnatural facts. Indeed, married women who dominated at home gave the neighbors a good reason to play *cencerrada* (rough music or skimmington). Every member of the household should be under the authority of the father-and-husband. In his turn, he should govern his home in a fair, prudent, and tolerant manner, which meant he was even expected to take into account the opinions of his wife.

Paternalism was the ideology of the household, but it extended well beyond that sphere. Due to such reasoning, matrimony was at the very center of the moral and political debate, and when moralists paid attention to matrimony, they basically thought of authority. Matrimony should be a relationship characterized by a perfect friendship between wife and husband, but every husband should have his wife under control as a minor under tutelage, because women were inferior to their husbands. Their lives were centered on domestic tasks, obedience to their husbands, farming, cooking, sewing, sweeping, scrubbing—in short, "they should be patient in suffering their husband's authority, loving mothers of their children, kind neighbors in their community and prudent in affairs of honor." The perfect married woman was "a good and honest companion" to her husband.[8] The first set of characteristics implied an inequality in the relationship of wife to husband. The last characteristics, however, pointed, if not at conjugal equality, at least at a sense of partnership. This notion of partnership was not only in the mind of sixteenth-century moralists and theorists. In the seventeenth and eighteenth centuries, these precepts had been appropriated by ordinary people. As late as 1802, a prosecutor in a trial for conjugal homicide in the small northern Spanish judicial district of Alfoz de Lloredo explained about a violent husband: "I will never be able to say how extreme the tyrannical despotism was that the accused acted out toward the victim of his violence [his wife] . . . Every husband should be a partner of his wife instead of her lord. His authority is limited by prudence and moderation. His conduct must be according to the precept of the apostle of Ephesus [according to St. Paul, every Christian should love his wife as Christ loved his Church: he gave his life for his Church]."[9]

Penal law as well as the writings of the moralists contributed to upholding paternalism. However, the criteria which distinguish virtuous from bad government at home were set by the neighborhood. It had the last word about the limits of authority of the *pater familias*. The neighbors' advice, gossip, and public rumor, even individual suggestions of qualified members of the community such as a relative, a parish priest, or a member of a respected family, were instruments to delineate the border between licit and illicit male government. Paternalism articulated order in the household and every sphere of sociability. However, the principles of mutualism and communalism were also at work within every family, social corps, and community. Paternalism legitimated patriarchal government rooted in prudence, tolerance, fidelity, and loyalty among those with an interest in social peace in the household and outside it. Obviously, sometimes paternalism did not suffice to avoid violence within the household and in the community, since about 4 percent of all criminal cases and 15 percent of assaults concerned conjugal violence.[10] Of course, these figures refer merely to marital violence registered in judicial archives, but they constitute a good sample, because they concerned the cases in which marital violence was rejected both by the neighborhood and the court.

In the last resort, the neighborhood's intolerance of aggressive males defined the border between prudent paternal authority and tyrannical patriarchy. This was also the border between scandalous behavior and tolerated behavior. In early modern Spain, scandal was an effect of "vile and reprehensible" conduct that had three main components. First, it constituted behavior transgressing the common customary ideals of social harmony and order; second, it was publicly considered social deviance; last, it set a negative example to the rest of the community. Spanish moralists of the eighteenth century emphasized the third of these features.[11] This was the landmark between social tolerance and intolerance toward violence.

The household formed part of the kinship group and the kinship group formed part of the neighborhood, which in turn formed part of a wider rural community or an urban district. This district belonged to a city, which lay in a kingdom. Spain as a whole—the Crown's rule—consisted of several kingdoms, each with its own political traditions and law. Paternalism was a major force at all these levels, from the household to the Crown. It was not only an ideology to keep order, peace, government, and hierarchy within the family, but also within these wider social and political spheres.

Family Types and Family Discipline

Family structures influenced the way in which family discipline could establish order and harmony and organize mutualism within the group. The Spanish Old Regime knew several family models. We can distinguish them by taking into account the location of the married couple and the inheritance system. According to these parameters, three large areas are visible: first, the northern Atlantic coast; second, interior Castile, Andalucía, and the Mediterranean coast except Cataluña, and third Cataluña and the north of Aragón. In the first region the stem family was the rule, but women could inherit; sometimes the dowry was their part of the inheritance. On the Atlantic coast there also existed some restrictions to nuptiality, while rates of fecundity and mortality were not high. In the second area the nuclear family was predominant and matrimony was a nearly universal option. Women as well as men married at a younger age than in the rest of the country, and rates of births and mortality were higher. In Cataluña and the north of Aragón, women married at a younger age than men, and the typical family was strongly dominated by the father's lineage.[12] Despite these peculiarities the three Spanish areas shared the general characteristics of the so-called western European family.[13]

Urban and rural factors also had an influence on family patterns, relationships, and discipline. Urban areas attracted rural emigrants. In the cities, mortality and natal rates were unbalanced in favor of the first, due to a greater share of single people such as soldiers, clergymen, students, servants, and prostitutes. As elsewhere in Europe, Spanish cities were great "people eating monsters." Moreover, in Spain those urban characteristics already applied to places with more than two thousand inhabitants, particularly on the north Atlantic coast.[14] This factor, together with other social features, affected family structure and organization. The highest aristocratic families intermarried and met each other in Madrid, sharing court life and culture. Yet, those noble families had their principal houses, emblems, and land in small Castilian towns. Urban culture radiated from those towns to the countryside. In these small urban places both the Crown and the Catholic Church had located their institutions: schools, law courts, and convents of mission preachers. Life cycles also affected family patterns. The domestic economy was most favorable when the children still contributed to it, before they married and left home. For each household, this was the golden period, enabling it at times to receive and help needy and old relatives as new members. This situation did not basically change when the Old Regime ended.[15]

Next to the general characteristics, every social group had a specific family structure. A first contrast was between noble and bourgeois families. The noble family was strongly centered on one of its male members, who had formal authority within the kinship group. The bourgeois family usually was nuclear, although it employed domestic servants quite frequently. Nobles and bourgeois developed similar marriage strategies. Social endogamy knew several versions, but it was always practiced to avoid division of the patrimony as well as to reinforce mutual aid and solidarity. The primogeniture system and social endogamy of the nobility tended to concentrate various portions of the inheritance in the hands of the same individual. All this strongly facilitated the social reproduction of the group. Bourgeois families did not usually favor primogeniture, but they practiced social and professional endogamy or they tried to marry into noble lineages. The elite of the northern Spanish commercial city of Santander adhered to professional endogamy, even extending their matrimonial strategies to Bilbao, Burgos, Palencia, Cádiz, and several places in America.[16] Their marriage links followed the same routes as their trade. The southern Mediterranean city of Cartagena had an important commercial and military harbor. In this city the richest merchants were foreigners, who practiced a type of endogamy that mainly took into account the national origin of the spouses. This sort of national endogamy was particularly strong among the group of Genoese merchants who made up the urban oligarchy.[17]

Noble families knew a strong mixture of authority, hierarchy, and discipline. Institutions like the primogeniture inheritance system (*mayorazgo*) reinforced a rigid family structure dominated by the oldest male. He even had the authority to decide on the life options of other family members. He negotiated about buying and selling land as well as who was to marry whom. During the eighteenth century this situation slowly changed. Increasingly, family members who had been excluded from the inheritance in the primogeniture system came to occupy a more important position within the kinship group or *parentela*. They acted as brokers of a kind within that group. They donated money to the primogeniture but for the benefit of family investments, to help pay for the education of relatives and, sometimes, to start colonial trade enterprises or even to raise women's dowries, so that they could obtain a better marriage. The brokers' activities created a mutual link of solidarity under their control. Although this change did not imply a total transformation of the family group, it was slightly and slowly diluting the power hierarchy within the family. In the second half of the eighteenth century, elite families still were engaged in a common enterprise to realize common goals, but they were no longer so clearly led by the oldest male.

Peasant families shared some characteristics with their social superiors. Here, too, members worked together to overcome the worst adversities and to protect the family honor. They offered each other help with building a house or making repairs, emigrating, getting out of prison, and attenuating the negative effects of a disease or physical incapacity. The father or the oldest brother usually had a measure of authority over the group of brothers and sisters, even when they were already married. However, his authority was not as strong as that of the noble family chief. The emigrant who sent money from America to help his relatives with necessities won some influence because of this. An organized way to secure mutual support consisted of the so-called company (*compañía de uso*), set up by a group of relatives from different households with the aim of pooling their inheritances instead of dividing them into parts. Everyone shared the profits and risks of the company, which fostered mutual solidarity. In the Aragonese Pyrenees and northern Cataluña, however, such affairs were subject to a family council, which meant that many domestic decisions were taken under the influence of the husband's and wife's relatives. Family councils still operated in these regions at the beginning of the twentieth century, when they had become extinct in other parts of Spain.[18] Less organized forms of mutual aid, however, were maintained in most of Spain at least until the end of the nineteenth century.

From the discipline as well as the mutual support, as practiced in early modern Spain, we can deduce how the family was conceived by its members. In the narrowest sense, "family" referred to the group of blood relatives living together in a household (*casa*). But the notion of family could further extend to include the group of bilateral relatives who were contemporaries and kept in touch with each other (*parentela*). This means that even though biological factors helped make a family, it was constituted primarily because people wanted to be members of a group. Emigrants had this notion of family in mind when they picked some of their relatives to correspond with. Those asking their relatives for help or to be assisted by them when they were in need had a similar idea of family. A set of relatives also partook of every family commemoration—baptisms, weddings, and funerals—and they were active as well when a person needed other members of the kinship group to protect his or her honor.[19] These conceptions of the family, wider than the nuclear family, the domestic community, and the household or casa, stood at the very center of the moralists' and political thinkers' critical writings. They stressed patriarchy as the guarantee of social peace and order, focusing their discourses on the household.

As already explained, it was the family of experience that had the greatest meaning in everyday social practice. Nevertheless, family discipline and solidarity linked every member of the family within the entire group to attain common goals. One of those was harmony within the group and loyalty to their common strategies to deal with everyday affairs. Family discipline was in favor of common and mutual support and defense against every possible external damage and risk. The family honor reinforced that sense of unity, at least up to the late-eighteenth century. That is why honor stood in the very center of family affairs. For example, in the eighteenth century still, the family group organized assaults (*pendenças*) against those who had offended family honor, in order to have it restored. This was done even by members of the popular classes. Social control within the Spanish early modern family was a result of different forces and projects but, in general, was accepted by family members and was developed according to common aims.

Life Cycles, Community, Gift Economy, and Social Control

The life cycles of peasants and fishermen converged on many points, although there were some differences.[20] Childhood, up to eleven or twelve years old, was a period of instruction. Instruction meant not only schooling but also education about customs, social conventions, and relationships. Young people had to start working soon, to contribute to the household economy. The second phase, youth, began around twelve years and lasted until twenty-four or twenty-five. In this period, men either got further education or started working outside the household. Men from the Atlantic coast in the north began to take part in seasonal migrations to Castile, the court of Madrid, Andalucía, or America. People looking for a better chance in life or wanting to emigrate to America flocked to the ports of Seville and Cádiz. Young fishermen's sons enlisted as ships' boys at the age of eleven and, slowly, they learned everything they needed to ensure a profitable future as a fisherman. Next, they practiced coast fishing, and when they had more experience, they participated in deep-sea fishing. Peasants' as well as fishermen's sons, and even the sons of poor artisans, had the additional option of entering well-to-do households as domestic servants. Family ties with wealthy people or any other personal link facilitated this option. Such a first contact with employment created a bond of personal dependence with the master. Under these circumstances, once more, paternalism functioned as an ideology of social control. Apprentices were tied to their masters, servants to household heads, ships' boys to skippers, as if they formed an artificial family under the fathers' rule. The transition from this phase of the life cycle to the next depended on three main factors associated with one another: age, economic position, and marriage.

The possession of some land or cattle or the ability to rent it or having the tools to start a career as a craftsman helped in obtaining a good marriage. In general, the lower the man's economic status, the more modest his marital prospects. Fishermen married when their earnings became more regular and predictable. This usually happened when the fisherman became a skipper. The word *skipper* did not necessarily refer to the owner of a ship.[21] Frequently, he took part in a company with others. In these companies, both the skipper and the ship owner shared risks and profits. Such an arrangement gave the skipper some stability of income, but a fisherman's life never was wholly stable. Because of this, probably, fishermen very often owned some land as well. If their projects went well, the fisherman, and even the coast-fishing skipper, took part in deep-sea fishing, thereby improving their earnings. Urban artisans had a chance to get married when their apprenticeships ended, although they were still subject to the master and the guild rule. When a young couple had children, they faced a real risk of impoverishment. Then, the increasing expenditure put the domestic budget to a test.

Only when a peasant, artisan, or fisherman was over forty years old, did the household economy really improve. By that time, the children had started their own labor career. Then a mere sharecropper could become a small land or cattle owner, and the fisherman had a chance to acquire his own ship or the artisan his own workshop. Slowly, the domestic economy improved, enabling the father to provide his sisters and daughters with good dowries and to help his sons attain greater professional stability. If these activities were successful, they raised the prospects for the children's future family alliances. Next to this, they provided the father with the authority to have a say in his relatives' personal decisions. When the children left the parental home, the household might take care of the husband's or the wife's parents, if they were in need. This was the prelude to their own old age, when personal need increased and individual capacities to face it decreased.

In these circumstances, peasants, artisans, and fishermen, apart from relying on family assistance, had the opportunity to receive complementary community aid from social institutions like confraternities and guilds. Such institutions, present in towns as well as villages, usually had ordinances regulating their structure of authority and internal corporate culture. The ordinances of guilds as well as confraternities dealt with a broad range of activities, including mutual help, the moral behavior of members, and religious practice, in particular the devotion to the institution's patron saint.[22] Furthermore, they usually obliged members to subject conflicts among them to internal arbitration, avoiding the Crown courts. All these prescriptions date back to the Middle Ages, but they were still valid at the end of the eighteenth century and in some cases even later, in spite of an attack from the enlightened administrations of the 1770s.[23]

Municipal relief and semiformal institutions that contributed to public order, such as guilds and confraternities, were complementary to family and neighborhood discipline. Guilds and confraternities were internally structured as a large family. As a rule, someone was appointed as the head of the corporate body, usually with a few members of the confraternity to assist him. The head arbitrated disputes between members of the institution, even in cases of adultery or physical assault. Every member of a confraternity was expected to submit a case to those arbitrators instead of taking it to the Crown court. The confraternity's peacemakers negotiated between the parties to avert a public scandal, and their settlement was supposed to be reached "with equity, fairness and Christianity."[24]

In the lives of peasants, small craftsmen, and fishermen, economic risks and insecurity were an ever present reality. That is the reason why they cherished family ties and relied on mutual assistance in the form of communal institutions like confraternities and guilds. Family and community solidarity and cooperative institutions supplemented each other. They implied different versions of the gift economy. According to Marcel Mauss, the donation of a gift established a bond between the donor and the receiver. With the gift, the donor presented to the receiver a part of the donor's personality. This meant that the gift also gave the donor a measure of power over the receiver, because the latter was left with a retributive obligation toward the donor.[25] Ethical values were central to gift giving. A gift economy contributed to overcoming social tensions, conflict, and interpersonal violence. Somehow, the exchange of gifts brought civilization, because it led people to surrender to each other instead of fighting. The Spanish early modern gift economy, however, was unlike the one Mauss describes, when the receiver transmitted the gift to a third person. In that case, this person had no retributive obligation toward the original donor. Anyway, all these exchanges required the fidelity of the parties to the bond that the gift created between them. This happened not only among the lower social groups but also among the nobility. Nobles, too, felt the need for a gift economy and for mutual fidelity, in order to maintain family discipline, exercise marriage strategies, and uphold the primogeniture system—in short, to ensure their social reproduction as an elite group. Of course, these activities were unsuccessful at times and provoked conflict between relatives, ending up in court.

Personal characteristics made the provision of community support either smoother or more difficult. A violent temper, alcoholism, offensive or rude behavior, insults, and outward signs of shameful disease (venereal in particular) could obstruct the family and community aid to the needy. This gives us a compelling view of the prejudices prevalent in popular culture, founded on the archetypes of the good neighbor and the bad neighbor. The community canalized the gift economy in many ways, through confraternities, guilds, parishes, and more spontaneous social

ANNUAL INCREASING DATA, 1591 –1830 (CANTABRIA)

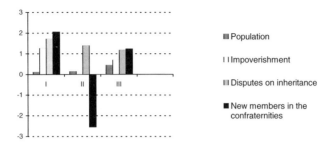

Period I. Population: 1591 –1752. The other indicators: 1650/70 –1730/50.
Period II. Population: 1752 –1787. The other indicators: 1730/50 –1771/90.
Period III. Population: 1787 –1822. The other indicators: 1770/90 –1810/30.

Sources: About confraternities, A(rchive) D(Diocesan) S(antander), *Cofradías*, sig. 5068,
5595, 5597, 3729, 60144 y 6015. On population, Lanza, *La población y el crecimiento*, p.
201. On inheritance disputes, Man tecón, *Conflictividad y disciplinamiento social,* 455.

Figure 1 Impoverishment, disputes on inheritance, new members in confraternities

organizations in urban districts. These social institutions took care of people in
cases where the family could not. The neighborhood also assisted persons in need
while they received family aid as well. A mad person or an alcoholic could be
cared for by his or her family group, but the latter needed the tacit consent of
the community to develop an effective aid because the community operated by
the fabrication of a common ethic that condemned buying things from the insane
or serving them wine or another alcoholic drink in a tavern. Such norms clearly
show how social control operated at the community level, in conjunction with
the gift economy.

Mutual aid among relatives was based not only on love, loyalty, solidarity, and
fidelity between donor and receiver but also on self-interest. Many times the donor
was motivated by the retributive dimension of the gift economy, and quite often
the retribution was specified on paper. Food, clothing, and other basic necessities were given to and tasks performed in the home of old, mad, or disabled people in exchange for their inheritance. In this way, the receiver of assistance became
a donor of his or her total belongings. Such an exchange did not amount to a gift
economy in the proper sense, because a clear material interest was involved. Perhaps
that is why Castilian law called these deals an improper gift (*donación impropia*),
because it concerned an economic exchange rather than a real donation.

In all the spheres just discussed—family, community, the gift economy, and
social control—there were changes over time (figure 1). This is indicated by such

factors as impoverishment of the population, the frequency of litigation within the family, and the vicissitudes of community solidarity. As a good indicator exists for each of these three factors, I am drawing the related arguments together in one discussion. The rate of impoverishment of the population is measured by considering the number of people buried at parish expense. Their names were inserted in the registers of deceased persons (*libros de finados*) that priests were required to keep according to the decrees of the Council of Trent. The second factor, family conflict, allows us a view of situations when family ties were put to a test. Probably the most sensitive family affairs were inheritance matters. Therefore, the incidence of inheritance disputes at the quarter sessions of the court is a good statistical indicator.[26] The level of community solidarity, finally, is indicated by the annual number of new members in the registers of religious confraternities. These numbers, of course, have to be adjusted for increases or decreases in the population.

The paucity of local studies makes it difficult to get a general idea on the situation in the kingdom of Castile. Cantabria, not quite urbanized and not totally rural either, was probably representative of the overall Castilian average. In any case, it was highly representative for the northern Atlantic coast. The population of Cantabria slightly increased between 1591 and 1752, more sharply between 1752 and 1787, and at an even faster pace up to 1822. During the second period of the graph, the rates of impoverishment were much lower than in the first, having dropped from a number ten times above the population rates to underneath them. At the turn of the eighteenth century, however, impoverishment increased again over the population statistics. This means that, from the mid-eighteenth century until the beginning of the nineteenth (including years of extreme poverty around 1800), the gift economy was put to a test. In those circumstances, did conflict or mutual help prevail in family and community relationships?

Inheritance disputes were very frequent over the whole period, but nevertheless they underwent a slight downward trend from the early-seventeenth century to the beginning of the nineteenth. This downward trend continued when the increase in impoverishment rates was higher than the increase in population. This means that family cohesion was more important than family conflict even in the worst circumstances. What about community assistance? The annual entry rates of new members in religious confraternities were extremely sensitive to the rise of impoverishment. When the increase in population was higher than the increase in impoverishment, many fewer new members entered a confraternity. By contrast, the higher the rates of impoverishment were over the population, the more new entries into confraternities we observe. This happened, for instance, in the last two decades of the seventeenth century and again at the turn of the eighteenth century.

The decrease in lawsuits concerning inheritance disputes in spite of the impoverishment of the population and, by contrast, the obvious sensitivity of the confraternities to increases in poverty clarify many points in our discussion. First, these trends confirm my claim that strong bonds of mutual assistance existed among relatives. These bonds constituted an essential but intangible patrimony, with the capacity to prevent adversity from striking too hard. In addition, people were very confident about receiving community aid to overcome periods of extreme economic difficulty. These trends make it easy to understand why relatives and neighbors drew up formal agreements specifying their gift exchange and social control. A bad neighbor or a scandalous member of a family and the community easily fell prey to adversity, because such a person was deprived of all mechanisms of communal and mutual aid. Communal social control existed in every urban quarter and rural hamlet. It operated not only to either withhold or facilitate mutual assistance and gift giving but also to ensure social order, harmony, and peace. This is why we can speak of social control from below and popular arbitration of disputes, even when the latter had already been taken to court. Social control in the sphere of family and community had its own lexicon.

The Popular Political Lexicon and Social Control from Below

Expressions like representation, usurpation, abuse of authority (*desviación de poder*), sedition, fidelity, and even honor were common among the popular classes when they complained about the damage done by individuals and institutions—including the Crown—with respect to the use of common land or the violation of customs, urban privileges, or the liberties of guilds and confraternities. These concepts were voiced in many local political discussions, struggles, and revolts, as well as in the agreements that ended them. Together, they made up the basic popular lexicon of social control. They provide clues to the character of the political culture of the common people. This political culture legitimated social control from below, in the form of resistance to what was felt as a usurpation of the customary rights of a rural community, an urban quarter, a guild, a confraternity, a town, or even one of the kingdoms of the Spanish Crown.

Honor was a sensitive issue in social relationships, certainly before the mid-eighteenth century. When a man was assured of the loyalty of a family and furthered its aims, he was the head of his *parentela*, which had an honor of its own that ought to be protected by common action. If that individual then managed to obtain the loyalty of persons other than kin, he acquired the position of faction leader or head of a *clientela*. A *cacique* (local ruler) frequently used these types of personal ties for his own benefit. Although the fidelity of the neighbors was concentrated on this chieftain, a permanent competition went on among social factions, each striving to control the others. The local chieftains were a feature of small communities in particular, although they could be found in urban areas as well. Because the Spanish monarchy consisted of several kingdoms with different legal and customary systems, the caciques sometimes presented themselves as defenders of local autonomy, common law, and tradition. What they primarily sought, however, was the furtherance of their own interests and that of their social factions. Thus, in the kingdom of Valencia in the first half of the seventeenth century, parish priests, protected by the bishop, led the opposition against the social faction that represented royal interests. As a social faction themselves, those priests were connected to local chieftains, members of the same *parentela* or *clientela*. To defend local autonomy, custom, laws, and ancient privileges as well as the interest of local chieftains, the priests protected criminals and sponsored violence and other crimes against the viceroy, his administrative servants, and social supporters. The viceroy's problems were not solved until 1648, when a new bishop arrived in Valencia and the king successfully requested the Pope to restrain the rebellious priests.[27]

Rural caciques controlled local services such as justice, administration, the supply of goods, and the labor market. Sometimes they owned or managed local workshops and foundries. Until the middle of the eighteenth century, lower officials of the Inquisition (*familiares* and *comisarios*) also acted as local caciques. In that period, caciques were able to organize large factions, every member of which had personal ties of obligation toward them. They acted as patrons, distributing favors to their clients. This scheme worked very well in rural peripheral areas of the kingdom such as the Basque country, Navarra, Cantabria, and Galicia.[28] Sometimes the local chieftain was responsible for maintaining the community's honor and furthering its aims. If he did so, he was able to rally the community behind him and to get common proposals accepted. Some caciques, however, exceeded the bounds of community tolerance. They were considered usurpers, because they had appropriated goods and rights from other individuals or from common property. In such cases, the community wished to instruct, discipline, and control its cacique.

Representation was realized when someone voiced the complaints of a faction (clientela), kinship group (parentela), a community, or any other institution or social group. In several riots and social struggles, one individual or a small group took the initiative in representing the entire community. A famous example is the case of *El Encubierto* (the Hidden Man) during the revolt of the *Germanías* of Valencia against the emperor Charles V in 1519–1521, but it happened also during events of a lesser magnitude. El Encubierto was a product of several circumstances, in particular the social convulsion after the plague in the summer of 1519, the flight of several aldermen and members of the nobility from the city of Valencia, fears of an upcoming Moorish invasion, and a more realistic concern for the activities of Moorish pirates in the coastal areas. Next, apocalyptic sermons of wandering preachers, who prophesied an invasion from Africa, heightened the public commotion, leading to the first outbreak of revolt on August 7, 1519. This was followed by a harsh repression, to which the craft guilds reacted by joining together in a *germanía* (fraternity). El Encubierto was the embodiment of all those forces. He was finally captured, tried, and decapitated in March 1522, but his fame outlasted him for at least twenty years. This mythical hero was reborn several times and imprisoned and punished again, until 1541 when the last Encubierto stood trial. By that time, the movement associated with his name still stood for community ideals of the common good.[29]

A comparable event took place in 1782 in a quite peripheral part of the kingdom of Castile, the valley of Soba in Cantabria. When two hundred inhabitants of the valley including a few aldermen revolted, they elected from their midst Nicolás Corral as the chief magistrate of the jurisdiction, replacing Manuel de la Puente who had been appointed by the duke of Frías. Soon, however, the duke managed to remove Corral. For a brief time, Nicolás Corral had represented the community's ideas of justice and good government. Many people considered De la Puente a corrupt tyrant, who extorted money from prisoners in exchange for their freedom and who requested sexual favors from young girls who came to assist their imprisoned relatives. Sometimes he even threatened these young girls when they resisted his advances. This man had been criticized by the community for years, but nobody felt strong enough to oppose him and put an end to his offensive behavior until the revolt of 1782.[30]

As different as the times and circumstances were, both El Encubierto and Nicolás Corral had been designated as their representative by rioters and rebels in the midst of social revolt. They had been selected by way of an extraordinary procedure from the bottom up, not according to law and custom. In the eyes of the country's rulers, this constituted deviant use of authority, part of the more general concept of usurpation. The rioters had usurped the Crown's and the duke's authority. These two incidents were cases of sedition, according to the law, because they implied a rejection of legal authority. The punishment for sedition was death and confiscation of half of the criminal's property. From the early-sixteenth century on, defendants were charged with sedition even when they had killed, assaulted, obstructed, or resisted a royal representative. A Castilian law of 1566 allowed the Council of Castile to commute capital punishment in public whipping and long-term galley servitude. After the 1766 riots in Madrid, two new laws (1766 and 1774) aggravated the penalty again, but actual practice remained more or less the same. The judges knew how complex social solidarity was in every conflict, and they refrained from imposing rigorous punishments. Indeed, the judicial sentence after the riot of 1782 was milder than the full rigor of the law would prescribe. Nicolás Corral was merely forbidden from ever assuming the function of chief magistrate of his district.

Deviant use of authority, then, referred to any illicit presumption of authority by people who did not possess a well-founded right in this respect. Daily life regularly produced circumstances perceived as usurpation or causing damage, to which neighbors reacted. This early modern society witnessed a permanently hazardous balance of forces and tensions. Violence not only led to usurpations and conflict but was also the cause of its resolution. Frequently, popular social control—in the form of gossip, rumors, advice from neighbors or relatives, or suggestions made by the peacemakers of a confraternity or guild—served to establish a new balance of tensions. Sometimes, the court took part as well. In that case, the court was the arena in which the parties negotiated and the judge served as a qualified mediator to find a resolution of the dispute. During the proceedings, every party used the lawsuit and the court in an effort to improve its position over the other. A solution was usually reached out of court, through a private agreement between the parties, in exceptional cases written down by a public notary.

As a result of this mechanism, not only the court and the law but also self-control and family and community discipline—sometimes within the household and very often within social institutions such as guilds or confraternities—provided early modern Spaniards with many options for dealing with daily disputes according to common customs. Thus, there was a vast intermediate area between extremes such as the *kinbut* in Scotland, the Finnish blood feud, and the Friulian vendetta and, on the contrary, the peaceful, well-ordered, and disciplined society, controlled by judicial institutions and the penal law, sought by the monarchy.[31] This intermediate area constituted a broad framework with quite diverse instruments and values to arbitrate disputes, which shows us what social control meant in this society. Popular culture and social control from below were the main ingredients in the solution of everyday problems, conflict, and crime in early modern Spain. However, social control could also provoke social discrimination.

The King's Paternalism versus Community Intolerance

Community values, rooted in popular culture and custom, often guaranteed social control and peace; however, sometimes, they produced intolerance aimed at people whom the community disapproved of. In such cases, the king's paternalism could be the outsider's rescue, ensuring a return into social life. This concerned one of the most fundamental royal prerogatives. Only the king had the right to pardon even the worst criminals, as a corollary to his paternal authority over every subject.[32] What happened to María González in the four months between September and December of 1630 in the town of Molina de Aragón constitutes an excellent specimen of the dialogue between popular and official justice, particularly with reference to deviance and social control.

The fate awaiting María González was the same as that of other persons who were banished, for several years or for life, from their village, town, kingdom, or the entire territory of the Spanish Crown. Every prostitute, quarrelsome neighbor, or beggar faced that risk. It is not necessary to explain here what banishment meant in those days: a loss of family and community identity and exclusion from the gift economy. Prostitutes, in particular, suffered from all prejudices that existed in a society based on patriarchal values. For all these reasons, María González's case is typical of every case in which the community's discrimination turned against a social deviant.

María González was tried in September 1630, condemned to a banishment of two years from her town in October, and pardoned by the king toward the end of the year. Before and after the royal pardon, María's neighbors rejected her and her husband and friends because of her lifestyle as a prostitute. Despite this, the pardon meant that the neighborhood and the entire town had to accept María and her husband and friends again. In fact, María and her friend and next-door neighbor Elvira de Espinosa, also a prostitute, had been in jail in Molina de Aragón more often. On several earlier occasions, while they were living with their husbands in the *Calle de los Escuderos,* María and Elvira had been prosecuted by the urban judge. Then their husbands already knew very well that they practiced prostitution, but they were not concerned at all about this. The husband's consent to his wife's prostitution was something the community always criticized. María and Elvira even received clients when their husbands were at home and clearly saw what was going on. This fact was known by the neighbors, provoking a public scandal.

María and Elvira were considered imprudent; they "didn't have God in their minds."[33] María told several of her neighbors that "she would always live as she wanted to" and once she told one of them: "What do you want me to do? My husband is so lazy that if I wish to eat every day, I have to earn my living with my body." María and Elvira both received their clients at any time, day or night. Elvira also caused a scandal by often using "awful and dishonest words," often screaming at home and in the streets. María had two young girls in her home. She claimed they were domestic servants, but nobody believed it. The clients, usually strangers to the neighborhood, came to see all these women. Afterward, the clients paraded through the neighborhood, and sometimes they had lunch and drinks together with the women and their husbands, which lasted until they were completely drunk. Most of the neighbors felt very offended. In their opinion, these activities damaged the neighborhood. One of them, Juan Núñez, who lived just opposite to María and Elvira, explained that he and his wife refused to look through their window, because they did not want to see the scandalous way of life of their neighbors. Gerónimo Vela and his wife even locked the doors of their house. They did not want to hear what the prostitutes, husbands, and clients told each other. Núñez was furious because Elvira and María had been sentenced to banishment several times before, but these sentences had never been executed. Núñez said he contemplated moving to another district of the town. Several other neighbors in *los Escuderos* professed the same intention.[34]

Gossip magnified every small detail of Elvira's and María's lives, creating an archetype of the social deviant who should be repressed and punished for the benefit of the neighborhood, community, and town. The urban judge decided to banish María González from Molina de Aragón for a couple of years. Nevertheless, the king, by using his royal grace, decided to overrule this sentence. All the community's arguments to punish María were not sufficient to actually get her out of town. Thus, the king's paternalism functioned to avert social prejudices and discrimination against outsiders and deviants who did not represent a real threat to the government.

Conclusion

To end this reflection on social control from below, let me just stress that the Spanish early modern experience shows the potent social forces, groups, and institutions that left an imprint on judicial and political institutions. Consequently, the arbitration of disputes resulted from the combination of all those forces, in order to preserve public peace within tolerable limits. Self-control and family and community discipline were fundamental ingredients of this process of keeping individuals within tolerable limits. Nevertheless, a dialogue went on between official and informal means, aims, and mechanisms of social control. Patriarchy stood at the base of the political structure, which gave the king the last word in terms of justice. This was crucial for people like María González and Elvira de Espinosa in 1630, to help them ward off community discrimination.

Nevertheless, it was clear that most cases were considered in other spheres of social control, outside the king's court. In those cases, social views and popular culture were important factors for handling disputes as well as solving conflict in and out of court. There was no real intensification of jurisdiction from above in early modern Spain that could be understood as a devolution of social control from the highest to the lowest courts, as Richard L. Kagan has argued.[35] What happened instead was that popular spheres, social forces, and customary institutions never ceded their own right to arbitrate disputes. Increasingly, they arbitrated everyday disputes by using local courts as the arena for discussion—even if the solution frequently took place out of court. The king, nevertheless, attempted to limit these spheres of social control from below by underlining the task of every local court to monopolize justice in their environment. Perhaps that is why the Spanish government attempted to control guilds and confraternities in the second half of the eighteenth century, while many people still relied on them to settle everyday problems and disputes. All these characteristics ensured that justice had a hybrid nature, official and popular, in Spain until the end of the Old Regime. Then, justice was the result of the dialogue between the king and popular culture on the meaning of social control.

Notes

Some ideas included in this study have been discussed during the first and second international conferences on social control in the early modern period at Menaggio (October 1997) and Amsterdam (November 1998), also within the framework of the Criminal Justice Network of the European Social Science History Conference in Amsterdam (1998 and 2000). I am thankful to the participants in all those meetings for their comments.

1. *Les rapports de pouvoir passent à l'interieur des corps,* interview by L. Finas in *La Quinzaine Littéraine* 247 (1–15 January 1977): 4–6; and in the interview published in *Les révoltes logiques* 4 (1st term 1977). I consulted both articles in Spanish translation: Foucault, *Microfísica del poder,* 153–74.

2. This appears in the research done on the Church courts of Castile, Extremadura, and Andalucía in the sixteenth–eighteenth centuries: Pérez, *Pecar, delinquir y castigar;* Candau-Chacón, *Los delitos y las penas;* Lorenzo Pinar, *Amores inciertos.* See also Fortea, *Furor et rabies.*

3. Kagan, *Lawsuits and Litigants.*

4. Peristiany, *Mediterranean Family Structures.*

5. Golberg, *The Inevitability of Patriarchy.* I have read the Spanish translation: *La inevitabilidad del patriarcado,* Madrid: Alianza, 1976. See in this version, particularly, 37–41. This viewpoint also has been stressed by feminist historians in studies of early modern witchcraft as a gendered phenomenon. Hester, *Lewd Women and Wicked Witches.*

6. Castillo Bovadilla, *Política para corregidores,* book 2, paragraph 17, 7.

7. Santander, *Doctrinas y sermones para misión,* vol. 1, 182–84.

8. See on this the opinion of Fr. Luis de León, *La perfecta casada.* This was the most influential book on this topic. Marcel Bataillon found eleven editions of León's book between 1550 and 1589. Bataillon, *Erasmo y España,* 634.

9. Mantecón, *La muerte de Antonia Isabel Sánchez,* 69 et seq.

10. Research on the northern Spanish coast, the interior of Castile, and Andalusia gives these results. See the quoted books written by F. J. Lorenzo, M. L. Candau-Chacón, and T. A. Mantecón.

11. Mantecón, *La muerte de Antonia Isabel Sánchez,* 77–78.

12. Rowland, "Sistemas matrimoniales," 73–137.

13. It had less than 10 percent single people and higher marriage ages than was common in eastern Europe. The western European family, constituted between 1650 and 1750, tended toward a nuclear form, was focused on the descendants and was dominated by an increasing affection between wife and husband, parents and children. This created the basis of individualist feelings in family experiences. Shorter, *Naissance de la famille moderne.* Furthermore, it contributed to women's sexual liberation and women's labor, mainly in the cities. Laslett and Wall, eds., *Household and Family in Past Time;* Schofield and Wrigley, *The Population History of England;* Ariés, *Centuries of*

Childhood; Goody, *La evolución de la familia y del matrimonio*; Stone, *Family, Sex and Marriage in England.*

14. Pérez and Reher, "La población urbana española", 129–64. Lanza, "Ciudades y villas en la Cornisa Cantábrica," 165–200.

15. Reher, *La familia en España,* 140–48.

16. Maruri, *La burguesía mercantil santanderina,* 43.

17. Velasco, "Lazo familiar, conexión económica e integración social," 221–39.

18. Violant i Simorra, *El Pirineo español,* 327. Moreno, "Pequeña nobleza rural," 72–73.

19. This refers to *honor* as well as *honra.* On this distinction, see Mantecón, "Honor and Everyday Life," 203–24.

20. See Martín, "Aprendices y domésticos," 197–209.

21. About 10 percent of the fishermen of Cantabria in the eighteenth century had their own ship. However, many fishermen were allowed to take part in association with others or to rent a ship. Ortega, *Gentes de mar,* 208–15. Frederic Le Play had explained it very well earlier. Le Play, *Campesinos y pescadores* (Spanish information from his report on *Les ouvriers européens, 1877–1879*).

22. Rumeu de Armas, *Historia de la previsión social en España,* 117–98; Molas, *Los gremios barceloneses*; Mantecón, *Contrarreforma y religiosidad popular;* López, *La labor benéfico-social de las cofradías;* Torras, "Gremios, familias y organización del trabajo," 171–80.

23. This was one of the main functions of medieval confraternities in Spain and Portugal. Mantecón, *Contrarreforma y religiosidad popular,* 175 et seq. Ruiz de la Peña, "Las solidaridades vecinales," 57–58; Da Cruz, "As confrarias medievais portuguesas," 163. Still this was a very angular point in the eighteenth-century Spanish confraternities according to many reports from the chief magistrates of different parts of Castile, Andalusia, Valencia, Extremadura, Galicia, and the Basque country. AHN (National Historical Archive), *Consejos,* sig. 7092 and 7094 (unnumbered pages).

24. This was said explicitly by the members of the confraternity dedicated to the Holy Rosary in the village of Riaño (Cantabria) in the eighteenth century. ADS (Santander Diocesan Archive), sig. 1590, 14–15.

25. Mauss, *The Gift.*

26. This includes cases in which families sued a convent. This institution kept the dowry of its nuns, which families considered a part of the divisible inheritance. See Lehfeldt, "Convents As Litigants," 645–64. Nevertheless, litigation on this point was an exception instead of a rule within the total rates of inheritance disputes.

27. Callado, "Los intentos de la Corona," 157–80.

28. Imízcoz and Floristán, "La comunidad rural vasco-navarra," 193–215; Mantecón, *Conflictividad y disciplinamiento social,* 213–84; Cristóbal, *Confianza, fidelidad y obediencia*; López Vela, "La Inquisición de la época confesional," 381–88; Torres, "Cantabria en la estructura inquisitorial del tribunal de Logroño," 47–79.

29. García Cárcel, *Las Germanías de Valencia,* 133–38; García, *Bandolers, corsaris i*

moriscos; Pérez García, "Conflicto y represión," 185–98. A recent book is the most complete study of El Encubierto and the social and political context of the movement, focusing on the last Encubierto, Don Enrique de Mendoza (1541) and including an edition of the most relevant documents of his trial: Pérez García and Catalá Sanz, *Epígonos del encubertismo.*

30. ARCHV (Archive of the Royal Court of Valladolid), *Pleitos Criminales*, doc. C-108–2. I've studied this and similar cases of the north of Spain in the eighteenth century in Mantecón, "Popular Culture."

31. On Scotland, Finland, and Friuli, see Wormald, "The Blood Feud"; Ylikangas, "Major Fluctuations in Crimes of Violence"; Muir, *Mad Blood Stirring*. Sweden makes a different Scandinavian example from that of Finland, because a judicial administration kept all those problems under control from the 1620s. Ylikangas, "Reasons for the Reduction of Violence," 165–73; Liliequist, "Violence, Honour and Manliness," 176; Ylikangas et al., *Five Centuries of Violence*, 17–58, 84–94, and 139–43.

32. I analyzed this in my contribution Mantecón, "Criminals and Royal Pardon," 477–506.

33. AGS (General Archive of Simancas), CC (Cámara de Castilla), leg. 1778, doc. 24, ff. 1–4.

34. Ibid., 4–6.

35. Kagan, *Lawsuits and Litigants.*

CHAPTER 15

Charivari and Shame Punishments: Folk Justice and State Justice in Early Modern England

Martin Ingram

Introduction

W hile historians of social control in early modern Europe have naturally devoted much attention to punishment, the coverage has been uneven. There has been a great deal of emphasis on the death penalty (in all its forms and manifestations from hanging to breaking on the wheel), and on the search for alternatives to capital punishment, such as transportation, from the seventeenth century onward. There has likewise been much interest in workhouses and houses of correction, which with their ostensible purpose of reforming as well as simply punishing the offender may be seen as precursors of the modern prison.[1] A theme that received considerable if unsystematic attention among historians and jurists in the nineteenth century but has only recently begun to be studied in depth by modern scholars is that of the shame punishments that were very frequently meted out by early modern authorities. The pre-Reformation Catholic Church and the church of the Counter-Reformation used public penance—involving such features as penitential garb, the bearing of a candle in procession, and an act of contrition before the image of a saint—as a means of disciplining sinners. Protestant churches for their part employed either a modified form of penance or analogous procedures of congregational confession. The various forms of church discipline were supposed to be primarily medicinal rather than retributive, rituals of repentance, reconciliation, and reintegration rather than simple punishments, but in practice their impact was often not much different from the shame penalties imposed by the secular courts.[2]

Foremost among these was the pillory, found in various forms all over Europe. Basically a device for exposing the offender in public, it sometimes involved a pair of wooden boards with holes to lock the head and hands in position, but there were many variants. The stocks, a pair of boards to hold the legs, were rather

Plate 1 *Riding the Ass,* from Claude Noirot, *L'Origine des Masques* (1609), repr. Paris 1838, in C. Leber, ed., Collections des meilleurs dissertations, notices et traités particuliers relatifs à l'histoire de France, vol. 9. Reference (shelfmark) 237 b.56. By permission of the Bodleian Library, University of Oxford.

similar but were often used as a holding device rather than as a punishment. Other implements were the cucking-stool, a means of ducking the offender (in England most commonly a female) in water, and a large whetstone or millstone that offenders had to carry in the German punishment of *Steinetragen.* Plainly these penalties were not simply shame punishments in that those subjected to them also endured a degree of physical pain, or at the least acute discomfort, and indeed public exposure was often associated with corporal punishments such as whipping, branding, blinding, and the cutting off of nose or ears. Expulsion from the community, or at least loss of civic rights, was also a frequent concomitant. Moreover, a feature of such punishments was maximum publicity and exposure. It was common, for example, for offenders to be paraded round the town before and after their period of exposure on the pillory; often drums were played, trumpets were sounded, or pots and pans were vigorously beaten to attract the crowd and mark the ignominy of the offender with cacophony.[3]

Such usages are highly reminiscent of charivari, a topic that has in fact received far more historical attention than official shame punishments. The phenomenon may be briefly defined as a set of popular customs, variants of which have existed in many parts of Europe and over many centuries down to the recent past, which characteristically involved a noisy, mocking demonstration usually occasioned by some anomalous social situation or infraction of community norms. If in form these customs had affinities with official shame punishments, they also embodied elements drawn from more festive contexts and in fact shaded off into a variety of popular customs associated with Carnival, Maytime, and other calendrical rituals. Often they were associated with youth groups and with festive associations such as Abbeys of Misrule. Charivaris varied greatly in scale and elaboration, while the mockery they invoked could range from mild and good hearted raillery to fiercely hostile derision. On occasion large numbers of people took part, and the proceedings could escalate into physical violence that put life, limb, and property at risk. The pretext for staging such demonstrations also varied. In France, the classic form of charivari—consisting essentially of discordant noise—was associated with the remarriage of widows and widowers and sometimes with such ill-sorted unions as when an old man married a young woman. Another kind of charivari, perhaps more properly called the *asouade* or riding the ass, took place when a wife beat her husband (plate 1). Indeed in many parts of Europe, the themes of female insubordination and of cuckoldry were very commonly associated with these customs.[4]

Charivari, or—to use the term mostly used by historians of eighteenth- and nineteenth-century England—"rough music," has traditionally been regarded as a bottom-up topic, quintessentially the manifestation of popular or plebeian culture. However, the accumulating work on official shame punishments invites a rather different perspective, stressing the interaction between popular and official forms and demanding further investigation into how far these popular customs were subject to official repression. The following detailed discussion focuses on England, but as will be seen there are affinities with the situation in France. Indeed the argument is probably relevant to other parts of Europe too, but a broader perspective will be possible only when more detailed research has been done for Spain, Germany, Italy, and elsewhere. As is appropriate for a topic concerned with the "world turned upside down," I shall start in the eighteenth century and work backward. The advantage of a reverse chronological approach is to show how a historiography based in eighteenth- and nineteenth-century evidence has tended to obscure features of the topic that would have been more salient if a fifteenth- and sixteenth-century perspective had shaped approaches to the subject.

Riding Skimmington: The English Charivari

The English form of charivari was generally referred to as a "riding" or "skimmington ride." Plate 2, an illustration to the 1710 edition of Samuel Butler's *Hudibras* (1664), portrays a fairly elaborate version; but manifestations could be much simpler. Whatever the degree of elaboration, the main elements were

Plate 2 *Skimmington Ride,* from Samuel Butler, *Hudibras;* in three parts, 1710. Engraving between pages 156–57. Reference (shelfmark) Douce B 12. By permission of the Bodleian Library, University of Oxford.

something to ride and one or more riders. The mount was variously represented by a real horse (occasionally an ass) or by a "cowlstaff" or "stang" (a stout pole) carried on men's shoulders. Sometimes the victims themselves were made to ride. On the way they might be pelted with filth and could end up by being ducked, with or without the aid of a cucking-stool, put in the stocks, or simply run out of town. But often a substitute rider was found, customarily the "next neighbor" or, to avoid ambiguity, the "next neighbor nearest the church." In other cases effigies were used. Very frequently, the rider was made to face backward, or if there were two figures they were set "bum to bum." Sometimes the riders carried distaffs or spinning wheels, or were made to act out a scene of domestic disharmony, as in the illustration to *Hudibras.* Often the rider or someone else threw grain, sometimes mixed with dung, over the accompanying crowds, which could be large or small depending on location and circumstance.

Supplementary symbols were often present. Very common was the display of animals' horns or horned heads, intimate female garments such as smocks or petticoats, and sometimes obscene pictures or other foul or suggestive objects such as rams' stones (testicles) or a bull's pizzle (penis). Another regularly occurring feature was a parade of armed men, sometimes elaborately accoutered with standards, armor, pikes, and guns, sometimes merely carrying staves or arms improvised from household or workshop tools like ovenlugs, coalrakes, and pitchforks (the last having the advantage of replicating the horns symbol). But by far the most common, indeed almost universal accompaniment to a riding was cacophony, also called "rough music," though this phrase appears not to have been generally current before the early-eighteenth century—an ear-splitting din

produced by the beating of pots and pans and other household utensils, the rau-
cous playing of drums and other musical instruments, the ringing of bells, and
the discharge of guns and fireworks.[5]

In England ridings were not particularly associated with youth groups,
though youngsters often took part. The sheer exuberance and elaboration of symbolism invites exercises in decoding, which many historians have attempted, and
though some elements remain obscure or controversial, there is much agreement
on the main issues. I have discussed these themes in detail elsewhere. Suffice to
say that demonstrations characteristically convey a sense of order in disorder and
that images of reversal, inversion, and the crossing of boundaries are everywhere
apparent. Skimmington rides were one impressive embodiment of the well-known
topos of the "world turned upside down."[6]

Print and Practice

Gazing at a contemporary engraving, such as that reproduced in plate 2, is a useful way to begin the study of skimmington rides. However, it must of course be
recognized that such a representation cannot be read as a simple depiction of
popular customs but is a cultural product of some complexity. Butler's
Hudibras, one episode in which was the basis for the illustration, was itself a sophisticated political satire. Written just after the collapse of the English republic, in
the early years of the Restoration regime of Charles II, it deliberately employed
a folk motif, the skimmington ride, to mock political enemies and more generally to deride the killjoy "fanatics" of the Puritan revolution who had turned the
traditional political world upside down. Interestingly, the riding motif was immediately reappropriated by Andrew Marvell, erstwhile servant of the
Protectorate, to serve the purpose of anticourt propaganda, exploiting the motif
in a scathing attack on the conduct of the Second Dutch War in his "Last Instructions
to a Painter" (written 1667, published 1689). This association of the skimmington
motif with partisan politics persisted: charivaresque elements were prominent
in the symbolism used in the years 1679–1681 by the Exclusionists and anti-
Exclusionists (those for and against the statutory exclusion from the throne of
James, Duke of York, on the grounds that he was a Roman Catholic); they were
also present in Jacobite, anti-Hanoverian, and anti-Walpolean agitation well into
the eighteenth century.[7]

Marvell's account appears to have been based on a real life incident, mentioned in Pepys's diary in 1667, when a riding was staged at Greenwich for a
local constable.[8] Here life may be said to have inspired art, but the reverse was
also true. There are indications that the publication of *Hudibras* reinforced, perhaps even revived, the practice of riding skimmington in and about London in
the late-seventeenth century. Thus a riding was staged in Whitechapel in

January 1664, a month or two following the publication of Part II of the poem, in which the encounter with the skimmington occurs.[9] Indeed, the literary connection was sometimes made explicit, as in a newspaper advertisement that promised that "at Hammersmith, near Kensington, tomorrow being Friday, will be rode a skimmington triumph, according to the manner described in Hudibras."[10] William Hogarth's publication in 1726 of highly detailed illustrations to accompany the work was a further stimulus. More specifically, the term *skimmington*—which had originally been a local usage, probably confined to the west country and perhaps referring to the large skimming ladle that sometimes featured in these demonstrations—was also publicized, not only in *Hudibras* but also in other printed literature and images in the seventeenth century.[11]

Widely publicized also was the normal occasion for a riding. It is true that there were some holiday usages for these customs, or something very like them; for example, the "riding" of people who refused to join in festivities. More generally, some of the forms had close affinities with holiday games and practices that involved mockery and mischief but were not necessarily directed against a specific offender. In particular, there were close linkages with Shrovetide and Lenten customs, Maytime, and (to a lesser extent) Christmas, New Year, and Epiphany. But there is no doubt that the characteristic occasion for staging a riding in sixteenth- and seventeenth-century England—attested both by the overwhelming majority of known examples and by a multitude of literary and iconographic references—was when a wife beat her husband or otherwise succeeded in dominating him. This was especially so if the matter became notorious—either because it was witnessed, because the man bore scratch marks or other signs of the assault upon his face, or because the wife openly vaunted her triumph or the man bewailed his fate in the presence of his companions. In 1678 an elderly clergyman of Bottle Claydon (Buckinghamshire), having been beaten by his wife, provoked a riding by being "so unadvised as to take notice of it yesterday in his pulpit." Indeed such open knowledge, making it a public matter, was almost of the essence. That female domination was not merely an occasion but virtually the only pretext for mounting skimmington rides requires explanation, a point to which I will return. But in itself the significance of the occasion is easy to grasp. For a wife to beat her husband was an extreme violation of contemporary patriarchal ideals and hence an assault on fundamental values that threatened to turn the world upside down. As such, it demanded a spectacular and determined response to set things right.[12]

In practice the morality of the situation was apt to be a little more complicated. It is noteworthy that in the illustration to *Divers Crabtree Lectures,* written by the popular poet and humorist John Taylor in 1639 (plate 3), the wife offers a reason for beating her husband: the man was a drunkard. The same theme emerges from many real-life examples of skimmington rides: the man was either drunk, a ne'er do well, sexually impotent, or otherwise unsatisfactory, or the marital relationship as a whole was profoundly dysfunctional. These traits might help to explain why the husband was unable to maintain the authority expected of him and might offer, at least implicitly, some shred of excuse for the wife. This ambivalence may be the reason why in some ridings the man appears to have been the main target of attack, in others the woman, while on other occasions it is either unclear which of them is being victimized, or both appear to bear the brunt. The deficient man is as much a "domestic danger" as the termagant wife. This complexity made it possible to include both the motif of the riding and the topos of the world turned upside down in moderately thoughtful treatments, in pictures or in words, of the perennial problems of marital relations and the means of achieving a satisfactory match. The point may be illustrated by a series of engravings issued in 1628 and known to have been reprinted during the Interregnum and again in 1672. Of the twelve prints, one represents the figure of Woman in relation to the Four Elements—Earth, Air, Fire, and Water—and underscores the importance of balance between ingredients "that powerful can preserve and kill" (plate 4). Another is a powerful evocation of the World Turned Upside Down, showing the husband at the spinning wheel and the wife in the act of pulling on the breeches. A third introduces the motif of the riding, with the wife beating her husband in the foreground, while the accompanying verse animadverts on a dangerous imbalance:

> Well worth to scourge, so weak a patch
> Who with so strong a whore would match,
> And cause the boys, thereat make games,
> By riding thus, to both their shames.[13]

Official Attitudes

Ridings and the ideas associated with them were thus a more complex phenomenon than might at first sight be supposed. They were not merely popular sanctions or folk punishments, but multivalent cultural products that could be manipulated in a variety of sophisticated ways. The attitudes of the authorities to the enactment of ridings were likewise not straightforward. In Gerd Schwerhoff's terms, ridings were both an "object" and a "medium" of social control, in an ambivalent relationship to the law.[14] The balance, moreover, changed over time. In the late seventeenth century, just as the idea of skimmington riding was being exploited for political ends by Butler and other authors, and as charivaresque elements were becoming stock motifs in populist politics, these customs were explicitly declared illegal by the Royal courts. To be sure, in practice little action was taken against them, but the fact of proscription is nonetheless significant. In 1676, on the basis of a case from Canterbury, the judges in King's Bench decided that riding skimmington constituted a riot; by 1683 it was also decided that an action

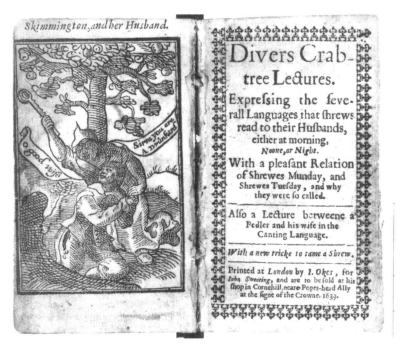

Plate 3 *Skimmington and her Husband,* from John Taylor, *Divers Crabtree lectures,* 1639, frontispiece and title page. Reference (shelfmark) Douce L 4. By permission of the Bodleian Library, University of Oxford.

for libel could be brought on the grounds of skimmington riding, and this was confirmed in a King's Bench judgment of 1693.[15] Even earlier, at least by the 1630s, Church court judges had been willing to recognize ridings as a form of defamation. This was made explicit in the opinion of the ecclesiastical lawyer Dr. Thomas Eden on a Cambridgeshire case in 1638, "that to say that a woman hath beaten her husband, or to raise a fame thereof, or to make a riding (as the custom is in some places) for it, or to prepare in a public or open manner for such a riding, is a defamation of the parties, especially of the woman: and that the woman thereupon may have remedy (vidzt public reclamation and acknowledgement of wrong in the ecclesiastical court)."[16]

Interestingly, Eden made explicit comparison with the French custom of charivari, which he described as "a like rude unmannerly custom." That he used such derogatory language was also part of a trend, traceable from around 1600—a tendency, if not to condemn, then at least to discountenance ridings as "rude and unmannerly," "uncivil," associated with "base persons" or "lewd boys." This tendency, which became more pronounced in the late-seventeenth and eighteenth centuries, represented a process of cultural distancing, but one that was only partial. On the one hand, the fundamental ideas underlying skimmington rides, focusing on the patri-

Plate 4 *Woman and the Four Elements,* from *English Customs,* London, 1628. By permission of the Folger Shakespeare Library.

archal ideal and the condemnation of termagant wives, remained culturally central and shared by all social ranks. On the other hand, the actual performance of ridings was coming to be seen as plebeian or puerile—though even so the split was never total, and patronage of (or even personal participation in) ridings by members of the gentry and other elite figures can be documented well into the eighteenth century. A similar evolution, and similar ambivalences, has been traced in France in the same period.[17]

In terms of legal action, the English authorities in the early- to mid-seventeenth century intervened only rarely. Not surprisingly, skimmington rides tended to arouse alarm in the unquiet circumstances of the civil wars and Interregnum, not least because there were suspicions that the custom could be used as a cloak for political action. Thus, it was reported to Cromwell in 1651 that "Captain Barker is returned from Kent, having, with his troop at Deptford, routed two thousand that rose on the pretence of riding skimmington."[18] In the same way, the government of James I had been exceptionally wary of public disturbances in the aftermath of the Midlands Revolt of 1607. In more normal circumstances, ridings were likely to attract the attention of justices of the peace or other officers of the law when they were associated with severe violence, damage, or disorder. That the potential for such disturbance was, however, not inconsiderable may be inferred from what is probably the most detailed account of skimmington riding to survive from the pre-1800 period, referring to two separate but related demonstrations on a vastly different scale at Quemerford near Calne (Wiltshire) in 1618. The first of them was, interestingly enough, repelled by the assertiveness of local women. But the force of the second was overwhelming. Thomas Mills of Quemerford, cutler, and Agnes his wife, deposed how about 8 or 9 A.M. on May 27:

> there came to Quemerford a young fellow of Calne named Croppe, playing upon a drum, accompanied with three or four men and ten or twelve boys; and Ralph Wellsteede of Quemerford, this examinant's landlord, and himself came to them as far as the bridge in Quemerford, and asked them what they meant, and they answered that there was a skimmington dwelling there, and they came for him. Whereupon Ralph Wellsteede answered them that the report of skimmingtons dwelling in Quemerford was false, and prayed them to depart the town, and the women of the town understanding that the drummer and his company came thither for a skimmington, they made towards the drummer and cut a part of his drum, whereupon he and his company departed homewards towards Calne. And about noon came again from Calne to Quemerford another drummer named William Wiatt, and with him three or four hundred men, some like soldiers, armed with pieces and other weapons, and a man riding upon a horse, having a white night cap upon his head, two shoeing horns hanging by his ears, a counterfeit beard upon his chin made of a deer's tail, a smock upon the top of his garments, and he rode upon a red horse with a pair of pots under him, and in them some quantity of brewing grains, which he used to cast upon the press of people, rushing over thick upon him in the way as he passed. And he and all his company made a stand when they came just against this examinant's house, and then the gunners shot off their pieces, pipes and horns were sounded, together with lowbells, and other smaller bells, which the company had amongst them, and rams' horns and bucks' horns, carried upon forks, were then and there lifted up and shown. And during the stand, some of the company, viz. William Wellwin of Calne, butcher, William Brooke and John Bray of the same, butchers, William Rawlins of the same, labourer, and Augustine Reynoldes of Yatesbury, husbandman, together with a great number of others, whose names neither of these examinants doth know, made towards their house. And they both fearing lest some violence and injury should be offered them (the rather because at their bending towards their house, divers stones were thrown in at their windows, whereof some did hit both of them), Thomas Mills the husband locks the street door, and locks his wife into her chamber where she lay, and the company pressing hard against his house, he

opened the street door to see whether he could persuade the company to depart from his house, and presently the parties abovementioned, viz. William Wellwin, William Brooke, John Bray, William Rawlins, Augustine Reynoldes and divers others, rushed in upon him into his entry, and thence into his hall, and brake open his chamber door upon his wife, and she offering to escape from them by climbing a pair of stairs to go up into an upper room, William Well[w]in plucked her down by the heels being half up the stairs. And then he and the rest took her up by the arms and the legs, and had her out through the hall into the entry, where being a wet hole, they threw her down into it, and trod upon her, and berayed her filthily with dirt, and did beat her black and blue in many places, with an intent, as these examinants have credibly heard, to have had her (viz. Agnes) out of their house to the horseman, and to have set her up behind him, to carry her to Calne and there wash her in the cucking-stool, and if she would not be still and sit quietly, then to stuff her mouth with grains.[19]

The chief actor in this disorderly demonstration, the butcher William Brooke, had a record of unneighborly offenses, and of course butchers tended to be men of powerful physique and not noted for their sensitive disposition. His wife, interestingly enough, was soon to be prosecuted as a common scold, that is a habitual brawler and quarreler with her neighbors. Nonetheless, the incident is ambiguous. The large scale of the proceedings implies considerable local support and access to resources, and the description of the accoutrements of the riders nicely matches surviving lists of the armor and weapons in the town armory around that time. There would appear to have been a close link with the militia and with muster organization, a point to which we shall return. Part of the dynamic, moreover, was evidently conflict or rivalry between the town of Calne and the neighboring community of Quemerford, a suburb situated across a bridge on the other side of the river; such intercommunity tensions feature quite frequently in the English versions of charivari. Furthermore, however disorderly they may have appeared, the Calne skimmington riders implicitly claimed a quasi-legal purpose: their stated aim was to subject Agnes Mills to the penalty of the cucking-stool, the official punishment for scolds.[20] Similarly, riders at Haughley and Wetherden (Suffolk) in 1604 claimed that the purpose of their demonstration was that "not only the woman which had offended might be shamed for her misdemeanour towards her husband, but other women also by her shame might be admonished [not] to offend in like sort"—a language of deterrence that paralleled numerous official pronouncements in courts of all kinds.[21]

It is instructive at this point to consider a plasterwork panel, dating from around 1600, which depicts both a wife beating her husband, who is forced to hold the baby and is presumably being punished for helping himself to beer, and the result-

Plate 5 "A Wife Beats Her Husband." Detail from a plasterwork panel in the Great Hall, Montacute House, Somerset, ca. 1600. Photograph by B. S. Evans.

ing riding (the main scenes are reproduced in plates 5 and 6). Interesting features include the presence of women in the demonstration, albeit in a back-up role; the representation of the way domestic disharmony became public knowledge; and the observation of the quarrelling couple by an authoritarian figure bearing a paper or parchment—perhaps the village constable. But the truly remarkable circumstance is that this frieze dominates the Great Hall of Montacute House (Somerset), built by Sir Edward Phelips, Master of the Rolls and Speaker of the House of Commons. That such a motif was included among the welter of Renaissance ornament that adorns the house suggests a remarkable degree of sympathy with this element of popular custom, even allowing that the frieze is situated in the hall—the interface with the outside world and the lower orders, not the great chamber where Sir Edward and his guests would dine in state, or the long gallery where they took their indoor recreation.[22]

Ridings and Official Shame Punishments

Whatever the motives of Sir Edward Phelips, it was not inconceivable to some contemporaries that the punishment of wives who beat their husbands might eventually be taken up by authority and incorporated into the structure of official sanctions; at least Thomas Lupton, an admittedly rather amateurish writer

Plate 6 "A Riding." Detail from a plasterwork panel in the Great Hall, Montacute House, Somerset, ca. 1600. Photograph by B. S. Evans.

on penal reform, seems to have thought so in 1580. Condemning the custom whereby the next neighbor was made to ride, he envisaged instead an official version of the penalty for the unruly spouse herself:

> she should have her husband's apparel put on her back, with a sword girded to her, and so should ride through every street in the town where she dwells; and the men that are her next neighbours shall guard her, and say in the streets as she rides, "This is the woman that hath beaten her husband"; and then she shall be put into a house appointed for unruly persons, where she shall have neither meat nor drink until she have earned it; and at the month's end, she shall go home to her husband again.[23]

This was not entirely fantasy, since beaten husbands and cuckolds were, or had been in the past, subjected to riding the ass and similar penalties as *official* shame punishments in some Continental countries. There are even occasional cases of the infliction of similar penalties in English court records. In the Cinque port of Rye (Sussex) in 1572, it was ordered that "Wodde's wife shall go about the town with a basin [ringing] afore her and a sword and buckler on her shoulder, and her husband to follow her with a broom on his shoulder, which punishment is for biting away a piece of her husband's ear and for fighting with him and other beastly using herself towards him."[24] Such a case was, however, very rare: in England the beating of a husband by his wife was as such not normally the subject of official legal action. The features of skimmington rides that were close to routine official action were not the occasions but the forms. The rough music of basins, pots, and pans; the ignominious ride, especially facing backward or with mimetic elements and symbolic trappings, or both; the parade of armed guards—these features were very characteristic of urban justice and are recorded in exceptional detail for the city of London. Its late-fourteenth-century customs prescribed an elaborate series of punishments for adulterers and adulteresses, whores, bawds, and scolds. The penalties were graduated and involved various elaborations. But basic to all of them was the provision that offenders should be paraded through the city to the accompaniment of minstrelsy. Examination of actual cases in the Court of Aldermen in the fifteenth and sixteenth centuries reveals that these punishments were interpreted in ways strikingly similar to what we think of as ridings and rough music. The minstrelsy was frequently referred to as "vile" and was made not only by musical instruments but also by the banging of utensils. Actual ridings, when the culprit was made to sit backward on a horse and paraded round the streets, were also used. This punishment was generally inflicted for perjury, forgery, and deception but could also be visited on sexual offenders.[25] The power of such penalties is suggested by the fact that, according to a contemporary annalist, three men ridden round the city and afterward pilloried for perjury and extortion in legal proceedings in 1509 "died all within seven days after for shame." Whether this lethal "shame" was the gnawing of their own consciences (the court record itself refers to "conscience" in this case); whether their sense of self was fatally destroyed by their public exposure; or whether the brickbats and ordure that probably assailed them while they rode and as they stood in the pillory had something to do with their demise, remains tantalizingly obscure.[26]

Although they were especially characteristic of London, similar penalties were also used in the sixteenth and early-seventeenth centuries in other towns. The backward facing ride, usually to the accompaniment of rough music and sometimes in association with the pillory, was also used by the Crown, particularly to punish cases of perjury, forgery, and official malfeasance. In 1543, when the notorious heretic hunter Dr. John London overreached himself by imprudently accusing some of the gentlemen of the Privy Chamber, the King's Council ordered that he and his two associates should, among other punishments, "ride about Windsor, Reading and Newbury, with papers on their heads, and their faces turned to the horse tails" for perjury (plate 7).[27] In fact riding backward became part of the normal repertory of punishments for Star Chamber, the Council in the Marches of Wales, and other prerogative courts, and cases were regularly reported throughout the sixteenth and early-seventeenth centuries. The punishment was also taken up by Parliament when it resumed its judicial function in the

Plate 7 *The Punishment of Dr John London and William Simons,* 1543, from John Foxe, *Actes and Monuments,* London, 1641. By permission of Brasenose College, Oxford.

1620s, employing the penalty against corrupt monopolists and speakers of slanderous words. A contemporary depiction of the parliamentary form of the penalty survives as "The manner and forme how Projectors and Patentees have rode a Tylting in a Parliament time." Illustrating a pamphlet directed against the notorious wine monopolists Alderman William Abell and Richard Kilvert in 1641, it was apparently intended to indicate the fate that might lie in store for them when the Long Parliament came to consider their misdeeds. The luckless victim is shown riding backward, holding the horse's tail. An attendant holds the bridle, while another goes before beating a dish; guards with halberds bring up the rear. Some people are watching from a window or gallery, others are in the open air, kept back by barriers. These arrangements suggest the crowd control that was surely necessary on these occasions, but figures in the background do appear to be aiming missiles—perhaps dung or other ordure—at the rider, whose gloomy expression tells its own story (plate 8).[28]

Two points have emerged from the preceding discussion: first, that action against wives who had beaten their husbands or the abject spouse himself, or both, were normally independent of formal court proceedings, though very occasionally official ridings of this type are found and, more generally, a quasi-legal purpose seems to have been assumed; second, that the forms that these demonstrations took were in many respects very similar to official shame sanctions meted out by Crown,

Plate 8 "The manner and forme how Projectors and Patentees have rode a Tylting in a Parliament Time" (1641), from Thomason Tracts, British Library Shelfmark E156(16), p. 8. By permission of the British Library.

Parliament, and civic authorities. These twin points may be illustrated further by comparing the City of London records with the diary of Henry Machyn, "merchant-taylor," for the years 1550–1563. Machyn was an undertaker or supplier of funeral furnishings. His diary was primarily an account of important funerals in the City of London, but he also recorded other notable ceremonies and, in addition, the carrying out of official shame punishments. Comparing the diary with the records of the Court of Aldermen, it emerges that many of the official penalties noted in the diary can be matched with the court records and vice versa. Machyn also recorded two cases of ridings occasioned by the beating of a husband by his wife, in March 1562 and February 1563. But neither of these entries has a counterpart in the official city record. There is an account of yet another London riding, in the handwriting of John Stow, very similar in form to the entries in Machyn's diary. Again there is no sign of this event in the city's surviving judicial archives.[29]

That these marital ridings were formally separate from the official punitive system is underscored by two features that emerge from Machyn's descriptions. The first is that the person ridden was neither the termagant wife nor the beaten husband but the next neighbor. There was a legal basis for this practice in Continental jurisprudence: in Gascony around 1400, for example, it was prescribed not only that husbands who had been beaten by their wives should be paraded on an ass,

face to tail, but also that the next neighbor should lead the animal.[30] This may
have been designed to symbolize the duty of neighborly surveillance. In unofficial contexts, where the neighbor actually took the place of the husband on the
horse or ass, the aim may have been to limit the possibility of violence toward
the beaten husband or his wife. However, such proxy punishments were never
ordered by the mayor and aldermen of London. The second point to note is that
in their form the ridings, though broadly similar, did not *precisely* follow the city's
usual arrangements either for rough music for harlots, bawds, and scolds, or for
the backward facing ride imposed on cheats and perjurers. There were some unusual
features, such as the use of a pole rather than a horse on which to ride the victim and the presence of some distinctive symbolic elements. Thus in 1562 Machyn
recorded that "the 9 day of March, being Monday, one Trestram a cook within
Westmorland Place within Silver Street, rode upon a cowlstaff with a basket of
grains before him, because that one of his neighbour[s'] wife broke her husband['s]
head, and cast grains on the people"; while in 1563 "the 22 day of February was
Shrove Monday, at Charing Cross, there was a man carried of four men, and
afore him a bagpipe playing, a shawm and a drum playing, and a score links burning about him, because his next neighbour's wife did beat her husband." The
references to Shrove Monday and the torches probably indicate a festive element
or occasion; as we shall see, this feature recurs.[31]

Though the city fathers did not prescribe these ridings for termagant wives,
they do not seem to have been particularly hostile to them. The ridings
recorded by Machyn in 1562 and 1563 apparently did not land the participants
in trouble, while the account for 1565 indicates a parade of such size and elaboration that it must have had the approval and support of virtually all the local
inhabitants, including the most substantial: "the 30 day of April one man rode
on two staves borne on four men's shoulders at S. Katherine's for that his next
neighbour suffered his wife to beat him; there went with him nigh three hundred men with handguns and pikes, well armed in corslets." The scale of this
manifestation is explained by special circumstances. In that year, at the petition
of the Armourers' Company, the Court of Aldermen ordered a special civic watch
of armed men to take place throughout London on May Eve. It was intended
to be a serious occasion, without "any manner of cresset light, drumslade or other
minstrelsy," but apparently the inhabitants of St. Katherine's saw this martial event,
a display of manly strength by the citizenry in arms, as an ideal opportunity to
shame a beaten husband and his wife. As in the case from Calne in 1618, it looks
as though skimmington riding was a by-product of muster organization.[32]

The St. Katherine's mentioned by Machyn was in all probability St.
Katherine's by the Tower, for this was one of the self-governing London liberties (areas exempt from civic authority) that had a long and firmly established
tradition of independent judicial action. But such independence was really only
a matter of degree. All the city wards and parishes that Machyn was writing

about operated to a large extent as self-governing communities. Presided over by the alderman and the alderman's deputy, policed by constables and other local officers assisted at all times by ordinary householders, they represented a world in which social control operated on a neighborhood basis, and many of the sanctions applied were informal ones. Official penalties were only invoked when informal ones were insufficient or had failed, or to make an example. Much the same was true of the wards and parishes of provincial towns and cities and, in a weaker but nonetheless still real sense, in small boroughs and country villages too. In the day-to-day keeping of the peace, they were to a large extent self-governing. To put the matter another way, though the actual administration of justice was (in our terms) the monopoly of the state, the maintenance of law and order was a much more widely diffused responsibility. In such worlds, it made sense to supplement the formidable battery of official shame punishments with a somewhat more jocular version. Though it would seem that these demonstrations could occur at any time of the year, the festive seasons of Shrovetide (associated with the purging of sins) and Maytime (linked both with the display of authority and the criticism of abuses) offered particularly suitable occasions as also did musters and watches, when virile virtues were on parade in a display of masculinity.

Yet this assumption of authority was a strictly limited one. It must be reemphasized that in this period unofficial ridings were not directed against offenders of all sorts but only (with the limited exceptions already noted) against dominant wives and their beaten husbands. The reason for this would seem to be not merely the unique cultural and political importance of this form of disorder but also its quasi-legal dimensions. It was a contemporary commonplace that the authority of the husband over his wife was analogous to that of the prince over his subjects: the two forms of authority were mutually validating reflections of a divinely ordained hierarchy. The maintenance of patriarchal authority was thus conceived to be a cornerstone of the commonwealth. Hence the termagant wife was guilty of something akin to petty treason. She was also responsible for breaking her marriage vow to love, honor, and obey; so there was an obvious link with the numerous civic punishments for perjury and deception. Moreover, "common scolds"—women who broke the public peace by continual brawling or contentious behavior—were legally subject to the cucking-stool or other penalty. It was really only a small step to the notion that termagant wives were also worthy of exemplary punishment.[33] Thus we find quasi-judicial touches to the language Machyn used, suggesting that the ridings he described, though strictly speaking unofficial, were closely linked in his mind with authorized punitive practice: he concluded his account of the incident of 1563 with the comment that "therefore *it is ordered* that his next neighbour shall ride about the place."[34]

Folk Justice and Official Punishments Drift Apart

The great pioneer in the study of charivari in England was the late Edward Thompson, whose point of vantage was the eighteenth and nineteenth centuries. By that period the associations between the popular customs of riding and rough music were much fainter than they had been earlier. The old civic punishments had gradually fallen out of use. The colorful parades of rough music and riding backward became routine as "carting" in the late-sixteenth and early-seventeenth centuries, then disappeared altogether after 1700; they had been replaced by the common law or statutory penalties of stocking, whipping, and incarceration. The abolition of the Star Chamber and other prerogative courts in 1641 was another blow to the official versions of ridings. More broadly, the framework of penal ideas and social values that had sustained both popular ridings and official shame punishments slowly altered, in ways that by the end of the seventeenth century had substantially diminished the communal element in the detection of offenders and the infliction of punishments, while as we have seen a process of cultural distancing tended to push the actual performance of skimmington rides and the like to the margins of society.

Partly through the work of early modernists, Thompson nonetheless grew increasingly aware of the links that these customs had had in an earlier period with official shame punishments, and in the reworked version of his ideas published shortly before his death he made some attempt to explore these associations. He was able to maintain his primary emphasis on the plebeian vitality and creativity of rough music, while acknowledging the strength of links with official forms, by suggesting that the phenomenon might be "ambivalent, . . . [moving] between the mockery of authority and its endorsement." On the one hand, he recognized, the symbolism "owes much to authority's pomp of awe and justice"; on the other hand, he insisted, it was "*anti*-processional, in the sense that horsemen, drummers, banners, . . . etc., mock, in a kind of conscious antiphony, the ceremonial of the processionals of state, of law, of civic ceremonial, of the guild and of the church." However, Thompson admitted that he did "not know whether the formal (legal) and the informal (customary) infliction of such punishments coincided in late medieval and early modern times or whether popular, self-regulating forms . . . took over to new uses forms that the authorities were ceasing to employ."[35]

On the basis of the information now available for the sixteenth and seventeenth centuries, some answers may be offered to these questions. Save for the occasional exception such as the Rye case of 1572, it would appear that in this period these charivaresque customs were distinctively nonofficial but ran parallel to and in very close association with legal shame sanctions that were in regular and lively use. It would probably be too much to say that the popular forms copied the official versions: rather the two were in a state of mutual interaction, both drawing on a repertory of motifs that, as was noted at the outset, have been very widely diffused in space and time. But certainly it can be said that, in the sixteenth- and seventeenth-century context, ridings for beaten husbands were a jocular supplement to, rather than a satirical parody of, the battery of official punishments. That these customs were so closely linked with establishment structures and values helps to explain why—as I have argued in more detail elsewhere[36]—there was no strong and sustained attempt to repress them. Admittedly, the custom of riding skimmington was likely to be undertaken with particular zest when the henpecked husbands occupied some position of authority, such as constable or minister, and, contrariwise, magistrates were inevitably wary of such occasions for ridicule. Instances of this kind may certainly be found—the derision of a constable in 1667 and the mockery of a clergyman in 1678 have already been noted in this essay—and may indeed have been especially likely to attract the attention of the authorities. In this sense, ridings did sometimes involve a touch of antiauthoritarian mischief. However, it must be concluded that in Tudor and early Stuart times such satire against the authorities was a relatively minor cadence in the theme of rough music. It was only by the eighteenth and nineteenth centuries, when the popular forms had drifted apart from the practice of official punishments, that they became more readily available for subversive purposes.

Notes

1. Foucault, *Discipline and Punish,* trans. Sheridan; Sharpe, *Judicial Punishment,* chap. 1; Evans, *Rituals of Retribution,* pt. 1.

2. Schilling, "'History of Crime' or 'History of Sin'?"; Mentzer, ed., *Sin and the Calvinists;* Ingram, "History of Sin or History of Crime?" 87–103.

3. Van Dülmen, *Theatre of Horror,* chap. 3; Ingram, "'Scolding Women Cucked or Washed'"; Schwerhoff, "Verordnete Schande?"; Rublack, *Crimes of Women,* chap. 2; Ingram, "Shame and Pain."

4. Le Goff and Schmitt, eds., *Le Charivari;* Davis, *Society and Culture,* chaps. 4–5; Fabre, "Families: Privacy versus Custom"; Schindler, "Guardians of Disorder."

5. For examples of all these features, see Ingram, "Ridings, Rough Music and the 'Reform of Popular Culture.'" Note that the beating of pots and pans was sometimes conducted without a riding, usually as a sanction against sexual transgression. However, there are complications in the interpretation of such cases: see Ingram, "Juridical Folklore," 64, 72–74.

6. Ingram in Le Goff and Schmitt, eds., *Le Charivari,* 251–64; Ingram, "Juridical Folklore," 64. On the world turned upside down, see Babcock, ed., *Reversible World,* esp. chap. 1; Burke, *Popular Culture,* 185–91.

7. Ingram, "Ridings, Rough Music and the 'Reform of Popular Culture,'" 107–8.

8. Pepys, *Diary,* ed. Latham and Matthews, 8: 257.

9. Lambeth Palace Library, Court of Arches, Eee 1, fols. 291–95; the case is cited in Foyster, *Manhood,* 154. For the date of publication of Hudibras, pt. 1, see Pepys, *Diary,* ed. Latham and Matthews, 4: 400.

10. Quoted in Ashton, *Social Life*, 1: 324.

11. Ingram, "Juridical Folklore," 65–66.

12. Ingram, "Ridings, Rough Music and the 'Reform of Popular Culture,'" 82–90; on the Bottle Claydon incident, see Verney, ed., *Verney Letters*, 1: 367–68.

13. *English Customs* (1628) [STC 10408.6]. The prints are discussed in Jones, "English Print, c.1550–c.1650," 353–54.

14. See Schwerhoff in this volume.

15. See Ingram, "Ridings, Rough Music and the 'Reform of Popular Culture,'" 101, and the references there cited.

16. Cambridge University Library, Cambridge University Archives, CUR 13, no. 29 (I owe this reference to Dr. Alex Shepard).

17. Ingram, "Juridical Folklore," 82; Ingram, "Ridings, Rough Music and the 'Reform of Popular Culture,'" 104–6; Fabre, "Families," 559–61.

18. Nickolls, ed., *Original Letters and Papers*, 66.

19. Wiltshire Record Office, Trowbridge, Quarter Sessions Great Rolls, Trinity 1618, no. 168. The document has several times been reprinted in abridged versions: for example, Cunnington, ed., *Records of the County of Wilts*, 65–66.

20. Ingram, "Ridings, Rough Music and the 'Reform of Popular Culture,'" 103–4; Mabbs, ed., *Guild Stewards' Book of the Borough of Calne, 1561–1688*, 100.

21. Public Record Office, London, STAC 8/249/19, m. 18.

22. Rogers, *Montacute House*, 7–8, 11, 16–17, 55–57.

23. Lupton, *Siuqila*, 49–50; cf. Rose, "Too Good to Be True," esp. 183–86, 193–94.

24. Flandrin, *Familles*, 22; Mayhew, *Tudor Rye*, 205.

25. Ingram, "Juridical Folklore in England," 69–71.

26. Dyboski, ed., *Songs, Carols and Other Miscellaneous Poems*, 155.

27. Foxe, *Actes and Monuments*, 2: 1398–99.

28. *A Dialogue or Accidental Discourse betwixt Mr. Alderman Abell and Richard Kilvert* . . . [British Library, Thomason Tracts, E. 156 (16)].

29. Based on comparison of Machyn, *Diary*, 278, 301 and passim and Gairdner, ed., *Three Fifteenth-Century Chronicles*, 132, with Corporation of London Record Office, Journals 16–18, Repertories 12–15, Letter Books R, S, T.

30. Flandrin, *Familles*, 122.

31. Machyn, *Diary*, 278, 301.

32. Gairdner, ed., *Three Fifteenth-Century Chronicles*, 132; Corporation of London Record Office, Repertory 15, fols. 347v, 348v–349r, 436v, 437r.

33. Petty treason was the killing of a husband by his wife or a master by his servant: see the statute 25 Edward III, 5 c. 2. On scolds, see Ingram, "'Scolding Women Cucked or Washed.'"

34. Machyn, *Diary*, 301 (my emphasis).

35. Thompson, *Customs in Common*, 478–80, 482.

36. Ingram, "Ridings, Rough Music and the 'Reform of Popular Culture,'" passim.

CHAPTER 16

Social Control and the Neighborhood in European Cities

CARL A. HOFFMANN

I n May 1600 the Augsburg council imprisoned the weaver[1] Marx Gropp for adultery and poor housekeeping (*Übelhausen*). During the trial, people from Gropp's neighborhood, including the neighborhood captain (*Gassenhauptmann*), and members of his guild presented a supplication in his favor. They defended him by referring to his wife's "spiteful complaints" (*gehässig anclagen*) and explained that although they did not know the actual accusations, they had heard that Gropp's former maidservant was also imprisoned. Then they begged for his release from prison, where he had already spent fifteen days. In case Gropp had actually done anything that deserved punishment—and they hoped this was not true—they asked for the council's mercy. In spite of their efforts, the defendant was convicted of his crimes in a trial lasting nearly three weeks. On May 20, 1600, Gropp was punished with a fine and made to swear an oath to live well with his wife.[2]

The story of this case is related here only briefly; our focus will be the position of the neighborhood and its role of social control in the urban context. As is usual in such cases, the perspective comes from the courts. As a first approach to the subject, we can learn a lot from this short example. First and foremost, the neighborhood appears as a formal institution between the urban government and the population, which provides an independent statement on the case. As we know from other examples, neighborhood intervention played a certain role in the reconciliation of the accused and his wife as expressed in his oath and in the chances for the convicted to become reintegrated into the community. In this context the neighborhood is also an informal means of social control. In having a hand in allowing Gropp the chance to return to his old social network, neighbors exert a certain power over him, obliging him to behave in accordance with the norms of the community.

I will analyze the neighborhood as a tool of social control in the early modern city from two different perspectives. The neighborhood was an instrument of urban or state authorities, as well as a local community of subjects with their own interests, norms, and values. Thus, the neighborhood in the urban context is to be interpreted both from the formal point of view, as an institution, and from the informal perspective, as a group of urban inhabitants that is not clearly defined. Moreover, the neighborhood was often part of the organizational structure in early modern cities. Thus, its position in this structure has to be analyzed. Social control in this context is formal, based on the instructions, regulations, and surveillances of the authorities. However, the neighborhood was also a sociological phenomenon, defined by "spatial proximity and permanent or temporary cohabitation."[3] Out of this perspective social control is informal. Exercise of control is not only the result of state legislation but also the interests of the cohabitants of a street or lane. Thus the values and norms not only of the state or the administration but also—and perhaps primarily— of the fellow lodgers or the surrounding society played a vital role in the day-to-day life of neighborhoods.

Central to this article are the following questions: In what ways and to what extent could urban neighborhoods exert social control on their cohabitants, and how did this control change during the early modern period? Due to the state of research, we have to concentrate on certain examples of early modern cities. Primary attention will be given here to the example of sixteenth-century Augsburg.[4]

Although historians up to now have shown little specific interest in urban neighborhoods, their organization, or their daily life, we do have a number of interesting case studies for the early modern period. Most deal with social and political life in neighborhoods in a general way or with neighborhood conflicts, but they do give us an idea about some specific developments in formal as well as in informal aspects of social control in this area. There have been no long-term or comparative studies, which would allow more general views on the subject. Research on individual cities (or parts of a city) in certain periods exists, but there is not even a single analysis on an individual city for the entire early modern period. Thus, we must glean our knowledge about long-term trends by comparing studies that usually have very different methodological approaches. Of particular value for our subject are the overviews of research on urban neighborhoods by Lis and Soly and by Roodenburg.[5] Nevertheless, we all walk on very thin ice if we compare sixteenth-century Dutch cities with eighteenth-century London or Paris, or even with sixteenth-century Augsburg. Simple comparisons of this kind cannot lead to satisfying results, for there are too many factors influencing the development of neighborhood life.

Some light on the subject of social control in the context of urban neighborhoods is also shed by work in the history of crime and of attitudes. Two fields of research with interesting results for our subject out of numerous others are the history of public houses and gender history. The study of social control by neighborhoods can be done for the most part only through sources produced by the authorities or the criminal justice system. Therefore, a broad picture of functioning neighborhood relations, and their positive influence or successful disciplining efforts, must be reconstructed indirectly. Nevertheless, it is possible to identify a wide variety of areas in which social control took place, ranging from consent and cooperation within the whole society to conflict between authorities and subjects.[6]

Very impressive studies also exist on church discipline in the urban context. We can learn a lot from these authors. Unfortunately, they concentrate primarily on the Calvinist denomination; we still have little information about church discipline in Lutheran or Catholic cities and towns.[7] Given the present state of research, any overview of social control in urban neighborhoods during the early modern period will remain a very rough sketch.

There are studies of neighborhood relations by sociologists. Although sociological analysis of urban neighborhoods is primarily inspired by an interest in defining future social policy, they often deal with historical perspectives to explain long-term dimensions. Nevertheless, "most do little more than offer clichés" in describing this perspective, because they remain in a simple "traditional-modern dichotomy."[8] But the interests and approaches of historians dealing with neighborhoods are often inspired by sociological questions, especially where they are connected with issues of informal relations between citizens in close living conditions.

In order to describe urban neighborhoods within the context of social control in the early modern period, it is necessary to take the main developments of early modern state building into consideration. The so-called process of modernization in historical research includes a wide spectrum of developments, from the extension of state institutions and their competence to disciplining ordinances that penetrated into many aspects of the daily life of all subjects. This catchphrase covers the concepts of social disciplining, confessionalization, civilization, and emancipation, but also the rise in state-controlled legal institutions (*Verrechtlichung*).[9] The problematic aspects of these concepts have been discussed for some time; we will need to continue to keep them in mind in the following pages.

Neighborhoods were very much dependent on the development of state or urban institutions. Thus, this development corresponded with many factors of the relationship between state legislation and urban society. Several researchers, and not only those dealing with neighborhoods, have suggested as a hypothesis that the more the modern state exerted power over its subjects, the more informal and nonstate institutions lost their importance for social control. The question that follows from this hypothesis is: To what extent was the position of urban neighborhoods affected by this phenomenon? Not only was modernization not a linear development but also—and this is true even in research on modern societies—the community never lost its importance for its residents (perspective from the bottom). The more the approach of the so-called infrajudiciary is explored, the more a simple model of modernization must be doubted, in our context as well as elsewhere.[10]

Neighborhoods As Formal Institutions of Social Control

The neighborhood as a formal institution within the urban administrative structure can be defined for our purposes more precisely, using the example of sixteenth-century Augsburg, an Imperial city in south Germany. In Augsburg sources, the subordinates of a neighborhood captain called themselves a "neighborhood" and normally consisted of the inhabitants of about ten to fifteen houses.[11] These individuals, who were primarily artisans and laborers, also served as officials with responsibilities in the military and administrative areas. Neighborhood captains had to register inhabitants, weapons, grain reserves, or special taxes. In the court records they were mentioned together with their neighborhoods as institutions of nonjudicial mediation in conflicts or at the first signs of offenses against order within their administrative district. The neighborhood in this sense becomes the institutionalization of social control. The duties of these neighborhoods will now be described in more detail.

First and foremost, citizens and other inhabitants had a general duty to pacify and to admonish in any case of conflict within their community. This was especially true in cases of blasphemers, squanderers of household goods, heads of household who were regularly drunken and abused their families, or similar offenders. The role of the neighbor was to draw the attention of these individuals to their misdemeanor and to give a friendly admonition in order to bring them back to accepted moral standards. Only in cases in which the individual failed to understand the personal or communal warning, or where a repetition of the offenses occurred, were the courts informed. Before a misdemeanor escalated to a punishable act, the fellow citizens had the obligation to find a satisfactory solution. In this way, the community, more specifically the neighborhood, was directly involved in social control by serving as an extra- or nonjudicial mediation committee. In these mediations and admonitions, the above mentioned neighborhood captains in Augsburg played a crucial role.

The following example of an innkeeper from Augsburg in 1552 shows clearly how such a procedure worked in practice. Zimprecht Grens was accused by his neighbors of housing "loose" women, of giving married and unmarried men access to them, and of entertaining guests beyond the regular closing time, thereby disturbing the general peace. After first trying verbal confrontations, the neighbors called in the neighborhood captain, who admonished Grens but could not impose sanctions. After all attempts at mediation between the parties failed, fifteen neighbors—that is, the entire neighborhood—informed the city council, which immediately arrested Grens.[12]

Second, it was the duty of all inhabitants to stop violent confrontations with the command that peace should be established (*Friedbieten*). In other words, eyewitnesses were expected to intervene in any case of violent behavior or confrontation, and to command that the participants stop what they were doing and make peace with one another. Of course, the bystanders, the visitors to an inn or the neigh-bors of a brutal husband, were also supposed to enforce this peace on the quar-relling parties. The command to make peace was exercised in the name of the mayor and became, therefore, of official importance, especially if the conflict could not be settled. To further support this, special punishments were given to those who ignored the bidding of peace by their fellow citizens.

The duty to admonish in cases of misdemeanors or to intervene in violent confrontations produced a gray area of involvement that could endanger or draw the mediator into the incident. An example of such circumstances is that of the wife of Andreas Widenman, a citizen of Nördlingen, who was nearly killed by her neighbor in 1584 when she tried to calm the drunken and furious man.[13] The understandable inclination to avoid any involvement in such quarrels was countered by the threat of harsh penalties for noncompliance. Conversely, the duty often also served as an excuse for participants who claimed that they only became involved in a confrontation after they had commanded peace and thus could be excused of guilt.

Third, citizens and the other dwellers of the city of Augsburg as well as those of other cities had the duty to inform authorities about offenses and violations of discipline ordinances as well as of the criminal law. This duty was observed so completely that one cannot discern much of a difference between the author-ities and the subjects in their understanding of norms. This can be shown through the protocols of the lower criminal courts (*Strafherren, Einunger,* etc.).[14] Besides the normal accusations and denunciations, people often made remarks that show how completely obliged they felt to bring further evidence forward in specific cases. Especially in cases involving sexual crimes, we get the impression of a nearly oppressive system of spying, suspicion, rumors, surveillance, and marginaliza-tion, which brought countless hints, accusations (true or false), or even concrete evidence to the attention of the authorities. In most cases victims were innkeep-ers who ran their houses more liberally than allowed, or women who lived alone because of the frequent absences of their husbands or because they were unmar-ried or widows. Often a short visit by a man to such a single woman, even dur-ing the day, was enough to inspire the fancy of the neighbors, and their suspicions of impropriety could ultimately result in the woman being brought to prison, put in irons, and examined by two councilors.

The incentive for bringing information or making an accusation to the mayor or the lower courts was further encouraged by a financial reward. The informer or denunciator (often called *informant,* or *Kundschafter*) received a fixed sum that was related to the degree of the judgment. This, of course, caused a lot of sus-picion and false accusations, often leading to the punishment of the informant himself. In many cases, neighborhood networks became extremely poisoned as a result of these actions, with accusation and counteraccusations producing an extended period of insults, investigations, and trials.

Finally, neighbors had the duty to appear at trial as witnesses of the crime or offense itself, as well as serving as character witnesses. In 1519, the Augsburg city council commanded such testimonies from neighbors for all the so-called St. Gall's people. Every year at St. Gall's day until 1536, a specific court day was held for prostitutes or other women or men accused of sexual offenses to be sentenced. If proved guilty, they were expelled from the city for at least a year. The mandate specifically stated, "if somebody is accused for exile, the neighbors shall be questioned about the habits of the accused. After this inquiry, everything shall be done, as is right."[15]

As the above duties of urban dwellers show, in order to enforce the state aims of peacekeeping, security, and discipline as protection for the community against the potential rage of God (which could be brought on by the sinful and wicked lives of the subjects), early modern authorities needed a surveillance instrument close to the people. Using a combination of persuasion, financial incentives, and the threat of punishment, the magistrates succeeded in making the town dwellers serve as instruments in the implementation and enforcement of their policy. This communal control in combination with quite efficient criminal courts and police created a system of discipline that expanded its efficiency in most cases through the cooperation between authorities and subjects. Conversely, where this cooperation did not work, we can assume some kind of opposition against legal provisions.

The institutions most similar to the Augsburg neighborhoods were those in Dutch cities. There are a number of interesting studies of these neighborhood communities (*gebuurten*), including Delft, Haarlem, Leiden, Rotterdam, The Hague, and Utrecht.[16] These communities were founded in the late Middle Ages by the people themselves who were living together on a street and originally organized informally for mutual help. Roodenburg explains their origins from the same roots as those of guilds and confraternities, with an ideal of sociability (*Vergemeinschaftungsideal*), resting on basic values (harmony, concord, peace, and reconciliation). The author does not want to draw a picture of pure harmony in late Medieval society but interprets these ideals as reactions to internal disruption.[17]

Dutch neighborhoods also had a formal structure similar to the neighborhoods in Augsburg, but with more staff. People living in a *gebuurte*, like the members of a guild, elected a dean and captains (*hoofdmannen*) and also had an informal judicature. These principals often had a secretary, and sometimes even an advocate. All neighborhoods had a servant who ensured the mutual rights of the inhabitants and served as mediators in case of conflicts. Between the fifteenth and the eighteenth centuries, clear changes in the responsibilities of the neighborhood officers and in the urban institutional structure can be recognized. During the early modern period the gebuurten increasingly came under the supervision of the city government, with an accompanying shift in the definition of their functions. The deans and captains became responsible for registering strangers or monitoring the local poor.[18]

For the Dutch cities also, a decline in participation in local government can be supposed. We know that in The Hague, the heads of poor families were excluded from the election of the deans and captains and that in Leiden rich and poor increasingly failed to cooperate with each other.[19] Aside from this marginalization of poor inhabitants, in Leiden the neighbors lost their right to elect their deans in 1593. The inhabitants of the neighborhood were allowed only to nominate three candidates, with the city court then making the final selection.[20] The development of the responsibilities and tasks of the deans in the southern Netherlands in the better analyzed example of Ghent seems in general to be very similar to the Dutch cities, although Lis and Soly suggest that in this city, local autonomy was preserved much longer than elsewhere in Western Europe.[21]

In contrast to our Augsburg example, the principals in The Hague and in Leiden had the right to sentence their neighbors to a broad variety of fines.[22] They were also tasked with intervening informally in local conflicts and pacifying the participants before escalation. At the end of the sixteenth century, ordinances required that quarrelsome neighbors explain their problems first to the principals of their neighborhood before going to the city court. As we know from other early modern cities, most of these quarrels were conflicts of honor and the task of the principals was to preserve peace within the neighborhood. Thus, the captains were also called "peacemakers." In case of verbal injuries, citizens could revoke their insults in front of the principals. A seventeenth-century contemporary described the scene: "then they shake hands, and are made friends."[23] It is possible that such settlements could also be made in front of Augsburg neighborhood captains, but we know of them only as they took place in front of the representatives of the city council.

One could interpret these changes as a development from the self-regulated local community within a city on the basis of the neighborhood to instrumental elected neighborhood representatives. This is also a step in the process of *Verrechtlichung* or increased legalism in many fields of early modern life, which is very much connected with the professionalization of civic administrative and juridical systems.

In comparison with what we know thus far about developments in other European cities, local autonomy in Paris was most restricted, at least in the eighteenth century. In Paris earlier than in other cities, "an extensive and professional police force was created."[24] In the French capital, the neighborhood (*le voisinage*) was never a clearly defined space with its own formally recorded rights and duties. In the first half of the sixteenth century, the city was divided into sixteen quarters, which were governed by local dignitaries elected by their elite citizens. During the following two centuries, the withdrawal of a significant number of members of the elite classes from community life changed the character of the quarters.

"With each successive withdrawal, with the spread of what were becoming mainstream values, and through other changes that were taking place simultaneously, the community itself was changing." One example of the loss of local autonomy is the change in the city militia, which was maintained by the citizens of the quarters until the middle of the eighteenth century, when it was replaced by a police force. According to David Garrioch, the centralization of the administration, and the reduction of local autonomy and the responsibilities of the local elites, also "significantly reduced the importance of the quarter as a social and psychological entity."[25]

Moreover, Martin Dinges has shown that at least since 1760, conflicts of honor underwent a process of decreasing judicial jurisdiction (*Entrechtlichung*) in Paris. The number of such quarrels declined in the courts, and instead quarrels were treated by the police. The author recognizes in this institutional change the reason for an increase in juridically unregulated violence. The background of this phenomenon, according to Dinges, is that in Paris the class most interested in defending its own position by protecting its honor, the middle class, was no longer interested in provocative honor quarrels, which were dealt with in higher courts. Quarrels of honor still existed but were increasingly ignored by the leading politicians of justice. Social control in this area was now treated primarily by the police and handled less and less between neighbors themselves.[26] What Dinges describes cannot be interpreted as a backward-oriented development in the period before the rise in legal procedures took place, but rather as a symptom of modern class society. Conflicts of honor to defend one's position in society were a declining model of the ancien régime, which no longer interested the courts in most cases.

Informal Social Control by Urban Neighborhoods

The definition of "neighborhood," stressing the informal use of the category, which Bernd Roeck has designated as a "soft" category and described as "generally marked by spatial proximity and permanent or temporary cohabitation," comes close to Max Weber's definition and that of other sociologists and anthropologists.[27] Scholars in these disciplines have reflected about interpersonal cooperation, tension, conflict, special codes of behavior, and so forth in towns and cities. The concepts of these community studies were adapted by historians.[28] For our purposes we could say that the neighborhood is not only a formal framework for institutionalized social control but also a source of conflicts within the community, which in turn lead to the need for control measures by the authorities or the society itself. These conflicts can result from the violation of one norm, but also from the tension between different norms, for example between socially accepted or even required behaviors and contradicting laws enacted by an authority.

The formal institution of a neighborhood originally was created by the neighbors themselves—at least we know this from the Dutch cities. Drawing on Karl-Sigismund Kramer, Roodenburg is convinced this institution rested on the corporative values of concord, brotherhood, and friendship.[29] These values led to a process of horizontal social control that was enforced by fellow citizens. Even if the formal social control exercised and initiated by the city authorities (or by state institutions) became more and more important in the early modern period, control on the horizontal level never lost its importance.

This was true also for eighteenth-century London or Paris. The tremendous mobility of the population and its enormous increase in number, combined with a segregation of the elites, has led to the hypothesis that the instruments of social control within the community lost their function in favor of centralized institutions, especially a modern police body. But modern research shows that the socially more homogeneous neighborhoods developed new forms of autonomous informal social control, parallel to the security institutions of the authorities.[30]

Examples of areas in which we can see neighborhoods as enforcers of social control include: interest conflicts arising from the narrow living conditions in cities, for example in connection with the building of houses or the use of wells; sexual infractions, such as adultery or procuring; intolerable living circumstances for wives and children with violent husbands and fathers; physical injuries in the alleys; and so on. Poor housekeeping, in Augsburg sources generally described as "bad housekeeping" (*Übelhausen*), caused neighbors to intervene personally and, in the case of failure, to press neighborhood captains or finally the council to restore Christian family life in their environment. Not only a sense of civic duty to act in the name of the authorities but also piety and moral and religious convictions, or less altruistic motives such as envy, economic advantage, or other aspects of personal relationships, led neighbors to act to control each other.[31]

Where the peace of the community or the security of its inhabitants was threatened, cooperation often occurred between the population and the authorities. There was a broad spectrum of legal, self-motivated neighborhood interventions in urban society to exert social control. In the vast majority of these cases, individuals within a neighborhood pressed the urban authorities to intervene because their personal living space was disturbed or their property or even person or family was endangered. This was the case in many examples where a neighbor challenged the head of a household for fighting outside his house, complained about fights leading to the stabbings of journeymen, or opposed the violence of drunken men in the streets. The number of trials, particularly those concerned with acts of violence and offenses against property, increased enormously in Augsburg during the sixteenth century. At the same time, trials of resistance and attacks against the urban authorities declined significantly. A first tentative hypothesis derived from these facts could be: The great increase in population in that century and the connected demographic, economic, and social crisis led to a great loss of security. This sense of insecurity—probably in conjunction with successes in the disciplining process—increasingly linked the interests of authorities and subjects at the beginning of the modern period.[32]

Especially under the perspective of informal or horizontal social control between members of a community, the substantial criticism against the concept of social discipline (*Sozialdisziplinierung*) in its narrow interpretation that has arisen in recent years is substantial. Since this theory was postulated, many authors have shown that there was a great deficit in the execution of disciplining measures by the authorities. On the other hand, there was a broad variety of horizontal mechanisms of social control at all levels of early modern society. A decisive link that confronted individuals with the norms and values of their vicinity was the neighborhood. Very often neighbors called for the help of the authorities, especially when their competence in effecting conciliation was exhausted. In this context, scholars have also found examples of critical surveillance of the authorities by their own subjects.[33] These results demonstrate an interaction between vertical and horizontal social control; more, they show that a clear distinction between the two areas is not realistic in an early modern town or city.

One opponent of the concept of social discipline and a prominent advocate of the contrary concept of negotiation (*Aushandeln*) of norms is Martin Dinges. It is not necessary here to discuss the pros and cons of this concept in detail. What is important for us is that he exemplifies his approach with Paris neighborhoods in the eighteenth century. In his 1994 study *Der Maurermeister und die Finanzrichter,* he objects to the notion that there was a general decline in regulation by autonomous face-to-face societies in favor of legal norms that did away with the validity of autonomous regulation. For this to be true, either two equal norms must have existed in the population and in the judicial system, or two competing norms. Dinges advocates the integration of investigations into social control in modern societies into historical research. One finding of these sociological works is that countercurrent processes of increasing and decreasing regulation (*Verrechtlichung* and *Entrechtlichung*) exist permanently in any society. He thus believes that a pure dichotomy between "community" and "society" is not a useful model. The advantage of the concept of social control is that the perspective is not fixed on state institutions. The question for Dinges is: To what potential sanctions do the respective actors have access? This approach is especially useful for the analysis of notions of conflicts of honor in early modern societies. In the context of his research, Dinges examines neighborhood and police on equal terms, and he is interested in the mutual influence of the population and the judicial system. This concept is fundamentally different from sociologist Max Weber's approach to *Verrechtlichung!*[34]

If norms are interpreted as the result of a process of negotiation within a society, the society itself takes on much greater importance than in a pure concept of social disciplining. Drawing on the sociologist Helge Peters, Dinges interprets social control as the "totality of measures that aim to prevent or restrict deviant behavior by a member of a society." Social control in this sense is a dependent variable, conditioned by social realities. The forms in this context are gossip, admonition, insult, quarrel of honor, action, and denunciation. The author's hypothesis is therefore that justice is only a special case of social control in a continuum of possible reactions to deviance. In his specific example people had a choice between a quarrel of honor or an accusation before the *commissaire*.[35] Possible reactions to any kind of offense ranged from informal to formal, at times functioning in a kind of staged model.

The study of Dinges is central to our topic. Loss, or the fear of loss, of honor can be understood as a result of social control within societies, and also within neighborhoods. By means of the "social capital" of honor—as defined by Pierre Bourdieu—men were kept within the networks of their community and either succeeded or were marginalized from their social environment. Conflicts of honor were normally one of the largest categories of legal proceedings in early modern societies. During the sixteenth century, legal proceedings caused by accusations of defamation increased dramatically.[36] And damage to one's reputation was the most common reason for complaints to the commissaire in eighteenth-century Paris.[37]

The continuum of possibilities for resolving conflicts of honor was not limited to informal settlements and secular courts. Ecclesiastical courts also dealt with the problem, as historians working on church discipline have noted. Particularly, works on Calvinist consistories and their role within a parish show that many aspects of their tasks overlapped with those of state or urban courts. As Roodenburg has shown for Amsterdam, the consistory played a crucial role in secular conflict management. According to Roodenburg, in Amsterdam, "church discipline was part of a spectrum of legal pluralism." Within this spectrum consistories concentrated not only on church discipline, but also on the security of peace within the city. Ministers and elders exerted discipline more effectively than other courts, because they were in close contact with neighbors, and asked them about the behavior of delinquents, and so forth. People lived under "mutual control, [and] the constant anxiety about their 'honor' and 'respectability'" was their primary concern. Within this duty of the consistory, the exertion of church discipline "was primarily exemplary." It was not the goal of the institution to bring all misdemeanors to court; rather, *De occultis Ecclesia non judicat* was the maxim. Although the consistory was not severe in Amsterdam, the city became more disciplined through the work of the ministers and elders. What is interesting in this context is that after 1680 the Amsterdam consistory concentrated mainly on marriage or other special ecclesiastical subjects.[38]

The Calvinist *seniorat* in its territory or town was responsible for the entire religious and moral life of the community. Thus, informal quarrels of honor also came to their courts. Sentences were only ecclesiastical, but there must have been effective cooperation between church and secular authorities. The competence to intervene in primarily secular offenses came from the Ten Commandments. For example, envy, hatred, and defamation were interpreted as offenses against the Sixth Commandment.[39] That in Amsterdam the consistory concentrated more and more on purely ecclesiastical cases at the end of the seventeenth century may be explained by an increasingly thematic separation of secular and ecclesiastical courts in Calvinist regions.

There could be two explanations for the huge number of proceedings in this area. First, as is quite often held by historians of crime, one can determine an increasing use of the courts by the "common man" for this purpose. Second, in modifying considerations of Paul Münch a bit, there could be a loss of competence in conflict resolution within neighborhoods. While the first idea is based on the explanation that people turned to the courts voluntarily in such cases, the second stresses that early modern authorities destroyed or undermined the ability of neighborhoods to deal with many of the problems of community life, which were now regulated by the modern institutions of social or church discipline—in Münch's case study, by the Calvinist *seniorat*. Michael Frank has suggested that during the second half of the seventeenth and the eighteenth centuries, only the secular courts had an adequate model of resolution for conflicts of honor. This was the chance for the early modern state to exert itself at the local level.[40]

As a result of his methodological approach, Martin Dinges shows that the concept of *Verechtlichung* was not just a one-dimensional process of steadily increasing responsibility of the courts for more and more areas of social life. In eighteenth-century Paris, conflicts of honor were of high public interest. Men of the middle classes and of middle age were the primary actors, but women can also be found in the statistics of court activity more than in all other crimes of violence. Accusations before the commissaire were an important means of social control within the urban neighborhood, but they often had a long prehistory and show a planned use of the judicial system. Insults remained an important form of conflict regulation within the community, combined with a high demand for regulation by the police or the courts. As the courts increasingly retreated from these cases at the end of the ancien régime, the neighborhoods themselves once again had to settle these conflicts. For Dinges this is a good example of *Entrechtlichung*.[41]

A number of studies in the last couple of years have stressed the importance of honor in verbal and nonverbal conflicts between neighbors. It is now clear that these conflicts were not only emotional outbursts of verbal injuries or even physical violence occurring without reflection; in many cases, they demonstrate control in the exercise of verbal and nonverbal attacks against the opponent, which allowed both parties to de-escalate the conflict at any phase. The primary aim was to preserve or to restore the honor of a person or of his house.[42] In keeping with the logic of safeguarding one's honor, insults only came to court when they were spoken publicly, for example when they were heard by neighbors.[43] These conflicts of honor within urban neighborhoods can also be interpreted within the broader concept of the infrajudiciary. Extrajudicial conflict settlements, of little interest for the history of law, belong to the early modern social system as much as do the courts of the early modern state with their pretension of a monopoly on justice. Research in the reality of neighborhood conflicts has demonstrated the consistent importance of this means.[44] What Dinges has shown in the example of neighborhood conflicts in Paris is the changing use of the courts within the development of social and state interests.

At the same time, these conflicts and their ritual aspects are the results of horizontal control, or even disciplining. Life in early modern society required keeping one's reputation alive. And this reputation was defined largely by fellow citizens, or even more so, by neighbors. Their code of honor was the standard on which behavior had to be based. Thus they exerted social control on their neighbors very effectively. One's honor provided an essential credit for difficult situations in life or, as Bourdieu put it, it was a form of social capital. It could be accumulated in the family, in the guild, or in the neighborhood. People who had a good reputation on their street could trust their neighbors to act as character witnesses if they were falsely accused. This was not only an advantage at the courts but enhanced social and economic status as members of the community as well.[45]

Reputation—or the capital of honor—in the neighborhood could be of essential importance for the economic existence of a citizen. Sources from sixteenth-century trials in Augsburg show an impressive influence of neighborhood testimonies and character references. Criminals of all sorts who hoped for the chance to be reintegrated into their old environment depended in many cases on their social capital. Intercessions were necessary in order to get a pardon, especially for those who had been exiled, as proof to the municipal council that the accused would be accepted within his or her old social network. Besides the family, guild members, friends, and often neighborhoods provided character testimony for the delinquent. One cannot underestimate this tool, because normally the length of the exile of a citizen was not fixed. Only if the city council had the impression that there was a good chance for reintegration could the exiled person hope to get permission to return. Together with the families, neighbors often pressed the authorities more than once in favor of their friends. In contrast, someone who was pardoned by the council could hardly hope to find peace or work without facing restrictions by the guild or other difficulties if his neighborhood and fellow craftsmen did not agree with the authorities' decision. The early modern judicial system was based not only on the cooperation of offender, victim, and tribunal. To a great extent, the delinquent's chances of resocialization and rehabilitation were influenced by, or even dependent upon, his social background.[46]

The fundamental importance of neighborhood testimonies can also be found in eighteenth-century Paris. Dinges stressed that established and well-integrated persons had the best chances of accumulating and defending their capital of honor. Such people were much more successful during conflicts in mobilizing allies who would agree to give positive declarations or testimonies to the commissaire or in front of a tribunal.[47]

The examples of Augsburg and Paris show some clear similarities, even though we have no detailed comparison of the influence of neighborhoods on court sentences. What is obvious is the element of social control that neighbors could exercise, even in legal transactions, throughout the entire early modern period. Their common memory was a factor in court decisions. In this context, Dinges coined the term "neighborhood public sphere."[48]

But in certain cases, the influence of neighbors could go even further, especially in difficult political or social situations. Supplications became more important if the urban council feared unrest within the city in relation to the sentence of a suspect. There were numerous cases in which punishments were not as severe as usual because of political considerations. This was especially true in times of religious unrest in the biconfessional city of Augsburg.[49] My example is also from Augsburg in 1596. The weaver Georg Kappel had written anonymous lampoons against the city council, the Augsburg merchants, and the principals of the weavers' guild.[50] During his trial, pleas were written from his family, his guild, and diverse neighborhoods. The arguments not only reflected the normal respectful formulations but also presented the clear message that Kappel was not wrong in his descriptions. The jurist who provided an expert opinion on the case took these pleas into serious consideration and used them to support his suggestion for a punishment. The argument was that if the council sentenced Kappel to death, a lot of people would oppose the decision, and the political situation could become dangerous. The council respected the suggestion and expelled the weaver from the city to fight against the Turks. The pleas in this case represented a threat to the council and had to be respected to a certain extent, although without losing authority in the city.

A spectacular institution of horizontal social control that was explicitly based on a norm system that differed from that of the secular and ecclesiastical courts was the charivari. The phenomenon, which was well-known all over Europe and a feature of towns as well as villages, belongs to a broad range of possible means of drawing public attention to misrule, misdeeds, or socially unacceptable behavior. Charivari can be seen as "an attempt to bring community pressure to bear on someone in order to make them redress a grievance."[51] The word has been in use since the high Middle Ages, very often in connection with sexual misbehavior and second marriages, "especially when there was a gross disparity in age between the bride and groom."[52] Nevertheless, charivaris are connected with a much broader spectrum of socially unacceptable behavior. Natalie Zemon Davis differentiates between charivaris in villages and towns. "The city charivari was used to mark other affronts to the sense of order or justice of the neighborhood." She cites sources from Dijon and Amiens where the phenomenon occurred in the context of theft, murder, seduction, bizarre marriage, or the selling of false wax.[53] Garrioch shows that traditional charivaris in Paris vanished after the mid-eighteenth century, partly because the authorities fought against it, and partly because the demographic development within the city meant that it no longer made sense. At the same time, Garrioch sees a "spread of the 'political charivari.'" He explains that the "disappearance or transformation of collective sanctions like the 'charivari' deprived the community of important mechanisms of self-regulation."[54] Davis gives examples of charivaris in French cities that in the sixteenth and seventeenth centuries had already "turned against the political authorities."[55] In that sense social control in the urban context was also social criticism, which was directed against the officials.[56]

In the context of our question of social control within urban neighborhoods, the charivaris can be interpreted as an independent instrument of the subjects to enforce their own norms on their fellow citizens. In France, charivaris most often occurred when the norms that were violated were not those of the authorities, but the moral convictions and social interests of the subjects. Although traditional charivari came to an end in eighteenth-century Paris, it was a popular counterpart of social control to that of the state throughout the early modern period.

Horizontal social control was often perceived as repressive. The great number of denunciations and accusations in the above description of the duties of citizens in sixteenth-century Augsburg was characteristic. One can assume that this often produced a difficult climate of distrust among neighbors. And in fact, many statements even in court protocols confirm this.[57] The situation presumably was worse in eighteenth-century Paris with its much greater population and dense living conditions. Garrioch describes an atmosphere of permanent vigilance and observation. Permanent fear of theft, threat to one's person, and endangerment of the social order through the violation of norms was an everyday experience.[58] There are examples of resistance against such permanent control. In the narrow living circumstances in the big cities especially, tenants tried to avoid the surveillance of their day-to-day lives and opposed interference with their freedom to come and go from their own flats whenever they chose. Paris tenants lived under the pressure of this long before the concierges began to appear at the end of the eighteenth century.[59] It is possible that these conditions were perceived more harshly in the century that marked the beginning of the privatization of life. But there are also hints that resistance against a too-strict control of movement already existed in the sixteenth century.

Conclusion

From the late Middle Ages to the eighteenth century, competences of neighborhoods in European cities increasingly moved from self-regulation to appointed duties. The external control of urban or state authorities increased from the sixteenth century. But beyond this general development, we have identified examples that are highly varied. In Paris the small entity of a neighborhood never had institutional importance for social control within the city but was only "the social context which was foremost in people's consciousness."[60] On the other side of the spectrum, Ghent presumably belonged to those cities in western Europe that preserved their local autonomy in a much better way than most others.

The development of the influence of social control by urban neighborhoods cannot be explained by institutional tasks alone. The perspective on the horizontal (informal) aspects of social control, and the interaction between the two approaches, gives an important insight into how early modern urban societies functioned. Neighbors had a great interest of their own in controlling their fellow citizens. Values and norms of the population were not always identical with those of the authorities. Thus, we can see a broad variety of reactions including cooperation, resistance, and demand between the two levels. Citizens called in the authorities whenever it was necessary and where the authorities had jurisdiction. But they kept away from formal institutions whenever it was useful for them. Thus, they turned to judicial instruments or police forces to protect life, honor, and property on the one hand and employed extrajudicial conflict settlements up to the level of charivaris on the other hand.

Research on these phenomena in the urban context is not broad enough to draw a clear picture of the development of interaction between vertical and horizontal social control, but a short sketch is possible: We can identify from the sixteenth century onward an increasing demand for professional conflict settlement by the courts. This developed parallel to the massive production of laws and ordinances by the state. At least in the seventeenth century, neighborhoods in most cities were integrated into the formal structure of the administrative and juridical body. Thus, they were supervised by the authorities. Nevertheless, there were aspects of social control in which the authorities no longer had any interest, or which they gave up on enforcing. This process is explained by Dinges in terms of *Entrechtlichung*. Parallel to these aspects, which were undergoing a permanent process of interaction between inhabitants and city authorities, there were always a great number of norm conflicts within the population that were of little or no interest for the authorities. These were completely subject to informal types of social control. These cases sometimes came to the regular courts indirectly, when the population used illegal means to enforce their own norms, for example with insults or even with charivaris.

Notes

I thank Prof. Ann Tlusty for the correction of the English manuscript and her critical hints.

1. Specifically, Gropp appears in the records as a "Barchentkarter."

2. Stadtarchiv Augsburg, Reichsstadt, Strafbuch des Rates 1596–1605, fol. 107r; Stadtarchiv Augsburg, Reichsstadt, Urgichten 1600b Nr. 185 (Marx Gropp).

3. See Roeck, "Neighborhoods and the Public," 196. Roeck draws on Weber, *Wirtschaft und Gesellschaft*, 215–18.

4. For a more general overview of institutions, society, and mentality of sixteenth century Augsburg, see Gottlieb et al., eds., *Geschichte;* Roeck, *Eine Stadt in Krieg und Frieden.*

5. Lis and Soly, "Neighborhood Social Change"; Roodenburg, "Freundschaft, Brüderlichkeit und Einigkeit"; Roodenburg, "Naar een etnografie"; see also Deceulaer, "Stadsbestuur en buurtbewoners"; Jütte, "Das Stadtviertel."

6. For research overviews of German, English, Belgian, Netherlandish, Luxemburgian, Italian, Scandinavian, and Polish publications on the history of crime, see in Blauert and Schwerhoff, eds., *Kriminalitätsgeschichte.* Examples of the history of public houses and gender history are Tlusty, *Bacchus and Civic Order;* Roper, *The Holy Household;* Roper, *Oedipus and the Devil.*

7. Schilling, "Die Kirchenzucht," 11–40; Roodenburg, Onder censuur; Roodenburg, "Reformierte Kirchenzucht und Ehrenhandel," 129–52; Schilling, "Sündenzucht und frühneuzeitliche Sozialdisziplinierung." For Catholic Cologne, see Chaix, "Die schwierige Schule der Sitten," 199–217.

8. Lis and Soly, "Neighborhood Social Change," 1–4.

9. For example see several contributions in Boškovska Leimgruber, ed., *Die Frühe Neuzeit in der Geschichtswissenschaft.*

10. Loetz, "L'infrajudiciaire. Facetten and Bedeutung eines Konzepts," 545–62.

11. For the the Augsburg example, see Hoffmann, "Nachbarschaften als Akteure und Instrumente," 187–202. On early modern Augsburg neighborhoods, see also Roeck, "Neighborhoods and the Public."

12. Stadtarchiv Augsburg, Reichsstadt, Urgichten 1552 Nr. 24 (Zimprecht and Apolonia Grens, 16./22.8.1552).

13. Stadtarchiv Nördlingen/Ainung straffbuch 1584–1599, 28.12.1584.

14. For the Augsburg judicial system, see Hoffmann, "Strukturen und Quellen."

15. Ibid.," 75.

16. For this see the overviews of Roodenburg, "Freundschaft, Brüderlichkeit und Einigkeit"; Lis and Soly, "Neighborhood Social Change."

17. Roodenburg, "Freundschaft, Brüderlichkeit und Einigkeit," 21.

18. See Roodenburg, "Freundschaft, Brüderlichkeit und Einigkeit"; Lis and Soly, "Neighborhood Social Change," 6.

19. Lis and Soly, "Neighborhood Social Change," 6.

20. Roodenburg, "Freundschaft, Brüderlichkeit und Einigkeit," 19.

21. Lis and Soly, "Neighborhood Social Change," 7.

22. Roodenburg, "Freundschaft, Brüderlichkeit und Einigkeit," 17.

23. Ibid., 13, 17–18; Roodenburg, *Onder censuur,* 22. A similar scene is described for Kiel in 1559 in front of the mayor of the city: Lorenzen-Schmidt, "Beleidigungen," 5.

24. Lis and Soly, "Neighborhood Social Change," 8.

25. Garrioch, *Neighborhood and Community in Paris,* 30, 206–11.

26. Dinges, Der Maurermeister, 213–15, 416f.

27. Roeck, "Neighborhoods and the Public," 196.

28. See Jütte, "Das Stadtviertel," 243–44.

29. Einigkeit, Brüderlichkeit, Freundschaft: Roodenburg, "Freundschaft, Brüderlichkeit und Einigkeit," 12.

30. Boulton, *Neighborhood and Society;* Garrioch, *Neighborhood and Community in Paris;* Dinges, *Der Maurermeister;* see also Lis and Soly, "Neighborhood Social Change."

31. Hoffmann, "Nachbarschaften als Akteure und Instrumente."

32. Hoffmann, "Bürgersicherheit und Herrschaftssicherung."

33. Especially for urban examples see Boulton, *Neighborhood and Society;* Dinges, *Der Maurermeister;* Schwerhoff, *Köln im Kreuzverhör;* Hoffmann, "Bürgersicherheit und Herrschaftssicherung"; Bleckmann, *Nachbarschaftskonflikte in einer Stadt,* 90, 199, 200.

34. Dinges, *Der Maurermeister,* 26–30, 174. The negotiation concept in the Augsburg example: Tlusty, "Water of Life"; Tlusty, *Bacchus and Civic Order.*

35. Dinges, *Der Maurermeister,* 174f.

36. See the research review of Schreiner and Schwerhoff, eds., "Verletzte Ehre," 1–28; see also Backmann et al., eds., *Ehrkonzepte.* Especially for the urban context, Dinges, "Die Ehre als Thema der Stadtgeschichte."

37. Garrioch, *Neighborhood and Community in Paris,* 37.

38. Roodenburg, *Onder censuur,* 421–23.

39. Münch, "Kirchenzucht und Nachbarschaft," 228–29.

40. Frank, "Ehre und Gewalt im Dorf."

41. Dinges, *Der Maurermeister,* 213–15.

42. Compare Walz, "Agonale Kommunikation."

43. Garrioch, *Neighborhood and Community in Paris,* 40.

44. Loetz, *L'infrajudiciaire.*

45. Garrioch, *Neighborhood and Community in Paris,* 37–38; Roodenburg, *Onder censuur,* passim; Roodenburg, "Freundschaft, Brüderlichkeit und Einigkeit," 11.

46. Hoffmann, "Der Stadtverweis"; Hoffmann, "Außergerichtliche Einigungen bei Straftaten als vertikale und horizontale soziale Kontrolle im 16. Jahrhundert," 563–79.

47. Dinges, *Der Maurermeister,* 420.

48. Nachbarschaftsöffentlichkeit: Dinges, *Der Maurermeister,* 297.

49. Hoffmann, "Konfessionell motivierte und gewandelte Konflikte in der zweiten Hälfte des 16. Jahrhunderts . . .," 99–120.

50. Stadtarchiv Augsburg, Reichsstadt, Urgichten 1596a Nr. 168 (Georg Kappel, January 1596).

51. Garrioch, *Neighborhood and Community in Paris,* 45.

52. Davis, *Society and Culture,* 105, 301 footnote 35; Davis, "Humanismus, Narrenherrschaft und die Riten der Gewalt," 106–35; Spierenburg, *The Broken Spell,* 68–72.

53. Davis, *Society and Culture,* 117.

54. Garrioch, *Neighborhood and Community in Paris,* 217–20.

55. Davis, *Society and Culture,* 117, 119, passim.

56. See Kaschuba, "Ritual und Fest," 253.

57. See Stadtarchiv Augsburg, Reichsstadt, Urgichten.

58. Garrioch, *Neighborhood and Community in Paris,* 16–55; Dinges, *Der Maurermeister,* 288–96.

59. Garrioch, *Neighborhood and Community in Paris,* 35–36.

60. Ibid., 31.

Bibliography

Primary Sources

Archief Kerkenraad van de Nederlands Hervormde Kerk te Delft. Kerkenraadsnotulen, inv. nos. 1–7, tuchtboeken, 276–77.

Archive of the Royal Court of Valladolid. *Pleitos Criminales*, doc. C-108–2.

British Library, Thomason Tracts, E. 156 (16).

Cambridge University Library, Cambridge University Archives, CUR 13, no. 29.

Essex Record Office, Court of the Archdeacon D/ACA (Act Books), 50.

Gemeente Archief Delft. Church council notes 276, 30 June, 2–25 August, 5 September 1664, fol. 119.

Gemeente Archief Delft. Church council notes 3, 4 December 1600.

Gemeente Archief Delft, Oude Rechterlijke Archieven. Confession books, inv. nos. 58–61.

Gemeente Archief Delft, Oude Rechterlijke Archieven. Sentence books, inv. nos.46–50.

Gemeente Archief Delft. Sentence books 46, 1562, fol. 35–36.

Gemeente Archief Rotterdam, Oude Rechterlijke Archieven. Confession books, inv. nos. 139–43.

Gemeente Archief Rotterdam, Oude Rechterlijke Archieven.Correction books, inv. nos. 266–68.

Gemeente Archief Rotterdam, Oude Rechterlijke Archieven.Sentence books, inv. nos. 244–52.

Gemeente Archief Rotterdam. Church council notes 5, 7 February 1661.

Gemeente Archief Rotterdam. Confession book 141, 1688.

Gemeente Archief Rotterdam. Confession book 142, 24 February 1696.

Gemeente Archief Rotterdam. Confessionbook 142, 24 December 1696.

Gemeente Archief Rotterdam. Sentence book 246, 1623, fol. 139.

Gemeente Archief Rotterdam. Sentence book 248, 1649, fol. 81.

Gemeente Archief Rotterdam. Sentence book 251, 1697, fol. 175.

Gemeente Archief Rotterdam. Sentence book 250, 1679, fol. 146.

Gemeente Archief Rotterdam. Sentence book 250, 1679, fol. 166–67.

Gemeente Archief Rotterdam. Sentence book 248, 1646, fol. 24–25.

General Archive .f Simancas, Cámara de Castilla. Leg. 1778, doc. 24, ff. 1–4.

Historisches Archiv der Stadt Köln. G 211, fol. 189v.

Historisches Archiv der Stadt Köln. G 227/8, February 1593.

Historisches Archiv der Stadt Köln. Verf. u. Verw. G 310, fol. 109r-116v.

Kerkenraadsacta van de Nederlands Hervormde Gemeente van Rotterdam. Kerkenraadsnotulen, inv. nos. 1–8.

Lambeth Palace Library, Court of Arches, Eee 1, fols. 291–95.

National Historical Archive. *Consejos*, sig. 7092 and 7094.

Public Records Office, London, STAC 8/249/19, m. 18.

Reformation Ordinances in Basel, 1529. ABR III, no. 473, 383.

Santander Diocesan Archive. Sig. 1590, 14–15.

Staatsarchiv Marburg 17. I no. 5125

Staatsarchiv Marburg. 17 I no. 5119, Beschwerde der Stadt Hersfeld wegen Hochzeitsordnung 1590.

Stadtarchiv Augsburg. Reichsstadt, Strafbuch des Rates 1596–1605, fol. 107r. Stadtarchiv Augsburg. Reichsstadt, Urgichten 1600b Nr. 185 (Marx Gropp).

Stadtarchiv Augsburg. Reichsstadt, Urgichten 1552 Nr. 24 (Zimprecht and Apolonia Grens, 16./22.8.1552).

Stadtarchiv Augsburg. Reichsstadt, Urgichten 1596a Nr. 168 (Georg Kappel, Januar 1596).

Stadtarchiv Augsburg. Reichsstadt, Urgichten.

Stadtarchiv Nördlingen. Ainung straffbuch 1584–1599, 28.12.1584.

Trinity College, Dublin Abstract of the State of the Church of Ireland, 1622, fol. 45.

Trinity College, Dublin, British Library, Additional Manuscript. MS 4756, "Entry Book of Reports of the Commissioners for Ireland, 1622," fol. 23r.

Trinity College, Dublin. MS 4756, "Entry Book of Reports of the Commissioners for Ireland, Appointed by James I in 1622," fol. 62v.

Trinity College, Dublin. MS 550, "State of Armagh Province, 1622, Visitation of Derry by George Downham," fols. 205–206.

Trinity College, Dublin. MS 582, "His Majesty's Instructions Concerning the Church of Ireland, Brought Over by Bishop Andrew Knox about 1620," fol. 136r.

Trinity College, Dublin. MS 806, "Remembrances to the Commissioners of the Regal Visitation, 1615," fol. 119r.

Trinity College, Dublin. MS 808, "Orders and Directions Concerning the State of the Church of Ireland, 1623," fols. 36, 38.

Books

A Dialogue or Accidental Discourse betwixt Mr. Alderman Abell, and Richard Kilvert . . . London, 1641 [British Library, Thomason Tracts, E. 156 (16)].

Agulhon, Maurice. *La sociabilité méridionale: Confréries et associations dans la vie collective en Provence orientale à la fin du 18e siècle.* Aix-en-Provence: La Pensée universitaire, 1966.

Alcalá, Angel, ed. *Inquisición española y mentalidad inquisitorial.* Barcelona: Ariel, 1984.

Allestree, Richard. *The Whole Duty of Man, Laid Down in a Plain and Familiar Way for the Use of All, But Especially the Meanest Reader.* London, 1678.

Anderson, Michael. *Family Structure in Nineteenth-Century Lancashire.* Cambridge: Cambridge University Press, 1971.

Ankum, Hans. "Le marriage et les conventions matriomoniales des mineurs." *The Legal History Review* 46 (1978): 204–49.

Anonymous. *The True Narrative of the Execution of John Marketman, Chyrurgian, of Westham in Essex, for Committing a Horrible and Bloody Murther.* London, 1680.

Archer, Ian. *The Pursuit of Stability: Social Relations in Elizabethan London.* Cambridge: Cambridge University Press, 1991.

Ariés, Philippe. *Centuries of Childhood: A Social History of Family Life.* New York: Vintage Books, 1962.

Aristotle. *The Politics,* VII, 11. 350 B.C. Translated by Benjamin Jowett. Mineola: Dover Publications, 2000.

Ashton, John. *Social Life in the Reign of Queen Anne.* 2 vols. London: Chatto and Windus, 1882.

Atkinson, E. D. *Dromore: An Ulster Diocese.* Dundalk: W. Tempest, 1925.

Babcock, Barbara A., ed. *The Reversible World: Symbolic Inversion in Art and Society.* Ithaca: Cornell University Press, 1978.

Backmann, Sybille, et. al., eds. *Ehrkonzepte in der Frühen Neuzeit: Identitäten und Abgrenzungen.* Berlin: Akademie Verlag, 1998.

Banker, James R. *Death in the Community: Memorialization and Confraternities in an Italian Commune in the Late Middle Ages.* Athens: University of Georgia Press, 1988.

Bänninger, Hans. *Untersuchungen über den Einfluss des Polizeistaates im 17. und 18. Jahrhundert auf das Recht der Eheschliessung in Stadt und Landschaft Zürich.* Ph.D. diss., Zurich, 1948.

Bataillon, Marcel. *Erasmo y España.* Madrid and Mexico: Fondo de Cultura Económica, 1986 (1st ed. Mexico: 1950).

Battenberg, J. Friedrich. "Seelenheil, gewaltsamer Tod und herrschaftliches Friedensinteresse: Zur Auswirkung eines kulturellen Codes auf die Sühne- und Strafpraxis der vormodernen Gesellschaft." In *Du guoter tôt: Sterben im Mittelalter Ideal und Realität,* edited by Markus J. Wenninger, 347–76. Friesach: Wieser Verlag, 1998.

Bayley, David H. "The Police and Political Development in Europe." In *The Formation of National States in Western Europe,* edited by Charles Tilly, 328–79. Princeton: Princeton University Press, 1975.

Beattie, J[ohn] M. *Crime and the Courts in England, 1660–1800.* Oxford: Clarendon Press, 1986.

Beck, Rainer. "Illegitimität und voreheliche Sexualität auf dem Land: Unterfinning, 1671–1770." In *Kultur der einfachen Leute,* edited by Richard van Dülmen, 112–50. Munich: C. H. Beck, 1983.

Becker, Eduard. "Zur Geschichte der Wiedertäufer in Oberhessen." *Archiv für hessische Geschichte und Altertumskunde* NF 10 (1914): 66–105.

Behrens, Ulrich. "Sozialdisziplinierung als Konzeption der Frühneuzeitforschung." *Historische Mitteilungen* 12 (1999): 35–68.

Behringer, Wolfgang. "Mörder, Diebe, Ehebrecher: Verbrechen und Strafen in Kurbayern vom 16. bis 18. Jahrhundert." In *Verbrechen, Strafen und soziale Kontrolle,* edited by Richard van Dülmen, Studien zur historischen Kulturforschung III, 85–132. Frankfurt am Main: Fischer, 1995.

Beier, A. L. *Masterless Men: The Vagrancy Problem in England, 1560–1640.* London: Methuen, 1985.

Belting, Hans. *Bild und Kult.* Munich: Beck, 1990.

Bennassar, Bartolomé, and Bernard Vincent. *Spanien: 16. und 17. Jahrhundert.* Stuttgart: Klett-Cotta, 1999.

Bennassar, Bartolomé, et al. *L'Inquisition Espagnole, 15e-19e siècle.* Paris: Hachette, 1979.

Bentmann, Reinhard, and Michael Müller. *Die Villa als Herrschaftsarchitektur: Versuch einer kunst- und sozialhistorischen Analyse.* Frankfurt am Main: Suhrkamp, 1970.

Berges, Wilhelm. *Die Fürstenspiegel des hohen und späten Mittelalters.* Leipzig: Hiersemann, 1938.

Bergsten, Torsten. *Balthasar Hubmaier: Seine Stellung zu Reformation und Täufertum, 1521–1528.* Kassel: Oncken, 1961.

Berlin, Michael. "'Broken All in Pieces': Artisans and the Regulation of Workmanship in Early Modern London." In *The Artisan and the European Town, 1500–1900,* edited by Geoffrey Crossick, 75–91. Aldershot: Scolar Press, 1997.

Bernard, George W. "The Church of England, c.1529 1642." *History* 75 (1990):185 206.

Bethencourt, Francisco. *L'Inquisition à l'époque moderne: Espagne, Italie, Portugal, 15e-19e siècle.* Paris: Fayard, 1995.

Bimbenet-Privat, M. *Les orfèvres Parisiens de la Renaissance (1502–1620).* Paris: Commission des Travaux Historiques de la Ville de Paris, 1992.

Binz, Louis. "Les Confréries dans le diocèse de Genève à la fin du Moyen Age." In *Le mouvement confraternel au Moyen Âge: France, Italie, Suisse,* edited by Agostino Paravincini Bagliani, 233–61. Geneva: Droz, 1987.

Black, Antony. *Guilds and Civil Society in European Political Thought from the Twelfth Century to the Present.* London: Methuen, 1984.

Black, Donald, ed. *Toward a General Theory of Social Control.* 2 vols. Orlando: Academic Press, 1984.

Blankenburg, Erhard, and Jan R. A. Verwoerd. "Prozeßhäufigkeiten in den Niederlanden und Nordrhein-Westfalen, 1970–1984." In *Prozeßflut: Studien zur Prozeßtätigkeit europäischer Gerichte in historischen Zeitreihen und im Zeitvergleich,* edited by Erhart Blankenburg, 257–333. Köln: Bundesanzeiger, 1989.

Blastenbrei, Peter. *Kriminalität in Rom, 1560–1586.* Tübingen: Max Niemeyer Verlag, 1995.

Blauert, Andreas, and Gerd Schwerhoff, eds. *Kriminalitätsgeschichte: Beiträge zur Sozial- und Kulturgeschichte der Vormoderne.* Konstanz: Universitätsverlag, 2000.

Blauert, Andreas. "Kriminaljustiz und Sittenreform als Krisenmanagement? Das

Hochstift Speyer im 16. und 17. Jahrhundert." In *Mit den Waffen der Justiz: Zur Kriminalitätsgeschichte des späten Mittelalters und der Frühen Neuzeit*, edited by Andreas Blauert and Gerd Schwerhoff, 115–36. Frankfurt am Main: Fischer, 1993.

Bleckmann, Maren. *Nachbarschaftskonflikte in einer Stadt der frühen Neuzeit: Warendorf im späten 16. und frühen 17. Jahrhundert*, Schriftliche Hausarbeit erste Staatsprüfung für das Lehramt der Sekundarstufe II/I, Universität Münster 1999 (forthcoming summary in *Warendorfer Schriften*).

Blécourt, A. S., and H. F. W. D. Fischer. *Klein plakkaatboek van Nederland, Verzameling van ordonnantiën en plakkaten betreffende regeeringsvorm, kerk en rechtspraak (14e eeuw tot 1749)*. Groningen: Wolters, 1919.

Blickle, Peter. *Kommunalismus: Skizzen einer gesellschaftlichen Organisationsform.* Vol. 1: *Oberdeutschland,* vol. 2: *Europa.* Munich: Oldenbourg, 2000.

Blickle, Peter. *Resistance, Representation and Community.* Oxford: Clarendon Press, 1997.

Blok, Anton. *De Bokkerijders: Roversbenden en geheime genootschappen in de Landen van Overmaas, 1730–1774.* Amsterdam: Prometheus, 1991.

Bock, Gisela. "Frauenräume und Frauenehre: Frühneuzeitliche Armenfürsorge in Italien." In *Frauengeschichte–Geschlechtergeschichte,* edited by Karin Hausen and Heide Wunder, 25–49. Frankfurt am Main: Campus Verlag, 1998.

Bos, Sandra. *'Uyt liefde tot malcander': Onderlinge hulpverlening binnen de Noord-Nederlandse gilden in internationaal perspectief (1570–1820).* Amsterdam: IISG, 1998 (with a summary in English).

Boschloo, Anton W. A. *Annibale Carracci in Bologna: Visible Reality in Art after the Council of Trent.* 2 vols. The Hague: Staatsuitgeverij, 1974.

Boškovska Leimgruber, Nada, ed. *Die Frühe Neuzeit in der Geschichtswissenschaft: Forschungstendenzen und Forschungserträge.* Paderborn: Ferdinand Schöningh, 1997.

Bossenga, Gail. *The Politics of Privilege: Old Regime and Revolution in Lille.* Cambridge: Cambridge University Press, 1991.

Bossy, John. "Blood and Baptism: Kinship, Community and Christianity in Western Europe, Fourteenth to Seventeenth Century." In *Sanctity and Secularity: The Church and the World,* edited by Derek Baker, 129–43. Oxford: Blackwell, 1973.

Bossy, John. "Holiness and Society." *Past and Present* 75 (1977): 119–37.

Bossy, John. "Postscript." In *Disputes and Settlements: Law and Human Relations in the West,* edited by John Bossy, 287–94. Cambridge: Cambridge University Press, 1983.

Bossy, John. "The Character of Elizabethan Catholicism." *Past and Present* 21 (1962): 39–59.

Bossy, John. *Christianity in the West, 1400–1700.* New York: Oxford University Press, 1985.

Bossy, John. *Peace in the Post-Reformation.* The Birkbeck Lectures 1995. Cambridge: Cambridge University Press, 1998.

Bossy, John. *The English Catholic Community, 1570–1850.* London: Darton, Longman and Todd, 1975.

Bottigheimer, Karl S. "The Hagiography of William Bedell." In *"A Miracle of*

Learning": Studies in Manuscripts and Irish Learning, Essays in Honour of William O'Sullivan, edited by Toby Barnard et al., 199–206. Aldershot: Ashgate, 1997.

Bottigheimer, Karl S., and Ute Lotz-Heumann. "The Irish Reformation in European Perspective." *Archiv für Reformationsgeschichte* 89 (1998): 268–309.

Boulton, Jeremy. *Neighbourhood and Society: A London Suburb in the Seventeenth Century.* Cambridge: Cambridge University Press, 1987.

Braddick, Michael J. "State Formation and Social Change in Early Modern England: A Problem Stated and Approaches Suggested." *Social History* 16 (1991): 1–17.

Braddick, Michael J. *State Formation in Early Modern England, 1550–1700.* Cambridge: Cambridge University Press, 2000.

Brady, W. Maziere. *Essays on the English State Church in Ireland.* London: Strahan, 1869.

Braudel, Fernand. "Sur une conception de l'histoire sociale." *Annales E.S.C.* 14 (1959): 308–19.

Breit, Stefan. *'Leichtfertigkeit' und ländliche Gesellschaft: Voreheliche Sexualität in der frühen Neuzeit.* Munich: R. Oldenbourg, 1991.

Brennan, Thomas. *Public Drinking and Popular Culture in Eighteenth-Century Paris.* Princeton: Princeton University Press, 1988.

Breuer, Stefan. "Sozialdisziplinierung: Probleme und Problemverlagerungen eines Konzeptes bei Max Weber, Gerhard Oestreich und Michel Foucault." In *Soziale Sicherheit und soziale Disziplinierung,* edited by Christoph Sachsse and Florian Tennstedt, 45–69. Frankfurt am Main: Suhrkamp Verlag, 1986.

Brigden, Susan. "Religion and Social Obligation in Early Sixteenth Century London." *Past and Present* 103 (1984): 67–112.

Briggs, Robin. "The Sins of the People: Auricular Confession and the Imposition of Social Norms." In *Communities of Belief: Cultural and Social Tension in Early Modern France,* edited by Robin Briggs, 277–338. Oxford: Clarendon Press, 1989.

Brink, Leendert. *De taak van de kerk bij de huwelijkssluiting.* Nieuwkoop: Uitgeverij Heuff, 1977.

Brooks, Christopher. "Apprenticeship, Social Mobility and the Middling Sort, 1550–1800." In *The Middling Sort of People: Culture, Society and Politics in England, 1550–1800,* edited by Jonathan Barry and Christopher Brooks, 52–83. London: Macmillan, 1994.

Brown, Jonathan, and Richard G. Mann. *Spanish Paintings of the Fifteenth through Nineteenth Centuries.* Washington, D.C.: Cambridge University Press, 1990.

Brown, Jonathan. "Murillo, pintor de temas eróticos: Una faceta inavertida de su obra." *Goya* (1982): 35–43, 169–71.

Brown, Jonathan. *Images and Ideas in Seventeenth-Century Spanish Painting.* Princeton: Princeton University Press, 1978.

Brundage, James. *Law, Sex and Christian Society.* Chicago: University of Chicago Press, 1987.

Bryson, Anna. *From Courtesy to Civility: Changing Codes of Conduct in Early Modern England.* Oxford: Clarendon Press, 1998.

Buckwalter, Stephen E. *Die Priesterehe in Flugschriften der frühen Reformation,*

Quellen und Forschungen zur Reformationsgeschichte 68, Gütersloh: Gütersloher Verlagshaus, 1998

Bullinger, Heinrich. *Der Christlich Eestand.* Zurich: Froschauer, 1540

Burdy, Jean-Paul. *Le soleil noir: Un quartier de Saint-Etienne, 1840–1940.* Lyon: Presses Universitaires de Lyon, 1989.

Burghartz, Susanna. "Disziplinierung oder Konfliktregelung? Zur Funktion städtischer Gerichte im Spätmittelalter: das Zürcher Ratsgericht." *Zeitschrift für historische Forschung* 4 (1989): 385–407.

Burghartz, Susanna. "Rechte Jungfrauen oder unverschämte Tochter? Zur weiblichen Ehre im 16. Jahrhundert." In *Frauengeschichte–Geschlechtergeschichte,* edited by Karin Hausen and Heide Wunder, 173–84. Frankfurt am Main: Campus Verlag, 1998.

Burghartz, Susanna. *Leib, Ehre und Gut: Delinquenz in Zürich Ende des 14. Jahrhunderts.* Zürich: Chronos, 1990.

Burghartz, Susanna. *Zeiten der Reinheit, Orte der Unzucht: Ehe und Sexualität in Basel während der frühen Neuzeit.* Paderborn: Ferdinand Schöningh, 1999.

Burgière, André, and François Lebrun. "Priest, Prince and Family." In *A History of the Family.* Vol. 2, *The Impact of Modernity,* edited by André Burguière et al., trans. Sarah Hanbury-Tenison, 95–158. Cambridge: Cambridge University Press, 1996.

Burke, Peter. *Popular Culture in Early Modern Europe.* New York: Harper & Row, 1978.

Burke, Peter. *The Historical Anthropology of Early Modern Italy: Essays on Perception and Communication.* Cambridge: Cambridge University Press, 1987.

Bustamante García, Agustín. "El Santo Oficio de Valladolid y los artistas." *Boletín del Seminario de Estudios de Arte y Arqueología* 61 (1995): 455–66.

Calendar of the State Papers Relating to Ireland, of the Reign of Elizabeth, 1596–1597. London: Public Record Office, 1893.

Calendar of the State Papers Relating to Ireland, of the Reign of James I, 1603–1606. London: Public Record Office, 1872.

Callado, E. "Los intentos de la Corona de reprimir la delincuencia del clero valentino durante el episcopado de Isidoro Aliaga." In *Conflictos y represiones en el Antiguo Régimen.* Departamento de Historia Moderna de la Universidad de Valencia, Valencia: Colección Monografías y Fuentes, 2000.

Candau-Chacón, María Luisa. *Los delitos y las penas en el mundo eclesiástico sevillano del siglo XVIII.* Sevilla: Diputación Provincial, 1993.

Cashmere, John. "The Social Uses of Violence in Ritual: Charivari or Religious Persecution?" *European History Quarterly* 21 (1991): 291–319.

Castan, Nicole. "Autorité familiale et criminalisation d'ordre public en France (XVIIe -XVIIIe siècles)." *IAHCCJ Bulletin* 17 (1992/3): 56–65.

Castan, Nicole. *Justice et répression en Languedoc à l'époque des Lumières.* Paris: Flammarion, 1980.

Castan, Yves. "Criminalisation et ménagement des règlements brutaux des conflits." *IAHCCJ Bulletin* 17 (1992/3): 46–55.

Castan, Yves. *Honnêteté et relations sociales en Languedoc, 1715–1780.* Paris: Plon, 1974

Castillo Bovadilla, Jerónimo. *Política para corregidores y señores de vasallos.* Madrid: Instituto de Estudios de la Administración Local, 1978 (1st ed. Madrid: Luis Sánchez, 1597).

Cavallo, Sandra, and Simona Cerutti. "Female Honor and the Social Control of Reproduction in Piedmont between 1600 and 1800." In *Sex and Gender in Historical Perspective,* edited by Edward Muir and Guido Ruggiero, 73–109. Baltimore: Johns Hopkins University Press, 1990.

Cerutti, Simona. "Group Strategies and Trade Strategies: The Turin Tailors' Guild in the Late Seventeenth and Early Eighteenth Centuries." In *Domestic Strategies: Work and Family in France and Italy, 1600–1800,* edited by S. Woolf, 102–47. Cambridge: Cambridge University Press, 1991.

Cerutti, Simona. *La ville et les métiers: Naissance d'un langage corporatif (Turin 17e-18e siècles).* Paris: Editions de l'EHESS, 1990.

Chaix, Gérald. "Die schwierige Schule der Sitten—christliche Gemeinden, bürgerliche Obrigkeit und Sozialdisziplinierung im frühneuzeitlicheen Köln, etwa 1450–1600." In *Kirchenzucht und Sozialdisziplinierung im frühneuzeitlichen Europa,* edited by Heinz Schilling, 199–217. Berlin, 1994.

Châtellier, Louis. *The Europe of the Devout: The Catholic Reformation and the Formation of a New Society.* Cambridge: Cambridge University Press, 1989.

Chiffoleau, Jacques. *La comptabilité de l'au-delà: Les hommes, la mort et la religion dans la région d'Avignon à la fin du Moyen Age (vers 1320-vers 1480).* Rome: Ecole française de Rome, 1980.

Christelle, Clement. "Les délits ordinaires dans le Baillage de Châtillon-sur-Seine au XVIIIe siècle: L'exemple des litiges de voisinage." In *La petite délinquance du Moyen Age à l'époque contemporaine,* edited by Benoît Garnot, 145–52. Dijon: Editions universitaires de Dijon, 1998.

Clarke, Aidan. "Bishop William Bedell (1571–1642) and the Irish Reformation." In *Worsted in the Game: Losers in Irish History,* edited by Ciaran Brady, 61–72. Dublin: Lilliput Press, 1989.

Claverie, Elisabeth, and Pierre Lamaison. *L'impossible mariage.* Paris: Hachette, 1982.

Clemen, Otto, ed. *Flugschriften aus den ersten Jahren der Reformation.* Vol. 4, no. 5. Leipzig: Halle, 1911.

Cobb, Richard. *The Police and the People: French Popular Protest, 1789–1820.* Oxford: Oxford University Press, 1970.

Cochrane, Eric. *Florence in the Forgotten Centuries.* Chicago: University of Chicago Press, 1973.

Cockburn, J. S., ed. *Western Circuit Assize Orders, 1629 - 1648: A Calendar.* Camden Society, 4th series, 17, 1976.

Coffin, Judith G. "Gender and the Guild Order: The Garment Trades in Eighteenth-Century Paris." *Journal of Economic History* 54 (1994): 768–93.

Cohen, Stanley, and Andrew Scull, eds. *Social Control and the State.* New York: St Martin's Press, 1983.

Cohen, Stanley. *Visions of Social Control: Crime, Punishment and Classification.* Cambridge: Polity Press, 1985.

Collinson, Patrick. "Elizabethan and Jacobean Puritanism As Forms of Popular Religious Culture." In *The Culture of English Puritanism, 1560–1700,* edited by Christopher Durston and Jacqueline Eales, 32–57. London: Macmillan, 1996.

Collinson, Patrick. "England and International Calvinism, 1558–1640." In *International Calvinism, 1541–1715,* edited by Menna Prestwich, 197–223. Oxford: Clarendon Press, 1985.

Collinson, Patrick. "England." In *The Reformation in National Context,* edited by Bob Scribner et al., 80–95. Cambridge: Cambridge University Press, 1994.

Collinson, Patrick. "The Cohabitation of the Faithful with the Unfaithful." In *From Persecution to Toleration,* edited by Ole Peter Grell et al., 51–76. Oxford: Clarendon Press, 1991.

Collinson, Patrick. "The Monarchical Republic of Queen Elizabeth I." *Bulletin of the John Ryland's University Library of Manchester* 69 (1986/87): 394–424.

Collinson, Patrick. *From Iconoclasm to Iconophobia: The Cultural Impact of the Second Reformation.* Reading: University of Reading Press, 1986.

Collinson, Patrick. *The Birthpangs of Protestant England: Religious and Cultural Change in the Sixteenth and Seventeenth Centuries.* New York: Macmillan, 1988.

Collinson, Patrick. *The Elizabethan Puritan Movement.* London: Cape, 1967.

Connolly, S. J. *Religion, Law and Power: The Making of Protestant Ireland, 1660–1760.* Oxford: Clarendon Press, 1992.

Constitutions and Canons Ecclesiastical Treated upon by the Archbishops and Bishops, and the Rest of the Clergy of Ireland. And Agreed upon by Royal License in the Synods Held at Dublin, A.D. 1634 and 1711. Dublin: Association for Discountenancing Vice and Promoting . . . the Christian Religion, 1864.

Contreras, Jaime. *Sotos contra Riquelmes: Regidores, Inquisidores y Criptojudíos.* Madrid: Anaya & Mario Muchnik, 1992.

Cooney, Mark. *Warriors and Peacemakers: How Third Parties Shape Violence.* New York: New York University Press, 1998.

Copia de los pareceres y censuras de los reverendísimos padres, maestros y señores catedráticos de las insignes universidades de Salamanca y Alcalá, . . . Madrid, 1632.

Cressy, David. *Literacy and the Social Order: Reading and Writing in Tudor and Stuart England.* Cambridge: Cambridge University Press, 1980.

Cristóbal, María Ángeles. *Confianza, fidelidad y obediencia. Servidores inquisitoriales y dependencias personales en la ciudad de Logroño (siglo XVII).* Logroño: Instituto de Estudios Riojanos, 1994.

Crowston, Clare. "Engendering the Guilds: Seamstresses, Tailors, and the Clash of Corporate Identities in Old Regime France." *French Historical Studies* 23 (2000): 339–71.

Crowston, Clare. *Fabricating Women: The Seamstresses of Old Regime France, 1675–1791.* Durham: Duke University Press, 2001.

Cunnington, B. H., ed. *Records of the County of Wilts.* Devizes: George Simpson and Co., 1932.

Cuperus, S. Het kerkelijke leven der Hervormden in Friesland tijdens de Republiek. 2 vols. Leeuwarden: Meijer & Schaafsma, 1920.

Curtis, Edmund, and R. B. McDowell, eds. *Irish Historical Documents, 1172–1922.* Reprint New York: Barnes & Noble, 1968.

Da Bisticci, Vespasiano. *Le Vite.* Aulo Greco, ed., vol. 2. Firenze: Istituto Nazionale di Studi sul Rinascimento, 1976.

Da Cruz Coello, María Helena. "As confrarias medievais portuguesas: espaços de solidariedades na vida e na morte." In *Cofradías, gremios, solidaridades en la Europa Medieval. XIX Semana de estudios medievales, Estella '92.* Pamplona: Departamento de Educación y Cultura, 1993.

Damsma, Dirk. "De dubbele revolutie en het gezin." In *Familie, huwelijk en gezin in West-Europa,* edited by Ton Zwaan, 165–92. Amsterdam: Boom, 1993.

Danker, Uwe. *Räuberbanden im alten Reich um 1700: Ein Beitrag zur Geschichte von Herrschaft und Kriminalität in der frühen Neuzeit.* 2 vols. Frankfurt am Main: Suhrkamp, 1988.

Darnton, Robert. "Workers Revolt: The Great Cat Massacre of the Rue Séverin." In idem, *The Great Cat Massacre and Other Episodes in French Cultural History,* 79–104. Harmondsworth: Allen Lane, 1984.

Davids, Karel. "From de la Court to Vreede: Regulation and Self-Regulation in Dutch Economic Discourse from c. 1660 to the Napoleonic Era." *Journal of European Economic History* 30 (2001): 245–89.

Davies, Julian. *The Caroline Captivity of the English Church.* Oxford: Clarendon Press, 1992.

Davies, M. Gay. *The Enforcement of English Apprenticeship, 1563–1642: A Study in Applied Mercantilism.* Cambridge: Harvard University Press, 1956.

Davis, Natalie Zemon. *Humanismus, Narrenherrschaft und die Riten der Gewalt: Gesellschaft und Kultur im frühneuzeitlichen Frankreich.* Frankfurt am Main: Fischer, 1987.

Davis, Natalie Zemon. *Society and Culture in Early Modern France.* Stanford: Stanford University Press, 1987 (reprint 1995).

De Boer, Wietse Thijs. *Sinews of Discipline: The Uses of Confession in Counter-Reformation Milan.* Ph.D. diss., Rotterdam, 1995.

De Giorgio, Michela, and Christiane Klapisch-Zuber, eds. *Storia del Matrimonio.* Rome: Laterza, 1996.

De Grazia, Diane. "Carracci Drawings in Britain and the State of Carracci Studies." *Master Drawings* 36, 3 (1998): 292–304.

De la Roncière, Charles M. "Les confréries à Florence et dans son contado." In *Le mouvement confraternel au Moyen Âge: France, Italie, Suisse,* edited by Agostino Paravincini Bagliani, 297–339. Geneva: Droz, 1987.

De las Heras Santos, Jose Luis. *La justicia penal de los Austrias en la Corona de Castilla.* Salamanca: Edicion de la Universidad de Salamanca, 1991.

De León, Fr. Luis. *La perfecta casada.* Madrid: Espasa-Calpe, 1992 (1st ed. 1583).

De Santander, Fr. Miguel. *Doctrinas y sermones para misión, del padre Fray Miguel de Santander.* 5 vols. Madrid: Imprenta de la Administración del Real Arbitrio de la Beneficencia, 1802–1803.

De Vries, Jan, and Ad van der Woude. *The First Modern Economy: Success, Failure, and Perseverance of the Dutch Economy, 1500–1815.* Cambridge: Cambridge University Press, 1997.

De Vries, Jan. *European Urbanization, 1500–1800.* London: Methuen, 1984.

Deceulaer, Harald and Bibi Panhuysen. "Schneider oder Näherinnen: Ein geslechts-bezogener Vergleich der Bekleidungshandwerke in den Nördlichen und Südlichen Niederlanden während der Frühen Neuzeit." In *Zunftlandschaften in Deutschland und den Niederlanden im Vergleich,* edited by Wilfried Reininghaus, 85–106. Münster: Aschendorf, 2000.

Deceulaer, Harald. "Guilds and Litigation: Conflict Settlement in Antwerp (1585–1796)." In *Statuts individuels, statuts corporatifs et statuts judiciaires dans les villes européennes (moyen âge et temps modernes),* edited by Marc Boone and Maar-ten Prak, 171–208. Leuven: Garant, 1996.

Deceulaer, Harald. "Stadsbestuur en buurtbewoners in Gent: Interactie, participatie, en publieke opinie, 1658–1668." *Bijdragen en mededelingen betreffende de geschiedenis der Nederlanden* 1, 110 (1995): 3–26.

Deceulaer, Harald. *Pluriforme patronen en eenverschillende snit: Sociaal-economische, insti-tutionele en culturele transformaties in de kledingsectorin Antwerpen, brussel en Gent, 1585–1800.* Amsterdam: Stichting beheer IISG, 2001.

Decker, Paul. *Fürstlicher Baumeister / oder: ARCHITECTURA CIVILIS: Wie Grosser Fürsten und Herren Palläste / mit ihren Höfen / Lust= Häusern / Gärten / Grotten / Orangerien / und anderen darzu gehörigen Gebäuden füglich anzulegen / und nach heutiger Art auszuzieren.* Augsburg, 1711–1716.

De Munck, Bert. *Leerpraktijken: Economische en sociaal-culturele aspecten van beroep-sopleidingen in Antwerpse ambachtsgilden, 16de-18de eeuw.* Ph.D. diss., Vrije Universiteit Brussel.

Denzler, Georg. *Päpste und Papsttum.* Vol. 5, parts I and II: *Das Papsttum und der Amtszölibat.* Stuttgart: Hiersemann, 1973 (part I) and 1976 (part II).

Diederiks, Herman. *In een land van justitie: Criminaliteit van vrouwen, soldaten en ambtenaren in de 18e-eeuwse Republiek.* Hilversum: Verloren, 1992.

Dietrich, David Henry. "Brotherhood and Community on the Eve of the Reformation: Confraternities and Parish Life in Liège, 1450–1540." Ph.D. diss., University of Michigan, 1982.

Dinges, Martin, ed. *Hausväter, Priester, Kastraten: Zur Konstruktion von Männlichkeit in Spätmittelalter und Früher Neuzeit.* Göttingen: Vandenhoeck & Ruprecht, 1998.

Dinges, Martin. "'Weiblichkeit' in 'Männlichkeitsritualen'? Zu weiblichen Taktiken im Ehrenhandel in Paris im 18. Jahrhundert." *Francia* 18 (1991): 257–79.

Dinges, Martin. "Aushandeln von Armut in der Frühen Neuzeit: Selbsthilfepotential, Bürgervorstellungen und Verwaltungslogiken." *Werkstatt Geschichte* 10 (1995): 7–15.

Dinges, Martin. "Die Ehre als Thema der Stadtgeschichte. Eine Semantik im Übergang vom Ancien Régime zur Moderne." *Zeitschrift für Historische Forschung* 16 (1989): 409–40

Dinges, Martin. "Ehrenhändel als kommunikative Gattungen: Kultureller Wandel in der frühen Neuzeit." *Archiv für Kulturgeschichte* 75 (1993): 359–93.

Dinges, Martin. "Frühneuzeitliche Armenfürsorge als Sozialdisziplinierung? Probleme mit einem Konzept." *Geschichte und Gesellschaft* 17 (1991): 5–29.

Dinges, Martin. "Frühneuzeitliche Armenfürsorge als Sozialdisziplinierung? Probleme mit einem Konzept." *Geschichte und Gesellschaft* 17 (1991): 5–29.

Dinges, Martin. "Policeyforschung statt 'Sozialdisziplinierung'"? *Zeitschrift für Neuere Rechtsgeschichte* 24 (2002): 327–44.

Dinges, Martin. "Residenzstadt als Sozialdisziplinierung? Zur Rekonstruktion eines kulturgeschichtlichen Forschungsgegenstandes." In *Disziplinierung im Alltag des Mittelalters und der frühen Neuzeit. Internationaler Kongreß.* 57–74. Vienna: Krems/Donau, 1999.

Dinges, Martin. "Michel Foucault, Justizphantasien und die Macht." In *Mit den Waffen der Justiz. Zur Kriminalitätsgeschichte des späten Mittelalters und der Frühen Neuzeit,* edited by Andreas Blauert and Gerd Schwerhoff, 189–212. Frankfurt am Main: Fischer, 1993.

Dinges, Martin. *Der Maurermeister und der Finanzrichter. Ehre, Geld und soziale Kontrolle im Paris des 18. Jahrhundert.* Göttingen: Vandenhoeck und Ruprecht, 1994.

Donajgrodzki, A[nthony] P., ed. *Social Control in Nineteenth-Century Britain.* London: Croom Helm, 1977.

Donnison, Jean. *Midwives and Medical Men: A History of Inter-Professional Rivalries and Women's Rights.* London: Heinemann, 1977.

Dorren, Gabriëlle. *Eenheid en verscheidenheid: de burgers van Haarlem in de Gouden Eeuw.* Amsterdam: Prometheus/Bakker, 2001.

Douglas, Mary. "Das Prinzip Reinheit und Verschmutzung." *Sozialwissenschaftliche Information* 11, 2 (1982): 67–78.

Douglas, Mary. *Purity and Danger: An Analysis of Concepts of Pollution and Taboo.* London: Routledge & Kegan, 1966.

Duffy, Eamon. "The Godly and the Multitude in Stuart England." *Seventeenth Century Journal* 1 (1986): 31–49.

Dunlop, O. J., and R. D. Dunman. *English Apprenticeship and Child Labour.* London: T. Fisher Unwin, 1912.

Dürr, E., and P. Roth, eds. *Aktensammlung zur Geschichte der Basler Reformation in den Jahren 1519 bis Anfang 1534.* 6 vols. Basel: Verlag der Historischen und Antiquarischen Gesellschaft, 1921–1950.

Dürr, Renate. *Mägde in der Stadt: Das Beispiel Schwäbisch Hall in der Frühen Neuzeit.* Frankfurt am Main: Campus Verlag, 1995.

Dwyer, Philip. *The Diocese of Killaloe from the Reformation to the Eighteenth Century.* Dublin: Hodges, Foster and Figgis, 1878.

Dyboski, R., ed. *Songs, Carols and Other Miscellaneous Poems, from . . . Richard Hill's Commonplace-Book.* Early English Text Society, Extra Series. Vol. 101. London: Oxford University Press, 1908.

Egmond, Florike. *Underworlds: Organized Crime in the Netherlands, 1650–1800.* Cambridge: Polity Press, 1993.

Ehmer, Josef. "Traditionelles Denken und neue Fragestellungen zur Geschichte von Handwerk und Zunft." In *Handwerk, Hausindustrie und die historische Schule der Nationalökonomie: Wissenschafts- und gewerbegeschichtliche Perspektiven,* edited by Friedrich Lenger, 19–77. Bielefeld: Verlag für Regionalgeschichte, 1998.

Ehmer, Josef. "Worlds of Mobility: Migration Patterns of Viennese Artisans in the Eighteenth Century." In *The Artisan and the European Town, 1500–1900,* edited by Geoffrey Crossick, 172–99. Aldershot: Scolar Press, 1997.

Ehrenpreis, Stefan, and Heinz Schilling, eds. *Konfessionelle und säkulare Trends frühneuzeitlicher Bildungsgeschichte: Forschungsperspektiven und Methodik.* Münster: Waxmann, 2003.

Eibach, Joachim. "Recht–Kultur–Diskurs. Nullum Crimen sine Scientia." *Zeitschrift für Neuere Rechtsgeschichte* 23 (2001): 102–20.

Eibach, Joachim. "Städtische Gewaltkriminalität im Ancien Régime: Frankfurt am Main im europäischen Kontext." *Zeitschrift für Historische Forschung* 25 (1998): 359–82.

Eichberg, Henning. "Geometrie als barocke Verhaltensnorm: Fortifikation und Exerzitien." *Zeitschrift für Historische Forschung* 4 (1977): 17–50.

Elias, Norbert. *The Civilizing Process: State Formation and Civilization.* Oxford: Blackwell, 1982.

Elias, Norbert. *Über den Prozeß der Zivilisation: Soziogenetische und psychogenetische Untersuchungen.* 2 vols. Frankfurt am Main: Suhrkamp, 1976.

Elkar, Rainer S. *Walz: Gesellenwanderungen in neuerer Zeit.* Stuttgart: Kohlhammer, 2000.

Elliott, J. H. "Yet Another Crisis." In *The European Crisis of the 1590s,* edited by Peter Clark, 301–11. London: Allen & Unwin, 1985.

Elliott, J. H., ed. *Hispanic World.* London: Thames and Hudson, 1991.

Elrington, C. R., and J. H. Todd, eds. *The Whole Works of the Most Rev. James Ussher . . . .* 17 vols. Dublin: n.p., 1847–1864.

Elton, Geoffrey. "Introduction." In *Crime in England, 1550–1800,* edited by J. S. Cockburn. London: Methuen, 1977.

Emsley, Clive. *Gendarmes and the State in Nineteenth Century Europe.* Oxford: Oxford University Press, 1999.

Emsley, Clive. *Policing and Its Context, 1750–1870.* London: MacMillan, 1983.

English Customs. London, 1628 [Folger Shakespeare Library, STC 10408.6].

Epstein, S. R. "Journeymen Mobility and Markets in Skilled Labour in Europe, 14th-18th centuries" (forthcoming).

Epstein, S. R. "Craft Guilds, Apprenticeship, and Technological Change in Preindustrial Europe." *Journal of Economic History* 58 (1998): 684–713.

Epstein, Steven A. *Wage Labor and Guilds in Medieval Europe.* Chapel Hill: University of North Carolina Press, 1991.

Esmein, A. *Le mariage en droit canonique.* 2 vols. Paris: Recueil Sirey, 1929–1935.

Estèbe, Jeanine, and Bernard Vogler. "La genèse d'une société protestante: Etude comparée de quelques registres consistoriaux Languedociens et Palatins vers 1600." *Annales ESC* 31 (1976): 362–88.

Evans, Richard. *Rituals of Retribution: Capital Punishment in Germany, 1600–1987.* Oxford: Oxford University Press, 1996.

Caravaggio. Exhibition catalog, Museo Nacional del Prado, 21.9.–21.11.1999. Madrid: Electa, 1999.

Los Inquisidores. Exhibition catalog, edited by Fundación Sancho el Sabio. Vitoria: Evagraf, 1993.

Saints and Sinners: Caravaggio and the Baroque Image. Exhibition catalog, edited by Franco Mormando. McMullen Museum of Art, Boston College, 1.2.–24.5.1999. Chicago: University of Chicago Press, 1999.

Faber, Sjoerd. *Strafrechtspleging en criminaliteit te Amsterdam, 1680–1811: De nieuwe menslievendheid.* Arnhem: Gouda Quint, 1983.

Fabre, Daniel. "Families: Privacy versus Custom." In *A History of Private Life: III. Passions of the Renaissance,* edited by Roger Chartier and translated by Arthur Goldhammer, 531–69. Cambridge: Harvard University Press, 1989.

Farge, Arlette, and Michel Foucault. *Familiäre Konflikte: Die "Lettres de cachet."* Frankfurt am Main: Suhrkamp, 1989.

Farr, James R. "On the Shop Floor: Guilds, Artisans, and the European Market Economy, 1350–1750." *Journal of Early Modern History* 1 (1997): 24–54.

Farr, James R. *Artisans in Europe, 1300–1914.* Cambridge: Cambridge University Press, 2000.

Farr, James R. *Hands of Honor: Artisans and Their World in Dijon, 1550–1650.* Ithaca: Cornell University Press, 1988.

Fehler, Timothy. "Social Welfare in Early Modern Emden: The Evolution of Poor Relief in the Age of the Reformation and Confessionalization." Ph.D. diss., University of Wisconsin-Madison, 1995.

Fehler, Timothy. *Poor Relief and Protestantism: The Evolution of Social Welfare in Sixteenth-Century Emden.* Brookfield, Vt.: Ashgate, 1999.

Flandrin, Jean-Louis. *Familles: parenté, maison, sexualité dans l'ancienne société.* Paris: Hachette, 1976.

Fletcher, Anthony, and John Stevenson, eds. *Order and Disorder in Early Modern England.* Cambridge: Cambridge University Press, 1985.

Florin, Franz Philipp. *Oeconomus prudens et legalis? Oder allgemeiner Kluger und Rechtsverständiger Haus-Vatter . . . .* Vol. 2. Nürnberg, 1719.

Flynn, Maureen. *Sacred Charity: Confraternities and Social Welfare in Spain, 1400–1700.* Ithaca: Cornell University Press, 1989.

Fontaine, Laurence. "Les villageois dans et hors du village: Gestion des conflits et contrôle social des travailleurs migrants originaires des montagnes françaises (fin XVIIe siècle - milieu du XIXe siècle." *Crime, Histoire et Sociétés/Crime, History and Societies* 1, 1 (1997): 71–85.

Ford, Alan. "The Protestant Reformation in Ireland." In *Natives and Newcomers: Essays on the Making of Irish Colonial Society, 1534–1641,* edited by Ciaran Brady and Raymond Gillespie, 50–74. Dublin: Irish Academic Press, 1986.

Fortea Pérez, José I., et al., eds. *Furor et rabies. Violencia, conflicto y marginación en la Edad Moderna.* Santander: Servicio de Publicaciones de la Universidad de Cantabria/Consejería de Cultura, Turismo y Deporte del Gobierno de Cantabria & Biblioteca Valenciana, 2003.

Foster, Stephen. *The Long Argument: English Puritanism and the Shaping of New England Culture, 1570–1700.* Chapel Hill: University of North Carolina Press, 1991.

Foucault, Michel. *Discipline and Punish: The Birth of the Prison,* translated by Alan Sheridan. London: Allen Lane, 1977.

Foucault, Michel. *Madness and Civilization: A History of Insanity in the Age of Reason.* Translated by Richard Howard. New York: Pantheon Books, 1965.

Foucault, Michel. *Microfísica del poder.* Edited and translated by J. Varela and F. Álvarez. Madrid: La Piqueta, 1991.

Foucault, Michel. *Überwachen und Strafen: Die Geburt des Gefängnisses.* Frankfurt am Main: Suhrkamp, 1976.

Foxe, John. *Actes and Monuments.* 2 vols. consecutively paginated. London: 1570.

Foyster, Elizabeth A. *Manhood in Early Modern England: Honour, Sex and Marriage.* London: Longman, 1999.

François, Etienne. "De l'uniformité à la tolérance: confession et société urbaine en Allemagne, 1650–1800." *Annales ESC* 37 (1982): 783–800.

François, Etienne. *Protestants et catholiques en Allemagne: identités et pluralisme, Augsbourg, 1648–1806.* Paris: Albin Michel, 1993.

Frank, Michael. "Ehre und Gewalt im Dorf der frühen Neuzeit. Das Beispiel Heiden (Grafschaft Lippe) im 17. und 18. Jahrhundert." In *Verletzte Ehre. Ehrkonflikte in Gesellschaften des Mittelalters und der Frühen Neuzeit,* edited by Klaus Schreiner and Gerd Schwerhoff, 320–38. Köln: Böhlau Verlag, 1995.

Frank, Michael. *Dörfliche Gesellschaft und Kriminalität: Das Fallbeispiel Lippe, 1650–1800.* Paderborn: Ferdinand Schöningh, 1995.

Franz, Günther, ed. *Urkundliche Quellen zur hessischen Reformationsgeschichte.* Vols. 1–4. Marburg: Elwert, 1951.

Fraser Jenkins, A. D. "Cosimo de Medici's Patronage of Architecture and the Theory of Magnificence." *Journal of the Warburg and Courtauld Institutes* 23 (1970): 162–70.

Freedberg, David. *The Power of Images: Studies in the History and Theory of Response.* Chicago: University of Chicago Press, 1989.

Freitag, Werner. *Volks- und Elitenfrömmigkeit in der Frühen Neuzeit: Marienwallfahrten im Fürstbistum Münster.* Paderborn: Schöningh, 1991.

Freitag, Winfried. "Mißverständnis eines, Konzeptes': Zu Gerhard Oestreichs,

Fundamentalprozeß' der Sozialdisziplinierung." *Zeitschrift für Historische Forschung* 28 (2001): 513–38.

Friedrichs, Christopher. "Politics or Pogrom? The Fettmilch Uprising in German and Jewish History." *Central European History* 19 (1986): 186–228.

Friedrichs, Christopher. *Urban Politics in Early Modern Europe*. London: Routledge, 2000.

Friess, Peer, and Rolf Kiessling, eds. *Konfessionalisierung und Region*. Konstanz: UVK Universitätsverlag, 1999.

Fuchs, Ralf-Peter. *Um die Ehre: Westfälische Beleidigungsprozesse vor dem Reichskammergericht, 1525–1805*. Paderborn: Schoeningh, 1999.

Gairdner, James, ed. *Three Fifteenth-Century Chronicles, with Historical Memoranda by John Stowe*. Camden Society, new series, vol. 28. London: 1880.

Gallego, Julián. *El pintor de artesano a artista*. Granada: Universidad de Granada, Departamento de Historia del Arte, 1976.

Gand, Roger. "De la signification des Initiales, Armes, Effigies et Emblèmes figurés sur les édifices civils et militaires aux XVe et XVIe siècles." *Mémoires de la Société Nationale des Antiquaires de France*, N.S. 3 (1954): 263–77.

García Cárcel, Ricardo. *Las Germanías de Valencia*. Barcelona: Península, 1975.

García Felguera, María de los Santos. "Saura, Millares und die 'Leyenda negra.'" *Kritische Berichte* 20, 1 (1992): 69–80.

García Hidalgo, José. *Principios para estudiar el nobilísimo y real arte de la pintura*. 1693. Reprint, Madrid: El Instituto de España, 1965.

García Martínez, Sebastià. *Bandolers, corsaris i moriscos*. Valencia: Eliseu Climent, 1980.

Garnot, Benoît, ed. *L'infrajudiciaire du Moyen Age à l'époque contemporaine. Actes du colloque de Dijon 5–6 octobre 1995*. Dijon: Presses Universitaires de Dijon, 1996.

Garnot, Benoît. "Justice, infrajustice, parajustice et extrajustice dans la France d'Ancien Régime." *Crime, Histoire et Sociétés/Crime, History and Societies* 4, 4 (2000): 103–20.

Garnot, Benoît. "L'ampleur et les limites de l'infrajudiciaire dans la France d'Ancien Régime (XVIe-XVIIe-XVIIIe siècle)." In *L'Infrajudiciaire*, edited by Benoît Garnot, 69–76. Dijon: Editions universitaires de Dijon, 1996.

Garrioch, David. "Verbal Insults in Eighteenth-Century Paris." In *The Social History of Language*, edited by Peter Burke and Roy Porter, 104–19. Cambridge: Cambridge University Press, 1987.

Garrioch, David. *Neighbourhood and Community in Paris, 1740–1790*. Cambridge: Cambridge University Press, 1986.

Gatrell, V. A. C. *The Hanging Tree: Execution and the English People, 1770–1868*. New York: Oxford University Press, 1994.

Gavitt, Philip. *Charity and Children in Renaissance Florence: The Ospedale degli Innocenti, 1410–1536*. Ann Arbor: University of Michigan Press, 1990.

Geertz, Clifford. "Centres, Kings and Charisma: Reflections on the Symbolics of Power." In *Culture and Its Creators*, edited by Joseph Ben-David and Terry N. Clark. Chicago: University of Chicago Press, 1977.

Geiger, Max. *Die Basler Kirche und Theologie im Zeitalter der Hochorthodoxie.* Zollikon-Zurich: Evangelischer Verlag, 1952.

Gellately, Robert. *Backing Hitler: Consent and Coercion in Nazi Germany.* Oxford: Oxford University Press, 2001.

Gellately, Robert. *The Gestapo and German Society: Enforcing Racial Policy, 1933–1945.* Oxford: Clarendon Press, 1990.

Geremek, Bronislaw. *Het Kaïnsteken: Het beeld van armen en vagebonden in de Europese literatuur van de 15e tot de 17e eeuw.* Baarn: Anthos, 1992.

Gillespie, Raymond. *Devoted People: Belief and Religion in Early Modern Ireland.* Manchester: Manchester University Press, 1997.

Godoy, Jack. *La evolución de la familia y del matrimonio en Europa.* Barcelona: Herder, 1986 (1st ed. 1983).

Goertz, Hans-Jürgen. *Die Täufer: Geschichte und Deutung.* München: Beck, 1980.

Golberg, Steven. *La inevitabilidad del patriarcado.* Madrid: Alianza, 1976 (1st ed.: *The inevitability of patriarchy.* New York: 1973).

Göttler, Christine. *Die Kunst des Fegefeuers nach der Reformation: Kirchliche Schenkungen, Ablaß und Almosen in Antwerpen und Bologna um 1600.* Mainz: von Zabern, 1996.

Gottlieb, Gunther, et al., eds. *Geschichte der Stadt Augsburg.* 2nd edition. Stuttgart: Konrad Theiss Verlag, 1984.

Gouge, William. *Of Domesticall Duties: Eight Treatises.* London, 1622.

Gowing, Laura. *Domestic Dangers: Women, Words and Sex in Early Modern London.* Oxford: Clarendon Press, 1996.

Grell, Ole Peter, and Andrew Cunningham. "The Reformation and Changes in Welfare Provision in Early Modern Northern Europe." In *Health Care and Poor Relief in Protestant Europe, 1500–1700,* edited by Ole Peter Grell and Andrew Cunningham, 1–42. London: Routledge, 1997.

Greschat, Martin. *Martin Bucer: Ein Reformator in seiner Zeit.* München: Beck, 1990.

Griffiths, Paul. *Youth and Authority: Formative Experiences in England, 1560–1640.* Oxford: Clarendon Press, 1996.

Groenendijk, L. F. *De nadere reformatie van het gezin: De visie van Petrus Wittewrongel op de christelijke huishouding.* Dordrecht: Van den Tol, 1984.

Gross, Jan T. "Social Control under Totalitarianism." In *Toward a General Theory,* edited by Donald Black, vol. 2, 59–77. Orlando: Academic Press, 1984.

Grotius, Hugo. *Inleidinge tot de Hollandsche Rechtsgeleertheid.* Arnhem: Universitaire Pers Leiden, 1939.

Gwynn, Lewis. "La terreur blanche et l'application de la Loi Decazes dans le département du Gard (1815–1817)." *Annales historiques de la Révolution française* 175 (1964): 174–93.

Hafter, Daryl. "Women Who Wove in the Eighteenth-Century Silk-Industry of Lyon." In *European Women and Preindustrial Craft,* edited by Daryl Hafter, 48–57. Bloomington: Indiana University Press, 1995.

Haks, Donald. *Huwelijk en gezin in Holland in de 17e en 18e eeuw: Processtukken en moralisten over aspecten van het laat zeventiende en achttiende eeuwse gezinsleven.* Assen: Van Gorcum, 1982.

Haliczer, Stephen, ed. *Inquisition and Society in Early Modern Europe.* London: Croom Helm, 1987.

Hamm, Berndt. "Von der spätmittelalterlichen reformatio zur Reformation: Der Prozeß normativer Zentrierung von Religion und Gesellschaft in Deutschland." *Archiv für Reformationsgeschichte* 84 (1993): 7–82.

Hanak, Gerhard, et al. *Ärgernisse und Lebenskatastrophen: Über den alltäglichen Umgang mit Kriminalität.* Bielefeld: AJZ Druck und Verlag, 1989.

Hanawalt, Barbara. "Keepers of the Lights: Late Medieval English Parish Gilds." *Journal of Medieval and Renaissance Studies* 14, 1 (1984): 21–37.

Hand, G. J., and V. W. Treadwell, eds. "His Majesty's Directions for Ordering and Settling the Courts within His Kingdom of Ireland, 1622." *Analecta Hibernica* 26 (1970): 177–212.

Hardtwig, Wolfgang, and Hans-Ulrich Wehler, eds. *Kulturgeschichte heute.* Göttingen: Vandenhoeck & Ruprecht, 1996.

Harrington, Joel. *Reordering Marriage and Society in Reformation Germany.* Cambridge: Cambridge University Press, 1995.

Härter, Karl. "Soziale Disziplinierung durch Strafe? Intentionen frühneuzeitlicher Policeyordnungen und staatliche Sanktionspraxis." *Zeitschrift für Historische Forschung* 3, 26 (1999): 365–79.

Hay, Douglas. "Property, Authority and the Criminal Law." *Albion's Fatal Tree: Crime and Society in Eighteenth-Century England,* edited by Douglas Hay et al. New York: Pantheon Books, 1975.

Heal, Felicia. *Hospitality in Early Modern England.* Oxford: Oxford University Press, 1990.

Hecht, Christian. *Katholische Bildertheologie im Zeitalter von Gegenreformation und Barock.* Berlin, 1997 (PhD. diss. Passau 1994).

Heers, Jacques. *Le clan familial au Moyen Age: Etude sur les structures politiques et sociales des milieux urbains.* Paris: Presses universitaires de France, 1974.

Heidrich, Hermann. "Grenzübergänge. Das Haus und die Volkskultur in der frühen Neuzeit." In *Kultur der einfachen Leute,* edited by Richard van Dülmen, 17–41. München: C. H. Beck Verlag, 1983.

Heinemeyer, Walter, ed. *Das Werden Hessens.* Marburg: Elwert, 1986.

Held, Jutta. *Caravaggio: Politik und Martyrium der Körper.* Berlin: Reimer, 1996.

Henderson, John. *Piety and Charity in Late Medieval Florence.* Oxford: Clarendon Press, 1994.

Herlihy, David. *Opera Muliebria: Women and Work in Medieval Europe.* New York: McGraw-Hill, 1990.

Herrero-García, Miguel. "Un dictamen pericial de Velázquez y una escena de Lope de Vega." *Revista Española de Arte* (1936): 66–68.

Herrup, Cynthia. *The Common Peace: Participation and the Criminal Law in Seventeenth-Century England.* Cambridge: Cambridge University Press, 1987.

Hesselink, Lidewij. "Goud- en zilversmeden en hun gilde in Amsterdam in de 17e en 18e eeuw." *Holland* 31 (1999): 127–47.

Hester, Marianne. *Lewd Women and Wicked Witches: A Study of the Dynamics of Male Domination.* London: Routledge, 1992.

Hildermeier, Manfred, et al., eds. *Zivilgesellschaft in Ost und West: Begriff, Geschichte, Chancen.* Frankfurt am Main: Campus Verlag, 2000.

Hill, Christopher. "The Many Headed Monster in Late Tudor and Early Stuart Political Thinking." In *From the Renaissance to the Counter Reformation: Essays in Honour of Garrett Mattingly,* edited by E. H. Carter, 296–324. London: Random House, 1966.

Hill, Christopher. "William Perkins and the Poor." In: idem, *Puritanism and Revolution,* 212–33. London: Secker & Warburg, 1984.

Hill, Christopher. *Society and Puritanism in Prerevolutionary England.* London: Secker & Warburg, 1964.

Hill, Jacqueline. *From Patriots to Unionists: Dublin Civic Politics and Irish Protestant Patriotism, 1660–1840.* Oxford: Clarendon, 1997.

Hindle, Steve. "The Keeping of the Public Peace." In *The Experience of Authority in Early Modern England,* edited by Paul Griffiths et al., 213–48. Basingstoke: Palgrave Macmillan, 1996.

Hindle, Steve. "The Shaming of Margaret Knowsley: Gossip, Gender and the Experience of Authority in Early Modern England." *Continuity and Change* 9 (1994): 391–419.

Hindle, Steve. *The State and Social Change in Early Modern England, c. 1550–1640.* Basingstoke: Palgrave Macmillan, 2000.

Hipp, Hermann, and Martin Warnke. *Architektur als politische Kultur: Philosophia practica.* Berlin: Reimer, 1996.

Hoffman, Carl A. "Au?ergerichtliche Einigungen bei Straftaten als vertikale und horizontale soziale Kontrolle im 16. Jahrhundert." In Kriminalitätsgeschichte. Beiträge zur Sozial- und Kulturgeschichte der Vormoderne, edited by Andreas Blauert and Gerd Schwerhoff, 563–79. Konstanz: Universitätsverlag, 2000.

Hoffmann, Carl A. "Bürgersicherheit und Herrschaftssicherung im 16. Jahrhundert: Das Wechselverhältnis zweier frühmoderner Sicherheitskonzepte." In *Unsichere Großstädte? Vom Mittelalter bis zur Postmoderne,* edited by Martin Dinges and Fritz Sack, 101–23. Konstanz: Universitätsverlag, 2000.

Hoffman, Carl A. "Konfessionell motivierte und gewandelte Konflikte in der zweiten Hälfte des 16. Jahrhunderts—Versuch eines mentalitätsgeschichtlichen Ansatzes am Biespiel der bikonfessionellen Reichsstadt Augsburg." In *Konfessionalisierung und Region,* edited by Peer Frie? and Rolf Kie?ling, 99–120. Konstanz: Universitätsverlag, 1999.

Hoffmann, Carl A. "Der Stadtverweis als Sanktionsmittel in der Reichsstadt Augsburg zu Beginn der Neuzeit." In *Neue Wege strafrechtsgeschichtlicher Forschung,* edited by Hans Schlosser and Dietmar Willoweit, 193–237. Köln: Böhlau Verlag, 1999.

Hoffmann, Carl A. "Strukturen und Quellen des Augsburger reichsstädtischen Strafgerichtswesens in der ersten Hälfte des 16. Jahrhunderts." *Zeitschrift des Historischen Vereins für Schwaben* 88 (1995): 57–108.

Hogan, Edmund, ed. *Ibernia Ignatiana Seu Ibernorum Societas Iesu Patrum Monumenta.* Dublin: Societas Typographica Dubliniensis, 1880.

Hogan, Edmund, ed. *Words of Comfort to Persecuted Catholics Written in Exile, Anno 1607 . . . by Father Henry Fitzsimon . . .* Dublin: M. H. Gill, 1881.

Hogan, Edmund. *Distinguished Irishmen of the Sixteenth Century.* London: Burns and Oates, 1894.

Höhlbaum, Konstantin, ed. *Das Buch Weinsberg: Kölner Denkwürdigkeiten aus dem 16. Jahrundert.* Vol. 1. Leipzig: Droste, 1886.

Honeyman, K., and J. Goodman. "Women's Work, Gender Conflict, and Labour Markets in Europe, 1500–1900." *Economic History Review* 2nd series 44 (1991): 608–28.

Hoogewerff, G. J. *De geschiedenis van de St. Lucasgilden in Nederland.* Amsterdam: Van Kampen & Zoon, 1947.

Horwitz, Allan V. *The Logic of Social Control.* New York: Plenum Press, 1990.

Houlbrooke, Ralph. *Church Courts and the People during the English Reformation, 1520–1570.* Oxford: Oxford University Press, 1979.

Howell, Martha. "Women, the Family Economy and the Structures of Market Production in Cities of Northern Europe during the Middle Ages." In *Women and Work in Pre-Industrial Europe,* edited by Barbara Hanawalt, 198–222. Bloomington: Indiana University Press, 1986.

Howell, Martha. *Women, Production, and Patriarchy in Late Medieval Cities.* Chicago: University of Chicago Press, 1986.

Hudson, Geoffrey L. "Negotiating for Blood Money: War Widows and the Courts in Seventeenth-Century England." In *Women, Crime and the Courts in Early Modern England,* edited by Jenny Kermode and Garthine Walker, 146–69. London: University College London Press, 1994.

Hufton, Olwen H. *The Poor of Eighteenth-Century France, 1750–1789.* Oxford: Clarendon Press, 1974.

Hugger, Paul, and Ulrich Stadler, eds. *Gewalt: Kulturelle Formen in Geschichte und Gegenwart.* Zürich: Unionsverlag, 1995.

Hull, Isabel V. *Sexuality, State, and Civil Society in Germany, 1700–1815.* Ithaca: Cornell University Press, 1996.

Hunt, William. *The Puritan Moment: The Coming of Revolution in an English County.* Cambridge: Harvard University Press, 1983.

Hutton, Ronald. *The Rise and Fall of Merry England: The Ritual Year, 1400–1700.* Oxford: Oxford University Press, 1994.

Huussen, A. H., Jr. *Veroordeeld in Friesland: Criminaliteitsbestrijding in de eeuw der Verlichting.* Leeuwarden: Hedeby Publishing, 1994.

Imízcoz, J. M., and A. Floristán. "La comunidad rural vasco-navarra (s. XV-XIX) ¿un modelo de sociedad?" *Mélanges de la Casa de Velázquez* 2, 29 (1993): 193–215.

Ingram, Martin. "History of Sin or History of Crime? The Regulation of Morality in England, 1450–1750." In *Institutionen, Instrumente und akteure: sozialer Kontrolle und Disciplinieiung in frühneuzeitlichen Europa,* edited by Heinz Schilling and Lars Behrisch, 87–103. Frankfurt: Main, 1999.

Ingram, Martin. "'Scolding Women Cucked or Washed': A Crisis in Gender Relations in Early Modern England?" In *Women, Crime and the Courts in Early Modern England,* edited by Jenny Kermode and Garthine Walker, 48–80. London: University College London Press, 1994.

Ingram, Martin. "Juridical Folklore in England Illustrated by Rough Music." In *Communities and Courts in Britain, 1150–1900,* edited by Christopher Brooks and Michael Lobban, 61–82. London: Hambledon Press, 1997.

Ingram, Martin. "Puritans and the Church Courts, 1560–1640." In *The Culture of English Puritanism, 1560–1700,* edited by Christopher Durston and Jacqueline Eales, 58–91. London: Macmillan, 1996.

Ingram, Martin. "Reformation of Manners in Early Modern England." In *The Experience of Authority in Early Modern England,* edited by Paul Griffiths et al., 47–88. London: Macmillan, 1996.

Ingram, Martin. "Religion, Communities and Moral Discipline in Late Sixteenth and Seventeenth Century England: Case Studies." In *Religion and Society in Early Modern Europe, 1500–1800,* edited by Kaspar von Greyerz, 177–93. London: Allen & Unwin, 1984.

Ingram, Martin. "Ridings, Rough Music and the 'Reform of Popular Culture' in Early Modern England." *Past and Present* 105 (1984): 79–113.

Ingram, Martin. "Shame and Pain: Themes and Variations in Tudor Punishments." In *Punishing the English: Essays on Penal Practice and Culture, 1500–1900,* edited by Paul Griffiths and Simon Devereaux, 36–62. Houndmills, Basingstoke: Palgrave Macmillan, 2004.

Ingram, Martin. "The Reform of Popular Culture? Sex and Marriage in Early Modern England." In *Popular Culture in Early Modern England,* edited by Barry Reay, 129–65. London: Macmillan, 1985.

Ingram, Martin. *Church Courts, Sex, and Marriage in England, 1570–1640.* New York: Cambridge University Press, 1987.

Irwin, Joyce L. *Womanhood in Radical Protestantism.* New York: Edwin Mellen Press, 1979.

Israel, Uwe. *Johannes Geiler von Kaysersberg (1445–1510): Der Straßburger Münsterprediger als Rechtsreformer.* Berlin: Duncker & Humblot, 1997.

Jacobs, Marc. "Sociaal kapitaal van buren: Rechten, plichten en conflicten in Gentse gebuurten (zeventiende - achttiende eeuw)." *Volkskundig Bulletin* 22 (1996): 149–77.

Jedin, Hubert. *Geschichte des Konzils von Trient.* 4 vols. Freiburg: Herder, 1949.

Jessen, Ralph. "Gewaltkriminalität im Ruhrgebiet zwischen bürgerlicher Panik und proletarischer Subkultur." In *Kirmes - Kneipe–Kino: Arbeiterkultur im Ruhrgebiet zwischen Kommerz und Kontrolle (1850–1914),* edited by Dagmar Kift, 226–55. Paderborn: Schöningh, 1992.

Johnson, Charles. *A General History of the Lives and Adventures of the Most Famous Highwaymen, Murderers, Street-Robbers, &c, to Which Is Added a Genuine Account of the Voyages of and Plunders of the Most Notorious Pirates.* London: 1734.

Johnson, Eric A. *Nazi Terror: The Gestapo, Jews and Ordinary Germans.* New York: Basic Books, 1999.

Joisten, Hartmut. *Der Grenzgänger Martin Bucer: Ein europäischer Reformator.* Speyer: Evangelischer Presseverlag, 1991.

Jones, Malcolm. "The English Print, c.1550–c.1650." In *A Companion to English Renaissance Literature and Culture,* edited by Michael Hattaway, 352–66. Oxford: Blackwell, 2000.

Jones, Thomas Wharton, ed. *A True Relation of the Life and Death of William Bedell.* London: Camden Society, 1872.

Joor, Johan. "Echtscheiding en scheiding van tafel en bed in Alkmaar in de periode, 1700–1810." *Tijdschrift voor Sociale Geschiedenis* 11 (1985): 197–230.

Jütte, Robert. "Das Stadtviertel als Problem und Gegenstand der frühneuzeitlichen Stadtgeschichtsforschung." *Blätter für deutsche Landesgeschichte* 127 (1991): 235–69.

Jütte, Robert. *Poverty and Deviance in Early Modern Europe.* New York: Cambridge University Press, 1994.

Kagan, Richard L. "A Golden Age of Litigation: Castille, 1500–1700." In *Disputes and Settlements: Law and Human Relations in the West,* edited by John Bossy, 145–66. Cambridge: Cambridge University Press, 1983.

Kagan, Richard L. *Lawsuits and Litigants in Castile, 1500–1700.* Chapel Hill: University of North Carolina Press, 1981.

Kamen, Henry. *La Inquisición española.* 1967. Reprint, Barcelona: Crítica, 1988.

Kaplan, Steven L. *La fin des corporations.* Paris: Fayard, 2001.

Kaplan, Steven L. "l'Apprentisage au XVIIIe siècle: le cas de Paris." *Revue d'Histoire Moderne et Contemporaine* 40 (1993): 436–79.

Kaplan, Steven Laurence. "Les corporations, les 'faux ouvriers' et le faubourg Saint-Antoine au XVIIIe siècle." *Annales ESC* 43 (1988): 353–78.

Kaplan, Steven Laurence. "Réflexions sur la police du monde du travail, 1700–1815." *Revue historique* 103 (1979): 17–77.

Kaplan, Steven Laurence. *The Bakers of Paris and the Bread Question, 1700–1775.* Durham: Duke University Press, 1996.

Karge, Henrik, ed. *Vision oder Wirklichkeit: Die spanische Malerei der Neuzeit.* Munich: Klinkhardt & Biermann, 1991.

Kaschuba, Wolfgang, and Carola Lipp. *Dörfliches Überleben: Zur Geschichte materieller und sozialer Reproduktion ländlicher Gesellschaft im 19. und frühen 20. Jahrhundert.* Ph.D. diss., Untersuchungen des Ludwig-Uhland-Instituts der Universität Tübingen 56. Tübingen: Tübinger Vereinigung für Volkskunde, 1992.

Kaschuba, Wolfgang. "Ritual und Fest. Das Volk auf der Straße." In *Dynamik der Tradition. Studien zur historischen Kulturforschung IV,* edited by Richard van Dülmen, 240–67. Frankfurt am Main: Fischer, 1992.

Keane, John. *Civil Society: Old Images, New Visions.* Cambridge: Polity Press, 1998.

Kent, Joan R. *The English Village Constable, 1580–1642: A Social and Administrative Study.* Oxford: Clarendon Press, 1986.

Keunen, A. and H. Roodenburg, eds. "Ongaarne beticht en bevlekt." In *Schimpen en schelden. Eer en belediging in Nederland, ca. 1600–1850* (a special volume of *Volkskundig Bulletin* 18,3 1992): 415–31.

King, Peter. *Crime, Justice and Discretion in England, 1740–1820.* Oxford: Oxford University Press, 2000.

Kingdon, Robert M. "Calvin and the Family: The Work of the Consistory of Geneva." *Pacific Theological Review* 17 (1984): 5–18.

Kingdon, Robert M. "Social Control and Political Control in Calvin's Geneva." In *Die Reformation in Deutschland und Europa: Interpretationen und Debatten,* edited by Hans R. Guggisberg and Gottfried G. Krodel, 521–32. Gütersloh: Gütersloher Verlagshaus, 1993.

Kingdon, Robert M. "The Control of Morals in Calvin's Geneva." In *The Social History of the Reformation,* edited by Lawrence P. Buck and Jonathan W. Zophy, 3–16. Columbus: Ohio State University Press, 1972.

Kingdon, Robert M. *Adultery and Divorce in Calvin's Geneva.* Cambridge: Harvard University Press, 1995.

Kloek, Els. *Wie hij zij, man of wijf: Vrouwengeschiedenis en de vroegmoderne tijd.* Hilversum: Verloren, 1990.

Knevel, Paul. *Burgers in het geweer: De schutterijen in Holland, 1550–1700.* Hilversum: Verloren, 1994.

Kobelt-Groch, Marion. "Unter Zechern, Spielern und Häschern: Täufer im Wirtshaus." *Aussenseiter* (1997): 111–27.

Köhler, Walther. *Zürcher Ehegericht und Genfer Consistorium.* 2 vols. Leipzig: Heinsius, 1932, 1942.

Koller, Heinrich, ed. *Reformation Kaiser Sigismunds.* Stuttgart: Hiersemann, 1964.

Konersmann, Frank. *Kirchenregiment und Kirchenzucht im frühneuzeitlichen Kleinstaat: Studien zu den herrschaftlichen und gesellschaftlichen Grundlagen des Kirchenregiments der Herzöge von Pfalz-Zweibrücken, 1410–1793.* Speyer: Verlag der Zechnerschen Buchdruckerei, 1996.

Kottmann, Peter. "Gogerichte in der Agrargesellschaft des Hochstifts Osnabrück (1500–1800)." *Historische Mitteilungen* 11 (1998): 1–22.

Krausman Ben-Amos, Ilana. "Failure to Become Freemen: Urban Apprentices in Early Modern England." *Social History* 16 (1991): 154–72

Krausman Ben-Amos, Ilana. "Women Apprentices in the Trades and Crafts of Early Modern Bristol." *Continuity and Change* 6 (1991): 227–52.

Krausman Ben-Amos, Ilana. *Adolescence and Youth in Early Modern England.* New Haven: Yale University Press, 1994.

Kruft, Hanno-Walter. *Städte in Utopia: Die Idealstadt vom 15. bis zum 18. Jahrhundert zwischen Staatsutopie und Wirklichkeit.* München: 1989.

Krug-Richter, Barbara. "Konfliktregulierung zwischen dörflicher Sozialkontrolle und patrimonialer Gerichtsbarkeit: Das Rügegericht in der Westfälischen Gerichtsherrschaft Canstein, 1718/1719." *Historische Anthropologie* 5 (1997): 212–28.

Krug-Richter, Barbara. "Von nackten Hummeln und Schandpflastern: Formen und Kontexte von Rauf- und Ehrenhändeln in der westfälischen Gerichtsherrschaft Canstein um 1700." In *Streitkultur(en): Studien zu Gewalt, Konflikt und Kommunikation in der ländlichen Gesellschaft, 16.-19. Jh.*, edited by Magnus Eriksson and Barbara Krug-Richter, 269–307. Köln: Böhlau, 2003.

Küch, Friedrich, ed. *Quellen zur Rechtsgeschichte der Stadt Marburg.* Vol. 1. Marburg: Elwert, 1918.

Kuhr, Olaf. *'Die Macht des Bannes und der Buße': Kirchenzucht und Erneuerung der Kirche bei Johannes Oekolampad (1482–1531).* Bern: Peter Lang, 1999.

Kümin, Beat. "Useful to Have, But Difficult to Govern: Inns and Taverns in Early Modern Bern and Vaud." *Journal of Early Modern History* 3 (1999): 153–75.

Küther, Carsten. *Menschen auf der Strasse: Vagierende Unterschichten in Bayern, Franken und Schwaben in der zweiten Hälfte des 18. Jahrhunderts.* Göttingen: Vandenhoeck & Ruprecht, 1983.

Labouvie, Eva. *Andere Umstände: Eine Kulturgeschichte der Geburt.* Köln: Böhlau, 1998.

Labouvie, Eva. *Zauberei und Hexenwerk: Ländlicher Hexenglaube in der frühen Neuzeit.* Frankfurt am Main: Fischer, 1991.

Labrot, Gérard. *Etudes Napolitaines: Villages-palais-collections XVI–XVII siècles.* Seyssel: Champ Vallon, 1993.

Lacour, Eva. "Faces of Violence Revisited: A Typology of Violence in Early Modern Rural Germany." *Journal of Social History* 35 (2001): 649–68.

Lacour, Eva. *Schlägereyen und Unglücksfälle: Zur Historischen Psychologie und Typologie von Gewalt in der frühneuzeitlichen Eifel.* Egelsbach: Dr. Hänsel-Hohenhausen, 2000.

Laing, David, ed. *The Work of John Knox.* Vol. 4. Edinburgh, 1855.

Lake, Peter. "'A Charitable Christian Hatred': The Godly and Their Enemies in the 1630s." In *The Culture of English Puritanism, 1560–1700*, edited by Christopher Durston and Jaqueline Eales, 145–86. London: Macmillan, 1996.

Lane, Joan. *Apprenticeship in England, 1600–1914.* London: University College London Press, 1996.

Lanza García, Ramón. "Ciudades y villas en la Cornisa Cantábrica." *Imágenes de la diversidad. El mundo urbano en la Corona de Castilla (s. XVI-XVIII)*, edited by José I. Fortea. Santander: Servicio de Publicaciones de la Universidad de Cantabria & Asamblea Regional de Cantabria, 1997.

Lanza García, Ramón. *La población y el crecimiento económico de Cantabria e el Antiguo Régimen.* Madrid: Ediciones de la Universidad Autónoma de Madrid/Servicio de Publicaciones de la Universidad de Cantabria, 1991.

Laqueur, Thomas. *Making Sex: Body and Gender from the Greeks to Freud*. Cambridge: Harvard University Press, 1990.

Laslett, Peter, and Richard Wall, eds. *Household and Family in Past Time: Comparative Studies in the Size and Structure of the Domestic Group Over the Last Three Centuries in England, France, Serbia, Japan and Colonial North America, with Further Materials from Western Europe*. London: Cambridge University Press, 1978 (1st ed. 1972).

Laslett, Peter. "Family, Kinship and Collectivity as Systems of Support in Pre-Industrial Europe: A Consideration of the 'Nuclear-Hardship' Hypothesis." *Continuity and Change* 3, 2 (1988): 153–75.

Laslett, Peter. *The World We Have Lost*. 2nd ed. London: Methuen, 1971.

Le Bras, Gabriel. "De la sociologie rurale à la sociologie urbaine." In *Etudes de sociologie religieuse*. Vol. 2, 418–89. Paris: Presses universitaires de France, 1955.

Le Goff, Jacques, and Jean-Claude Schmitt, eds. *Le charivari: Actes de la table ronde organisée à Paris*. Paris: Ecole des Hautes Etudes en Sciences Sociales, 1981.

Le Play, Pierre G. Frédéric. *Campesinos y pescadores en el Norte de España*. Madrid: Publicaciones del Ministerio de Agricultura, Pesca y Alimentación, 1990 (Spanish information from his report on *Les ouvriers européens, 1877–1879*).

Leeson, R. A. *Travelling Brothers: The Six Centuries' Road from Craft Fellowship to Trade Unionism*. London: Allen and Unwin, 1979.

Lehfeldt, Elizabeth A. "Convents As Litigants: Dowry and Inheritance Disputes in Early Modern Spain." *Journal of Social History* 3, 33 (2000): 645–64.

Leineweber, Luise. *Bologna nach dem Tridentinum: Private Kunststiftungen und Kunstaufträge im Kontext der katholischen Konfessionalisierung*. Hildesheim: Olms, 2000.

Leneman, Leah. "Defamation in Scotland, 1750–1800." *Continuity and Change* 15 (2000): 209–34.

LeNeve, John. *Fasti Ecclesiae Anglicanae*. London: Historical Institute, 1716.

Lenman, Bruce, and Geoffrey Parker. "The State, the Community and the Criminal Law in Early Modern Europe." In *Crime and the Law: The Social History of Crime in Western Europe since 1500,* edited by V. A. C. Gatrell et al., 11–48. London: Europa Publications, 1980.

Lennon, Colm. "Dives and Lazarus in Sixteenth-Century Ireland." In *Luxury and Austerity: Historical Studies XXI,* edited by Jacqueline Hill and Colm Lennon, 46–65. Dublin: University College Dublin Press, 1999.

Lennon, Colm. *The Lords of Dublin in the Age of Reformation*. Dublin: Irish Academic Press, 1989.

Lessing, Doris. "The Temptation of Jack Orkney." In idem, *Collected Stories*. Vol. 2, 7–26. London: Cape, 1979.

Leuker. "Schelmen, hoeren." In *Schimpen en schelden,* edited by Keunen and Roodenburg, 314–39 (further: see p. 529).

Liebig, Heinz. "Confessio Augustana De rebus civilibus - Ordnungen für den

Menschen: Unterrichtung der Gewissen im Gebrauch christlicher Freiheit." In *Humanismus - Reformation–Konfession,* edited by Wolfgang Bienert and Wolfgang Hage. Marburg: Elwert, 1986.

Liliequist, J. "Violence, Honour and Manliness in Early Modern Northern Sweden." In *Crime and Control in Europe from the Past to the Present,* edited by M. Lappalainen and P. Hirvonen. Helsinki: Publications of the History of Criminality Research Project, Academy of Finland, 1999.

Lillo, George. *The London Merchant: Or, the History of George Barnwell.* London, 1731.

Lindenberger, Thomas, and Alf Lüdtke, eds. *Physische Gewalt: Studien zur Geschichte der Neuzeit.* Frankfurt am Main: Suhrkamp, 1995.

Lis, Catharina, and Hugo Soly. "An 'Irresistible Phalanx': Journeymen Associations in Western Europe, 1300–1800." In *Before the Unions: Wage Earners and Collective Action in Europe, 1300–1850,* International Review of Social History, supplement 2, edited by Catharina Lis et al., 11–52. Cambridge: Cambridge University Press, 1994.

Lis, Catharina, and Hugo Soly. "De macht van 'vrije arbeiders': collectieve acties van hoedenmakersgezellen in de Zuidelijke Nederlanden (zestiende-negentiende eeuw)." In *Werken volgens de regels: Ambachten in Brabant en Vlaanderen, 1500–1800,* edited by Catharina Lis and Hugo Soly, 15–50. Brussels: VUB Press, 1994.

Lis, Catharina, and Hugo Soly. "Entrepreneurs, corporations et autorités publiques au Brabant et en Flandre à la fin de l'Ancien Régime." *Revue du Nord* 76 (1994): 725–44.

Lis, Catharina, and Hugo Soly. "Neighborhood Social Change in West European Cities, Sixteenth to Nineteenth Centuries," *International Review of Social History* 38 (1993): 1–30.

Lis, Catharina, and Hugo Soly. *Poverty and Capitalism in Pre-Industrial Europe.* Atlantic Highlands, N.J.: Humanities Press, 1979.

Little, Lester K. *Liberty, Charity, Fraternity: Lay Religious Confraternities at Bergamo in the Age of the Commune.* Bergamo: P. Lubrina, 1988.

Little, Lester K. *Religious Poverty and the Profit Economy in Medieval Europe.* Ithaca: Cornell University Press, 1978.

Llorens, Tomás. "Zwei Anmerkungen über die spanische Kunst." In exhibition catalog, *Spanische Kunst am Ende des Jahrhunderts,* 35–51. Museum Würth, Künzelsau, 24.1.–26.5.1999. Sigmaringen: Thorbecke, 1999.

López Muñoz, Miguel Luis. *La labor benéfico-social de las cofradías en la Granada Moderna.* Granada: Servicio de Publicaciones de la Universidad de Granada, 1994.

López Torrijos, Rosa. *La mitología en la pintura española del Siglo de Oro.* Madrid: Cátedra, 1985.

López Vela, Roberto. "La Inquisición de la época confesional en el mundo urbano (1550–1740)." In *Imágenes de la diversidad. El mundo urbano en la Corona de Castilla (s. XVI-XVIII),* edited by José I. Fortea. Santander: Servicio de Publicaciones de la Universidad de Cantabria & Asamblea Regional de Cantabria, 1997.

Lopez, Roberto S. "Hard Times and Investment in Culture." In *The Renaissance: A Symposium,* edited by Wallace C. Ferguson, 29–54. New York: Metropolitan Museum of Art, 1953.

Lopez, Roberto S. "The Crossroads within the Wall." In *The Historian and the City,* edited by O. Handlin and J. Burchard, 27–43. Cambridge: Harvard University Press, 1963.

López-Rey, José. "Goya's Drawing of Pietro Torrigiano." *Gazette des Beaux-Arts* 27 (1945): 165–70.

Lorenzen-Schmidt, Klaus-J. "Beleidigungen in schleswig-holsteinischen Städten im 16. Jahrhundert. Soziale Norm und soziale Kontrolle in Städtegesellschaften." *Kieler Blätter zur Volkskunde* 10 (1978): 5–27.

Lorenzo Pinar, Francisco J. *Amores inciertos, amores frustrados. Conflictividad y transgresiones matrimoniales en Zamora en el siglo XVII.* Zamora: Semuret, 1999.

Lorenz-Schmidt, Sabine. *Vom Wert und Wandel weiblicher Arbeit: Geschlechtsspezifische Arbeitsteilung in der Landwirtschaft in Bildern des Spätmittelalters und der Frühen Neuzeit.* Stuttgart: Steiner Verlag, 1998.

Lottes, Günther. "Disziplin und Emanzipation: Das Sozialdisziplinierungskonzept und die Interpretation der frühneuzeitlichen Geschichte." *Westfälische Forschungen* 42 (1992): 63–74.

Lotz-Heumann, Ute. *Die doppelte Konfessionalisierung in Irland: Konflikt und Koexistenz im 16. und in der ersten Hälfte des 17. Jahrhunderts.* Tübingen: Mohr Siebeck, 2000.

Lotz-Heumann, Ute. *Konfessionalisierung in Irland: Religion, Gesellschaft und staatlich-politischer Wandel im 16. und in der ersten Hälfte des 17. Jahrhunderts.* Berlin: Mohr Siebeck, 1998.

Lourens, Piet, and Jan Lucassen. "Ambachtsgilden binnen een handelskapitalistische stad: aanzetten voor een analyse van Amsterdam rond 1700." *NEHA-Jaarboek voor Economische, Bedrijfs- en Techniekgeschiedenis* 61 (1998): 121–62.

Lucassen, Jan. "Het welvaren van Leiden (1659–1662): de wording van een economische theorie over gilden en ondernemerschap." In *De kracht der zwakken: studies over arbeid en arbeidersbeweging in het verleden,* edited by Boudien de Vries et al., 13–48. Amsterdam: IISG, 1992.

Lupton, Thomas. *Siuqila: Too Good to Be True.* London: 1580.

Luther, Martin. "An den christlichen Adel deutscher Nation von des christlichen Standes Besserung." In idem, *Werkausgabe.* Vol. 6, 405–69. Weimar: Böhlau, 1888.

Mabbs, A. W., ed. *Guild Stewards' Book of the Borough of Calne, 1561–1688.* Wiltshire Record Society, vol. 7. Devizes, 1953.

MacCavitt, John. "Lord Deputy Chichester and the English Government's 'Mandates Policy' in Ireland, 1605–1607." *Recusant History* 20 (1991): 320–35.

MacErlean, John. *The Sodality of the Blessed Virgin Mary in Ireland: A Short History.* Dublin: Office of the *Irish Messenger,* 1928.

Machyn, Henry. *The Diary of Henry Machyn, Citizen and Merchant-Taylor of London, from AD 1550 to AD 1563.* Edited by John Gough Nichols. Camden Society, old series, vol. 42. London, 1848.

MacKenney, Richard. *Tradesmen and Traders: The World of the Guilds in Venice and Europe, c.1250-c.1650.* London: Croom Helm, 1987.

Mâle, Emile. *L'art religieux en France aprés la Concile de Trente.* Paris: [no publisher], 1932.

Mantecón Movellán, Tomás A. "Criminals and Royal Pardon in 18th-Century Spain." *Le pardon. Cahiers de l'insitut d'Anthropologie Juridique* 3 (1999): 477–506.

Mantecón Movellán, Tomás A. "El peso de la infrajudicialidad en el control del crimen durante la Edad Moderna." *Estudis* (2003): 43–75.

Mantecón Movellán, Tomás A. "Popular Culture and Arbitration of Disputes in the Northern Spanish 18th Century." In *Crimes, Punishment and Reform in Europe,* edited by Louis A. Knafla. Westport, Conn.: Praeger Publishers, Greenwood Publishing Group, 2003.

Mantecón Movellán, Tomás A. *Conflictividad y disciplinamiento social en la Cantabria rural del Antiguo Régimen.* Santander: Servicio de Publicaciones de la Universidad de Cantabria & Fundación Marcelino Botín Sanz de Sautuola, 1997.

Mantecón Movellán, Tomás A. *Contrarreforma y religiosidad popular en Cantabria. Las cofradías religiosas.* Santander: Servicio de Publicaciones de la Universidad de Cantabria & Asamblea Regional de Cantabria, 1990.

Mantecón Movellán, Tomás A. *La muerte de Antonia Isabel Sánchez. Tiranía y escándalo en una sociedad rural del Norte español en el Antiguo Régimen.* Alcalá de Henares: Centro de Estudios Cervantinos de la Universidad de Alcalá de Henares, 1998.

Marsh, Peter, and Anne Campbell, eds. *Aggression and Violence.* Oxford: Blackwell, 1982.

Martín, E. "Aprendices y domésticos en el Alto Palancia: una estrategia familiar." In *Familia, casa y* trabajo, edited by F. Chacónand L. Ferrer i Alós. Murcia: Servicio de Publicaciones de la Universidad de Murcia, 1997.

Martínez Ripoll, Antonio. "Control inquisitorial y figuración artística: Villafranca mejorado por Murillo." *Cuadernos de Arte e Iconografía* 2, 4 (1989): 20–29, plates 5–7.

Martschukat, Jürgen. *Inszeniertes Töten: Eine Geschichte der Todesstrafe vom 17. bis zum 19. Jahrhundert.* Köln: Böhlau, 2000.

Maruri Villanueva, Ramón. *La burguesía mercantil santanderina, 1700–1850.* Santander: Servicio de Publicaciones de la Universidad de Cantabria & Asamblea Regional de Cantabria, 1990.

Maurer, Wilhelm. "Luther und die Schwärmer." In *Luther und die europäischen Bekenntnisse,* edited by Ernst-Wilhelm Köhls and Gerhard Müller, 103–33. Göttingen: Vandenhoeck & Ruprecht, 1970.

Mauss, Marcel. *The Gift: The Form and Reason for Exchange in Archaic Societies,* translated by W. D. Halls, foreword by Mary Douglas. London: Routledge, 1990 (1st ed. 1923).

Mayhew, Graham. *Tudor Rye.* Falmer: Centre for Continuing Education, University of Sussex, 1987.

McBurney, William H., ed. *The London Merchant.* London: Edward Arnold, 1965.

McCarthy, Daniel, ed. *Collections on Irish Church History, from the Manuscripts of the Late . . . Laurence F. Renehan.* Vol. 1. Dublin: C. M. Warren, 1861.

McIntosh, Marjorie Keniston. *A Community Transformed: The Manor and Liberty of Havering, 1500–1620.* Cambridge: Cambridge University Press, 1991.

McIntosh, Marjorie Keniston. *Controlling Misbehavior in England, 1370–1600.* Cambridge: Cambridge University Press, 1998.

McIntosh, Marjorie. "Local Change and Community Control in England, 1465–1500." *Huntington Library Quarterly* 49 (1986): 219–42.

McMahon, Sean H. *Social Control and Public Intellect: The Legacy of Edward A. Ross.* New Brunswick, NJ: Transaction Publishers, 1999.

McNeill, Charles, ed. *The Tanner Letters: Original Documents and Notices of Irish Affairs in the Sixteenth and Seventeenth Centuries.* Dublin: Stationary Office, 1943.

McRee, Ben R. "Religious Gilds and Regulation of Behavior in Late Medieval Towns." In *People, Politics, and Community in the Later Middle Ages,* edited by Joel Rosenthal and Colin Richmond, 221–33. Gloucester: Alan Sutton, 1987.

McRee, Ben. "Religious Gilds and Civic Order: The Case of Norwich in the Late Middle Ages." *Speculum* 21, 67 (1992): 69–97.

Meldrum, Tim. "A Women's Court in London: Defamation at the Bishop of London's Consistory Court, 1700–1745." *London Journal* 19 (1994): 1–20.

Memoria Benedicta Dn. D. Theodori Zvingeri à Joh. Rodolpho Wetstenio S.S. Theol. Doct. and Professore. Basel: 1655.

Mentzer, Raymond A. "Disciplina Nervus Ecclesiae: The Calvinist Reform of Morals at Nîmes." *Sixteenth-Century Journal* 18 (1987): 89–115.

Mentzer, Raymond A. *Blood and Belief: Family Survival and Confessional Identity among the Provincial Huguenot Nobility.* West Lafayette, Ind.: Purdue University Press, 1994.

Mentzer, Raymond A., ed. *Sin and the Calvinists: Morals Control and the Consistory in the Reformed Tradition.* Kirksville, Mo.: Sixteenth Century Journal Publishers, 1994.

Mentzer, Raymond A., Jr. "Organizational Endeavour and Charitable Impulse in Sixteenth-Century France: The Case of Protestant Nîmes." *French History* 5, 1 (1991): 1–29.

Mergel, Thomas, and Thomas Welskopp, eds. *Geschichte zwischen Kultur und Gesellschaft: Beiträge zur Theoriedebatte.* München: Beck, 1997.

Meumann, Markus, and Dirk Niefanger, eds. *Ein Schauplatz herber Angst. Wahrnehmung und Darstellung von Gewalt im 17. Jahrhundert.* Göttingen: Wallstein, 1997.

Miedema, Hessel, ed. *De Archiefbescheiden van het St. Lucasgilde te Haarlem, 1497–1798.* Alphen a/d Rijn: Canaletto, 1980.

Miller, Pavla. *Transformations of Patriarchy in the West, 1500–1900.* Bloomington: Indiana University Press, 1998.

Milward, Peter. *Religious Controversies of the Elizabethan Age: A Survey of Printed Sources.* London: Scolar Press, 1977.

Mitchell, D., ed. *Goldsmiths, Silversmiths and Bankers: Innovation and the Transfer of Skill, 1550–1750.* Phoenix Mill: Alan Sutton, 1995.

Mitchison, Rosalind, and Leah Leneman. *Sexuality and Social Control: Scotland, 1660–1780.* Oxford: Blackwell, 1989.

Mitteraurer, Michael. *Ledige Mütter. Zur Geschichte illegitimer Geburten in Europa.* München: Beck, 1983.

Molas Ribalta, Pedro. *Los gremios barceloneses del siglo XVIII: la estructura corporativa ante el comienzo de la Revolución Industrial.* Madrid: Confederación Española de Cajas de Ahorros, 1970.

Monter, E. William. "The Consistory of Geneva, 1559–1569." *Bibliothèque d'Humanisme et Renaissance* 38 (1976): 467–84.

Monter, William. *Frontiers of Heresy: The Spanish Inquisition from the Basque Lands to Sicily.* Cambridge: Cambridge University Press, 1990.

Montias, John Michael. "Art Dealers in the Seventeenth-Century Netherlands." *Simiolus* 18 (1988): 244–56.

Montias, John Michael. *Artists and Artisans in Delft: A Socio-Economic Study of the Seventeenth Century.* Princeton: Princeton University Press, 1982.

Moran, Patrick Francis, ed. *Memoirs of the Most Rev. Oliver Plunkett, Archbishop of Armagh, and Primate of All Ireland.* Dublin: James Duffy, 1861.

Moran, Patrick Francis. *History of the Catholic Archbishops of Dublin since the Reformation.* Dublin: James Duffy, 1864.

Morard, Nicholas. "Une charité bien ordonnée: La confrérie du St-Esprit à Fribourg à la fin du Moyen Age (XIVe-XVe siècles)." In *Le mouvement confraternel au Moyen Âge: France, Italie, Suisse,* edited by Agostino Paravincini Bagliani, 275–96. Geneva: Droz, 1987.

Moreno, A. "Pequeña nobleza rural, sistema de herencia y estructura de la propiedad de la tierra de Plasencia del Monte (Huesca), 1600–1850." In *Poder, familia y consanguinidad en la España del Antiguo Régimen,* edited by F. Chacón and J. Hernández. Barcelona: Anthropos, 1992.

Muchembled, Robert. *Culture populaire et culture des élites dans la France moderne, 15e-18e siècles.* Paris: Flammarion, 1978.

Muchembled, Robert. *Die Erfindung des modernen Menschen: Gefühlsdifferenzierung und kollektive Verhaltensweisen im Zeitalter des Absolutismus.* Reinbeck bei Hamburg: Rowohlt, 1990.

Muchembled, Robert. *L'invention de l'homme moderne : Sensibilités, moeurs et comportements collectifs sous l'Ancien Régime.* Paris: Hachette, 1988.

Muir, Edward. "The Double Binds of Manly Revenge in Renaissance Italy.'" In *Gender Rhetorics: Postures of Dominance and Submission in History,* edited by Richard G. Trexler, 65–82. Binghamton, N.Y.: Cemers, 1994.

Muir, Edward. *Mad Blood Stirring: Vendetta and Factions in Friuli during the Renaissance.* Baltimore: Johns Hopkins University Press, 1993.

Münch, Paul. "Kirchenzucht und Nachbarschaft: Zur sozialen Problematik des calvinistischen Seniorats um 1600." In *Kirche und Visitation: Beiträge zur Erforschung des frühneuzeitlichen Visitationswesens in Europa,* edited by Ernst Walter Zeeden and Peter Thaddeus Lang, 216–48. Tübingen: Klett-Cotta, 1984.

Münch, Paul. *Zucht und Ordnung: Reformierte Kirchenverfassungen im 16. und 17. Jahrhundert.* Stuttgart: Klett-Cotta, 1978.

Münkler, Herfried, and Harald Bluhm, eds. *Gemeinwohl und Gemeinsinn: Historische Semantik politischer Leitbegriffe.* 2 vols. Berlin: Akademie-Verlag, 2001.

Musgrave, Elizabeth. "Women and the Craft Guilds in Eighteenth-Century Nantes." In *The Artisan and the European Town, 1500–1900,* edited by Geoffrey Crossick, 151–71. Aldershot: Scolar Press, 1997.

Myers, W. David. *Poor, Sinning Folk: Confession and Conscience in Counter-Reformation Germany.* Ithaca: Cornell University Press, 1996.

Neuschäfer, Hans-Jörg. *Macht und Ohnmacht der Zensur: Literatur, Theater und Film in Spanien (1933–1976).* Stuttgart: Metzler, 1991.

Nickolls, J., ed. *Original Letters and Papers of State, Addressed to Oliver Cromwell.* London: 1743.

Nolde, Dorothea. *Gattenmord: Macht und Gewalt in der frühneuzeitlichen Ehe.* Köln: Böhlau, 2003.

O'Malley, John W. *Trent and All That: Renaming Catholicism in the Early Modern Era.* Cambridge: Harvard University Press, 2000.

Oberli, Matthias. *Magnificentia Principis: Das Mäzenatentum des Prinzen und Kardinals Maurizio von Savoyen (1593–1657).* Weimar: VDG Verlag, 1999.

Octavio Picón, Jacinto. *Observaciones acerca del desnudo y su escasez en el arte español.* Madrid, 1902.

Oestreich, Gerhard. *Geist und Gestalt des frühmodernen Staates.* Berlin: Duncker & Humblot, 1969.

Ortega, José. *Gentes de mar.* Santander: Servicio de Publicaciones de la Universidad de Cantabria, 1996.

Osborough, W. N. "Ecclesiastical Law and the Reformation in Ireland." In *Canon Law in Protestant Lands,* edited by Richard H. Helmholz, 223–52. Berlin: Duncker & Humblot, 1992.

Österberg, Eva, and Sölvi Sogner, eds. *People Meet the Law: Control and Conflict-Handling in the Courts: The Nordic Countries in the Post-Reformation and Preindustrial Period.* Oslo: Universitetsforlaget, 2000.

Oyer, John S. *Lutheran Reformers against Anabaptists.* The Hague: Nijhoff, 1964.

Ozment, Steven E. *The Reformation in the Cities: The Appeal of Protestantism to Sixteenth-Century Germany and Switzerland.* New Haven: Yale University Press, 1975.

Ozment, Steven. *When Fathers Ruled: Family Life in Reformation Europe.* Cambridge: Harvard University Press, 1983.

Pacheco, Francisco. *Arte de la pintura.* Edited by Bonaventura Bassegoda y Hugas. Madrid: Cátedra, 1990.

Packull, Werner O. "The Melchiorites and the Ziegenhain Order of Discipline, 1538–1539." In *Anabaptism Revisited,* edited by Walter Klaassen, 11–28. Scottdale, Pa.: Herald Press, 1991.

Packull, Werner O., and Peter Tasch. "From Melchiorite to Bancrupt Wine Merchant." *Mennonite Quarterly Review* 62 (1988): 276–95.

Paiva, José Pedro, ed. *Religious Ceremonials and Images: Power and Social Meaning, 1400–1750,* Coimbra: Palimage Editors, 2002.

Palladio, Andrea. *I quattro libri dell'architettura.* Venezia, 1570 (new edition by Erik Forssman).

lmen, Eric. "De gilden en hun sociale betekenis." In *Geschiedenis van Dordrecht van 1572 tot 1813,* edited by Willem Frijhoff et al. Hilversum: Verloren, 1998.

Palomino de Castro y Velasco, Antonio. *El museo pictórico y escala óptica.* 2 vols. Madrid, 1715–1724.

Palomino de Castro y Velasco, Antonio. *Vidas.* Edited by Nina Ayala Mallory. Madrid: Alianza, 1986.

Panhuysen, Bibi. *Maatwerk: Kleermakers, naaisters, oudkleerkopers en de gilden (1500–1800).* Amsterdam: Stichting beheer IISG, 2000.

Panofsky, Erwin. "Die Perspektive als symbolische Form." *Vorträge der Bibliothek Warburg 1924/25,* 258–330. Leipzig/Berlin, 1937.

Panofsky, Erwin. *Grundfragen der Kunstwissenschaft.* Berlin, 1964.

Park, Robert E., and E. W. Burgess. *Introduction to the Science of Sociology.* Chicago: University of Chicago Press, 1924.

Parker, Charles H. *The Reformation of Community: Social Welfare and Calvinist Charity in Holland, 1572–1620.* Cambridge: Cambridge University Press, 1998.

Parry, G. J. R. *A Protestant Vision: William Harrison and the Reformation of Elizabethan England.* Cambridge: Cambridge University Press, 1987.

Peltonen, Markku. *The Duel in Early Modern England: Civility, Politeness and Honour.* Cambridge: Cambridge University Press, 2003.

Pepys, Samuel. *The Diary of Samuel Pepys.* Edited by Robert C. Latham and William Matthews. 11 vols. London: G. Bell and Sons, 1970–1983.

Pérez García, P., and J. A. Catalá Sanz. *Epígonos del encubertismo. Proceso contra los agermanados de 1541.* Valencia: Biblioteca Valenciana, Colección Historia, 2000.

Pérez García, Pablo. "Conflicto y represión: la justicia penal ante la Germanía de Valencia (1519–1523)." *Estudis* 22 (1996): 185–98.

Pérez Villanueva, Joaquín, and Bartolomé Escandell Bonet, eds. *Historia de la Inquisición en España y América.* Vol. 1. Madrid: La Editorial Católica, 1984.

Pérez, Isabel. *Pecar, delinquir y castigar: el tribunal eclesiástico de Coria en los siglos XVI y XVII.* Cáceres: Institución Cultural 'El Brocense,' 1992.

Pérez, V., and D. Reher. "La población urbana española entre los siglos XVI y XVIII. Una perspectiva demográfica." In *Imágenes de la diversidad. El mundo urbano en la Corona de Castilla (s. XVI-XVIII),* edited by José I. Fortea. Santander: Servicio de Publicaciones de la Universidad de Cantabria & Asamblea Regional de Cantabria, 1997.

Peristiany, John. *Mediterranean Family Structures.* Cambridge: Cambridge University Press, for the Social Research Centre of Cyprus, 1976.

Peters, Edward. *Inquisition.* New York: The Free Press, 1988.

Peters, Jan. "Leute-Fehde: Ein ritualisiertes Konfliktmuster des 16. Jahrhunderts." *Historische Anthropologie* 8 (2000): 62–97.

Pettegree, Andrew. *Emden and the Dutch Revolt: Exile and the Development of Reformed Protestantism.* Oxford: Clarendon Press, 1992.

Peveri, Patrice. "'Cette ville était alors comme un bois . . . 'Criminalité et opinion publique à Paris dans les années qui précèdent l'affaire Cartouche (1715–1721)." *Crime, Histoire et sociétés/ Crime, History and Societies* 1 (1997): 51–73.

Pitt, Jess R. "Social Control: I The Concept." In *International Encyclopedia of the Social Sciences,* edited by David L. Sills, vol. 14, 381–95. 18 volumes. New York: Macmillan and The Free Press, 1968.

Pohl, Susanne. "'Ehrlicher Totschlag' - 'Rache' - 'Notwehr': Zwischen männlichem Ehrcode und dem Primat des Stadtfriedens (Zürich 1376–1600)." In *Kulturelle Reformation: Semantische Umordnung und soziale Transformation, 1400–1600,* edited by Bernhard Jussen and Craig Koslofsky, 239–83. Göttingen: Vandenhoeck & Ruprecht, 1999.

Pollock, Linda A. *Forgotten Children: Parent - Child Relations from 1500 to 1900.* Cambridge: Cambridge University Press, 1983.

Poni, Carlo. "Local Market Rules and Practices: Three Guilds in the Same Line of Production in Early Modern Bologna." In *Domestic Strategies: Work and Family in France and Italy, 1600–1800,* edited by Stuart Woolf, 69–101. Cambridge: Cambridge University Press, 1991.

Prak, Maarten. "Corporate Politics in the Low Countries: Or, Guilds As Institutions (14th–18th Century)" (forthcoming).

Prak, Maarten. "The Carrot and the Stick: Social Control and Poor Relief in the Dutch Republic, Sixteenth to Eighteenth Centuries." In *Institutionen, Instrumente und Akteure sozialer Kontrolle und Disziplinierung im frühneuzeitlichen Europa* (Instruments and Agents of Social Control and Discipline in Early Modern Europe), edited by Heinz Schilling, 149–66. Frankfurt am Main: Vittorio Klosterman, 1999.

Prak, Maarten. "Individual, Corporation and Society: The Rhetoric of Dutch Guilds, Eighteenth Century." In *Statuts individuels,* edited by Marc Boone and Maarten Prak, 255–79. Apeldoorn: Garant, 1996.

Prak, Maarten. "Politik, Kultur, und politische Kultur: die Zünfte in den Nördlichen Niederlanden." In *Zunftlandschaften in Deutschlnd und den Niederlanden im Vergleich,* edited by Wilfried Reininghaus, 71–83. Münster: Aschendorff, 2000.

Prak, Maarten. "The Politics of Intolerance: Citizenship and Religion in the Dutch Republic, Seventeenth–Eighteenth Centuries." In *Calvinism and Religious Toleration in the Dutch Golden Age,* edited by Ronnie Po-chia Hsia and Henk van Nierop, 159–75. Cambridge: Cambridge University Press, 2002.

Priever, Andreas. "Paolo Veronese's Banquet in the House of the Levi: On a Rediscovered Drawing from the Collection of the Duc de Tallard." *Pantheon* 51 (1993): 92–100.

Pröve, Ralf. "Gewalt und Herrschaft in der Frühen Neuzeit: Formen und Formenwandel der Gewalt." *Zeitschrift für Geschichtswissenschaft* 47 (1999): 792–806.

Puff, Helmut. "ein schul / darinn wir allerlay Christliche tugend vnd zucht lernen. Ein Vergleich zweier ehedidaktischer Schriften des 16. Jahrhunderts." In *Geschlechterbeziehungen und Textfunktionen: Studien zu Eheschriften der Frühen Neuzeit,* edited by Rüdiger Schnell, 59–88. Tübingen: Max Niemeyer, 1998.

Puff, Helmut. *Sodomy in Reformation Germany and Switzerland, 1400–1600.* Chicago: University of Chicago Press, 2003.

Pullan, Brian S. *Rich and Poor in Renaissance Venice: The Social Institutions of a Catholic State, to 1620.* Cambridge: Harvard University Press, 1971.

Quast, Jenneke. "Vrouwen in gilden in Den Bosch, Utrecht en Leiden van de 14e tot en met de 16e eeuw." In *Fragmenten vrouwengeschiedenis,* vol. 1, edited by Wantje Fritschy, 17–27. The Hague: Nijhoff, 1980.

Quataert, Jean H. "The Shaping of Women's Work in Manufacturing: Guilds, Households, and the State in Central Europe, 1648–1870." *American Historical Review* 90 (1985): 1122–48.

Quint, David. "Duelling and Civility in Sixteenth-Century Italy." *I Tatti Studies* 7 (1997): 231–78.

Rabe, Horst. *Reich und Glaubensspaltung: Deutschland, 1500–1600.* München: Beck, 1989.

Radbruch, Gustav, ed. *Die Peinliche Gerichtsordnung Kaiser Karls. V. von 1532 (Carolina).* Stuttgart: Reclam, 1980.

Raff, Thomas. *Die Sprache der Materialien: Anleitung zu einer Ikonologie der Werkstoffe.* München: Deutscher Kunstverlag, 1994.

Rappaport, Steve. *Worlds within Worlds: Structures of Life in Sixteenth-Century London.* Cambridge: Cambridge University Press, 1989.

Reher, David. *La familia en España. Pasado y presente.* Madrid: Alianza, 1996.

Reinhard, Wolfgang. "Reformation, Counter-Reformation, and the Early Modern State: A Reassessment." *Catholic Historical Review* 75, 3 (1989): 383–404.

Reinhard, Wolfgang. "Zwang zur Konfessionalisierung? Prolegomena zu einer Theorie des konfessionellen Zeitalters." *Zeitschrift für historische Forschung* 10 (1983): 257–77.

Reinhard, Wolfgang. "Sprachbeherrschung und Weltherrschaft: Sprache und Sprachwissenschaft in der europäischen Expansion." In idem, *Ausgewählte Abhandlungen,* 404–36. Berlin: Duncker & Humblot, 1997.

Reininghaus, Wilfried. "Migrationen von Handwerkern: Anmerkungen zur Notwendigkeit von Theorien, Konzepten, und Modellen." In *Handwerk in Europa: Vom Spätmittelalter bis zur Frühen Neuzeit,* Schriften des Historischen Kollegs, vol. 41, edited by Knut Schulz, 194–212. Munich: Oldenbourg, 1999.

Reininghaus, Wilfried. *Die Entstehung der Gesellengilden im Spätmittelalter.* Vierteljahrschrift für Wirtschafts- und Sozialgeschichte, Vol. 71. Wiesbaden: Steiner, 1981.

Reith. "Apprentices in the German Crafts in Early Modern Times." Paper presented at the conference Apprenticeship (Middle Ages–2000), Alden Biesen, Belgium, December 8–9, 2000.

Remling, Ludwig. *Bruderschaften in Franken: Kirchen- und sozialgeschichtliche Untersuchungen zum spätmittelalterlichen und frühneuzeitlichen Bruderschaftswesen.* Würzburg: Kommissionsverlag F. Schöningh, 1986.

Repgen, Konrad. "Ferdinand III (1637–1657)." In *Dreißigjähriger Krieg und Westfälischer Friede,* edited by Franz Bosbach and Christoph Kampmann, 319–43. Paderborn: Schöningh, 1998.

Rexroth, Frank. "Der rechte und der unrechte Tod: Über die gesellschaftliche Deutung von Gewaltverbrechen in London, 1276–1340." In *du guoter tôt: Sterben im Mittelalter–Ideal und Realität,* edited by Markus J. Wenninger, 51–80. Friesach: Wieser, 1998.

Richardson, S. *The Apprentice's Vade Mecum.* London, 1733.

Robisheaux, Thomas. *Rural Society and the Search for Order in Early Modern Germany.* Cambridge: Cambridge University Press, 1989.

Roeck, Bernd. "Die Ohnmacht des Dogen und die Macht der Kunst: Marco und Agostino Barbarigo (1485–1501)." In *Architektur als politische Kultur: Philosophia practica,* edited by Hermann Hipp and Ernst Seidl, 79–92. Berlin: Reimer, 1996.

Roeck, Bernd. "Macht und Ohnmacht der Bilder: Die historische Perspektive." In *Macht und Ohnmacht der Bilder: ReFormatorisch er Bildersturm im Kontext der europäischen Geschichte,* edited by Peter Blickle, 32–63. München: Oldenbourg.

Roeck, Bernd. "Neighborhoods and the Public in German Cities of the Early Modern Period: A Magician and the Neighborhood Network." In *Private Domain, Public Inquiry, Families and Life-Style in the Netherlands and Europe, 1550 to the Present,* edited by Anton Schuurman and Pieter Spierenburg, 193–209. Hilversum: Verloren, 1996.

Roeck, Bernd. "Stadtgestalt und Macht in der europäischen Renaissance." In *Städtische Formen und Macht: Veröffentlichungen der Interdisziplinären Arbeitsgruppe Stadtkulturforschung,* edited by Michael Jansen and Werner Joël, 109–26. Aachen: n.p., 1994.

Roeck, Bernd. "Visual turn? Die neue Kulturgeschichte und die Bilder." *Geschichte and Gesellschaft* 2, 29 (2003): 294–315.

Roeck, Bernd. "Wirtschaftliche und soziale Voraussetzungen der Augsburger Baukunst zur Zeit des Elias Holl." *Architectura* 14 (1994): 119–38.

Roeck, Bernd. *Als wollt die Welt schier brechen: Eine Stadt im Zeitalter des dreissigjärigen Krieges.* München: Beck, 1991.

Roeck, Bernd. *Eine Stadt in Krieg und Frieden: Studien zur Geschichte der Reichsstadt Augsburg zwischen Kalenderstreit und Parität.* 2 vol. Göttingen: Vandenhoeck and Ruprecht, 1989.

Roeck, Bernd. *Kunstpatronage in der Frühen Neuzeit: Studien zu Kunstmarkt, Künstlern und ihren Auftraggebern in Italien und im Heiligen Römischen Reich (15.- 17. Jahrhundert).* Göttingen: Vandenhoeck & Ruprecht, 1999.

Rogers, Malcolm. *Montacute House, Somerset.* London: The National Trust, 1991.

Roodenburg, Herman. "Freundschaft, Brüderlichkeit und Einigkeit: Städtische Nachbarschaften im Westen der Republik." In *Ausbreitung bürgerlicher Kultur in den Niederlanden und Nordwestdeutschland,* edited by T. Dekker et al., 10–24. Münster: T. Coppenrath Verlag, 1991.

Roodenburg, Herman. "Naar een etnografie van de vroegmoderne stad: De 'gebuyrten' in Leiden en Den Haag." In *Cultur en maatschappij in Nederland, 1500–1850. Een historisch-antropologisch perspectief,* edited by Peter Te Boekhorst, Peter Burke, and Willem Frijhoff, 219–43. Boom: Open universiteit, Meppel en Amsterdam, Heerlen, 1992.

Roodenburg, Herman. *Onder censuur: De kerkelijke tucht in de Gereformeerde gemeente van Amsterdam, 1578–1700.* Hilversum: Verloren, 1990.

Rooijakkers, Gerard, and Tiny Romme, eds. *Charivari in de Nederlanden: Rituele sancties op deviant gedrag.* Amsterdam: P. J. Meertens Instituut, 1989.

Roper, Lyndal. *Oedipus and the Devil: Witchcraft, Sexuality and Religion in Early Modern Europe.* London: Routledge, 1994.

Roper, Lyndal. *The Holy Household: Women and Morals in Reformation Augsburg.* Oxford: Clarendon Press, 1989.

Rose Wagner, Isodora Joan. *Manuel Godoy: Patrón de las artes y coleccionista.* Madrid, 1983.

Rose, Elliot. "Too Good to Be True: Thomas Lupton's Golden Rule." In *Tudor Rule and Revolution: Essays for G. R. Elton from His American Friends,* edited by DeLloyd J. Guth and John W. McKenna, 183–200. Cambridge: Cambridge University Press, 1982.

Rosenberg, Charles M. *Art and Politics in Late Medieval and Early Renaissance Italy: 1250–1500.* Notre Dame, Ind.: University of Notre Dame Press, 1990.

Ross, Edward Alsworth. *Sin and Society: An Analysis of Latter-Day Iniquity, with a Letter from President Roosevelt.* Boston: Houghton Mifflin Company, 1907.

Ross, Edward Alsworth. *Social Control: A Survey of the Foundations of Order.* London: Macmillan, 1939 (orig. ed. 1901).

Rosser, Gervase. "Crafts, Guilds and the Negotiation of Work in the Medieval Town." *Past and Present* 154 (1997): 3–31.

Rossi, Paolo L. "The Writer and the Man, Real Crimes and Mitigating Circumstances: il caso Cellini." In *Crime, Society and the Law in Renaissance Italy,* edited by Trevor Dean and K. J. P. Lowe, 157–83. Cambridge: Cambridge University Press, 1994.

Roucek, Joseph S. and Associates. *Social Control.* Second Edition. Westport, Conn.: Greenwood Press, 1970.

Rousseaux, Xavier. "Inititative particulière et poursuite d'office: L'action pénale en Europe (XIIe-XVIIIe siècles)." *IAHCCJ Bulletin* 18 (1993): 58–92.

Rousseaux, Xavier. "Ordre moral, justices et violence: L'homicide dans les sociétés européennes. XIIIe-XVIIIe siècle." In *Ordre moral et délinquance de l'Antiquité au XXe siècle,* edited by Benoît Garnot, 65–82. Dijon: Editions universitaires de Dijon, 1994.

Rousseaux, Xavier. "From Case to Crime: Homicide Regulation in Medieval and Modern Europe." In *Die Entstehung des öffentlichen Strafrechts: Bestandsaufnahme eines europäischen Forschungsproblems,* edited by Dietmar Willoweit, 143–75. Köln: Böhlau, 1999.

Rowland, Robert. "Sistemas matrimoniales en la Península Ibérica (siglos XVI-XIX). Una perspectiva regional." In *Demografía histórica en España,* edited by V. Pérez and D. Reher. Madrid: El Arquero, 1988.

Rublack, Ulinka. *Magd, Metz' oder Mörderin: Frauen vor frühneuzeitlichen Gerichten.* Frankfurt am Main: Fischer, 1998.

Rublack, Ulinka. *The Crimes of Women in Early Modern Germany.* Oxford: Oxford University Press, 1999.

Ruiz de la Peña, J. I. "Las solidaridades vecinales en la Corona de Castilla (siglos XII-XV)." In *Cofradías, gremios, solidaridades en la Europa Medieval. XIX Semana de estudios medievales, Estella '92.* Pamplona: Departamento de Educación y Cultura, 1993.

Rumeu de Armas, Antonio. *Historia de la previsión ocial en España (cofradías, gremios, hermandades, montepíos).* Barcelona: El Albir, 1981 (1st ed. Madrid: Revista de Derecho Privado, 1944).

Rummel, Walter. "'Die Ausrottung des abscheulichen Hexerey Lasters': Zur Bedeutung populärer Religiosität in einer dörflichen Hexenverfolgung des 17. Jahrhunderts." In *Volksreligiosität in der modernen Sozialgeschichte,* edited by Wolfgang Schieder, 51–72. Göttingen: Vandenhoeck & Ruprecht, 1986.

Rummel, Walter. "Verletzung von Körper, Ehre und Eigentum: Varianten im Umgang mit Gewalt in Dörfern des 17. Jahrhunderts." In *Mit den Waffen der Justiz: Zur Kriminalitätsgeschichte des späten Mittelalters und der frühen Neuzeit,* edited by Andreas Blauert and Gerd Schwerhoff, 86–114. Frankfurt am Main: Fischer, 1993.

Ryter, Annamarie. *Als Weibsbild bevogtet: Zum Alltag von Frauen im 19. Jahrhundert. Geschlechtsvormundschaft und Ehebeschränkungen im Kanton Basel-Landschaft.* Liestal: Kantonsverlag, 1994.

Sabean, David Warren. "Family and Land Tenure: A Case Study of Conflict in the German Peasants' War (1525)." *Peasant Studies Newsletter* 3 (1974): 1–15.

Sabean, David Warren. *Power in the Blood: Popular Culture and Village Discourse in Early Modern Germany.* Cambridge: Cambridge University Press, 1984.

Sack, Fritz. "Strafrechtliche Kontrolle und Sozialdisziplinierung." *Jahrbuch für Rechtssoziologie und Rechtstheorie* 15 (1993): 16–45.

Safley, Thomas M. "Canon Law and Swiss Reform: Legal Theory and Practice in the Marital Courts of Zurich, Bern, Basel, and St. Gall." In *Canon Law in Protestant Lands,* edited by Richard H. Helmholz, Comparative Studies in Continental and Anglo-American Legal History, no. 11, 187–201. Berlin: Duncker & Humblot, 1992.

Safley, Thomas M. "Civic Morality and the Domestic Economy." In *The German People and the Reformation,* edited by R. Po-chia Hsia, 173–92. Ithaca: Cornell University Press, 1988.

Safley, Thomas M. *Let No Man Put Asunder: The Control of Marriage in the German Southwest: A Comparative Study, 1550–1600.* Kirksville, Mo.: Sixteenth Century Journal Publishers, 1984.

Sälter, Gerhard. "Lokale Ordnung und soziale Kontrolle in der frühen Neuzeit." *Kriminologisches Journal* 32 (2000): 19–42.

Scamozzi, Vincenzo. *Idea dell'architettura universale.* Vol. 2, pt. 6. Venezia, 1615.

Schama, Simon. *The Embarrassment of Riches: An Interpretation of Dutch Culture in the Golden Age.* London: Collins, 1987.

Scheerer, Sebastian, and Henner Hess. "Social Control: A Defence and Reformulation." In *Social Control and Political Order,* edited by Roberto Bergalli and Colin Sumner, 96–130. London: Sage Publications, 1997.

Schilling, Heinz, and Marie-Antoinette Gross, eds. *"Minderheiten" und "Erziehung" im Spannungsfeld von Staat und Kirche,* Zeitschrift für Historische Forschung, Beiheft. Berlin: Duncker & Humblot, 2003.

Schilling, Heinz. "Profil und Perspektiven einer interdisziplinären und komparatistischen Disziplinierungsforschung jenseits einer Dichotomie von Gesellschafts—und Kulturgeschichte." In *Institutionen, Instrumente und Akteure sozialer Kontrolle und Disziplinierung im frühneuzeitlichen Europa* (Instruments and agents of social control and discipline in early modern Europe), edited by Heinz Schilling, 3–36. Frankfurt am Main: Vittorio Klosterman, 1999.

Schilling, Heinz. "Die Kirchensucht im frühneuzeitlichen Europa in interkonfessionell vergleichender und interdisziplinärer Perspektive—eine Zwischenbilanz." In *Kirchenzucht und Sozialdisziplinierung im frühneuzeitlichen Europa,* edited by Heinz Schilling, 11–40. Berlin: Duncker & Humblot, 1994.

Schilling, Heinz, ed. *Institutionen, Instrumente und Akteure sozialer Kontrolle und Disziplinierung im frühneuzeitlichen Europa/ Institutions /Instruments and agents of social control and discipline in early modern Europe,* Ius Commune, Sonderheft nr. 127. Frankfurt am Main: Vittorio Klostermann, 1999.

Schilling, Heinz, ed. *Kirchenzucht und Sozialdisziplinierung im frühneuzeitlichen Europa.* Berlin: Duncker & Humblot, 1994.

Schilling, Heinz. "Confessional Europe." In *Handbook of European History, 1400–1600: Late Middle Ages, Renaissance, and Reformation,* edited by Thomas A. Brady, Jr., Heiko A. Oberman, and James D. Tracy, vol. 2, 641–81. Leiden: E. J. Brill, 1995.

Schilling, Heinz. "Die Konfessionalisierung von Kirche, Staat und Gesellschaft: Profil, Leistung, Defizite und Perspektiven eines geschichtswissenschaftlichen Paradigmas." In *Die katholische Konfessionalisierung: Wissenschaftliches Symposion der Gesellschaft zur Herausgabe des Corpus Catholicorum und des Vereins für Reformationsgeschichte,* edited by Wolfgang Reinhard and Heinz Schilling, 1–49. Gütersloh: Gütersloher Verlagshaus, 1995.

Schilling, Heinz. "Disziplinierung oder 'Selbstregulierung der Untertanen'? Ein Plädoyer für die Doppelperspektive von Makro- und Mikrohistorie bei der Erforschung der frühmodernen Kirchenzucht." *Historische Zeitschrift* 264 (1997): 675–91.

Schilling, Heinz. "History of Crime or History of Sin: Some Reflections on the Social

History of Early Modern Church Discipline." In *Politics and Society in Reformation Europe: Essays for Sir Geoffrey Elton on His Sixty-Fifth Birthday*, edited by E. I. Kouri and Tom Scott, 289–310. London: Macmillan, 1987.

Schilling, Heinz. "Sündenzucht und frühneuzeitliche Sozialdisziplinierung: Die calvinistische, presbyteriale Kirchenzucht in Emden vom 16. bis 19. Jahrhundert." In *Stände und Gesellschaft im Alten Reich*, edited by Georg Schmidt, 265–302. Stuttgart: Steiner, 1989.

Schilling, Heinz. "'Geschichte der Sünde' oder ,Geschichte des Verbrechens'?: Überlegungen zur Gesellschaftsgeschichte der frühneuzeitlichen Kirchenzucht." *Annali dell'Istituto Storico Italo-Germanico in Trento* 12 (1986): 169–92.

Schilling, Heinz. "Die Kirchenzucht im frühneuzeitlichen Europa in interkonfessionell vergleichender und interdisziplinärer Perspektive–eine Zwischenbilanz." In *Kirchenzucht und Sozialdisziplinierung im frühneuzeitlichen Europa*, edited by Heinz Schilling, 11–40. Berlin: Duncker & Humblot, 1994.

Schilling, Heinz. "Reformierte Kirchenzucht als Sozialdisziplinierung? Die Tätigkeit des Emder Presbyteriums in den Jahren, 1557–1562 (mit vergleichenden Betrachtungen über die Kirchenräte in Groningen und Leiden sowie mit einem Ausblick ins 17. Jahrhundert)." In *Niederlande und Nordwestdeutschland*, edited by Wilfried Ehbrecht and Heinz Schilling, 261–327. Köln: Böhlau, 1983.

Schilling, Heinz. *Civic Calvinism in Northwestern Germany and the Netherlands, Sixteenth to Nineteenth Centuries.* Kirksville, Mo.: Sixteenth Century Journal Publishers, 1991.

Schilling, Heinz. *Die neue Zeit. Vom Christenheitseuropa zum Europa der Staaten, 1250 bis 1750*, Siedler Geschichte Europas, vol. 3. Berlin: Siedler, 1999.

Schilling, Heinz. *Religion, Political Culture, and the Emergence of Early Modern Society: Essays in German and Dutch History.* Leiden: E. J. Brill, 1992.

Schindler, Norbert. "Guardians of Disorder: Rituals of Youthful Culture at the Dawn of the Modern Age." In *Ancient and Medieval Rites of Passage: A History of Young People in the West*, edited by Giovanni Levi and Jean-Claude Schmitt and translated by Camille Naish, 240–82, 364–77. Cambridge: Harvard University Press, 1997.

Schindler, Norbert. *Widerspenstige Leute: Studien zur Volkskultur in der frühen Neuzeit.* Frankfurt am Main: Fischer, 1992.

Schlumbohm, Jürgen, et al., eds. *Rituale der Geburt: Eine Kulturgeschichte.* München: Beck, 1998.

Schmale, Wolfgang. *Archäologie der Grund- und Menschenrechte in der Frühen Neuzeit: Ein französisch-deutsches Paradigma.* München: Oldenbourg Verlag, 1997.

Schmidt, Heinrich Richard, and Thomas Brodbeck. "Davos zwischen Sünde und Verbrechen: Eine Langzeitstudie über die Tätigkeit der geistlichen und weltlichen Gerichtsbarkeit, 1644–1800." *Jahrbuch der Historischen Gesellschaft von Graubünden* (1997–1998): 143–83.

Schmidt, Heinrich Richard. "Gemeinde und Sittenzucht im protestantischen Europa der frühen Neuzeit." In *Theorien kommunaler Ordnung in Europa,* edited by Peter Blickle, 181–214. München: Oldenbourg, 1996.

Schmidt, Heinrich Richard. "Sozialdisziplinierung? Ein Plädoyer für das Ende des Etatismus in der Konfessionalisierungsforschung." *Historische Zeitschrift* 265 (1997): 639–82.

Schmidt, Heinrich Richard. *Konfessionalisierung im 16. Jahrhundert,* Enzyklopädie deutscher Geschichte, vol. 12. München: Oldenbourg, 1992.

Schmidt, Heinrich-Richard. "Das Bernische Sittengericht zwischen Sozialdisziplinierung und kommunaler Selbstregulation." In *Bäuerliche Frömmigkeit und kommunale Reformation,* Itinera, fasc. 8, edited by Hans von Rütte, 85–121. Basel: Schwabe, 1988.

Schmidt, Heinrich-Richard. "Die Ächtung des Fluchens durch reformierte Sittengerichte." In *Der Fluch und der Eid,* edited by Peter Blickle and André Hohlenstein, 65–120. Berlin: Duncker & Humblot, 1993.

Schmidt, Heinrich-Richard. "Emden est partout: Vers un modèle interactif de la confessionnalisation." *Francia* 26 (1999): 23–45.

Schmidt, Heinrich-Richard. *Dorf und Religion: Reformierte Sittenzucht in Berner Landgemeinden der Frühen Neuzeit.* Stuttgart: Fischer, 1995.

Schnyder-Burghartz, Albert. *Alltag und Lebensformen auf der Basler Landschaft um 1700: Vorindustrielle, ländliche Kultur und Gesellschaft aus mikrohistorischer Perspektive - Bretzwil und das obere Waldenburger Amt von 1690 bis 1750.* Liestal: Kantonsverlag, 1992.

Schofield, R. S., and E. A. Wrigley. *The Population History in England, 1541–1871: A Reconstruction.* Cambridge: Cambridge University Press, 1981.

Scholz-Hänsel, Michael. "El Santo Niño de La Guardia: La pintura como medio de propaganda inquisitorial." *La balsa de la medusa* [Madrid] 30/31 (1994): 43–62.

Scholz-Hänsel, Michael. "Künstler als Gastarbeiter in Spanien: Vom Reiz des Fremden sowie dem Leiden unter und dem Leben mit der Inquisition." In *Kunst in Spanien im Blick des Fremden,* edited by Gisela Noehles-Doerk, 73–86. Frankfurt am Main: Vervuert, 1996.

Scholz-Hänsel, Michael. "Pictorial Propaganda against the Others: Spanish Art in the Context of the Tolerance Discussions of the Peace of Westphalia." In *War and Peace in Europe,* vol. 2, *Art and Culture,* edited by Klaus Bußmann and Heinz Schilling, 131–39. Münster: Bruckmann, 1998.

Scholz-Hänsel, Michael. "Neapolitanische Malerei und 'Konfessionalisierung': Veränderungen im Bild der Armen von Caravaggio zu Ribera." *Archiv für Reformationsgeschichte* 93 (2002): 339–68.

Scholz-Hänsel, Michael. *El Greco "Der Großinquisitor": Neues Licht auf die Schwarze Legende.* Frankfurt am Main: Fischer, 1991.

Scholz-Hänsel, Michael. *Jusepe de Ribera.* Köln: Könemann, 2001.

Schreiner, Klaus, and Gerd Schwerhoff, eds. *Verletzte Ehre: Ehrkonflikte in Gesellschaften des Mittelalters und der Frühen Neuzeit.* Köln: Böhlau 1995.

Schröter, Michael. "Staatsbildung und Triebkontrolle: Zur gesellschaftlichen Regulierung des Sexualverhaltens vom 13. bis 16. Jahrhundert." In *Macht und Zivilisation,* edited by Peter Gleichmann et al., 148–92. Frankfurt am Main: Suhrkamp, 1984.

Schröter, Michael. *"Wo zwei zusammenkommen in rechter Ehe. . . ." Sozio- und psychogenetische Studien über Eheschließungsvorgänge vom 12. bis. 15. Jahrhundert.* Frankfurt am Main: Suhrkamp, 1985.

Schulte Beerbühl, Margrit. *Vom Gesellenverein zur Gewerkschaft: Entwicklung, Struktur und Politik der Londoner Gesellenorganisationen, 1550–1825,* Göttinger Beiträge zur Wirtschafts- und Sozialgeschichte, vol. 16. Göttingen: Otto Schwartz & Co, 1991.

Schulte, Regina. *Das Dorf im Verhör: Brandstifter, Kindsmörderinnen und Wilderer vor den Schranken des bürgerlichen Gerichts Oberbayern, 1848–1910.* Reinbek bei Hamburg: Rowohlt, 1989.

Schulz, Knut. *Handwerksgesellen und Lohnarbeiter: Untersuchungen zur oberrheinischen und oberdeutschen Stadtgeschichte des 14. bis 17. Jahrhunderts.* Sigmaringen: Jan Thorbecke, 1985.

Schulze, Winfried. "Gerhard Oestreichs Begriff 'Sozialdisziplinierung' in der frühen Neuzeit." *Zeitschrift für Historische Forschung* 14 (1987): 265–302.

Schulze, Winfried. *Bäuerlicher Widerstand und feudale Herrschaft in der Frühen Neuzeit.* Stuttgart: Frommann-Holzboog, 1980.

Schuster, Beate. *Die freien Frauen: Dirnen und Frauenhäuser im 15. und 16. Jahrhundert.* Frankfurt am Main: Campus Verlag, 1995.

Schuster, Peter. *Das Frauenhaus: Städtische Bordelle in Deutschland (1350–1600).* Paderborn: Schöningh, 1992.

Schuster, Peter. *Der gelobte Frieden: Täter, Opfer und Herrschaft im spätmittelalterlichen Konstanz.* Konstanz: UVK, 1995.

Schuster, Peter. *Eine Stadt vor Gericht: Recht und Alltag im spätmittelalterlichen Konstanz.* Paderborn: Schoeningh, 2000.

Schütte, Ulrich. "Die Lehre von den Gebäudetypen." In *Architekt und Ingenieur: Baumeister in Krieg und Frieden,* edited by Ulrich Schütte, 156–267. Wolfenbüttel: Herzog August Bibliothek, 1984.

Schwarz, L. D. *London in the Age of Industrialisation: Entrepreneurs, Labour Force and Living Conditions.* Cambridge: Cambridge University Press, 1992.

Schwerhoff, Gerd. "Criminalized Violence and the Civilizing Process–A Reappraisal." *Crime, Histoire et Sociétés/ Crime, History and Societies* 6 (2002): 103–26.

Schwerhoff, Gerd. "Verordnete Schande? Spätmittelalterliche und frühneuzeitliche Ehrenstrafen zwischen Rechtsakt und sozialer Sanktion." In *Mit den Waffen der Justiz: Zur Kriminalitätsgeschichte des Spätmittelalters und der Frühen Neuzeit,* edited by Andreas Blauert and Gerd Schwerhoff, 158–88. Frankfurt am Main: Fischer, 1993.

Schwerhoff, Gerd. "Zivilisationsprozess und Geschichtswissenschaft. Norbert Elias' Forschungsparadigma in historischer Sicht." *Historische Zeitschrift* 266 (1998): 560–605.

Schwerhoff, Gerd. "'Mach, daß wir nicht in eine Schande geraten!' Frauen in Kölner

Kriminalfällen des 16. Jahrhunderts." *Geschichte in Wissenschaft und Unterricht* 44 (1993): 451–73.

Schwerhoff, Gerd. "Vom Alltagsverdacht zur Massenverfolgung: Neuere deutsche Forschungen zum frühneuzeitlichen Hexenwesen." *Geschichte in Wissenschaft und Unterricht* 46 (1995): 359–80.

Schwerhoff, Gerd. *Aktenkundig und Gerichtsnotorisch: Einführung in die historische Kriminalitätsforschung.* Tübingen: Edition Diskord, 1999.

Schwerhoff, Gerd. *Köln im Kreuzverhör. Kriminalität, Herrschaft und Gesellschaft in einer frühneuzeitlichen Stadt.* Bonn: Bouvier Verlag, 1991.

Scott, John Paul, and Sarah F. Scott, eds. *Social Control and Social Change.* Chicago: University of Chicago Press, 1971.

Scribner, Robert. "Practical Utopias: Pre-Modern Communism and the Reformation." *Comparative Studies in Society and History* 36 (1994): 743–74.

Scribner, Robert. *For the Sake of Simple Folk: Popular Propaganda for the German Reformation.* Oxford: Clarendon Press, 1994.

Seebaß, Gottfried. "Der linke Flügel der Reformation." In idem, *Die Reformation und ihre Außenseiter: Gesammelte Aufsätze und Vorträge,* 151–64. Göttingen: Vandenhoeck und Ruprecht, 1997.

Sharpe, J. A. "'Last Dying Speeches': Religion, Ideology and Public Execution in Seventeenth-Century England." *Past and Present* 107 (1985): 144–67.

Sharpe, J. A. "Such Disagreement between Neighbours." In *Disputes and Settlements: Law and Human Relations in the West,* edited by John Bossy, 169–87. Cambridge: Cambridge University Press, 1983.

Sharpe, J[ames] A. *Judicial Punishment in England.* London: Faber and Faber, 1990.

Sharpe, James A. *Defamation and Sexual Slander in Early Modern England: The Church Courts of York.* York: Borthwick Papers, 1980.

Sheehan, Michael. "The European Family and Canon Law." *Continuity and Change* 6, 3 (1991): 347–60.

Shoemaker, Robert B. *Prosecution and Punishment: Petty Crime and the Law in London and Rural Middlesex, c. 1660–1725.* Cambridge: Cambridge University Press, 1991.

Shoemaker, Robert. "The Decline of Public Insult in London, 1660–1800." *Past and Present* 169 (2000): 97–131.

Shorter, Edward. "Illegitimacy, Sexual Revolution and Social Change in Modern Europe." *Journal of Interdisciplinary History* 2 (1971): 235–72.

Shorter, Edward. *Naissance de la famille moderne.* Paris: Editions du Seuil, 1977 (1st ed. 1975).

Sibeth, Uwe. *Eherecht und Staatsbildung: Ehegesetzgebung und Eherechtsprechung in der Landgrafschaft Hessen (-Kassel) in der frühen Neuzeit,* Quellen und Forschungen zur hessischen Geschichte, 98. Darmstadt: Selbstverlag der Hessischen Historischen Kommission Darmstadt und der Historischen Kommission für Hessen, 1994.

Sieferle, Rolf Peter, and Helga Breuninger, eds. *Kulturen der Gewalt: Ritualisierung und Symbolisierung von Gewalt in der Geschichte.* Frankfurt am Main: Campus Verlag, 1998.

Simon, Christian. *Untertanenverhalten und obrigkeitliche Moralpolitik: Studien zum Verhältnis zwischen Stadt und Land im ausgehenden 18. Jahrhundert am Beispiel Basels.* Basel: Helbing und Lichtenhahn, 1981.

Simon-Muscheid, Katharina. *"Was nutzt die Schusterin dem Schmied?" Frauen und Handwerk vor der Industrialisierung.* Frankfurt am Main: Campus Verlag, 1998.

Slack, Paul. *Poverty and Policy in Tudor and Stuart England.* London: Longman, 1988.

Sleebe, Vincent C. *In termen van fatsoen: Sociale controle in het Groningse kleigebied, 1770–1914.* Assen: Van Gorcum, 1994.

Smith, A. G. R. *The Emergence of a Nation State: The Commonwealth of England, 1529–1660.* London: Longman, 1984.

Smith, Adam. *The Wealth of Nations.* Edited by Andrew Skinner. Harmondsworth: Penguin, 1986.

Smith, Alexander. *The History of the Lives of the Most Noted Highway-Men, Foot-Pads, Housebreakers, Shop-Lifts and Cheats of Both Sexes, in and About London, and Other Places in Great Britain, for Above Fifty Years Past.* London, 1714.

Smith, Steven R. "The London Apprentices As Seventeenth-Century Adolescents." *Past and Present* 61 (1973): 149–61.

Snell, K. D. M. *Annals of the Labouring Poor: Social Change and Agrarian England, 1660–1900.* Cambridge: Cambridge University Press, 1985.

Sofsky, Wolfgang. *Traktat über die Gewalt.* Frankfurt am Main: Fischer, 1996.

Sohm, Walther. *Territorium und Reformation in der hessischen Geschichte, 1526–1555.* Marburg: Elwert, 1957.

Sonenscher, Michael. "Journeymen's Migrations and Workshop Organization in Eighteenth-Century France." In *Work in France: Representations, Meaning, Organization, and Practice,* edited by Steven Laurence Kaplan and Cynthia J. Koepp, 74–96. Ithaca: Cornell University Press, 1986.

Sonenscher, Michael. *The Hatters of Eighteenth-Century France.* Berkeley: University of California Press, 1987.

Sonenscher, Michael. *Work and Wages: Natural Law, Politics and the Eighteenth-Century French Trades.* Cambridge: Cambridge University Press, 1989.

Spicker-Beck, Monika. *Räuber, Mordbrenner, umschweifendes Gesind: Zur Kriminalität im 16. Jahrhundert.* Freiburg i. Br.: Metropol, 1995.

Spierenburg, Pieter, ed. *Men and Violence: Gender, Honor, and Rituals in Modern Europe and America.* Columbus: Ohio State University Press, 1998.

Spierenburg, Pieter. "Faces of Violence: Homicide Trends and Cultural Meanings: Amsterdam, 1431–1816." *Journal of Social History* 4, 27 (1994): 701–16.

Spierenburg, Pieter. "How Violent Were Women? Court Cases in Amsterdam, 1650–1810." *Crime, Histoire et Sociétés/ Crime, History and Societies* 1 (1997): 9–28.

Spierenburg, Pieter. "Lange termijn trends in doodslag." *Amsterdam Sociologisch Tijdschrift* 20 (1991): 66–106.

Spierenburg, Pieter. "The Body and the State: Early Modern Europe." In *The Oxford History of the Prison,* edited by Norval Morris and David J. Rothman, 48–77. New

York: Oxford University Press, 1995.

Spierenburg, Pieter. "Violence and the Civilizing Process: Does It Work?" *Crime, Histoire et Sociétés/Crime, History and Societies* 2, 5 (2001): 87–105.

Spierenburg, Pieter. *The Broken Spell: A Cultural and Anthropological History of Preindustrial Europe.* New Brunswick: Rutgers University Press, 1991.

Spierenburg, Pieter. *The Prison Experience: Disciplinary Institutions and Their Inmates in Early Modern Europe.* New Brunswick: Rutgers University Press, 1991.

Spierenburg, Pieter. *The Spectacle of Suffering: Executions and the Evolution of Repression, From a Preindustrial Metropolis to the European Experience.* Cambridge: Cambridge University Press, 1984.

Spittler, Gerd. "Streitregelung im Schatten des Leviathan." *Zeitschrift für Rechtssoziologie* 1 (1980): 4–32.

Spufford, Margaret. "Puritanism and Social Control?" In *Order and Disorder in Early Modern England,* edited by Anthony Fletcher and John Stevenson, 41–57. Cambridge: Cambridge University Press, 1985.

Spufford, Margaret. "The Importance of Religion in the Sixteenth and Seventeenth Centuries." In *The World of Rural Dissenters, 1520–1725,* edited by Margaret Spufford, 1–102. Cambridge: Cambridge University Press, 1995.

Spufford, Margaret. *Contrasting Communities: English Villagers in the Sixteenth and Seventeenth Centuries.* Cambridge: Cambridge University Press, 1974.

Spufford, Margaret. *Small Books and Pleasant Histories: Popular Fiction and Its Readership in Seventeenth-Century England.* London: Methuen, 1981.

Sreenivasan, Govind. "The Land Family Bond at Earls Colne (Essex), 1550–1650." *Past and Present* 131 (1991): 3–37.

Stayer, James M. "Luther und die Schwärmer." In *Aussenseiter zwischen Mittelalter und Neuzeit: Festschrift für Hans Jürgen Goertz,* edited by Norbert Fischer and Marion Kobalt-Groch, 269–88. Leiden: Brill, 1990.

Stayer, James M. *Anabaptists and the Sword.* Lawrence: Coronado Press, 1976.

Stayer, James M., *The German Peasant's War and the Anabaptist Community of Goods.* Montreal: McGill-Queen's University Press, 1991.

Steffensen, James L., ed. *The Dramatic Works of George Lillo.* Oxford: Clarendon Press, 1993.

Stekl, Hannes. "Labore et fame: Sozialdisziplinierung in Zucht- und Arbeitshäusern des 17. und 18. Jahrhunderts." In *Soziale Sicherheit und soziale Disziplinierung: Beiträge zu einer historischen Theorie der Sozialpolitik,* edited by Christoph Sachße and Florian Tennstedt, 119–47. Frankfurt am Main: Suhrkamp, 1986.

Stone, Lawrence. *The Family, Sex and Marriage in England, 1500–1800.* London: Weidenfeld and Nicholson, 1977.

Storch, Robert D. "The Plague of the Blue Locusts: Police Reform and Popular Resistance in Northern England, 1840–1857." *International Review of Social History* 20 (1975): 61–90.

Storch, Robert D. "The Policeman as Domestic Missionary." *Journal of Social History*

4, 9 (1976): 481–509.

Storme, Hans. *Die trouwen wil voorsichtelijck: Predikanten en moralisten over de voorbereiding op het huwelijk in de Vlaamse bisdommen (17e-18e eeuw)*. Leuven: Universitaire Pers Leuven, 1992.

Strasser, Ulrike. *State of Virginity: Gender, Religion and Politics in an Early Modern Catholic State*. Ann Arbor: University of Michigan Press, 2003.

Stupperich, Robert. "Melanchthon und die Täufer." *Kerygma und Dogma* 3 (1957): 150–69.

Stupperich, Robert. *Schriften von evangelischer Seite gegen die Täufer.* Münster: Aschendorff, 1983.

Sturm, Leonhard Christoph. *Vollständige Anweisung, Regierungs-, Land- und Rath-Häuser, wie auch Kauff-Häuser und Börsen starck, bequem und zierlich anzugeben . . . .* Augsburg, 1718.

Stutzer, Dietmar, and Alois Fink. *Die irdische und die himmlische Wies.* Rosenheim: Rosenheimer Verlag, 1982.

Sutter, Eva. *"Ein Act des Leichtsinns und der Sünde": Illegitimität im Kanton Zürich: Recht, Moral und Lebensrealität (1800–1860)*. Zurich: Chronos, 1995.

Swanson, Heather. "The Illusion of Economic Structure: Craft Guilds in Late Medieval English Towns." *Past and Present* 121 (1988): 29–48.

Taverne, E. "Salmon de Bray and the Reorganization of the Haarlem Guild of St. Luke in 1631." *Simiolus* 6 (1972): 50–69.

Terpstra, Nicholas. *Lay Confraternities and Civic Religion in Renaissance Bologna.* New York: Cambridge University Press, 1995.

Thompson, E. P. "Time, Work-Discipline and Industrial Capitalism." *Past and Present* 38 (1967): 56–97.

Thompson, E. P. *Customs in Common.* London: The Merlin Press, 1991.

Thompson, E. P. *Whigs and Hunters: The Origins of the Black Act.* Harmondsworth: Penguin, 1977.

Tlusty, Ann. "Water of Life, Water of Death: The Controversy over Brandy and Gin in Early Modern Augsburg." *Central European History* 31 (1998): 1–30.

Tlusty, Ann. *Bacchus and Civic Order: The Culture of Drink in Early Modern Germany.* Charlottesville: University Press of Virgina, 2001.

Todd, Margo. *The Culture of Protestantism in Early Modern Scotland.* New Haven. Yale University Press, 2002.

Tomlinson, Janis A. "Burn It, Hide It, Flaunt It: Goya's Majas and the Censorial Mind." *Art Journal* 4, vol. 50 (winter 1991): 59–64.

Torras, J. "Gremios, familias y organización del trabajo. Las cofradías de oficio en los siglos XVII y XVIII." In *El trabajo a través de la historia,* edited by Santiago Castillo. Madrid: Asociación de Historia Social & Centro de Estudios Históricos de la Unión General de Trabajadores (U.G.T.), 1996.

Torres Arce, Marina. "Cantabria en la estructura inquisitorial del tribunal de Logroño." In *De peñas al mar. Sociedad e instituciones en la Cantabria Moderna,* edited by Tomás A. Mantecón. Santander: Ayuntamiento de Santander & Librería Stvdio, Colección Pronillo, 1999.

Truant, Cynthia M. "Independent and Insolent: Journeymen and Their 'Rites' in the Old Regime Workplace." In *Work in France: Representations, Meaning, Organization, and Practice*, edited by Steven Laurence Kaplan and Cynthia Koepp, 131–75. Ithaca: Cornell University Press, 1986.

Truant, Cynthia Maria. "Parisian Guildswomen and the (Sexual) Politics of Privilege: Defending Their Patrimonies in Print." In *Going Public: Women and Publishing in Early Modern France,* edited by Elisabeth C. Goldsmith and Dena Goodman, 46–61. Ithaca: Cornell University Press, 1995.

Truant, Cynthia Maria. *Rites of Labor: Brotherhoods of Comapgnonnage in Old and New Regime France.* Ithaca: Cornell University Press, 1994.

Turner, David. "'Nothing Is So Secret but Shall Be Revealed': The Scandalous Life of Robert Foulkes." In *English Masculinities, 1660–1800,* edited by Tim Hitchcock and Michèle Cohen, 169–92. London: Longman, 1999.

Ulbricht, Otto, ed. *Von huren und Rabenmüttern: Weibliche Kriminalität in der Frühen Neuzeit.* Köln: Böhlau, 1995.

Van Apeldoorn, L. J. *Geschiedenis van het Nederlandsche huwelijksrecht vóór de invoering van de Fransche wetgeving.* Amsterdam: Uitgeversmaatschappij Holland, 1925.

Van der Heijden, Manon. "Criminaliteit en sexe in 18e-eeuws Rotterdam: De verschillen tussen vrouwen- en mannencriminaliteit tussen, 1700 en 1750." *Tijdschrift voor Sociale Geschiedenis* 1, 21 (1995):1–36.

Van der Heijden, Manon. "Secular and Ecclesiastical Marriage Control: Rotterdam, 1550–1700." In *Private Domain, Public Inquiry: Families and Life-Styles in the Netherlands and Europe, 1550 to the Present,* edited by Anton Schuurman and Pieter Spierenburg, 39–60. Hilversum: Verloren, 1996.

Van der Heijden, Manon. "Women As Victims of Sexual and Domestic Violence in Seventeenth-Century Holland: Criminal Cases of Rape, Incest, and Maltreatment in Rotterdam and Delft." *Journal of Social History* (spring, 2000): 97–118.

Van der Heijden, Manon. *Huwelijk in Holland: Wereldlijke rechtspraak en kerkelijke tucht, 1550–1700.* Amsterdam: Bert Bakker, 1998.

Van der Vlis, Ingrid. *Leven in armoede: Delftse bedeelden in de zeventiende eeuw.* Amsterdam: Prometheus/Bert Bakker, 2001.

Van Deursen, A. Th. *Bavianen en slijkgeuzen: Kerk en kerkvolk ten tijde van Maurits en Oldebarnevelt.* Assen: Van Gorcum, 1974.

Van Dülmen, Richard, ed. *Entdeckung des Ich: Die Geschichte der Individualisierung vom Mittelalter bis zur Gegenwart.* Köln: Böhlau, 2001.

Van Dülmen, Richard, ed. *Erfindung des Menschen: Schöpfungsträume und Körperbilder, 1500–2000.* Vienna: Böhlau, 1998.

Van Dülmen, Richard. *Theatre of Horror: Crime and Punishment in Early Modern Germany,* translated by Elisabeth Neu. Cambridge: Polity Press, 1990.

Van Eupen, Th. A. G.. "Kerk en gezin in Nederland." In *Gezinsgeschiedenis: Vier eeuwen gezin in Nederland,* edited by G. A. Kooy, 7–28. Assen: Van Gorcum, 1985.

Van Lieburg, F. A. *De Nadere Reformatie in Utrecht ten tijde van Voetius.* Rotterdam: Lindenberg, 1989.

Velasco, F.: "Lazo familiar, conexión económica e integración social: la burguesía carta-genera de origen extranjero en el siglo XVIII." *Familia, casa y trabajo: Seminario familia y elite de poder en el reino de Murcia, siglos 15.–19.,* edited by Chacón Jiménez, Francisco & Llorenc Ferrer i Alòs. Murcia: Servicio de Publicaciones de la Universidad de Murcia, 1997.

Verney, Lady Margaret Maria, ed. *Verney Letters of the Eighteenth Century from the MSS. at Claydon House.* 2 vols. London: E. Benn Ltd, 1930.

Vincent, Catherine. *Des charités bien ordonnées: Les confréries normandes de la fin du XIIIe siècle au début du XVIe siècle.* Paris: Ecole normale supérieure, 1988.

Vincent, Catherine. *Les confréries médiévales dans le royaume de France: XIIIe-XVe siècle.* Paris: A. Michel, 1994.

Violant i Simorra, Ramón. *El Pirineo español. Vida, usos, costumbres, creencias y tradiciones de una cultura milenaria que desaparece.* Barcelona: Alta Fulla, 1986 (1st ed. Madrid: Plus Ultra, 1949).

Vitruvius. *De architectura libri decem / Zehn Bücher über die Architektur,* edited by Curt Fensterbusch, vol. 1, pt. 2. Darmstadt, 1981.

Vocelka, Karl. *Die politische Propaganda Kaiser Rudolfs II. (1576–1612).* Vienna: Österreichishen Akademie der Wissenschaften, 1981.

Von Friedeburg, Robert. "Reformation of Manners and the Social Composition of Offenders in an East Anglian Cloth Village: Earls Colne, Essex, 1531–1642." *Journal of British Studies* 29 (1990): 347–85.

Von Friedeburg, Robert. "Social and Geographical Mobility in the Old World and New World Communities: Earls Colne, Ipswich and Springfield, 1636–1685." *Journal of Social History* 28 (1995): 375–400.

Von Friedeburg, Robert. "Village Strife and the Rhetoric of Communalism: Peasants and Parsons, Lords and Jews in Hesse, Central Germany, 1646–1672." *The Seventeenth Century* 7 (1992): 201–26.

Von Friedeburg, Robert. *Ländliche Gesellschaft und Obrigkeit: Gemeindeprotest und politische Mobilisierung im 18. und 19. Jahrhundert.* Göttingen: Vandenhoeck & Ruprecht, 1997.

Von Friedeburg, Robert. *Self Defence and Religious Strife in Early Modern Europe: England and Germany, 1530–1680.* Aldershot: Ashgate, 2002.

Von Friedeburg, Robert. *Sündenzucht und sozialer Wandel.* Stuttgart: Steiner, 1993.

Von Friedeburg, Robert. The Public of Confessional Identity: Church and Church Discipline in Eighteenth Century Hesse." In *Cultures of Communication from Reformation to Enlightenment: Constructing Publics in Early Modern German Lands,* edited by James Melton, 104–18. Aldershot: Ashgate, 2002.

Von Trotha, Trutz, ed. *Soziologie der Gewalt.* Opladen: Westdeutscher Verlag, 1997.

Walker, Mack. *German Home Towns: Community, State, and General Estate,*

1648–1871. Ithaca: Cornell University Press, 1971.

Walter, Tilmann. *Unkeuschheit und Werk der Liebe: Diskurse über Sexualität am Beginn der Neuzeit in Deutschland,* Studia Linguistica Germanica 48. Berlin: Walter de Gruyter, 1998.

Walz, Rainer. "Agonale Kommunikation im Dorf der frühen Neuzeit." *Westfälische Forschungen* 42 (1992): 215–51.

Wandel, Lee Palmer. *Always among Us: Images of the Poor in Zwingli's Zurich.* New York: Cambridge University Press, 1990.

Ward, Joseph P. *Metropolitan Communities: Trade Guilds, Identity and Change in Early Modern London.* Stanford: Stanford University Press, 1997.

Warnke, Martin, ed. *Politische Architektur in Europa vom Mittelalter bis heute: Repräsentation und Gemeinschaft.* Köln: DuMont, 1984.

Warnke, Martin. "Politische Ikonographie." In *Die Lesbarkeit der Kunst,* edited by Andreas Beyer, 23–38. Berlin: Klaus Wagenbach, 1992.

Warnke, Martin. "Praxisfelder der Kunsttheorie: Über die Geburtswehen des Individualstils." *Jahrbuch der Hamburger Kunsthalle* 1 (1982): 54–71.

Watkins, Owen C. *The Puritan Experience.* London: Routledge & Kegan Paul, 1972.

Watt, Jeffrey. *The Making of Modern Marriage: Matrimonial Control and the Rise of Sentiment in Neuchâtel, 1550–1800.* Ithaca: Cornell University Press, 1992.

Weber, Max. *Wirtschaft und Gesellschaft: Grundriß der verstehenden Soziologie.* 5th ed. Tübingen: Mohr Verlag, 1985.

Weinburg, Julius. "Ross, Edward A." In *International Encyclopedia of the Social Sciences,* edited by David L. Sills, vol. 13, 560–62. 18 vols. New York: Macmillan and the Free Press, 1968.

Weinstein, Donald. "Fighting or Flyting? Verbal Duelling in Mid-Sixteenth-Century Italy." In *Crime, Society and the Law in Renaissance Italy,* edited by Trevor Dean and K. J. P. Lowe, 204–20. Cambridge: Cambridge University Press, 1994.

Weiß, Ruth. "Herkunft und Sozialanschauungen der Täufergemeinde im westlichen Hessen." *Archiv für Reformationsgeschichte* 52 (1961): 162–89.

Weissman, Ronald F. E. *Ritual Brotherhood in Renaissance Florence.* New York: Academic Press, 1982.

Wensky, Margret. "Women's Guilds in Cologne in the Later Middle Ages." *Journal of European Economic History* 11 (1982): 630–50.

Wesoly, Kurt. *Lehrlinge und Handwerksgesellen am Mittelrhein: Ihre sozial Lage und Organisation vom 14. bis ins 17. Jahrhundert,* Studien zur Frankfurter Geschichte, vol. 18. Frankfurt am Main: Kramer, 1985.

Westlake, H. F. *The Parish Gilds of Mediæval England.* London: Society for Promoting Christian Knowledge, 1919.

Wettmann-Jungblut, Peter. "Gewalt und Gegen-Gewalt: Gewalthandeln, Alkoholkonsum und die Dynamik von Konflikten anhand eines Fallbeispiels aus dem frühneuzeitlichen Schwarzwald." In *Streitkultur(en): Studien zu Gewalt, Konflikt und Kommunikation in der ländlichen Gesellschaft, 16.-19. Jahrhundert.,* edited by Magnus Eriksson and Barbara Krug-Richter, 17–58. Köln: Böhlau, 2003.

White, Peter. *Predestination, Policy and Polemic: Conflict and Consensus in the English Church from the Reformation to the Civil War.* Cambridge: University Press, 1992.

Wiesner, Merry E. "Guilds, Male Bonding, and Women's Work in Early Modern Germany." *Gender and History* 1 (1989): 125–37.

Wiesner, Merry E. *Christianity and Sexuality in the Early Modern World: Regulating Desire, Reforming Practice.* London: Routledge, 2000.

Wiesner, Merry E. *Gender, Church and State in Early Modern Germany.* London: Longman, 1998.

Wiesner, Merry E. *Women and Gender in Early Modern Europe.* Cambridge: Cambridge University Press, 1993.

Wiesner, Merry E. *Working Women in Renaissance Germany.* New Brunswick: Rutgers University Press, 1986.

Williams, Penry. *The Tudor Regime.* Oxford: Clarendon Press, 1979.

Willis Bund, J. W., ed. *Calendar of the Quarter Sessions Papers,* vol. 1, 1591–1643. Worcester County Records, Division I. Documents Relating to Quarter Sessions, 1900.

Wimmer, Michael, et al., eds. *Das zivilisierte Tier: Zur historischen Anthropologie der Gewalt.* Frankfurt am Main: Fischer, 1996.

Wolff, Christian. *Vernünftige Gedanken von dem gesellschaftlichen Leben.* Frankfurt, 1736.

Woodward, Donald. *Men at Work: Labourers and Building Craftsmen in the Towns of Northern England, 1450–1750.* Cambridge: Cambridge University Press, 1995.

Wormald, Jenny. "The Blood Feud in Early Modern Scotland." In *Disputes and Settlements: Law and Human Relations in the West,* edited by John Bossy. Cambridge: Cambridge University Press, 1983.

Wrightson, Keith, and David Levine. *Poverty and Piety in an English Village: Terling, 1525–1700.* London: Clarendon Press, 1979.

Wrightson, Keith. "Aspects of Social Differentiation in Rural England, c.1580–1660." *Journal of Peasant Studies* 5 (1978): 53347.

Wrightson, Keith. "The Politics of the Parish in Early Modern England." In *The Experience of Authority in Early Modern England,* edited by Paul Griffiths et al., 10–46. Basingstoke and London: MacMillan, 1996.

Wrightson, Keith. "The Social Order of Early Modern England: Three Approaches." In *The World We Have Gained: Histories of Population and Social Structure,* edited by Lloyd Bonfield, 177–202. Oxford: Blackwell, 1986.

Wrightson, Keith. "Two Concepts of Order: Justices, Constables and Jurymen in Seventeenth-Century England." In *An Ungovernable People: The English and Their Law in the Seventeenth and Eighteenth Centuries,* edited by John Brewer and John Styles. London: Hutchinson, 1980.

Wrightson, Keith. *English Society 1580–1680.* London: Hutchinson, 1982.

Wrigley, Edward A., and Roger Schofield. *The Population History of England 1541–1871: A Reconstruction.* London: Arnold, 1981.

Wunder, Heide. *'Er ist die Sonn,' sie ist der Mond' Frauen in der Frühen Neuzeit.* München:

C. H. Beck Verlag, 1992.

Wunder, Heide. "'Justitia, Teutonice Fromkeyt': Theologische Rechtfertigung und bürgerliche Rechtschaffenheit." In *Die frühe Reformation im Umbruch,* edited by Bernd Moeller, 307–32. Gütersloh: Gütersloher Verlagshaus, 1997.

Wunder, Heide. "Normen und Institutionen der Geschlechterordnung am Beginn der Frühen Neuzeit." In *Geschlechterperspektiven: Forschungen zur Frühen Neuzeit,* edited by Heide Wunder and Gisela Engel, 57–78. Frankfurt am Main: Ulrike Helmer, 1998.

Würgler, Andreas. "Diffamierung und Kriminalisierung von Devianz in frühneuzeitlichen Konflikten." In *Devianz, Widerstand und Herrschaftspraxis in der Vormoderne: Studien zu Konflikten im südwestdeutschen Raum (15.-18. Jahrhundert),* edited by Mark Häberlein, 317–47. Konstanz: UVK, 1999.

Yeo, Eileen, and Stephen Yeo, eds. *Popular Culture and Class Conflict, 1590–1914.* Brighton, Sussex: Harvester Press, 1981.

Ylikangas, H. "Major Fluctuations in Crimes of Violence in Finland: A Historical Analysis." *Scandinavian Journal of History* 1 (1976).

Ylikangas, H., P. Karonen, and Martti Lehti. *Five Centuries of Violence in Finland and the Baltic Area.* Helsinki: Publications of the History of Criminality Research Project, Academy of Finland, 1998.

Ylikangas, H. "Reasons for the Reduction of Violence in the 17th Century." In *Crime and Control in Europe from the Past to the Present,* edited by M. Lappalainen and P. Hirvonen. Helsinki: Publications of the History of Criminality Research Project, Academy of Finland, 1999.

Zapperi, Roberto. "La corporation des peintres et la censure des images à Bologne au temp des Carrache." *Revue d'Histoire Moderne et Contemporaine* 38 (1991): 387–400.

Zapperi, Roberto. *Eros e Controriforma: Preistoria della galleria Farnese.* Turin: Bollati Boringhieri, 1994.

Zdekauer, C., and O. Sella, eds. *Statuti di Ascoli: Piceno.* Rome, 1910.

Zeeden, Ernst Walter. "Grundlagen und Wege der Konfessionsbildung im Zeitalter der Glaubenskämpfe." *Historische Zeitschrift* 185 (1958): 249–99.

Zückert, Hartmut. *Die sozialen Grundlagen der Barockkultur in Süddeutschland.* Stuttgart: Fischer, 1988.

Zysberg, André. *Les galériens: Vies et destins de 60,000 forçats sur les galères de France, 1680–1748.* Paris: Sueil, 1987.

Index

HISTORY OF CRIME AND CRIMINAL JUSTICE SERIES
David R. Johnson and Jeffrey S. Adler, Series Editors

The series explores the history of crime and criminality, violence, criminal justice, and legal systems without restrictions as to chronological scope, geographical focus, or methodological approach.

Written in Blood: Fatal Attraction in Enlightenment Amsterdam
Pieter Spierenburg

Rethinking Southern Violence: Homicides in Post–Civil War Louisiana, 1866–1884
Gilles Vandal

Five Centuries of Violence in Finland and the Baltic Area
Heikki Ylikangas, Petri Karonen, and Martti Lehti